THE GOOD NON RETIREMENT GUIDE 2010

Everything you need to know about health, property, investment, leisure, work, pensions and tax

24TH EDITION

EDITED BY FRANCES KAY

KoganPage

LONDON PHILADELPHIA NEW DELHI

Publisher's note

Every possible effort has been made to ensure that the information contained in this book is accurate at the time of going to press, and the publishers and author cannot accept responsibility for any errors or omissions, however caused. No responsibility for loss or damage occasioned to any person acting, or refraining from action, as a result of the material in this publication can be accepted by the editor, the publisher or the author.

This 24th edition published in Great Britain in 2010 by Kogan Page Limited

Kogan Page Limited
120 Pentonville Road
London N1 9JN
United Kingdom
www.koganpage.com

© Kogan Page, 2010

British Library Cataloguing in Publication Data

A CIP record for this book is available from the British Library.

ISBN   978 0 7494 5882 9
E-ISBN 978 0 7494 5896 6

Typeset by Saxon Graphics Ltd, Derby
Printed and bound in Great Britain by MPG Books Ltd, Bodmin, Cornwall

British Model Flying Association

Do you have an interest in aviation? Would you like the satisfaction of building and flying an aircraft of your own?

The British Model Flying Association (BMFA) is the national governing body for the sport of model flying and is mandated by the Civil Aviation Authority and the Royal Aero Club. The BMFA dates back to 1922 and we currently represent 36,000 members and over 800 clubs throughout the U.K.

Our members build and fly a wide variety of models ranging from WW1 aircraft right up to modern day fighter aircraft powered by miniature jet engines. The BMFA covers all aspects of model flying including aerobatics, helicopters, scale models, pylon racers, gliders, rockets and balloons.

BMFA membership benefits include a bi-monthly magazine, a comprehensive membership handbook, access to training and achievement schemes and membership insurances. Two types of insurance are provided – Third Party Civil Liability cover (£10 million cover) and Personal Accident cover.

Please visit www.bmfa.org or call 0116 2440028 for further details of how to join the BMFA or find your nearest club.

advertisement feature

What better gift could you give than the gift of

life?

The Institute of Cancer Research is one of the world's leading cancer research organisations and is internationally renowned for the quality of its science.

By leaving a gift in your Will to The Institute, you can help our scientists to reach the ultimate goal that one day people may live their lives free from the fear of cancer as a life-threatening disease.

The Institute of Cancer Research: 123 Old Brompton Road, London, SW7 3RP

Tel: 020 7153 5000 | Fax: 0207 153 5313 | Email: legacy@icr.ac.uk | Web: www.icr.ac.uk

A charity, not for profit. Company limited by guarantee. Registered in England No. 534147.

The Institute of Cancer Research was founded in 1909 to investigate the causes, diagnosis and treatment of cancer. With 850 scientists on its two sites on the Fulham Road in central London and at Sutton in Surrey, it ranks today as one of the world's top four cancer research centres and it is the only one of these outside the USA. Its internationally leading research into genetics, molecular biology and drug development is unrivalled anywhere in the world.

In 2009 we celebrate our Centenary. Over the years, *we have grown to become one of the largest cancer research foundations in the world, the best in Europe and a global leader in developing treatments and in controlling the disease.*

The Institute of Cancer Research discoveries have not only fuelled its own continuing research but also informed and influenced other discoveries at other institutions around the world.

Some of our Achievements :

1910 – The Institute of Cancer Research founds a specialist radio-therapy department – one of the first in the world

1930s – The Institute of Cancer Research identifies the suspected link between smoking and lung cancer.

1950s – The Institute of Cancer Research develops the drugs busulphan, chlorambucil and melphalan – all of them outstandingly successful in treating cancer and which are still used today.

1960s – The Institute of Cancer Research scientists show that carcinogens act by damaging DNA, leading to the dramatic discovery that the basic cause of cancer is a DNA malfunction.

1970s – The Institute of Cancer Research develops carboplatin, the use of which becomes the global standard of care for patients with a wide range of solid tumours, and leads to the high cure rate for testicular cancer.

1995 – The Institute of Cancer Research identifies the breast cancer gene BRCA2, mutations in which predispose carriers to high risk of breast cancer. The finding provides the opportunity to initiate breast cancer prevention studies.

2000 – The Institute of Cancer Research scientists initiate the Cancer Genome Project with the aim of identifying genes that have relevance to particular cancers. The project, being conducted at the Wellcome Trust's Sanger Institute, has so far discovered over 350 genes associated with cancer.

You could help make our first centenary our last by remembering The Institute of Cancer Research in your Will. Your Legacy could save lives.

Making a Will is perhaps more important than you think, because if you die without one then everything does not automatically pass to your partner or spouse. Making a Will is easy and by doing so you can make sure that all your wishes are fully reflected within the document. You may think that there is no need to write a Will because you do not have very much to leave. Make a list of your assets and you will be surprised at how much you do have. You can use your Will to leave a gift to a charity such as The Institute of Cancer Research. People often chose to do this as they are not in the position to donate to charity during there lifetime. By leaving a gift to The Institute of Cancer Research in your Will, you could help fund our ground breaking work and save lives. Making a Will does not take much time, but its effects are long-lasting and far-reaching.

Remember that any gift you leave to charity in your Will are exempt from Inheritance Tax, so the tax burden on your estate is reduced.

Here at The Institute of Cancer Research we offer a Will for Free scheme where you can receive independent, professional advise allowing you to make a basic Will or update an existing one for free using one of your local participating solicitors.*

We make this offer in the hope that you could help fund our vital research although you are under no obligation to do so and providing for your family and friends must of course take priorty.

We would be delighted if you could support our work by leaving a legacy to The Institute of Cancer Research. However, to ensure that your intended gift is received your solicitor must ensure that our full details are specified correctly within your Will.

The Institute of Cancer Research
123 Old Brompton Road
London
SW7 3RP

X 90004 – Charity exemption number

For more information about The Institute of Cancer Research or further legacy Information, please contact us on : 0207 153 5387 or E-mail legacy@icr.ac.uk

Contents

Preface

Welcome to the 24th edition of *The Good Non Retirement Guide 2010*. As usual it has all the latest information and suggestions on where to get best advice on how to plan, prepare and enjoy a fulfilling and rewarding retirement. This year there is one omission to which the publishers wish to draw the readers' attention. Due to the unusually late scheduling of the Chancellor's Pre-Budget Statement (towards late November/early December 2009), it has not been possible to include the usual 'Stop Press' section with this edition. However, the Stop Press section has been prepared in web-ready format and readers are able to view the latest information online at: www.koganpage.com/gnrg.

We apologise for this departure from the norm; however, the prevailing circumstances were beyond our control.

1

Are you looking forward to retirement?

Welcome to the 24th and latest edition of *The Good Non Retirement Guide*, revised and updated for 2010. Are you looking forward to retiring? Is it something you have been thinking about for ages? Or have the years just slipped by and now that life-changing event is just around the corner? A research project carried out by scientists at University College London, which studied the lives of thousands of people over 50, found that men and women at or around retirement age view their quality of life differently. They are consequently influenced by slightly different things. Retirement in some cases improves the quality of life for men, while affecting life negatively for some women. According to the UCL scientists it is best to be married (or in a long-term partnership), to be educated to degree level and to have been employed in a managerial position to score highest in the satisfaction levels. There is also evidence that wealth and health often go hand in hand. The study reveals that exercise increases life expectancy (no surprise there) and that the longer you work, or keep mentally active, the fitter you remain.

If we are to get the best that life has to offer after 50, it pays to make some effort in advance. Important events always require some preparation if we are to make the most of them. The good news about *The Good Non Retirement Guide* is that it gives you all the help you'll need. It is packed with information, suggestions and advice on every aspect of retirement and beyond. It will inspire you to do things you've never thought of, and help you to sort out the practicalities if you don't already have the knowledge or contacts. It is an invaluable resource book, and its purpose is to help you enjoy your retirement to the full.

The majority of people retiring today are fitter, more skilled and financially better off than previous generations. Also, thanks to improved lifestyles and medical advances, a great many of us can realistically look forward to 25 years or more of active life: 60 could be the new 30. As a result, planning for the future has become critically important. *The Good Non Retirement Guide* is not designed to offer you a ready-made philosophy or some rose-tinted assurances that 'Life begins at 50'. Its aim is to be an antidote to any midlife crisis that might be looming on the horizon, and set you thinking along constructive lines. This book shows what is possible, advises on the best sources of relevant information available and helps you avoid the pitfalls that can catch the unwary. Key concerns are most likely to be money and what to do with your time. Other issues may well include where you live, how to keep healthy and how your retirement affects your nearest and dearest.

You don't have to be an accountant to know that once you stop earning your income will drop. But in Chapter 7 you will find our useful Budget Planner. Completing this is time well spent. You may be pleasantly surprised to find that the difference in income pre- and post-retirement is far less than you'd feared. On the plus side, you will probably save on travel and other work-related expenses, as well as gaining a welcome reduction in tax.

As with all questions affecting retirement, planning ahead makes good sense. Assessing your likely savings, including lump sums from your pension or any insurance policies you may have, can give you a clearer idea of the future. From this you can draw up a plan as to how to maximize their value. You will have to consider carefully how to invest your money, whether it would make sense to buy an annuity, and what tax planning should be considered. Best advice is to consult a good accountant, stockbroker or other professional adviser. Should you not have one already, there is advice in the book on how to find a reputable person to assist you and explain the options available to you.

Your retirement income may well depend on whether you start a new career, especially if – as happens to thousands of people – you were made redundant with no immediate job prospects on offer. While starting afresh is not easy and may not be appropriate for everyone, a large number of people over retirement age do find work rewarding. While some individuals turn their talents to something entirely new, others go freelance or become consultants in their existing area of expertise. There is some sound advice in Chapter 11, Looking for Paid Work, which gives many useful leads and suggestions.

There are an increasing number of people who start their own business in retirement. This is something that requires serious consideration, as it is not without risk. Entrepreneurs of any age can find they've never worked so hard in their life. But despite that it is exciting and invigorating. Being your own boss (perhaps for the first time in your life) is a heady prospect and, though it means sacrificing some of your social life, doing without a salary and having to post your own letters, it is immensely satisfying. If you are married, make sure your partner is supportive, as there could be domestic tensions – especially if you run the business from home. There are many who, having taken the plunge, derive enormous satisfaction from building up a profitable family enterprise. If you are seriously considering the idea, Chapter 10, Starting Your Own Business, provides some basic information that could help you decide whether this course of action is right for you.

A worthwhile alternative to becoming a business tycoon is to devote your energies to voluntary work. There are literally scores of opportunities for retired people to make a valuable contribution within their own community covering many different types of work, or nationally with larger not-for-profit organizations. Whether you can spare only the occasional day or can help on a regular basis, Chapter 12, Voluntary Work, has a wealth of suggestions you might like to consider.

Of paramount importance, whether you are thinking of paid or unpaid work, or for that matter simply planning to devote more time to your hobbies, is to remain fit and healthy. Good health is the most valuable possession we have. Without it, energy is lacking, activities are restricted and the fun goes out of life. No amount of money can compensate for poor health. While anyone can be unfortunate enough to be struck down by an unexpected illness, your future good health is largely in your own hands. The reason why people in their 70s are so often dogged by aches and pains is that insufficient care has been taken by them during their 50s and 60s. As well as all the obvious advice about not smoking, becoming overweight or drinking to excess, there is the important question of exercise. This book has suggestions for a number of interesting ways of keeping fit.

There are opportunities around the country for almost every kind of sport, with 50-plus beginners especially welcome. Additionally, dancing, yoga, keep-fit-to-music and relaxation classes are readily available through most local authorities. They are also offered by the many specialist bodies listed in the Leisure Activities and Health chapters (Chapters 9 and 13). The only problem is likely to be fitting everything in. The choice of leisure pursuits is enormous. If you have ever wanted to learn about computers, take a degree, join a choir, become proficient in a craft, play competitive Scrabble, start a coin collection or become a beekeeper, you will find an organization that caters for your enthusiasm.

The type of activities you enjoy may affect your decision as to where you will live. Lots of people are conditioned towards thinking of retirement as being the time for selling up and moving to a new home. It is something that should be considered carefully, as many people relocate without giving enough thought to such essentials as proximity to family and friends and whether there is the same scope for pursuing their interests. An all-too-common mistake is for people to retire to a place where they once spent an idyllic holiday, perhaps 15 or 20 years previously, without further investigation. Resorts that are glorious in midsummer can be bleak and damp in winter, as well as pretty dull when the tourist season is over. Equally, many people sell their house and move somewhere smaller without sufficient thought. It may be that when spending more time at home they actually want more space rather than less. This is particularly true of anyone planning to work from home or who has a hobby, such as carpentry, that requires a separate workroom.

While moving may be the right solution, especially if you want to realize some capital to boost your retirement income, there are plenty of ways of adapting a house to make it more convenient and labour-saving. Likewise, you may be able to cut the running costs, for example with better insulation. These and other possibilities, including taking in a paying guest or creating a granny flat, are explored in Chapter 8, Your Home. On the subject of granny flats, if you are caring for elderly parents there may come a time when a little bit of outside help could make all the difference. The range of organizations that can provide you with back-up is far more extensive than you might realize. For single people especially, who may feel that they have no choice but to give up a career, knowing what facilities are available could prove a veritable godsend.

While there may be pressure if a parent, however much loved, requires an undue amount of attention, a more commonplace problem is the effect of retirement on a couple's relationship. Many people find a period of settling down is necessary, particularly when for a number of years they have spent most of their days apart. From the abstract longing to be able to spend a little more time with the family the reality can be somewhat different. As one recently retired 62-year-old put it: 'I had hardly had a chance to enjoy a couple of days pottering in the garden for the first time in years, when my wife was nagging me to go out and find something to do. She was the one who wanted me to take early retirement. Now she is wishing that I was back at work.' The reverse situation can also apply, especially if the wife had a high-powered career. Although in general the evidence suggests that it is usually the man's retirement that provokes most friction, this will change as more of today's working women turn 60 and find themselves facing the same need to make adjustments.

Either way, the point is that, after years of seeing relatively little of each other, retirement suddenly creates the possibility of a couple having much more togetherness. Put in blunt terms, many women grumble that having a partner at home during the day means an extra meal to cook and inevitable disruption to their normal routine. And while this may not apply in an 'equal opportunity' marriage or partnership, where the domestic jobs are shared between both parties, in the majority of households women still do the lion's share of the housework. Sometimes a cause for resentment is that one or other party feels guilty about meeting friends or pursuing usual weekly activities unless the other partner is also busy. Should a wife still work, with a newly retired husband, the situation can be even more fraught as, apart from the extra housework, she may find her loyalties uncomfortably divided. Furthermore, quite irrationally, some retired husbands begin to harbour dire suspicions about their wives' working colleagues, imagining romantic entanglements that had never crossed their mind before. Sometimes too, retired people subconsciously label themselves as 'old' and start denying themselves and their partner the pleasures of intimacy that had been previously enjoyed. According to well documented medical research, a healthy sex life in middle age can positively help to promote good health and longer life expectancy.

Usually, problems that coincide with retirement can be fairly simply overcome by a willingness to discuss them frankly and to work out a solution that suits both partners. The situation is very much easier today than a few decades ago when male and female roles were far more stereotyped and many couples felt that they had to conform to a set pattern for the sake of convention.

Many single people also find that adjusting to retirement is not always that easy. Relatives may impose new pressures once you are no longer at work. Likewise, close friendships sometimes alter when one friend retires and not the other. Additionally, many people who live on their own admit that they had not realized how much they relied on their job for companionship and sometimes even for part of their weekend social life.

Pre-retirement courses

If you are considering what to do when you retire, talk to other people who have recently stopped working or ask friends about how they tackled the challenges and opportunities of retirement. Any advice is useful and a large number of companies recognize this need by offering pre-retirement courses. If you are in a firm where this is not offered, or if you are self-employed, there are a number of organizations that can give you advice and help. Before deciding on a particular course, it is worth thinking about the most appropriate time for you to attend one and the subjects that it should cover. The traditional view is that the ideal time is somewhere between one and two years before you are due to retire. While this is probably true for most people, it is also important to remember that preparing for retirement is best taken in stages. Some financial decisions, such as those affecting company or personal pension planning, need to be taken as early as possible. Others, such as whether to move house, can probably only be made much later.

The basic subjects that the best courses address are: finance, health, activity, leisure, housing and the adjustments that will need to be made by both you and your family when you retire. The crucial test, however, is not so much the amount of factual information the course contains but the extent to which it helps to focus and stimulate your own thoughts on the various issues and to lead to discussion with your partner and others in the same situation.

The following is a list of some organizations offering pre-retirement courses and advice:

Life Academy, 9 Chesham Road, Guildford, Surrey GU1 3LS; Tel: 01483 301170; e-mail: info@life-academy.co.uk; website: www.life-academy.co.uk. Life Academy is an educational charity. As the national centre for life planning, it helps individuals to prepare for life's next steps. Its courses are independent and free from commercial bias, and partners are encouraged to attend. They are held in London, Slough, Guildford, Godalming and Leeds. The cost (2009) is £270 per person or £430 per couple (excluding VAT), for a two-day non-residential course. For more information on this and other courses and how to book a place on a course, visit the website.

Retirement Education Services, 16 St Mary's Street, Wallingford, Oxfordshire OX10 0EW; Tel: 01491 833 696; e-mail: training@retirementeducationsers. co.uk; website: www.retirementeducationsers.co.uk. This organization is one of the biggest specialist training consultancies in the field of planning for retirement. It runs around 100 courses/seminars a year. Its head office is in Oxfordshire, but it has branches in Tyne & Wear and Edinburgh.

Scottish Pre-Retirement Council, 260 Bath Street, Glasgow G2 4JP; Tel: 0141 332 9427; e-mail: info@sprc.org.uk; website: www.sprc.org.uk. This is a charitable organization that runs pre-retirement education courses in all areas of Scotland to facilitate the change from working life to retirement. Courses are normally two one-day sessions held over consecutive weeks.

Another useful website to look at is **www.laterlife.com,** which has lots of relevant information and useful links.

Should you wish to see which useful government bodies and support organizations there are for the over-50s, look at **www.direct.gov.uk** and search 'Over 50s contacts'. The information and advice includes sections on work and career, learning and technology, retirement, financial advice and support, care and community, home, travel and leisure and veterans.

A number of **universities** run retirement planning courses. These are typically held once or twice a year and are normally arranged by the department of extramural studies.

Commercial organizations

The following organizations offer an attractive mix of courses with something to suit almost everyone. There are residential and day courses. Several are specifically for senior executives:

Millstream International, Harting, Petersfield, Hants GU31 5NS; Tel: 01730 825 711; e-mail: info@mill-stream.com; website: www.mill-stream.co.uk. Millstream helps senior people make the most of new opportunities when they leave their main employment, whether on retirement or for a career change. The residential courses last two and a half days and topics include personal adjustments, health considerations, finance (totally independent) and new opportunities.

Retirement Counselling Service, Apex House, Chiltern Avenue, Amersham, Bucks HP6 5AE; Tel: 01494 433553. The Retirement Counselling Service is an independent organization offering a range of in-house and external retirement seminars and services throughout the UK. For further information, contact Derek Wildey; e-mail: Dwildey@call-rcs.co.uk; website: www.the-retirement-site.co.uk.

Adult education

If you wish to consider further education in retirement, you could consult:

Workers' Educational Association, 3rd Floor, 70 Clifton Street, London EC2A 4HB; Tel: 020 7426 3450; e-mail: national@wea.org.uk; website: www.wea.org.uk. The WEA is the UK's largest voluntary provider of adult education. It was founded in 1903 to support the educational needs of working men and women. Today WEA runs over 10,000 courses each year, providing learning for more than 110,000 adults of all ages and drawn from all walks of life. There are nine regions in England, a Scottish association and over 450 local branches.

New focus for the retired

There are now a growing number of organizations to represent the interests of retired people. The over-50s represent a large proportion of the population, and it is essential that they have a means of putting forward their views on issues that affect their lives at both national and local levels. Two of the best known, which in addition to their campaigning role arrange a variety of social and other events, are:

Age Concern England's ActivAge Unit, free helpline: 0800 00 99 66; e-mail: aau@ace.org.uk; website: www.ageconcern.org.uk. ActivAge Unit, Age Concern England works to promote a more positive concept and approach to healthy, active ageing through a variety of programmes, including Technology and Communications, Ageing Well, Volunteering, and Intergenerational Work, and through the management of a five-year Big Lottery Well-Being project across England to increase the well-being of older people. All of these programmes offer people over 50 access to new opportunities and the scope to improve their own lives through increased well-being and the opportunity to make a meaningful contribution to their community.

National Pensioners Convention, 19–23 Ironmonger Row, London EC1V 3QN; Tel: 020 7553 6510; e-mail: info@npcuk.org; website: www.npcuk.org. The NPC is the umbrella group for pensioner associations throughout the country, which collectively have a membership of around 1.5 million retired people. While each group is autonomous and so organizes its own programme of events, a main aim of affiliated organizations is to act as a pressure group to improve facilities and opportunities for older people, including in particular a substantial improvement in the basic state pension, better long-term care for older people and free nationwide travel. For further information and addresses of local groups, contact the NPC at the address above or visit its website.

And finally, if you hadn't already realized the huge industry geared to the over-50s, there is now an exhibition especially for you. It's called *The Retirement Show* (sponsored by Prudential) and is held every year in three locations – Manchester, London and Glasgow. For further information and details of the 2010 shows, contact The Retirement Show, Tel: 01372 743 837; website: www.theretirement show.com.

2

Money in general

If you were to ask people approaching retirement what kept them awake at night, many would say 'having enough money'. Some people may be fortunate enough to have no worries; they have planned the event for years, made maximum pension contributions, carefully invested their savings, covered themselves and their family in insurance policies and carefully worked out forecasting budgets. They may even have a 'to do' list of what they are going to spend their money on as soon as their new life begins.

For a large number, however, this is not the case. After years of giving little if any thought to their pension, they are consumed with anxiety and fear as the day they will no longer be drawing a regular salary draws closer. There is nothing worse than the fear of not having enough to live on and having to make drastic lifestyle changes to make ends meet. In most cases anticipation is far worse than reality. Retirement can be, and often is, better than many people imagine. The current economic situation is not good from anyone's point of view but most people reaching retirement age are well aware of the difficulties. The key to managing your retirement well is to know how to make whatever money you have go as far as possible. Get clued up as to what is coming in and what has to go out, make what savings and assets you have work for you and you may be agreeably surprised. As long as people are realistic, it is unlikely that drastic economies will have to be made. For many men and women who have only a rough idea as to their likely income and expenditure, the best advice is to do your sums.

Doing the sums

Those who profess total ignorance of their financial situation have no excuse. It is far more sensible to be a wise owl than a headless chicken. Be prepared, get to know the facts, do some figures – these are the essential first steps in your pre-retirement planning. To make a proper assessment, you need to draw up several lists:

- expected sources of income on retirement;
- essential outgoings;
- normal additional spending (such as holidays and other luxuries).

Second, have a think about these options:

- possible ways of boosting your retirement income;
- spending now for saving later;
- your wish list, if affordable.

Most difficult of all to compile is a third list of variables and unknowns. It is impossible to predict the future, but for those who wish to be prudent certain things should be taken into account in any long-term budget planning. The two most important items are tax and inflation. Other things to bear in mind are rising energy prices, which can lead to higher heating and fuel bills. Emergency situations can and do arise, such as health issues for example, so if possible special provisions should be made. The other imponderable is predicting how long you, your partner or any dependants are likely to live, so it pays to consider such matters when budgeting in retirement.

Planning for the future is never a waste of time, neither can it be done too early. With regard to your pension and any savings or investment plans, you could start as much as five or even 10 years before you retire. When doing the sums, it helps to be realistic. Don't make the mistake of basing your calculations on current commitments and expenditure, because a number of your requirements are bound to change. To get the figures into perspective, imagine yourself already retired. While some items will probably take a heftier slice of your budget, others will certainly be cheaper or no longer cost you anything at all. So it's not all bad news.

The possible areas where savings can be made and extra outgoings need to be considered are discussed below. The most practical way of using the list is to tick off the items that will definitely apply to you and, where possible, write down the expenditure involved (see Budget Planner, page 128). While this will be no more than a draft – since there will obviously be gaps – the closer you are to retirement, the more sensible it is to do this exercise.

Possible savings

There's no doubt that going out to work costs money; it involves a fair number of expenses, not least travelling and clothes. When you leave your job, you could easily save quite a few pounds a week on average. Items for which you will no longer have to pay include: your travelling costs to work, bought lunches and special clothes, out-of-pocket incidentals such as drinks with colleagues, trade magazines and collections for co-workers' presents or the Christmas party. More good news is that you won't have to pay any more National Insurance Contributions and, unless you choose to invest in a private plan, your pension payments will also cease. Additionally, when you retire, you may be in a lower tax bracket.

At the same time you may have reached the stage when your children are now independent, your mortgage is substantially paid off and you have stopped subscribing to a life assurance policy. One of the most enjoyable aspects of reaching state retirement age is that you become eligible for a variety of benefits. These include, for example, concessionary travel, free NHS prescriptions, cheaper theatre and cinema tickets (usually matinees), reduced entrance charges for exhibitions and a wide choice of special holiday offers. Some benefits apply to both men and women from age 60.

Another point worth mentioning is that many insurance companies give discounts to mature drivers. In some instances, discounts apply to those aged 50; other companies restrict eligibility to those aged 55 or even 60. Normally, but again this varies, the scheme is terminated when the policy holder reaches 75. Most companies, but not all, extend the cover to a spouse or other named person with a good driving record. The discount for people over 50 ranges from 10 to 15 per cent. There are considerable extra savings for drivers with a five-year claim-free record.

The best advice is to approach your existing insurance company first and ask what terms they will give you. If these do not seem good, it could pay to shop around. Among those that offer special rates for mature drivers are Zurich Insurance, Direct Line, Saga Services and Age Concern Insurance Services. It is also worth checking the internet, as a growing number of insurers give discounts to those buying a policy online.

Extra outgoings

There is no escaping the fact that when you retire some of your expenses will be heavier than at present. First, you will probably be spending more time at home, so items like heating and lighting are liable to increase.

If you received any perks with your job, such as a company car or health insurance, then unless you have a very generous employer these will have to come out of your own pocket in future. Equally, any business entertaining you enjoyed will probably cease, so no more free lunches. Entertaining will now have to be paid for out of the domestic housekeeping.

Another very important consideration is all that extra leisure. With more time available, you may be tempted to spend more on outings, your hobbies and longer holidays from home. To avoid having to make serious cutbacks, these need to be budgeted for well in advance. Most people say that in an ideal world they would expect to be spending roughly double on entertainment of all kinds, compared with when they were working. Even voluntary activities have hidden expenses, for example more use of the telephone, petrol costs and supporting fund-raising occasions.

Looking ahead, most older people want more home comforts. You may have to consider paying other people to do some of the jobs, such as the decorating or gardening, that you previously managed yourself. Anticipating such areas of additional expenditure is not being pessimistic. On the contrary, it is the surest way of avoiding future money worries. You may find, once you have sat down and worked out your retirement income and expenditure in detail, that you'll manage very well.

Expected sources of income on retirement

Your list will include at least some of the following. Once you have added up the figures in the Budget Planner, you will have to deduct Income Tax to arrive at the net spending amount available to you:

- State basic pension;
- State graduated pension;
- SERPS;
- State second pension;
- occupational pension;
- personal pension;
- stakeholder pension;
- State benefits.

Additionally, you may receive income or a capital sum from some of the following:

- company share option scheme;
- sale of business or personal assets;
- investments (stocks and shares, unit trusts, etc);
- other existing income (from a trust, property, family business);
- bank/building society savings;
- National Savings & Investments bond or certificate;
- endowment policy.

You might also be in receipt of income from an annuity. However, since at this stage you will be unlikely to have purchased one, this really belongs in the category of investment decisions.

Unavoidable outgoings

One person's priority is another person's luxury – and vice versa. For this reason, the divide between 'unavoidable outgoings' and 'normal additional expenditure' (see section following) is likely to vary with each individual. For example, pet owners would consider pet food and veterinary bills as an essential item of expenditure, whereas those who do not have a pet are able to disregard such costs. Almost everyone will want to juggle some of the items between the two lists or add their own particular requisites or special enthusiasms.

Our suggestions are simply intended to prompt thought and discussion – and are not a guide to what should, or should not, constitute a luxury. What matters is the basic principle behind the exercise. If at some stage budgeting choices have to be made, decisions will be very much easier if you already know your total outgoings. This includes what you are spending on each item individually and those you variously rate as important or marginal.

Whatever your own essentials, some of the following items will certainly feature on your list of unavoidable expenses:

- food;
- rent or mortgage repayments;
- Council Tax;
- repair and maintenance costs;
- heating;
- lighting and other energy;
- telephone/mobile and internet connection;
- postage (including Christmas cards);
- TV licence/Sky/digital subscriptions;
- household insurance;
- clothes;
- domestic cleaning products;
- laundry, cleaners' bills, shoe repairs;
- miscellaneous services, ie property maintenance, such as plumber, window cleaner;
- car, including licence, petrol, road rescue such as RAC or AA, servicing;
- other transport;
- regular savings and life assurance;
- HP/other loan repayments;
- outgoings on health.

Normal additional expenditure

This may well include:

- gifts;
- holidays;
- newspapers/books/CDs/DVDs;
- computer expenses (including broadband);
- drink;

- cigarettes/tobacco;
- hairdressing;
- toiletries/cosmetics;
- entertainment (hobbies, outings, DVD purchase/rental, home entertaining, etc);
- miscellaneous subscriptions/membership fees;
- charitable donations;
- expenditure on pets;
- garden purchases;
- other.

Work out the figures against these lists. Then, in order to compare your expenditure against likely income, jot them down on the Budget Planner (see page 128).

Possible ways of boosting your retirement income

Other than luck – winning the lottery or coming into a legacy – there are three main possibilities for providing you with extra money: your home, work and investment skill.

Your home

Your home offers several different options.

Moving somewhere smaller

You could sell your present home, move into smaller accommodation and end up with the double bonus of pocketing a lump sum and reducing your running costs. Leaving aside such considerations as whether you would still be able to have your grandchildren to stay and looking at the matter strictly in financial terms, it is as well to realize from the outset that the cash difference on the exchange – in other words, your profit – will invariably be less than you expect. What with removal charges and lawyers' fees, moving home is a very expensive business. Additionally, you will probably have some decorating expenses and there is bound to be a period of overlap when you will be paying two lots of telephone rental, extra electricity bills and so on.

If you are planning to buy, you may need to add Stamp Duty. New thresholds in force until 31 December 2009 (see the Stop Press section for the latest information) mean that if you buy property and the purchase price is £175,000 or less you don't pay any stamp duty land tax at all. If it's more than £175,000, you pay between 1 and 4 per cent of the whole purchase price. Since October 2007 there is Stamp Duty relief for most buyers of new zero-carbon homes. Moving may well be an excellent decision, but if money is the main criterion you need to be thoroughly realistic when calculating the gains.

A particular point to be aware of is that it becomes hugely expensive if you buy a new home before selling your existing one. You could easily dissipate a large proportion of any profits you hope to realize on the exchange. Ideally, you should try to dovetail selling and buying at the same time. If this is not possible, as so often happens, the best advice is to sell first and rent a property for a short period of time rather than risk lumbering yourself with the expense of having to borrow for several months or possibly longer.

If you do decide to move, you might consider transferring an existing mortgage to your new property or getting a new one, even if you could afford to buy the property outright. You may think that you are too old but, today, mortgages are available to people over retirement age. However, there may be good reasons why a mortgage would not be sensible for you. Do your sums carefully to see whether there is any real gain. If in doubt, consult an accountant or solicitor who will help you work out the details.

Taking in lodgers

If your children have left home and you have more space than you need, you could consider taking in lodgers, either as paying guests or, if your property lends itself to the creation of a separate flatlet, in a tenancy capacity. When assessing the financial rewards, it is wise to assume that there will be times when the accommodation is empty – so you will not be receiving any rent. The good news is that you may be able to keep more of any earnings you make.

You can, under the government's Rent a Room scheme, let out a furnished room in your home and claim tax relief of up to £4,250 a year (£2,125 if letting jointly). Any excess rental over £4,250 will be assessed for tax in the normal way. The scheme does not apply if you let unfurnished accommodation in your home. You don't even have to be a homeowner to take advantage of the Rent a Room scheme, but if you are renting you should check whether your lease allows you to take in a lodger. If you're paying a mortgage, it is best to check the mortgage lender's and insurer's terms too. The relief applies only to accommodation that is 'part of your main home', so if you are thinking of creating a separate flatlet you will need to take care that this qualifies and that it is not at risk of being assessed as a commercial let. Since the dividing line is somewhat hazy, check with your architect or other professional adviser that he or she fully understands the technical requirements.

Raising money on your home

A third option is to part-sell your home for either a capital sum or regular payments, under an equity-release scheme, and continue to live in it for as long as you wish. Sounds wonderful? There are both attractions and drawbacks that need to be considered carefully, and you would be strongly advised to discuss the matter with your solicitor.

All these possibilities are explored in greater detail in Chapter 8, Your Home. If you think any of the ideas sound interesting, see the following sections in Chapter 8: 'Moving to a new home', 'Raising money on your home' and 'Letting rooms in your home'.

Work

You might wish to continue working. If this is the case, one of the simplest solutions is for you to talk to your employer to see if it is agreeable for you to remain with your present organization. The age discrimination legislation should be a point in your favour, as it strengthens the rights of individuals who want to postpone their retirement. If you stay, you could either defer your pension (see page 30) or, if you prefer and the scheme rules allow it, you could start drawing your pension benefits – perhaps as a way to boost your income if you ease down to part-time work.

Alternatively, you may look on retirement as the opportunity for a job switch or the chance you have always wanted of setting up on your own. When assessing your budget plans, it is as well to err on the side of caution with regard to any additional income you will be likely to earn. Although things are improving, many so-called 'retirement jobs' are notoriously badly paid. If, instead of paid work, you are thinking of becoming self-employed or setting up a business, not only will you have to meet the start-up costs but, as you may well be aware, very few new enterprises make a profit during the first two or three years.

Consider the effects of continuing to work or of setting up your own enterprise. While you are working, you may not be spending money on entertainment. Also, particularly if you are self-employed or own a business, there may be certain tax advantages as well as possible scope for improving your pension. Lastly, of course, you may be one of the lucky ones for whom work after retirement really pays. Quite apart from the money, work can be thoroughly enjoyable and rewarding in its own right. For ideas and information, see Chapter 11, Looking for Paid Work, and Chapter 10, Starting Your Own Business.

Investment

Contrary to what some people believe, you do not need to be very rich, or young, to think about investing. Those over the age of 55 can find it fascinating and rewarding. As you will see from Chapter 5, investment can take many different forms, and among the list of different options there should be something to suit almost everyone. Although you may consider this to be specialist reading, it is worth taking a look. Maximizing your income in retirement could make all the difference between being able to enjoy life and a few luxuries and worrying about money.

Spending now for saving later

You may normally take the view that there is never a best time for spending money. But, remember, retirement planning is different in that sooner or later you will need, or want, to make certain purchases. These could include paying off outstanding commitments, such as a mortgage. Most people's basic list – at least to think about – under this heading includes one or more of the following:

- expenditure on their home;
- the purchase of a car;
- the termination of HP or other credit arrangements.

Additionally, there may be a number of general domestic or luxury items that you have been promising yourself you would buy for some time. The question is simply one of actual timing: that is, determining the right moment to buy. Typical examples might include a microwave, gardening equipment, a DVD recorder, a new computer, hobby materials and so on. To help you decide whether a policy of 'spending now' is sensible, or possibly self-indulgent, there are two very simple questions you should ask: Can I afford it more easily now – or in the future? By paying now rather than waiting, will I be saving money in the long run? True, the issue may be complicated by tax and other considerations, but for most choices this very basic analysis helps greatly to clarify the financial arguments on both sides.

Home improvements

If you plan to stay where you are, the likelihood is that at some point you will want to make some changes or improvements: install double glazing, insulate the loft, modernize the kitchen or perhaps convert part of the house to a granny flat for an elderly parent who is becoming too frail to live alone. It is normally accepted that any significant expenditure on your home is best undertaken several years prior to retirement. However, in our experience the matter is less clear cut and what may be right for some is not the solution for others. As with many other important decisions, the question largely depends on individual circumstances. Some people find it easier, and more reassuring, to pay major household bills while they are still earning. Others specifically plan to use part of the lump sum from their pension to create a dream home.

To arrive at the answer that makes best financial sense, present commitments have to be weighed against likely future expenditure (together with what money you will have available). Equally, as with insulation for example, you will need to work out what long-term savings you could make by taking the plunge now. There is also the safety aspect: if you have bad lighting or dangerously worn carpet on part of the staircase, waiting for a few years to tackle the problem (because it is all part of the grand plan) could prove a very false economy indeed.

Another very important consideration is to make sure you know how long you intend to stay in your present home. Investing a fortune in a property and then moving a couple of years later is not wise. Despite what people may think, it is rare to recoup all your expenditure on a property you've modified to your own taste.

Though it involves a few minutes' paperwork, a worthwhile exercise is to jot down your own personal list of pros and cons under the headings 'spending now' and 'spending later'. If still in doubt, waiting is normally the more prudent course.

Purchasing a car

There could be two good reasons for buying a new car ahead of your retirement. One is that you have a company car that you are about to lose; the other is that your existing vehicle is getting old and is beginning (or will probably soon start) to give you trouble. If either of these applies, then it probably makes sense to buy a replacement while you are still feeling relatively flush.

However, on the principle of 'look before you leap', company car owners should first check whether they might be entitled to purchase their present car on favourable terms. A number of employers are quite happy to allow this. Also, dreary though the suggestion sounds, if economies look like being the order of the day, two-car families might assess whether, come retirement when husband and wife may be doing more things together, two cars are really as essential as before.

Paying off HP and similar

In general, this is a good idea, since delay is unlikely to save you any money – and may in fact actually cost you more. The only precaution is to check the small print of your agreement, to ensure that there is no penalty for early repayment. A further exception to the rule could be your mortgage. An accountant could advise you; or, if you are thinking of moving (and the issue is really whether to transfer an existing mortgage – or possibly acquire a new one), include this among the points to raise with your solicitor.

Cherished plans, if affordable

The Budget Planner (page 128) may help you work out whether the various luxuries and plans of which nearly all of us dream could be affordable or are destined to remain on the wish list. Fun as it might be to compile, there would be little purpose in discussing the practicalities, or otherwise, of going on a cruise, owning a racehorse, installing a swimming pool, buying a caravan or whatever. Even among married couples there would be huge differences in choice and it would be difficult to apply in terms of normal budgeting wisdom. This does not mean that you should promptly forget the whole idea of noting items that come into this category. Perhaps as this is such a very personal decision area, only you can really make the assessments. However, if you plan your finances with a specific objective in view, you may find that against expectations an idea that first seemed impossible is actually affordable. Or, when you really think about the choices, some of your earlier priorities will seem less important.

Money – if you become redundant

Much of the information in the earlier part of the chapter is equally valid whether you become redundant or retire in the normal way. However, there are several key points with regard to money that it could be to your advantage to check:

You may be entitled to statutory redundancy pay

Your employer is obliged to pay the legal minimum, which is calculated on your age, length of service and weekly pay. To qualify, you will need to have worked for the organization for at least two years. The maximum weekly pay taken into account is £350 a week (this figure is revised annually, normally around February, to reflect any changes in the Retail Prices Index). For further information, see the Redundancy Help website: www.redundancyhelp.co.uk.

Ex gratia payments

Many employers are prepared to be more generous. HM Revenue & Customs (HMRC) allows individuals to receive up to £30,000 in redundancy pay/benefits free of tax, provided this is not one of the terms and conditions included in the contract of employment. Amounts over this are taxed under the PAYE system, so there could be an advantage in requesting that some of the payment be made into your pension scheme. For tax relief to apply, this must be done before your departure.

Benefits that are not part of your pay

Redundancy may mean the loss of several valuable benefits, such as a company car, life assurance and health insurance. Your employer may let you keep your car as part of your pay-off and might be willing to extend any health/other insurance cover for a few months after you leave. Some insurance companies allow preferential rates to individuals who were previously insured with them under a company scheme.

Holiday entitlement

You could be owed holiday entitlement for which you should be paid.

Your mortgage

Your mortgage lender should be notified as soon as possible and might agree to a more flexible repayment system. Check whether your mortgage package includes insurance against redundancy. If you have a very low income, you may be able to obtain Income Support (IS) to help with your mortgage costs. If your mortgage was taken out before 2 October 1995, IS would be obtainable after eight weeks. If it was taken out after 2 October 1995, you will normally have to wait for about nine months.

Other creditors/debts

Any creditors that you may have difficulty in paying (electricity, gas, a bank overdraft) should be informed as early as possible in the hope of agreeing easier payment terms. There could be an argument for paying off credit card bills immediately, even if this means using some of your redundancy pay. People who have taken out insurance to cover debts in the event of unemployment no longer have the money taken into account in calculating their eligibility for income-related benefits, provided the money is actually used to pay off past debts. Previously, this only applied if the money was paid direct to a creditor, as opposed to being received by the individual.

Company pension

Company pension scheme members normally have several choices. See the 'Early leavers' section in Chapter 3, Pensions, page 46.

Jobseeker's allowance (JSA)

Even if you are hoping to get another job very soon, you should sign on without delay, since as well as the allowance itself (£60.50 a week) your National Insurance Contributions will normally be credited to you. This is important to protect your State pension. To qualify for JSA you need to be under State pension age and must either have paid sufficient Class 1 National Insurance Contributions or have a low income. You must also be both available for and actively seeking work. For further information about JSA and other benefits, contact your local Jobcentre or Jobcentre Plus office, or look on the Directgov website (www.direct.gov.uk).

Redundancy helpline

The helpline can answer queries on all aspects of redundancy; Tel: 0845 145 0004; website: www.redundancyhelp.co.uk.

Money left unclaimed

Many people lose track of their financial assets, either because they have forgotten about them or because they do not know how to contact the relevant organizations that owe them money. If you think this could apply to you, the Unclaimed Assets Register might be able to help. The products it covers include life policies, pensions, unit trusts and dividends. There is a small search fee, of £18, which is payable whether or not the search is successful. For further information, contact the **Unclaimed Assets Register**, PO Box 9501, Nottingham NG80 1WD; Tel: 0870 241 1713; e-mail: search@uar.co.uk; website: www.uar.co.uk.

Another helpful website is www.mylostaccount.org.uk. (e-mail: info@mylostaccount.org.uk). This site gives information on the **British Bankers' Association** Lost Accounts Manager (Tel: 020 7216 8909; website: www.bba.org.uk); and the **Building Societies Association** Lost Savings (Tel: 020 7520 5900; website: www.bsa.org.uk) provides free services to help individuals trace forgotten current and deposit accounts; the **Pension Service** (Tel: 0845 600 2537; website: www.thepensionservice.gov.uk/tracing/) offers a similar service to help owners of old pension schemes trace their holdings. Also **National Savings & Investments** (Tel: 0845 964 5000; website: www.nsandi.com) has its own tracing service for lost bonds, certificates or accounts. For insurance policies, try the **Association of British Insurers** (Tel: 020 7600 3333; website: www.abi.org.uk).

There are plans, backed by MPs, for the Treasury to seize dormant assets and donate money towards good causes, including National Savings & Investments (NS&I) schemes. An account is deemed dormant when it has been left untouched for 15 years or more. With fixed-term accounts, the 15 years begin at the end of the fixed term. Cash ISAs will be included. Should you find a passbook for an old savings account long forgotten, take it to the relevant bank or building society. If your address has changed, you will need to take proof of your current address, such as a utility bill. If you can't remember the specific bank or building society, contact the **British Bankers' Association** or the **Building Societies Association** – see above. If you were to find account details while sorting out the paperwork of a deceased relative, you would need to take a copy of the statutory declaration or probate form when you claim the money.

Extra income

There are a great many State benefits and allowances available to give special help to people in need. Definition of need covers a very wide range and applies, among others, to problems connected with health, housing and care of an elderly or disabled relative, as well as widowhood and problems encountered by the frail elderly who, for example, may require extra heating during the winter. While many of these benefits are 'means-tested', in other words are given only to people whose income is below a certain level, some – such as Disability Living Allowance – are not dependent on how poor, or how wealthy, you are. Moreover, even when means-testing is a factor, for some of the benefits income levels are nothing like as low as many people imagine. Because this information is not widely enough known, many individuals – including in particular over a million pensioners – are not claiming help to which they are entitled and for which in many cases they have actually paid through their National Insurance Contributions. The main benefits and allowances are listed in their appropriate chapters: for example, housing benefit appears in Chapter 8, Your Home; carer's allowance is briefly described in Chapter 15, Caring for Elderly Parents. A number of voluntary organizations also provide assistance to individuals, sometimes in cash or sometimes in the form of facilities, such as special equipment for disabled people. Details are given in the relevant chapters.

For further advice and information, you could contact the following organizations:

Jobcentre Plus Office, Tel: 0800 055 6688; website: www.jobcentreplus.gov.uk.
Department for Work and Pensions, Richmond House, 79 Whitehall, London SW1A 2NS; Tel: 020 7210 3000; website: www.dwp.gov.uk.
Citizens Advice Bureau, 115–123 Pentonville Road, London N1 9LZ; website: www.citizensadvice.org.uk.
Age Concern, National Helpline, Tel: 0800 00 99 66; website: www.ageconcern. org.uk. National offices:
England, Astral House, 1268 London Road, London SW16 4ER; Tel: 020 8765 7200.
Northern Ireland, 3 Lower Crescent, Belfast BT7 1NR; Tel: 028 9024 5729.
Scotland, Causewayside House, 160 Causewayside, Edinburgh EH9 1PR; Tel: 0845 833 0200.
Cymru, Ty John Pathy, Units 13 and 14 Neptune Court, Vanguard Way, Cardiff CF24 5PJ; Tel: 029 2043 1555.

Making your money go further

Utility Warehouse is a company that offers telephone, broadband, mobile, gas and electricity at very competitive rates. There is also the opportunity to use a 'cashback' card for your shopping that will lessen the cost of your other bills. Tel: 0800 131 3000, or full details of all that is on offer can be found at www.utility-warehouse.co.uk.

You can also access all age-specific discounts and promotions in the **Seniors Discounts** Directory if you register as a member of Seniors Discounts. All new discounts are automatically added to the home page under 'Latest Discounts' so it pays to check regularly. To enrol, go to www.seniorsdiscounts.co.uk and follow the instructions.

Useful reading

The Pensioners' Guide is an easy-to-read booklet that provides information on the range of government benefits and services for pensioners, obtainable from Jobcentre Plus or social security offices, Citizens Advice Bureau and Post Offices. It is also available in pdf downloadable format from the website: www.thepensionservice.gov.uk.

Another excellent book for those wanting detailed information about planning their finances is *Talking about Retirement* by Lyn Ashurst, published by Kogan Page, March 2009. The author is an authority in her field and gives a comprehensive and detailed study of a careful and planned approach to the retirement process, based on about 50 case studies. This is an interesting book that covers a lot of ground. For more information and other recommended titles on retirement and associated issues published by Kogan Page see its website (www.koganpage.com).

Association of British Insurers, Website: www.abi.org.uk. 51 Gresham Street, London, EC2V 7HQ. Consumer hotline number: 020 7216 7455.

The ABI is the influential voice of Britain's Insurance Industry. It also provides practical guidance for consumers on all types of insurance products.

3

Pensions

Pensions are no longer providing the sums of money they used to. There are many people coming up to retirement whose pension schemes have been wound up and who have lost a large chunk of their savings. This is one of the most difficult situations to cope with. But despite this, next to your home your pension is still almost certainly your most valuable asset. It is therefore important to check where you stand – and what you can best do if damage limitation is required – to ensure that when you retire you receive the maximum benefit.

State pensions

You can get a pension if you are a man of 65 or a woman of 60, provided you have paid (or been credited with) sufficient National Insurance Contributions. In time the age for women will alter, as the government has published plans to equalize the State pension age for men and women at 65. This change is being phased in over 10 years, beginning this year, 2010. This will affect younger women only. Those born before 6 April 1950 have no need to alter their retirement plans.

Your right to a State pension

Your right to a State pension depends on your (or your spouse's) National Insurance Contributions (NIC). Most people have to pay contributions into the NIC scheme while they are working. If you are an employee, your employer will have automatically deducted Class 1 NIC from your salary, provided your earnings were above a certain limit (2009/10: £110 a week – the 'earnings threshold'). If you are self-employed, you will have been paying a flat-rate Class 2 NIC of £2.40 every week and possibly the earnings-related Class 4 NIC as well. You may also have paid Class 3 voluntary contributions at some point in your life in order to maintain your contributions record. If you are over pension age (65 for men and 60 for women) you do not pay NIC. There may have been times during your working life when you have not – either knowingly or unwittingly – paid NIC. If you have not paid sufficient contributions to qualify for a full-rate basic pension you may be entitled to a reduced rate of pension. However, your NIC record will have been maintained in the following circumstances.

If you have lived or worked outside Great Britain

If you have lived in Northern Ireland or the Isle of Man, any contributions paid there will count towards your pension. The same should also apply in most cases if you have lived or worked in an EU country or any country whose social security is linked to Britain's by a reciprocal arrangement. However, there have sometimes been problems with certain countries so, if you have any doubts, you should enquire what your position is at your pension centre.

If you have received Home Responsibilities Protection (HRP)

If you have not worked regularly at some time since 1978, because you have had to stay at home to care for either a child or a sick or elderly person, you may have protected your right to a pension by claiming HRP. This benefit allows you to deduct the years when you were required to give up work from the normal qualifying period for a basic pension and so, in effect, shorten the number of years when you would otherwise have been required to make contributions.

There are two important points to note. First, if you are a woman and were claiming Child Benefit, HRP should have been credited to you automatically, whereas a man staying at home to care for a child would have needed to arrange the transfer of Child Benefit to himself. Second, HRP is available only for complete tax years in which earnings were less than 52 times the lower earnings limit.

Although HRP can be claimed by both sexes, it predictably applies more frequently to women. For more information, see 'Pensions for women' at the end of this chapter, or obtain leaflet CF411, *How to Protect Your State Pension if You Are Looking after Someone at Home*, available from your pension centre; or see website: www.thepensionservice.gov.uk.

If you have been in any of the following situations

You will have been credited with contributions (instead of having to pay them) if:

* you were sick or unemployed (provided you sent in sick notes to your social security office, signed on at the unemployment benefit office or were in receipt of Jobseeker's Allowance);

- you were a man aged 60–64 and not working;
- you were entitled to maternity allowance, invalid care allowance or unemployability supplement;
- you were taking an approved course of training;
- you had left education but had not yet started working;
- since April 2000, your earnings had fallen between what are known as the lower earnings limit and the primary threshold, ie between £95 and £110 a week (2009/10).

Married women and widows

Married women and widows who do not qualify for a basic pension in their own right may be entitled to a basic pension on their husband's contributions at about 60 per cent of the level to which he is entitled (see 'Pensions for women' at the end of this chapter).

Since the introduction of independent taxation, husband and wife are assessed separately for tax. As a result, a married woman is now entitled to have her section of the joint pension offset against her own personal allowance – instead of being counted as part of her husband's taxable income. For many pensioner couples, this should mean a reduction in their tax liability.

Reduced-rate contributions note: many women retiring today may have paid a reduced-rate contribution under a scheme that was abolished in 1978. Women who were already paying a reduced-rate contribution were, however, allowed to continue doing so. These reduced-rate contributions *do not count* towards your pension and you will not have had any contributions credited to you. If you are still some years away from retirement, it could be to your advantage to cancel the reduced-rate option, as by doing so you may be able to build up a wider range of benefits without paying anything extra. This applies if you are currently (2009/10) earning between £95 and £110 a week, ie between the lower earnings limit and the primary threshold. If you are earning above the primary threshold (£110), to get the same extra benefits you would have to start paying extra contributions. For advice, contact your local tax office or see website: www.hmrc.gov.uk.

How your pension is worked out

Your total pension can come from three main sources: the basic pension, the additional pension and the graduated pension. Anyone wanting to work out what they are due can write to their pension centre for a 'pension forecast'. This is normally expressed in percentage terms so, for instance, someone with full contributions will get 100 per cent of pension. You can also get a forecast of the additional earnings-related pension to which you are entitled. To obtain a forecast, ring the pension service on 0845 3000 168 and request the form BR19, Pension Forecast Application Form. Or, if more convenient, you can print off the form from the Pension Service website: www.thepensionservice.gov.uk.

It is worth getting an early estimate of what your pension will be, as it may be possible to improve your NI Contribution record by making additional Class 3 voluntary contributions. See website: www.thepensionservice.gov.uk.

Basic pension

The full basic pension for a man or woman (April 2009/10) is £95.25 a week, and is £152.30 for a married couple (unless your spouse is entitled to more than the £57.05 spouse's addition on his or her own contributions, in which case you will receive more). Pensions are uprated in April each year. Up-to-date rates are contained in leaflet RM1, *Retirement – A Guide to Benefits for People Who Are Retiring or Have Retired*, obtainable from your pension centre and main Post Offices (website: www.dwp.gov.uk). All pensions are taxable other than one or two special categories, such as war widows and the victims of Nazism. If, however, your basic pension is your only source of income, you will not have to worry, as the amount you receive is below the Income Tax threshold.

The rate of basic pension depends on your record of NIC over your working life. To get the full rate you must have paid (or been credited with) contributions for roughly nine-tenths of your working life, although widows can also be entitled to a full basic pension on their husband's contributions. If you are divorced, you may be able to use your former spouse's contributions to improve your own pension entitlement, provided that you have not remarried before reaching pension age.

Your working life, for this purpose, is normally considered to be 39 years for a woman and 44 years for a man (ie age 16 until pension age), but it may be less if you were of working age but not in insurable employment when the National Insurance scheme started in 1948.

In 2006 the government announced a cut in the number of years' NIC needed to qualify for the full basic pension, which is 30 from this year, 2010. Those who reached pension age earlier than the date these rules came into force, however, did *not* benefit.

Due to improvements in service arrangements, you only need to claim a State pension two months before your State pension birthday date, rather than the three to four months previously required. The telephone number on which you make your claim has now been changed to 0800 731 7898. The Department for Work and Pensions (DWP) has also launched an online service where you can now claim benefits from home or abroad.

Reduced-rate pension

If you do not have full contributions but have maintained your contributions record for between a quarter and nine-tenths of your working life, you may get a pension at a reduced rate. The amount is calculated according to the number of years for which you have paid contributions. However, to get any basic pension you must satisfy two conditions. First, you must actually have paid enough full-rate contributions in any one tax year, from 6 April 1975, for that year to count as a qualifying year; or have paid 50 flat-rate contributions, in any one year, before 6 April 1975. Second, your total contributions must be enough to have entitled you to at least 25 per cent of the full basic rate.

Additional pension: SERPS

SERPS, the additional State pension scheme, was discontinued by the government in April 2002 and has been replaced by a new additional scheme, called the State Second Pension. Those formerly contracted into SERPS will not suffer any loss, as they will still keep the benefit of any contributions made. Equally, of course, those already in receipt of a SERPS pension will continue to receive their payments as normal. If you paid into the scheme, you probably know that the amount of additional pension you will get depends on your earnings above an annually adjusted 'lower earnings limit' for each complete tax year since April 1978.

If you have not already done so, it would be sensible to apply for a statement of your savings in SERPS by completing form BR19, Pension Forecast Application Form, obtainable from any pension centre. Full details and examples of how SERPS is worked out can be found in leaflet PM2, *State Pensions – Your Guide*, obtainable by calling the Pensions Info-Line on 0845 731 3233/0845 606 0265 or see the website of the Pension Service: www.thepensionservice.gov.uk.

In practical terms, the fact that SERPS has been discontinued may make very little difference to your plans. You can remain in the additional State pension scheme, ie the State Second Pension; or, if you think you can do better by making independent provision, you can invest instead in either a personal pension or a stakeholder pension. For details, see 'Personal pensions for employees and 'Stakeholder pensions', pages 53 and 56.

SERPS benefits for surviving spouses

The rules about inheriting a SERPS pension changed in October 2002, so they may have changed since you last worked out what pensions you will get. The changes are being gradually phased in up till October 2010. Additionally, anyone who was over State pension age on 5 October 2002 will be exempt from any cuts and will keep the right to pass on his or her SERPS pension in full to a bereaved spouse or civil partner, however many years away the bereavement may be. Equally, any younger widow, widower or civil partner who had already inherited a late spouse or civil partner's SERPS entitlement before 6 October 2002 will not be affected and will continue to receive the full amount. The DWP table below shows how the cuts apply to those reaching State pension age between October 2002 and 2010 (for further information, see leaflet SERPSL1, *Important Information for Married People – Inheritance of SERPS*) available from your local pension centre, Tel: 0845 606 0265; website: www.thepensionservice.gov.uk:

% SERPS passing to surviving spouse	Date when contributor reached State pension age
100	5 October 2002 or earlier
90	6 October 2002 – 5 October 2004
80	6 October 2004 – 5 October 2006
70	6 October 2006 – 5 October 2008
60	6 October 2008 – 5 October 2010
50	6 October 2010 or later

State Second Pension (S2P)

The State Second Pension replaced SERPS from April 2002. If you were previously contributing to SERPS, you are unlikely to notice very much difference. Your future additional pension will continue to be worked out on earnings on which you have paid Class 1 contributions as an employee. Class 1 contributions are paid (or credited) as a percentage of earnings, currently (2009/10) between £95 and £844 a week.

In time this will change as, a few years from now, the pension payments are planned to become flat-rate instead of earnings-related. The State Second Pension gives employees earning up to a certain amount (£31,800 in 2009/10) a better pension than SERPS, whether or not they are contracted out into a private pension, with most help going to those on the lowest earnings.

The main beneficiaries of the S2P will be: 1) people earning up to around £13,500, who will be able to save towards a much better pension; and 2) some carers and people with a long-term illness or disability, who will receive credits, equivalent to their earning £13,500, for periods when, owing to their caring responsibilities or health, they are unable to work. Others likely to gain are employees with earnings up to about £31,800, who should be able to look forward to a more generous additional pension than with SERPS.

The State Second Pension is not applicable to the self-employed, for whom the alternative pension choices are either a personal pension or a stakeholder pension (see pages 53 and 56). However, this may change, as the government has announced proposals to allow the self-employed to join S2P in return for higher National Insurance Contributions.

If you are a member of a contracted-out occupational pension scheme, you are legally entitled either to a pension that must be broadly the same as, or better than, the one you would have got under the State scheme, or to what are known as 'protected rights' (ie your and your employer's compulsory contributions to your pension together with their accumulated investment growth).

Graduated pension

This pension existed between April 1961 and April 1975. The amount you receive depends on the graduated NIC you paid during that period. Anyone over 18 and earning more than £9 a week at that time will probably be entitled to a small graduated pension. This includes married women and widows with reduced contribution liability. A widow or widower whose spouse dies when they are both over pension age can inherit half of the graduated pension based on his or her late spouse's contributions.

Ways to increase your pension

Deferring your pension

Your pension will be increased if you delay claiming it past State retirement age. You can do so whether you are still in work or not. For every year you defer taking your pension, there will be an increase in its value. For example, if you put off claiming your State pension for a year, when you do finally claim it you could get an extra 10.4 per cent added to your weekly state pension for life – that's just over an extra £1 for every £10 of State pension.

You can continue deferring your pension for as long as you like. The extra money will be paid to you when you eventually decide to claim your pension. You can choose whether to take it as a taxable lump sum or in higher weekly pension payments. If you choose to receive higher weekly payments, you will need to defer your pension for at least five weeks. If you go for the lump sum, deferral must be for at least one year; the rate of interest paid will be 2 per cent over bank rate. For further information, see leaflet SPD1, *Your Guide to State Pension Deferral: Putting off Your State Pension to Get Extra State Pension or a Lump Sum Payment Later*, obtainable by ringing 0845 731 3233 (website: www.thepensionservice.gov.uk). *Warning:* If you plan to defer your pension, you should also defer any graduated pension to which you may be entitled – or you risk losing the increases you would otherwise obtain.

Increases for dependants

From 6 April 2010 it will no longer be possible to claim an increase of your State pension for another adult. If you are already entitled to this increase on 5 April 2010 you will be able to keep it until you no longer meet the conditions for the increase, or until 5 April 2020, whichever is first. If you claim your State pension on or after 6 April 2010 you will not be able to claim an increase for an adult who depends on you financially when you finally claim your State pension. This is because you cannot claim this increase before you have started claiming your State Pension. For further information on adult dependency increases contact your pension centre or go to the website: www.thepensionservice.gov.uk.

Age addition

Your pension will be automatically increased once you reach 80. The current rate is 25p a week.

Income Support

If you have an inadequate income, you may qualify for Income Support. There are special premiums (ie additions) for lone parents, disabled people, carers and pensioners.

A condition of entitlement is that you should not have capital, including savings, of more than £16,000. To qualify for maximum Income Support, the capital limit is £6,000. For every £500 of capital over £6,000, individuals are deemed to be getting £1 a week income – so the actual amount of benefit will be reduced accordingly.

A big advantage is that people entitled to Income Support receive full help with their rent and should also not have any Council Tax to pay. See 'Housing benefit' and 'Council Tax benefit', in Chapter 8.

Pension Credit

All pensioners are guaranteed at least a minimum income. The Pension Credit was introduced in October 2003. This used to be known as 'Minimum Income Guarantee' (MIG), which has been superseded by the Pension Credit and is officially called Pension Credit Guarantee Credit. The basic rate for the standard minimum guarantee for 2009/10 is £130 a week for single people and £198.45 for couples. These totals exclude mortgage interest and disregarded income, for example attendance allowance. It incorporates a guaranteed element (ie the previous MIG) plus an addition designed to reward pensioners with modest savings. If you were previously receiving MIG, you should now automatically be getting the guaranteed element of Pension Credit. If you are not already receiving Pension Credit but think you would be entitled to do so, or if this is not happening for some reason, even though previously eligible you failed to claim it, ring the Pension Credit Helpline on 0800 991 234 or check its website: www.thepensionservice.gov.uk.

If you prefer, you can get an application form from any pension centre. At the same time, you might like to ask for leaflet PC1L, *Pension Credit – Pick It Up, It's Yours*. To help ensure that no one entitled to the credit misses out, claims can be backdated 12 months.

Other sources of help

Social Fund. If you are faced with an exceptional expense you find difficult to pay, you may be able to obtain a budgeting or crisis loan, or funeral payment, from the Social Fund. Ask at your social security or Jobcentre Plus office (website: www.jobcentreplus.gov.uk).

There are two other online sources of help relating to information on benefits. These are **Turn2Us** (www.turn2us.org.uk). This is a relatively new charity identifying potential sources of funding for those struggling with money. The second is **EntitledTo** (www.entitledto.co.uk), which will help you see if you qualify for certain benefits.

Working after you start getting your pension

This used to be a problem for many people because of the earnings rule. At the time, men between the ages of 65 and 69 and women between the ages of 60 and 64 who earned more than £75 a week had their basic State pension reduced. Happily, this does not apply any more, and today there is no longer any limit to the amount pensioners can earn.

Early retirement and your pension

Because so many people retire early, there is a widespread belief that it is possible to get an early pension. While the information is correct as regards many employers' occupational pension schemes, as well as for stakeholder and personal pensions, it does not apply to the basic State pension. If you take early retirement before the age of 60, it may be necessary for you to pay voluntary Class 3 NIC to protect your contributions record for pension purposes. If you are a man over 60, however, you will automatically get contribution credits from the tax year in which you reach 60.

How you get a pension

You should claim your pension a few months before you reach State pension age. The Department for Work and Pensions (DWP) should send you a claim form (BR1) at the proper time, but if this doesn't arrive it is your responsibility to contact the DWP. Remember, it will send the claim form to the last recorded address it holds for you, so if you have moved and not informed it, do make sure it has your current address. You should apply for the form about four months before you are due to retire. Or, if you prefer, instead of using a claim form you can ring the Pension Service claim line on 0845 300 1084 and give your details over the phone or you can get in touch online (www.thepensionservice.gov.uk). After you claim, you are told in writing exactly how much pension you will get. You will also be told what to do if you disagree with the decision. The information you are given should include the name and address of the organization responsible for paying you any guaranteed extra pension (ie the equivalent of what you would have received from the additional State pension).

How your pension can be paid

Pensions are usually paid direct into a bank account, rather than by order books and giros. You can choose whether it is a bank or building society account or, if you prefer, a Post Office Card Account. Those who want to do so can still collect their pension from the Post Office, although if you have a bank or building society account you will need to check whether your account offers this facility. All recipients whose pension is not already being paid direct will be notified by letter when they need to decide on an account and how, if necessary, they can arrange to open one. In the meantime, if you have a pension book or use giros, you can continue collecting your pension as normal.

NB: while most people who have already made the switch to direct payment find it safer and more convenient, there were fears that some more vulnerable pensioners would genuinely be unable to manage an account. The government has recognized this and individuals in this situation can still receive their money every week by cheque, which can be cashed at the Post Office or paid direct into a Post Office Card Account.

Other situations

If your pension is £5 a week or less, it will normally be paid once a year in arrears by a crossed order that you can pay into a bank or building society account. Payment is made each year shortly before Christmas. Pensions can be paid to an overseas address, if you are going abroad for six months or more. For further details see leaflets NI38, *Social Security Abroad*, obtainable from HMRC (NI Contributions) offices and GL29, *Going Abroad and Social Security Benefits*, obtainable from social security and pension centre offices (website: www.thepensionservice.gov.uk).

If you are in hospital, your pension can still be paid to you. Until recently, the amount was reduced if you were in hospital for more than 52 weeks but, since April 2006, this is no longer the case. You now can receive your pension in full for the duration of your stay, regardless of how long you have to remain in hospital. Leaflet GL12, *Going into Hospital?* (obtainable from Jobcentre Plus offices and NHS hospitals), provides full information (website: www.jobcentreplus.gov.uk).

Christmas bonus

Pensioners usually get a small tax-free bonus shortly before Christmas each year. The amount and due date are announced in advance. For many years the sum has been £10. The bonus is combined with your normal pension payment for the first week in December. From January 2009 every pensioner receives a £60 one-off payment, rising to £120 for couples, on top of the £10 bonus to help pay for energy bills.

Advice

If you have any queries or think you may not be obtaining your full pension entitlement, you should contact the Pension Service as soon as possible. If you think a mistake has been made, you have the right to appeal and can insist on your claim being heard by an independent tribunal.

Before doing so, you would be strongly advised to consult a solicitor at the Citizens Advice Bureau or the Welfare Advice Unit of your social security office. Some areas have special Tribunal Representation Units to assist people to make claims at tribunals. If you are contacting the Pension Service with a query, you should quote either your National Insurance number (or your spouse's) or your pension number if you have already started receiving your pension.

For further information about pensions, see leaflets RM1, *Retirement – A Guide to Benefits for People Who Are Retiring or Have Retired*, and PM2, *State Pensions – Your Guide*, obtainable by calling the Pensions Information Line on 0845 731 3233, or see the website: www.thepensionservice.gov.uk.

Private pensions

The importance of persuading individuals to save for their own pension instead of just relying on the State has been recognized by successive governments. Encouragement has been made through tax incentives so that, despite recent problems, pension savings are still one of the most tax-effective investments available:

- You get Income Tax relief on contributions at your highest tax rate.
- The pension fund is totally exempt from Income Tax and Capital Gains Tax, providing good growth prospects for your money.
- Part of the pension can be taken as a cash sum when you retire, and that too is tax-free.

Private pension schemes fall into two broad categories: those arranged by employers, for example company pension schemes, and those you can arrange for yourself.

Company pension schemes

Employee pension enrolment and employer contributions are to be made compulsory as part of the government's attempt to take control of the UK's impending demographic crisis. Provisions are contained in the Pensions Act 2008, which is due to come into force in 2012. It covers the automatic enrolment of qualifying workers into a qualifying workplace pension scheme. It also requires employers to make contributions to such a scheme. To make sure that employers are able to comply with such duties a universal personal account scheme is being created. Consultations and regulations will continue to be issued that will make it clearer what is expected of employers and pensions schemes in anticipation of the new regime in 2012.

The pensions industry has long been aware of the impending demographic crisis that threatens to leave millions with little or no additional pension provision above the basic State pension. The Turner Report (its full title is The Pension Commission Full Report) in 2005 called for urgent changes in the reform of the State pension system; boosting private savings and longer working. The government's response was two acts – The Pensions Act 2007 and the Pensions Act 2008. Those most likely to suffer under the new rules are high earners, since the personal account regime has a limit of £3,600 per annum. Neither does it assist in respect of the removal of higher rate tax relief for these employees.

About 10 million people are now participating in company schemes. While these can vary considerably, the following basic features apply to all of them.

Pension fund

Pension contributions go into a pension fund that is quite separate from your employer's company. It is set up under trust and run by trustees, appointed from management and from pension scheme members. It is the job of the trustees to manage the fund and its investments and to ensure that the benefit promises are kept.

Payments into the fund

Your scheme may or may not ask for a contribution from you. For this reason, schemes are known as 'contributory' or 'non-contributory'. If (as is normally the case) you are required to make a contribution, this will be deducted from your pay before you receive it.

Your employer's contributions to the scheme represent the money your employer is setting aside for your pension and other benefits. In some schemes the amount is calculated as a fixed percentage of your earnings. In others the scheme actuary will estimate the amount that your employer needs to pay to ensure your (and other members') benefits in the future.

Benefits from the scheme

All pension scheme members should be given a booklet describing how the scheme works, what benefits it provides and other information, including the address of the Pensions Ombudsman. If you do not receive one, you should ask the person in the company responsible for the pension scheme – this is often the personnel manager – to supply you with a booklet. You can also ask to see a copy of the trust deed as well as the latest annual report and audited accounts. The key benefits applicable to most pension schemes include:

* A pension due at whatever age is specified by the scheme, usually somewhere between 60 and 65 (although many companies offer early retirement provision).

- Death benefit (sometimes known as 'lump sum life assurance'), paid out if you die before retirement age.
- A widow's or widower's pension paid for life no matter when you die. NB: since December 2005, same-sex couples who enter a civil partnership by officially registering their relationship are treated the same as married couples, which among other benefits entitles them to receive an equivalent survivor's pension to that of a married person on the death of their partner.

Contribution and benefit limits

The government sets limits (for tax relief) on the contributions that individuals can invest in their pension plan and on the pension benefits they can receive. Prior to April 2006, the rules differed between one type of scheme and another. These anomalies have now been swept away, as the government has brought all company and personal pension schemes under a single tax regime.

Among other important changes, the earnings cap is no longer a factor. Instead, individuals can now invest up to 100 per cent of annual earnings into their plan (or plans) with the benefit of tax relief, up to a maximum figure – known as the annual allowance – of £235,000. Higher contributions are allowed but without any tax relief on the excess. There is also a lifetime limit of £1.65 million for total pension funds, including any fund growth. Funds in excess of the lifetime limit are subject to a 25 per cent recovery charge (ie tax) if taken as income, or 55 per cent if taken as a lump sum. Both the annual allowance and the lifetime limit will be increased in stages, rising respectively to £255,000 and £1.8 million by 2010/11. The ceiling on tax relief given to people with pension funds up to £1.8 million will be maintained until 2015/16.

Tax-free lump sum

Provided your scheme rules allow it, you can take up to a maximum of 25 per cent of the value of your fund – including Additional Voluntary Contributions (AVCs) and contracted-out benefits from the State Second Pension scheme – from age 55 without having to retire. Furthermore, unless you are in a final salary scheme, you are no longer obliged to take any pension income when accessing your lump sum but can leave the money in the fund to continue to grow. A major new benefit for those nearing retirement is that they can ease into part-time work, take their lump sum and, if they wish to do so, start drawing some pension income.

Scheme rules

The fact that HMRC has changed the rules is unfortunately no guarantee that individuals will be able to take full advantage of all the new options that have become available. Their employer's pension scheme rules will also need to have been altered accordingly, which may not always be the case. Before making any definite plans, it is advisable first to check with whoever is responsible for the company scheme.

Types of scheme

Due to the difficulties in the financial climate many firms are finding final salary pension schemes unsustainable. The future trend will be that people will have to do far more for themselves for pension provision than has been seen in the past. There are other types of pension schemes such as average earnings and flat-rate schemes.

Final salary scheme

Now increasingly rare, this is where your pension is calculated as a proportion of your final pay, which could mean literally the last year you work, or possibly for controlling directors the average of three consecutive years during the last 10. The amount you receive depends on two factors: the number of years you have worked for the organization and the fraction of final pay on which the scheme is based, typically 1/60th or 1/80th. So if you have worked 30 years for a company that has a 1/60th pension scheme, you will receive 30/60ths of your final pay – in other words, half. Final pay schemes can be contracted into or out of the additional State pension scheme. If a scheme is contracted out, it must provide a pension that is broadly equal to, or better than, its State equivalent.

Money purchase scheme

Unlike final salary schemes, the amount of pension you receive is not based on a fixed formula but (within HMRC limits) is dependent on the investment performance of the fund into which your own and your employer's contributions on your behalf have been paid. Although there is an element of risk with money purchase schemes, in that no one can forecast with certainty how well or badly a pension fund might do, in practice most trustees act very conservatively.

Different schemes have different ways of determining how members' pension entitlements are calculated. You should enquire what the rules are and additionally (if you have not already received one) you should request a statutory money purchase illustration (SMPI), which should give you an idea of what size pension you might realistically expect once inflation has been taken into account. You should receive a fresh SMPI statement every year, based on the actuarial assumptions that have been used to calculate its growth and the (inflation-adjusted) income it should yield on purchase of an annuity. One of the more important changes of the new rules is that it is no longer compulsory to purchase an annuity. Individuals who prefer to keep their fund invested can opt, at 75, for an alternatively secured pension (see page 43).

Group personal pension scheme

Employers sometimes arrange group schemes for employees wishing to build up a personal pension. They are usually more advantageous than individual personal pensions because employers normally make contributions of 3 per cent (or more) into all participants' pension funds. Also, because of the group savings, the charges tend to be lower than for individually administered schemes. All personal pensions, whether group or individual, are a form of money purchase scheme.

Contracted-out mixed benefit scheme (COMBS)

This is a mixed scheme that combines elements of salary-related and money purchase schemes.

Average earnings scheme

As its name implies, this is based on your average earnings over the total period of time that you are participating in the scheme. Every year, an amount goes into the scheme on your behalf, calculated in accordance with your level of earnings. As your salary increases, so too do your potential benefits. Each year, your 'profits' from the scheme are worked out from a formal table and the total of all these annual sums constitutes your pension.

Flat-rate pension scheme

Your level of pay is not a factor. Instead, the same flat rate applies to everyone, multiplied by the number of years in which they have been participants of the scheme. So, for example, if the flat rate is £500 a year of pension and you have been a member of the scheme for 20 years, your pension will be £10,000 a year.

Additional or other schemes

There may be one scheme that applies to everyone in the organization or there may be a variety of schemes for different grades of employee. For example, there may be a works scheme and a staff scheme operating side by side. It is also quite common for there to be a special pension scheme for executives and directors. The government recently announced details of a landmark new savings scheme to give all employees the right to a workplace pension with a contribution from their employer. Research has shown strong support for plans to tackle savings inertia by automatically enrolling employees into the new scheme. The proposed personal pensions savings accounts would be run as an occupational pensions scheme managed by a board of trustees – placing the interests of members at its heart. Trustees would be advised by a members' panel and an employers' panel – to ensure that the voices of both individuals saving in the scheme and contributing employers are heard. There would be an annual contribution limit which would be uprated by earnings year on year. It is estimated that between 6 and 10 million people will save in personal accounts from 2012. Employees will see their savings accounts matched pound for pound by a combination of contributions from their employer and the government. The employees will put in a minimum of 4 per cent of their salary, the employer will put in a minimum of 3 per cent, and 1 per cent will come from the government in tax relief.

There is an organization that is committed to helping anyone who has an occupational pension in the UK. It has over 100,000 members who benefit from having a powerful voice representing their interests. **Unite** is the largest member of the Occupational Pensioners' Alliance and offers support to its members through campaigns, helplines, networks and representation. For further information contact Unite, Tel: 01582 663880; e-mail: info@pensioneronline.com; website: www.pensioneronline.com.

Executive pension plans

These are individual pension plans arranged by an employer for the benefit of some or all executives above a certain grade. In some companies, executive pension plans apply only to directors; in others, they may also include senior and middle management. Equally, there may be a separate policy for each individual, or a master policy covering everyone in the scheme.

One of the attractions of executive pension plans is their potential flexibility. They can be tailored to cater for differing retirement ages as well as for varying contribution levels, which explains why some organizations are able to offer early retirement on very attractive terms.

Historically, executive pension plans are of the money purchase type, and the same government-allowable contribution and benefit rules apply equally to them as to other pension schemes. Normally, one of the following four types of investment policy is used: with profits, unit linked, deposit administration and non-profit. These are described in the section 'Personal pension schemes' on page 53. See also 'Top-up schemes' on page 40.

Possible changes to your scheme

Unfortunately, as mentioned earlier, more and more employers have closed their final salary schemes to new entrants and even, in some cases, discontinued them for existing members – replacing them instead with money purchase schemes. While there is no pretending that money purchase schemes are as good as final salary ones, you will almost certainly be better off remaining in your employer's scheme than leaving it in favour of, say, a personal pension. Your employer will still be making contributions into the scheme on your behalf, which very few employers do in the case of personal pensions, and additionally you will not have any management charges to pay, which, if you had a personal pension, would come out of your own fund. Also, if you fear that your pension will be insufficient, you have several possible ways of helping to improve it: you can make AVC contributions (see page 44); you can invest in a stakeholder scheme (this is now allowed even if you have earnings of more than £30,000); or you can invest in a personal pension. If you like, you can do all three.

Focus on high earners

Most of the previous rules affecting high earners, in particular the earnings cap and the allowable tax-free lump sum, have been swept away. In common with everyone else, their maximum tax-free lump sum is now limited to 25 per cent of their fund value or 25 per cent of their lifetime limit, whichever is lower. For many high earners, this is likely to be a positive gain. But not all pension schemes have changed their rules accordingly, so when it comes to the lump sum this might well be a point to check. Equally, a couple of other former rules may well still apply. In particular, until recently, high earners who joined a new pension scheme were required to base their final salary assessment on their average earnings over any three consecutive years during their last 10. Similarly, controlling directors were not permitted to resign just before retirement to boost their salary but, instead, had to use the three-year average method of calculation. Also, gains from share options in the final year of employment were not allowed in the calculation of final salary.

Accelerated accrual rates

Some schemes allow individuals to enjoy an enhanced accrual scale to qualify for full pension benefits after an agreed minimum number of years' service.

Top-up schemes

Employers can still set up 'top-up' pension schemes to provide additional benefits above the HMRC limits, but such schemes are now taxable and their former advantages have largely gone as a result of the new pension rules introduced in 2006. There is some transitional relief for individuals with existing schemes. If you have a FURBS (funded, unapproved retirement benefit scheme), SUURBS (secured, unfunded, unapproved retirement benefit scheme) or similar, expert advice is strongly recommended to explore your best course of action.

Compulsory purchase annuities

Until April 2006, virtually everyone with a personal pension, section 226 policy, retirement annuity, contracted-out company money purchase scheme (COMPS) or AVC arrangement was required by law to purchase an annuity. Although today individuals have greater choice in the matter – see 'Alternatively secured pension', below – for most people the purchase of an annuity (though no longer compulsory) will still be the most sensible arrangement, since annuities offer greater security than most other ways of providing you with an income in retirement. Even if you are not planning to buy an annuity at the present time, it is still worth understanding how annuities work and the amount of choice you have to determine which of the varied possibilities suits you best.

The basics

An annuity is a regular income paid in exchange for a lump sum, usually the result of years of investing in an approved, tax-free pension scheme. There are different types of annuity; the vast majority are conventional and pay a risk-free income that is guaranteed for life. The amount you will receive depends on your age, whether you are male or female, the size of your pension fund and, in some circumstances, the state of your health. You have the choice of using the whole of your accumulated pension fund or you can first take all, or part, of your tax-free lump sum. If you take your lump sum, this will reduce the size of your annuity and the amount of annual income you receive.

Other important factors that can affect your annuity 'earnings' include: what add-on options you may choose, the timing of when you buy your annuity, and the choice of provider. A further consideration could be your life expectancy. Some providers offer annuities that pay enhanced rates to people suffering from ill health or who have been regular smokers for some years.

Add-on options

The most typical options that you will be offered include: a spouse's pension; annual increases, which may either be fixed at, say, 3 or 5 per cent or may be linked to retail price inflation; and a return of some of the capital (either in the form of a lump sum or in annual payments over five or 10 years) should you die unexpectedly early. Wise as such options usually are to protect your and your dependants' long-term security, there will almost invariably be some additional cost that, if you were to go for all the possible extras, could reduce the annual income by around 50 per cent.

Timing

Today everyone with a money purchase scheme, including those with a free-standing AVC (FSAVC), can choose when they wish to purchase an annuity between the ages of 50 and 75, or whether on reaching 75, instead of purchasing an annuity, they would prefer to extend a drawdown scheme (see below) and opt for an alternatively secured pension.

The two key factors when it comes to a question of timing are what age you are when you purchase an annuity and what the level of interest rates are at the time. As a general rule, the older you are and the higher the level of interest rates, the bigger the annual income you will receive. *NB:* the government has now raised the earliest age at which you can take a pension (or benefit from the income withdrawal option) to 55 – this change came into effect in 2009.

If you choose to wait, you have what is known as the *income withdrawal option,* or *drawdown* as it is sometimes called. This allows you to take your tax-free lump sum any time from age 55 to 75, and to withdraw a limited income from the fund (the maximum permitted is broadly equal to the annuity your fund could have provided) during the deferral period. The rest of the money has to remain in the fund, where it can continue to be invested and grow tax-free. In case of death, the fund may pass to the surviving spouse, who can either continue with the income withdrawal option or purchase an annuity. Alternatively, the fund can be paid out to the surviving spouse (or to the estate of the deceased) as a lump sum, minus a 35 per cent tax charge.

Attractive as this sounds, income withdrawal is not a decision to be entered into lightly. While the big gain of the withdrawal option is that it allows individuals both to delay purchase of an annuity until interest rates are favourable and to obtain their lump sum and – if wanted – an income in the meantime, there are also very considerable risks. In particular: the stock market could fall, reducing the capital value of your pension fund; interest rates could be even less favourable when you eventually need to purchase an annuity; commission rates are usually high compared with those for conventional annuities and there could also be substantial administration charges to pay; and some plans are more tax-efficient than others.

Not only is independent financial advice very strongly recommended if you are considering deferring the purchase of an annuity, but many experts advise that the income withdrawal option is not suitable for anyone with less than £250,000 in their pension fund. The issue is not that clear cut, however, and those with smaller funds may be advised to use income withdrawal to give themselves greater flexibility together with some additional income if, for example, they move to part-time work. Sensible as this may be in certain circumstances, you would need to ensure that you do not run down your fund too far and so risk ending up with an inadequate pension.

An alternative to drawdown, for those who have no need to take their tax-free lump sum up front, is *phased retirement.* It is, however, not available to people in an employer's scheme but only to those with personal pensions. The scheme works broadly as follows. In effect, your pension fund is divided into slices – say 1,000 – and each year you can withdraw a number of these to purchase an annuity or income drawdown scheme, while at the same time taking up to 25 per cent of the money as tax-free income. The remainder of your money stays in the fund and can continue to be invested.

As well as allowing you greater control over your annuity purchase (since, as opposed to just one, you would be buying a series of smaller annuities), one of the major advantages of phased retirement is that all money left in your pension fund on death can (unless the present rules are changed) be passed on to your spouse, or other beneficiaries, free of tax.

However, as with drawdown, there are risks as well as advantages, and expert advice is strongly recommended. For further information about withdrawal schemes, you might find it useful to read *Income Withdrawal – A Retirement Option for You?*, obtainable free from the Financial Services Authority, Tel: 0845 606 1234; website: www.fsa.gov.uk.

Choice of provider

Whether you intend to buy a normal retirement annuity, a drawdown pension plan as described above or one of the newer with-profits or unit-linked annuities, this is one area above all where expert independent advice is essential. Annuity rates offered by life companies can vary by as much as 25 per cent, and the difference between the best and worst choice could affect your income by hundreds of pounds a year or more. There is no obligation to buy your annuity from the company that has been managing your pension plan. Indeed, the best people for pension plans are not usually the most competitive for annuities and, while there may be attractions in remaining with the same company (some offer loyalty bonuses), your decision will need to be based on the best all-round terms you can get at the time of purchase. But once you have made a choice, it is extremely difficult to switch.

Alternatively secured pension

If you dislike the idea of tying up your money for good, you may be attracted to limited period annuities or value protected annuities, introduced by the government in 2006 to allow individuals greater flexibility. The *alternatively secured pension (ASP)*, which is a variation on the drawdown scheme, is available to individuals over age 75 who would rather keep their fund invested than buy a conventional annuity. When first announced, a major attraction of ASPs was that pension assets remaining on death could be transferred to the pension funds of other members in the scheme, free of inheritance tax. A further advantage of having an ASP was that individuals who did not require their pension benefits for a while had the choice of leaving all the money in their fund, as opposed to withdrawing part of it as annual income.

Since 6 April 2007, all this has changed. While the remaining assets on death can still be passed on to spouses, civil partners, financial dependants or a charity free of IHT, in all other cases the money is subject to an 'unauthorized payment' charge of up to 70 per cent plus inheritance tax – effectively adding up to a tax of 82 per cent. It is also no longer possible to leave all the money in the fund.

Instead there is now a requirement to withdraw a minimum income every year, equivalent to the annual amount that could have been obtained from a comparable annuity at age 75. The maximum allowed is 70 per cent of what an annuity would have paid. An ASP is not necessarily for life: if you change your mind, you can buy an annuity at any time.

You are advised to take advice from an independent financial adviser, a pensions consultant or from one of the several companies that specialize in tracking annuity rates. **The Annuity Bureau,** for example, monitors the rates on a daily basis and will track the optimum rate that best suits your particular circumstances. Depending on the amount of personalized advice you require, there may be a fee for using this service. If you would like it to do so, the Annuity Bureau can also arrange the purchase and deal with the paperwork both for normal retirement annuities and for drawdown pensions. For a copy of a free guide, *Maximising Retirement Money*, and further information, contact The Annuity Bureau Ltd, Tel: 0845 602 6263; website: www.alexanderforbes.co.uk.

Another annuity specialist that offers similar services is **Annuity Direct,** Tel: 020 7684 5000; website: www.annuitydirect.co.uk. A free guide with information about with-profit and investment-linked annuities and drawdown is available by calling Freephone 0500 506575.

Pension pot of less than £15,000

People with a pension pot of under £15,000 are not required to buy an annuity. Instead, once they reach 60, they can take all the money as a lump sum – with a quarter of their lump sum being tax-free and the remainder subject to Income Tax. If annuity rates are still at their current low, some individuals might be better off paying the tax. Your pension provider, or an independent financial adviser (IFA), should be able to advise you at the time. An important point if you have more than one pension plan is that the 'exempt' amount of £15,000 does not apply to each of them but is the total aggregate value of all your plans. If you wish to take a lump sum from all of them, this will need to have been arranged within a 12-month period, at any time between age 60 and 75.

Additional voluntary contributions (AVCs)

If, as you approach retirement, you become aware that you are not going to have a big enough pension to live as comfortably as you would like, you might seriously consider the possibility of making AVCs. Although no longer as valuable as they once were, because the 2006 rule changes allow individuals similar ways of boosting their pension, nevertheless for some people AVCs might still offer the best solution. Their particular attractions are, first, that AVCs – as well as the growth of the plan – enjoy full tax relief, so for basic-rate taxpayers HMRC is in effect paying £20 of every £100 invested. A further advantage is that some AVCs allow you to purchase 'added years', to make up any shortfall in your entitlement to benefit under a company scheme.

However, an option known as 'free-standing AVCs' (FSAVCs) is also on offer. As the name implies, these are not linked to a company scheme but can be purchased independently from insurance companies, building societies, banks, unit trusts, friendly societies and IFAs. Individuals can, if they wish, contribute both to company AVCs and to a free-standing plan or plans. To enjoy the tax relief, the total of all your AVCs plus other contributions to the pension plan is not allowed to exceed your annual earnings, or your annual allowance if this is lower.

Rule changes

Over the years, there have been several rule changes of which you should be aware:

- Previously, individuals had to make a commitment to pay regular contributions for a period of at least five years. This requirement has been abolished and (provided the actual scheme rules permit) both the amount and the timing of payments can be varied to suit members according to their personal circumstances.
- AVCs purchased between April 1987 and 5 April 2006 can now go towards your pension or towards your lump sum, as you prefer.
- AVC benefits, provided your scheme rules allow, can now be taken at any time between ages 50 and 75 (or earlier if an individual is forced to leave employment owing to incapacity). If you choose to draw your AVC benefits before you retire, they would normally have to be taken as part of your tax-free lump sum or in the form of income drawdown (see page 42).

Choosing an AVC plan

The best schemes can yield excellent value and for many individuals can be one of the most effective ways of increasing their security in retirement. All scheme providers (ie both company AVC and FSAVC schemes) must give prospective investors 'key features' information, including in particular details of the charges. Also, anyone advising you about the purchase of FSAVCs must at the very least explain the basic differences between the FSAVCs being recommended and the AVCs offered by your employer's scheme.

IFAs must go further and give you an analysis of the specific differences to help you decide which type of scheme – or possible alternative type of investment – would be in your best financial interest. When discussing the options, a particular question you might ask is whether it would be more sensible for you to invest in an ISA. In general, the charges are likely to be lower with a collective AVC scheme offered by an employer than for free-standing contracts. Also, some employers match members' contributions to a company AVC scheme with extra contributions to the occupational scheme. Against this, if the performance is pedestrian or if there are early retirement penalties, you might still be better off with FSAVCs or a SIPP (Self-Invested Personal Pension; see page 59) or other personal pension.

As with any other important investment decision, you would be well advised to take your time, do some basic research into the track record of any policies you might be considering (specialist publications such as *Money Management* provide a good starting point) and on no account sign any document without first being absolutely certain that you fully understand all the terms and conditions. Finally, if you are already subscribing to company AVCs, before investing in a new plan check on your present level of contributions and the benefits that these are expected to yield. You should be aware that current taxation, legislation and HMRC practice are all liable to change without notice, and the impact of taxation (and any tax reliefs) depends on individual circumstances. Please check details with your company pension adviser or IFA, who should be only too happy to answer any questions.

Early leavers

In the past early leavers tended to do very badly, owing to the heavy financial penalties of withdrawing from a scheme in mid-term. In recent years, however, the government has introduced new rules that help considerably. For example, employers can now pay a full pension, without actuarial reduction, at any age between 50 and 70. Companies are under no obligation to do so but, for those people lucky enough to work for an organization that has amended its pension scheme rules accordingly, this provision could make an immense difference to the financial position of early retirees. It has to be said, however, that most employers still apply actuarial reductions (although these are sometimes waived in special cases such as redundancy), so if you are thinking of taking early retirement it is advisable to work out very carefully how this might affect your pension.

Another important change concerns what are known as your *preserved rights* – in other words, your financial rights with regard to your pension. Previously you were entitled to these rights only if you had been in an employer's scheme for at least five years. Today, the qualifying period is two years. If you leave earlier but have at least three months' qualifying service in the scheme, you now have a choice. Whereas previously the best you might have hoped for was a refund of contributions, today, if you prefer, you can request to have a cash sum transferred to another scheme. But, as you may realize, the amount of money involved is not likely to be very large.

There are three choices available to people with preserved rights who leave a company to switch jobs: leaving your pension with the scheme, taking your pension to a new scheme, or taking your pension to an insurance company.

1. Leaving the pension with the scheme

You remain a member of the scheme and receive a pension at the scheme's normal retirement age. If the scheme is a final salary one, the value would probably be calculated on 1/60th (or 1/80th) of your earnings at the time of your leaving and the number of years you have worked for the company. Whereas previously most pensions were frozen, today company schemes are obliged to increase the accrued pension rights by 2.5 per cent (5 per cent until 2005) a year or the rate of inflation, whichever is lower. Another advantage of remaining in the scheme is that you keep any benefits – such as a widow's pension and possibly others – that are already included. Also, once you start receiving your pension, you would be entitled to any extra increases that may be given. In the case of money purchase schemes, your accumulated assets would normally remain invested in the fund, hopefully growing every year to buy you a bigger pension on retirement. You would also be entitled to any benefit that the scheme provided under the rules.

2. Taking your pension to a new scheme

You do not have to make an immediate decision. You can transfer your pension scheme at any time, provided you do so over a year before you retire. If you wish to switch to a new scheme, this could be to another company scheme, a personal pension or a stakeholder pension. Personal and stakeholder pensions are described later in this chapter, so if you are interested in taking advantage of either of these you should read the sections carefully. Here, we explain the various possibilities if you wish to join a scheme run by your new employer.

Early leavers now have the right to move their pension – or, more precisely, its transfer value – to a new employer's scheme willing to accept it. The transfer value is the cash value of your current pension rights. Calculating this, however, can be problematic, and early leavers are often at a disadvantage compared with those who remain in the scheme. Joining a new employer's scheme does not necessarily oblige you to transfer your previous benefits. In some circumstances, there may be very good arguments for leaving your existing benefits with your former scheme and joining your new employer's scheme from scratch for the remaining years that you are working. Since you could be at risk of giving up more than you stand to gain by transferring your benefits to a new scheme, expert advice is strongly recommended.

3. Taking your pension to an insurance company

If neither of the two previous options appeal, or your new company will not accept your old pension value into its own scheme, you can go independent and have the transfer value of your pension invested by a life company into a personal scheme. After deducting its charges, the life company would invest the balance of the money in the fund, or funds, of your choice.

Advice

Deciding on your best option is not easy, so before taking action you should at least consult your company pension scheme manager to give you an assessment of the likely value of your pension if you leave it in the scheme. An important point to bear in mind is that your present company scheme may include valuable extras, such as a spouse's pension, life cover and attractive early retirement terms in the event of ill health.

If you are planning to switch, you will need to decide between a section 32 buy-out, a personal pension and a stakeholder pension. Although for a majority of employees a personal or stakeholder pension is usually likely to offer a higher return, there are certain limitations, and the accepted wisdom seems to be that the older the employee and the larger the transfer value, the more attractive a section 32 buy-out becomes. Because this is a complex area – and making the wrong decision could prove expensive – independent expert advice is very strongly recommended. Particularly if a large sum of money is involved, it could pay you to get the advice of a pension consultant. For a list of those operating in your area, contact the **Society of Pension Consultants,** Tel: 020 7353 1688; email: john.mortimer@spc.uk.com; website: www.spc.uk.com.

Becoming self-employed

If, as opposed to switching jobs, you leave paid employment to start your own enterprise, you are allowed to transfer your accumulated pension rights into a new fund. There are three main options. The most obvious solution is to invest your money with an insurance company, as mentioned above, or to take either a personal or a stakeholder pension. Alternatively, if you expect to be in a high earning bracket, you might consider setting up a limited company, even if you are the only salaried employee, rather than launching the same business as a self-employed individual. The company could set up a self-administered pension scheme with loan-back facilities plus other advantages. However, there are various pros and cons that will need to be weighed up carefully depending on the transfer value of your earlier pension and the anticipated annual amount available for investing in your new scheme. Since this is rather a complex area, before taking any action you are strongly advised to consult your financial adviser. A third possibility, which might be more attractive if you are fairly close to normal retirement age, is to leave your pension in your former employer's scheme. See above, 'Leaving the pension with the scheme'.

Useful reading

Transferring a Pension to Another Scheme and *Ill-Health Early Retirement*, obtainable from the Pensions Advisory Service, Tel: 0845 601 2923; website: www.pensionsadvisoryservice.org.uk.
Leaflet PM4, *Personal Pensions – Your Guide*, obtainable by calling the Pensions Info order line on 0845 731 3233; website: www.thepensionservice.gov.uk.
Stakeholder Pensions and Decision Trees, obtainable from the Financial Services Authority, Tel: 0300 500 5000; website: www.fsa.gov.uk.

Minimum retirement age

The minimum age at which you are allowed to take early retirement and draw your pension has just risen to 55 – effective 6 April 2010.

Questions on your pension scheme

Most people find it very difficult to understand how their pension scheme works. However, your pension is a valuable asset, especially as you approach retirement, and it is important that you should know the main essentials, including any options that may still be available to you.

If you have a query or if you are concerned in some way about your pension, you should approach whoever is responsible for the scheme in your organization. If the company is large, there may be a special person to look after the scheme on a day-to-day basis: this could be the pensions manager or, quite often, it is someone in the personnel department. In a smaller company, the pension scheme may be looked after by the company secretary or managing director. The sort of questions you might ask will vary according to circumstance, such as: before you join the scheme, if you are thinking of changing jobs, if you are hoping to retire early and so on. You will probably think of plenty of additional points of your own. The questions listed are simply an indication of some of the key information you may require in order to plan sensibly ahead.

If you want to leave the organization to change jobs

- Could you have a refund of contributions if you were to leave shortly after joining?
- How much will your deferred pension be worth?
- Should you wish to move the transfer value to another scheme, how long would you have to wait from the date of your request? (This should normally be within three to six months.)

If you leave for other reasons

- What happens if you become ill – or die – before pension age?
- What are the arrangements if you want to retire early? Most schemes allow you to do this if you are within about 10 years of normal retirement age, but your pension may be reduced accordingly. Many schemes, in fact, operate a sliding scale of benefits, with more generous terms offered to those who retire later rather than earlier.

If you stay until normal retirement age

- What will your pension be on your present salary? And what would it be assuming your salary increases by, say, 5 or 10 per cent before you eventually retire?
- What spouse's pension will be paid? Can a pension be paid to other dependants?
- Similarly, can a pension be paid to a partner, male or female?
- What happens if you continue working with the organization after retirement age? Normally, any contributions you are making to the scheme will cease to be required and your pension (which will not usually be paid until you retire) will be increased to compensate for its deferment. NB: Since April 2006, provided their scheme rules allow it, members of occupational pension schemes can draw their pension benefits, if they wish, without having to wait until after they leave.
- What are the arrangements if you retire from the organization as a salaried employee but become a retained consultant or contractor?

If you just want information

- Are any changes envisaged to the scheme? For example, if it is a final salary one, is there any chance that it might be wound up and a money purchase one offered instead?
- If there were a new money purchase scheme, would the company be making the same contributions as before or would these be lower in future?
- Is there any risk that benefits – either members' own or those for dependants – could be reduced?
- Is there a possibility that members might be required to pay higher contributions than at present?

What to do before retirement

In addition to understanding your current pension scheme, you may also need to chase up any previous schemes of which you were a member. This is well worth pursuing, as you could be owed money from one or more schemes, which will all add to your pension on retirement day.

You may be able to get the information from your previous employer(s). If you have difficulty in locating them – perhaps because the company has been taken over – contact the **Pension Tracing Service,** which assists individuals who need help in tracing their pension rights. This is a free service, run by the Pension Service, part of the Department for Work and Pensions. Its database contains the details of over 200,000 occupational and personal pension scheme administrators. Applicants can either write to the Pension Tracing Service, giving as much detail about the employer and pension scheme as possible, or alternatively request a trace application form (PTI) to complete. Call the Pension Tracing Service, Tel: 0845 600 2537 (if you have difficulty with your hearing or speech, you can call 0845 300 0169). It is also possible to fill in a tracing request form online by visiting the website (www.thepensionservice.gov.uk) and choosing the link to the Pension Tracing Service.

Other help and advice

If you have any queries or problems to do with your pension, in addition to the Pension Tracing Service there are three main sources of help available to you. These are the trustees or managers of your pension scheme, the Pensions Advisory Service and the Pensions Ombudsman.

Trustees or managers

These are the first people to contact if you do not properly understand your benefit entitlements or if you are unhappy about some point to do with your pension. Pensions managers (or other people responsible for pensions) should give you their names and tell you how they can be reached.

The Pensions Advisory Service

This is an independent voluntary organization with a network of 500 professional advisers throughout the UK. It can give free help and advice, other than financial advice, on all matters to do with any type of pension scheme. The service is available to any member of the public who either has a specific query or just needs general information. It operates a local call rate helpline on 0845 601 2923; website: www.thepensionsadvisoryservice.org.uk.

Pensions Ombudsman

You would normally approach the Ombudsman *only* if neither the pension scheme manager (or trustees) nor the Pensions Advisory Service is able to solve your problem. The Ombudsman can investigate: 1) complaints of maladministration by the trustees, managers or administrators of a pension scheme or by an employer; 2) disputes of fact or law with the trustees, managers or an employer. The Ombudsman does not, however, investigate complaints about mis-selling of pension schemes, a complaint that is already subject to court proceedings, one that is about a State social security benefit, or a dispute that is more appropriate for investigation by another regulatory body. There is also a time limit for lodging complaints, which is normally within three years of the act, or failure to act, about which you are complaining.

Provided the problem comes within the Ombudsman's orbit, he will look into all the facts for you and will inform you of his decision, together with his reasons. There is no charge for the Ombudsman's service. The Pensions Ombudsman has now also taken on the role of Pension Protection Fund Ombudsman and will be dealing with complaints about, and appeals from, the Pension Protection Fund. He will also be dealing with appeals from the Financial Assistance Scheme. Contact the **Pensions Ombudsman,** Tel: 020 7834 9144; website: www.pensions-ombudsman.org.uk. If you have a personal pension, contact the **Financial Ombudsman Service (FOS),** Tel: 0845 080 1800. It is possible you may be referred to the Pensions Ombudsman, but if so you will be informed very quickly.

Protection for pension scheme members

New rules have been introduced to protect pension scheme members in the event of a company takeover or proposed bulk transfer arrangement. A welcome reform is that, in the event of a scheme in deficit being wound up, the deficiency becomes a debt on the employer that the trustees can pursue. As an additional safeguard, self-investment by occupational pension funds is now restricted to 5 per cent. Equally important, solvent companies choosing to wind up their scheme on or since 11 June 2003 will need to protect members' accrued pension rights in full.

The regulatory system has also become much more stringent since April 2005, with the creation of the **Pensions Regulator**, a body with wide powers and a proactive approach to regulation, whose top priority is to identify and tackle risks to members' benefits. There is now also a *Pension Protection Fund (PPF)* to help final salary pension scheme members who are at risk of losing their pension benefits owing to their employer's insolvency. Members over the normal pension age will receive 100 per cent of their current benefits plus annual increases (the lower of RPI and 2.5 per cent) on pensions accrued from 6 April 1997. Members below the scheme's normal retirement age will receive 90 per cent of the Pension Protection Fund level of compensation plus annual increases, subject to a cap and the standard Fund rules. There is more help too for members who lost pension savings in a company scheme before the introduction of the Pension Protection Fund. The *Financial Assistance Scheme (FAS)* offers help to some people who have lost out on their pension. The scheme is managed by the Department for Work and Pensions and is administered by the FAS Operational Unit (FAS OU). It makes payments to top-up scheme benefits to eligible members of schemes that are winding up or have wound up. Assistance is also payable to the survivor of a pension scheme member. It is payable from normal retirement age (subject to a lower age limit of 60 and an upper age limit of 65).

Personal pensions for employees

A main aim behind personal pensions is to give people working for an employer the same freedom as the self-employed to make their own independent pension arrangements, should they wish to do so. Before making any decision, a basic point to understand is that nearly everyone who pays NI Contributions as an employee is already contributing towards an additional pension: either to the State Second Pension or to a contracted-out company pension scheme.

You have the right to take a personal pension (PP) in place of the State Second Pension or, alternatively, in place of your employer's scheme (whether this is contracted in or out). If you like you can also invest in a personal pension in addition to your employer's scheme, provided the total of your contributions does not exceed your annual allowance.

To judge whether a personal pension is a good idea, you need to understand the advantages and possible limitations of your present arrangements compared with the attractions – but also risks – of a PP. *If you are a member of a good contracted-out final salary scheme – or have the opportunity of joining one – it is very unlikely that a PP would be in your best interest.* If, however, your employer does not have a pension scheme, if you are ineligible to join, if the scheme is contracted into the State scheme, if you think you could do better for yourself than your current scheme, or if you think that it could be to your advantage to have an extra pension, then a PP might be worth considering.

A main advantage of a personal pension is that if you change jobs you can take it with you without penalty. You will have real choice as to how your pension payments are invested. If you have built up a big enough fund, you can retire at any age between 55 and 75. Also, if you change your mind after having taken a personal pension, you can switch back into the State scheme or, if the scheme rules allow it, you can transfer your payments into a company contracted-out scheme.

The biggest drawback of a personal pension, particularly for an older person, is that it may not offer you such attractive benefits as your present scheme. For a start, most employers do not make extra contributions to a personal pension so, other than your rebate from the State Second Pension (see 'Minimum contributions', below), all the investment towards your pension will need to come out of your earnings. You may also lose out on valuable extra benefits that are often included in an employer's scheme, including a pension before normal age were you to become ill, protection for your dependants should you die, attractive early retirement terms if you were made redundant, and any increases in pension payments that the scheme may give to help offset inflation.

Before taking a decision, a first essential is to understand how personal pensions work.

Starting date

You can decide to start a personal pension at any time you want and then, in order to receive all the minimum contributions that will be paid into your pension plan, backdate it to the start of the tax year on 6 April. The formalities involved are very easy.

Contributions into your pension plan

There are three possible ways (previously four, see 'Special incentive payments', below) of building up savings in your pension plan:

1. *Minimum contributions.* These will be paid into your new scheme automatically. They are worked out according to the level of NIC that both you and your employer are required to pay by law. Instead of going into either the State Second Pension or a contracted-out company pension scheme, they will be paid directly into your personal pension plan at the end of the Income Tax year to which they relate. The older you are, the bigger the contribution rebate. Whereas previously there was a fixed percentage for all personal pension members (with those over 30 receiving an extra 1 per cent), since April 1997 contribution rebates are calculated on an age and earnings-related basis.
2. *Extra contributions made by you.* You can make extra contributions into your pension plan. If you do so, you will not only build up more savings for your retirement but you also enjoy full tax relief on these contributions.
3. *Voluntary contributions by your employer.* Your employer might decide that it wishes to help you improve your pension by making contributions over and above the statutory NI Contributions into your pension plan. If you are considering leaving a company pension scheme, this could be one of the questions you should ask as a means of comparing the value of a personal pension against your existing scheme. The total of your and your employer's contributions is not allowed to exceed your annual earnings.
4. *Special incentive payments.* An extra 2 per cent payment was given by the government as part of the launch of personal pensions. These payments have now ceased. Anyone who previously received them can look forward to enjoying the benefit when they retire.

Your pension receipts

As with all money purchase schemes, the amount of pension you eventually receive will depend on two main factors: the size of the fund you have been able to build up and the fund's investment performance. Generally speaking, the longer you have been saving towards a personal pension and the bigger the total contributions paid, the larger your pension will stand to be. Many pension advisers suggest that a useful formula is to halve your age at the time of first starting to save for your pension and use this figure as a percentage of your gross salary that you should invest annually in your pension for the remainder of your working life.

Thanks to the new rules, you can average this out over the years, making lower contributions when money is tight and higher ones when you can more easily afford to do so. You have a great deal of choice in the matter, but there are also certain rules designed to protect you.

A basic rule concerns what are known as your *protected rights*. These are the minimum contributions (including the value of the extra 2 per cent introductory payment) and tax relief you may have received – together with their accumulated investment growth. Your protected rights can only be invested in a single contract, in contrast to your and your employer's extra or voluntary contributions, which can be invested in as many different personal plans as you please. You can choose whether to use your protected rights towards your annuity or towards your tax-free lump sum, as you prefer.

Choosing a pension plan

Personal pensions are offered by insurance companies, building societies, unit trusts, friendly societies and IFAs. Before you make up your mind, you should aim to look at a variety of plans. Furthermore, you should not hesitate to ask as many questions as you want about any points that are unclear or any technical term that you do not fully understand – including in particular any questions you may have about the level of charges.

Understanding the figures has become very much easier over the past few years. Today, not only are all life and pension policy providers required to state their charges in writing but they must also disclose any salesperson's commission – stated in cash terms – in advance of any contract being signed. These, together with other essential 'consumer' information about the policy, should be included in what are called the 'key facts' documents. Advisers must now also state in writing their reasons for any recommendations to you.

Because choosing both the right type of investment and the particular institution with which you are likely to feel happiest is such an important decision, even after you have chosen a scheme you will have a *14-day cooling-off period* that gives you a chance to change your mind.

Is a personal pension a wise decision?

This is a question that only you, or an adviser who knows your personal circumstances, can answer. As a general rule, if you are in a good company pension scheme the advice is to stay there. Those for whom opting out is likely to be least advised are older people in a good company or public sector pension scheme.

The key issue is how your existing pension arrangements compare with the alternatives. You will therefore need to know what the value of your pension would be if you stay in the additional State pension scheme or in your company scheme, whichever is applicable. For information about the value of your state scheme rights, complete form BR19, *State Pension Forecast*, obtainable from your pension centre, or check the Pension Service website: www.thepensionservice. gov.uk.

In the case of an employer's scheme, ask the pensions department or the person responsible for pensions (this could be the personnel manager or company secretary) to provide you with full information about your pension and future benefits, including details of death and disability cover.

Other points you will need to consider include: what type of investment policy would suit you; what size contributions (within HMRC-allowed limits) you could realistically afford; and what, after deduction of administrative and other charges, your plan might be worth when you come to retire. This is not to say that taking a personal pension is either a right or a wrong decision, simply that you need to be aware of all the various factors before opting out of your present arrangements. Since the sums are often very complex, if you are thinking of making a change you would be strongly advised to consult an independent pensions specialist.

Useful reading

Leaflets QG1, *A Quick Guide to Pensions*; PM3, *Occupational Pensions – Your Guide*; PM4, *Personal Pensions – Your Guide*; and PM5, *Pensions for the Self-Employed – Your Guide*, obtainable by ringing the Pensions Info-Line, Tel: 0845 731 3233; website: www.thepensionservice.gov.uk.
Stakeholder Pensions and Decision Trees and *FSA Guide to Pensions*, obtainable free from the FSA Money Made Clear information line, Tel: 0845 606 1234; website: www.fsa.gov.uk.

Stakeholder pensions

Stakeholder pensions were launched in April 2001 with the aim of encouraging more people to begin saving towards a pension. While essentially targeted at more modest earners, anyone else should they wish to do so can start, or switch to, a stakeholder pension. (The rule excluding individuals in occupational schemes with earnings over £30,000 was abolished in April 2006.)

Stakeholders are very similar to personal pensions but with the advantage that they are required to meet specified government standards, including limiting maximum annual charges (excluding financial advice) to 1.5 per cent for the first

10 years of the policy. This was increased from 1 per cent in April 2005, but if you were investing in a stakeholder prior to this date the maximum charge you would have to pay for the next few years is held at 1 per cent.

Whereas until fairly recently pension contributions were always linked to earnings, anyone with a stakeholder policy can invest up to £3,600 a year, regardless of how much or how little they earn – or even if they have no earnings at all. A husband or wife could make contributions for a non-earning partner. Those wishing to contribute more than £3,600 a year to their own scheme can do so, provided they have earnings of over £3,600 a year. Also, savers can stop, start or alter payments without penalty.

All contributions paid will be net of basic-rate tax, with the pension provider reclaiming the tax from HM Revenue & Customs. Higher-rate taxpayers will need to reclaim the excess tax through the self-assessment system. From April 2008, when basic-rate tax reduced to 20 per cent, the cost for basic-rate taxpayers increased to £2,880. Most higher-rate taxpayers should be unaffected. However, as now, they will only be able to claim the excess relief if the stakeholder scheme is in their own name, rather than that of a partner or other person.

Early retirees who are already drawing an occupational pension can, if they wish, start contributing to a stakeholder pension. A good reason for doing so might be to take advantage of an immediate self-vesting pension or series of immediate self-vesting pensions. As with personal pensions, stakeholder pensions can be taken at any age between 55 and 75.

How to obtain

Stakeholder pensions are available from banks, Post Offices, insurance companies and other financial institutions. Although the basic charges may not be very different between one provider and another, you are nevertheless strongly advised to investigate at least two or three plans and ask for much the same sort of information as you would if you were considering a personal pension. This is even more important if you are actually thinking of switching from a PP to a stakeholder pension or, as is possible, having a stakeholder as well as a PP.

Advantages and drawbacks

Some experts are of the view that, if you are happy with your present arrangements, you might be best staying as you are. Though stakeholder policies are usually cheaper, you could face penalties if you terminate your existing scheme early. Equally, if you are thinking of switching from an employer's money purchase scheme, you will lose the extra contributions that your employer is making on your behalf. Against this, the flexibility you would get with a stakeholder to alter or stop payments without penalty is attractive. Since weighing up the pros and cons of making a change is not easy, you are strongly recommended to get expert advice or, if you have a particular query, contact the Pensions Advisory Service Helpline, Tel: 0845 601 2923; website: www. pensionsadvisoryservice.org.uk. Remember, this organization cannot give financial advice.

Useful reading

PM8, *Stakeholder Pensions – Your Guide,* obtainable from the Pensions Information order line, Tel: 0845 731 3233; website: www.thepensionservice.gov.uk.

Types of investment policy

There are four different types of investment policy: with-profits, unit-linked, deposit administration and non-profit policies. Brief descriptions of each follow.

With-profits policies

These are one of the safest types of pension investments. They guarantee you a known minimum cash fund and/or pension on your retirement and, although the guaranteed amount is not usually very high, bonuses are added at regular intervals, according to how the investments in the fund perform. Additionally, a terminal (or final) bonus is given when the pension policy matures. Over the past few years most terminal bonuses have been lower than projected, reflecting low interest rates and a patchy performance by equities. However, an important feature is that once bonuses are given, they cannot later be withdrawn or put at risk due to some speculative investment.

Unit-linked policies

These are less safe than with-profits policies but they offer the attraction of potentially higher investment returns. Unit-linked policies by and large have performed fairly well over the last 15 years and have consequently been growing in popularity. However, as illustrated by the recent upsets on the stock market, there is a risk that they will not perform as well in future, and the size of your pension will obviously be affected. For this reason, many advisers recommend that their clients swap their unit-linked policies to the with-profits type about five years before they retire, provided market conditions are favourable at the time. The decision as to what is best will very much depend on timing. Clearly if the stock market is depressed, then cashing in equity-based contracts before you need could lose you money, unless of course your adviser takes the view that the stock market is likely to plunge even further. Another factor that should be taken into account is the prevailing level of interest rates, since these affect annuity rates.

Deposit administration policies

These lie somewhere between with-profits and unit-linked policies in terms of their risk/reward ratio. They operate rather like bank deposit accounts, where the interest rate is credited at regular intervals.

Non-profit policies

These have lost favour in recent years. Although they provide a guaranteed pension payment, the return on investment is usually very low. As a rule, they tend only to be recommended for people starting a plan within five years of their retirement.

Choosing the right policy

This is one area where it really pays to shop around. Great care is needed when choosing the organization with which to invest your pension savings. Once you have committed yourself to a policy, you will not usually be able to move your money without considerable financial penalty. As a general rule, it is sensible to select a large, well-known company that has been in the market for a long time. Before deciding, you should compare several companies' investment track records. What you should look for is evidence of good, consistent results over a period of 10 to 20 years.

You should aim at the very least to talk to two or three financial institutions or independent financial advisers (IFAs) and make it clear to all of them that you are doing so. If you need further advice – and particularly if a large sum of money is involved – there could be a strong argument for consulting an independent pension consultant or IFA who charges fees rather than earns commission.

Self-Invested Personal Pension

Another possibility is to set up your own Self-Invested Personal Pension (SIPP). These are do-it-yourself schemes that among other assets can include directly held shares and commercial property. Residential property cannot be held in a SIPP nor can luxury items such as antiques, wine, classic cars and yachts. The big advantage of SIPPs is that they offer greater flexibility than ordinary pensions. On the other hand, administration costs are usually higher. Pension experts advise that such schemes are only suitable for fairly sophisticated investors with at least £100,000 in their pension fund. This is not to say that you should necessarily rule out SIPPS, simply that before you go ahead you should ensure that you understand the drawbacks as well as the advantages.

Complaints

If you have a complaint about advice you have received in relation to your SIPP or other personal pension, contact the Financial Ombudsman Service (FOS; Tel: 0845 080 1800).

Opting back into the State scheme

You may have been told by a financial adviser that, rather than continue with your personal pension, you might be better off switching into the State Second Pension (S2P). One reason you may have been given is that the rebates paid to those who have contracted out of the State scheme are insufficient in the light of increased longevity and the expected return on equity investments. Another reason, quite simply, could be that your present fund is unlikely to yield you as good a pension as S2P, especially as the age-related rebates paid to those with personal pensions (and other money purchase schemes) have been reduced from 10.5 per cent to 7.4 per cent since April 2007.

The advice is most likely to be pertinent if you are already over 43 and have average, or modest, earnings. However, if you can afford to do so, there is nothing to stop you from contracting back into the State scheme and also having a personal pension. Before you decide, check that your adviser has taken account of all the factors. Particular points you might want to discuss include:

- the likely value of your pension if:
  - you stay as you are,
  - you contract back into the State scheme,
  - you contribute to both S2P and a personal pension;
- what contributions you would need (or be advised) to make in each of the above situations;
- whether there would be a penalty if you stopped paying into your personal pension;
- how easy it would be to restart the plan should a PP be more advantageous when the S2P changes from being earnings-related to flat-rate, as the government has planned should happen in the next few years.

Another point to take into account could be your financial adviser's charges, as these may come out of the fund that you are building towards your pension. As guidance, many PP managers have recently reduced their fees to around 1.5 per cent – in line with the norm (excluding financial advice) for stakeholder pensions.

A lump sum?

All pension scheme members, whether in an employer's scheme or having a private pension plan, are entitled to take a tax-free lump sum from their fund.

The maximum amount allowed is 25 per cent of their fund or 25 per cent of their lifetime limit, whichever is lower. While those with personal pensions have up till now been able to take their lump sum at any age between 50 and 75, members of employers' schemes normally had to wait until they retired; this is no longer so. The minimum age at which you can retire or take your lump sum now is 55.

Taking a lump sum reduces the pension you receive, but on the other hand, if you invest the money wisely, you could end up with a higher income. The first priority, however, is to ensure that you will have enough income for your own needs.

If you take a lump sum, the amount by which your pension will be reduced is mainly determined by your age. The younger you are, the smaller the reduction. Another consideration is your tax status. Since the lump sum is tax-free, as a general rule the higher your top rate of tax after retirement, the greater the advantage in opting for a lump sum. Your life expectancy can also be an important factor. The shorter this is, the more sense it makes to take the lump sum, rather than deny yourself for a longer-term pension that you will not be around to enjoy.

Before consulting an expert, it would be helpful to both of you if you could work out – at least in very general terms – what your financial priorities are. The sort of questions your adviser will ask are: whether you are investing for income now or capital growth in the future; whether you need to go for absolute security with every penny you have or whether you can afford slightly more risky investments in the hope of making more money in the long run; and what other sources of income you have or might expect to receive. As is normal conservative practice, you will probably find that you will be recommended to spread your lump sum across a mixture of investments.

Pension rights if you continue to work after retirement age

When you reach normal retirement age, you will usually stop making contributions into your company pension scheme, even if you decide to carry on working. Your employer, of course, would have to agree to your continuing to work but, thanks to the age discrimination legislation, this should not normally be a problem if you are under 65 and are physically and mentally capable of doing your job. Even if you are over 65, you may find that your employer will be only too happy for you to stay – and, even then, if your employer wants you to leave, it will have to give you at least six months' notice in writing. If you are facing such a decision, here are some points to bear in mind:

- You can continue working, draw your company pension and put some (or possibly all) of your earnings into a separate scheme.

- You can leave your pension in the fund, where it will continue to earn interest until you retire. In most private schemes, you could expect to receive in the region of an extra 8 per cent for every year that you delay retirement. If you continue working, say, for an additional five years, your pension would then be 40 per cent higher than if you had started taking it at the normal age. You will also have been earning a salary meanwhile, so you are likely to be considerably better off as a result.
- You can leave your pension in the fund, as described above, and additionally contribute to a personal or stakeholder pension, provided your contributions do not exceed the (2010/11) £255,000 annual allowance. (This level will be maintained until 2015/16 – announced by the Chancellor in the pre-budget report in November 2008.)

Since April 2006, provided your scheme rules allow, you can continue working for your existing employer and draw your pension benefits, as opposed to – as previously – having to defer them until you left the organization.

Equal pension age

Employers are required to treat men and women equally with regard to retirement and pension issues. This means that by law they must have a common retirement age that applies equally to both sexes. Similarly, they must also have a common pension age, and pension schemes must offer the same benefits to their male and female members. The State pension age is being equalized for men and women to 65, starting this year. Any woman born before 6 April 1950 has no need to alter her retirement plans.

Divorce

Until recently, a long-standing grievance of many divorcees (ex-wives especially) was that the courts did not normally take pension benefits into account when deciding the financial arrangements between the couple. To help overcome these problems, a new provision known as 'pension-sharing' has now been made legally available in respect of divorce or annulment proceedings commenced on or after 1 December 2000. While a main advantage of pension-sharing is that it allows a clean break on divorce, many experts believe that it may well have the effect of so diminishing the pension scheme member's retirement fund that he or she may not have sufficient left to rebuild an adequate pension. The situation could apply to men or women. Although women usually benefit most from pension-sharing, the legislation equally allows an ex-husband to have a share in his former wife's pension rights.

If sadly you are in the throes of a divorce, the question of pension-sharing could be a subject to raise with your solicitor. But however much in favour he or she may be, in the final analysis it is up to the court to decide on what they see as the fairest arrangement – and pension-sharing is only one of several options available to them.

Divorced wives

If you have a full basic pension in your own right, this will not be affected by divorce. However if, as applies to many women, despite having worked for a good number of years you have made insufficient contributions to qualify for a full pension, you should contact your pension centre, quoting your pension number and NI number. It is possible that you may be able to obtain the full single person's pension, based on your ex-husband's contributions.

Your right to use your ex-husband's contributions to improve or provide you with a pension depends on your age and/or whether you remarry before the age of 60. As a general rule, you can use your ex-husband's contributions towards your pension for the years you were married (ie until the date of the decree absolute). After that, you are expected to pay your own contributions until you are 60, unless you remarry.

If you are over 60 when you divorce, then whether you remarry or not you can rely on your ex-husband's contributions. If you remarry before the age of 60, then you cease absolutely being dependent on your former husband and instead your pension will be based on your new husband's contribution record.

NB: the same rules apply in reverse. Although it happens less frequently, a divorced man can rely on his former wife's contribution record during the years they were married to improve his basic pension. A divorced wife might have some claim to her former husband's occupational pension benefits.

Pension-sharing

As previously mentioned, provisions to enable the court to share occupational or personal pension rights at the time of divorce or annulment came into law on 1 December 2000. The legislation now equally applies to the additional State pension. Sharing, however, is only one option for dealing with pension rights and would not necessarily apply in all cases.

Separated wives

Even if you have not lived together for several years, from an NI point of view you are still considered to be married. The normal pension rules apply including, of course, the fact that, if you have to depend on your husband's contributions, you will not be able to get a pension until he is both 65 and in receipt of his own pension.

If you are not entitled to a state pension in your own right, you will receive the dependant's rate of benefit, which is about 60 per cent of the full rate (or less if your husband is not entitled to a full pension). In such a case, you can apply for Income Support to top up your income. Once you are 60, you can personally draw the wife's pension of £57.05 a week, without reference to your husband.

If your husband dies, you may be entitled to bereavement benefits in the same way as other widows. If there is a possibility that he may have died but that you have not been informed, you can check by contacting the **General Register Office**, Tel: 0845 603 7788; e-mail: gro.communications@ons.gsi.gov.uk; website: www.gro.gov.uk. The indexes to all birth, marriage and death entries in England and Wales are available at the **National Archives**, Tel: 020 8876 3444; website: www.nationalarchives.gov.uk.

Widows

There are three important benefits to which widows may be entitled: Bereavement Benefit, Bereavement Allowance and Widowed Parent's Allowance. All are largely modelled on the former widows' benefits (Widow's Payment, Widow's Pension and Widowed Mother's Allowance), with the important difference that all are now also applicable to widowed men. To claim the benefits, fill in form BB1, obtainable from any social security or Jobcentre Plus office. You will also be given a questionnaire (BD8) by the registrar. It is important that you complete this, as it acts as a trigger to help speed up payment of your benefits.

NB: widows who were already in receipt of the Widow's Pension before it was replaced by Bereavement Allowance in April 2001 are not affected by the change and will continue to receive their pension as normal.

Bereavement Benefit

This has replaced what used to be known as 'Widow's Payment'. It is a tax-free lump sum of £2,000, paid as soon as a woman is widowed, provided that: 1) her husband had paid sufficient NI contributions; 2) she is under state retirement age; or 3) if she is over 60, her husband had not been entitled to a retirement pension. Her claim will not be affected if she is already receiving a State pension, provided this is based on her own contributions. Bereavement Benefit applies equally to widowers. In such cases, the male State retirement age (65) applies and receipt is dependent on the wife's NI contributions.

Bereavement Allowance

This has replaced the Widow's Pension. As stated earlier, women already in receipt of Widow's Pension before 6 April 2001 are not affected and will continue to receive their pension as normal. Bereavement Allowance is for those aged between 45 and State pension age who do not receive Widowed Parent's Allowance. It is payable for 52 weeks and, as with Widow's Pension before, there are various levels of payment: the full-rate and age-related Bereavement Allowance. Receipt in all cases is dependent on sufficient NI contributions having been paid.

Full-rate Bereavement Allowance is paid to widows and widowers between the ages of 55 and 59 inclusive. The weekly amount is £95.25, which is the same as the current pension for a single person. Age-related Bereavement Allowance is for younger widows and widowers who do not qualify for the full rate. It is payable to widowed persons who are aged between 45 and 54 inclusive when their partner dies. Rates depend on age. Bereavement Allowance is normally paid automatically once you have sent off your completed form BB1, so if for any reason you do not receive it you should enquire at your social security or Jobcentre Plus office. In the event of your being ineligible, owing to insufficient NI contributions having been paid, you may still be entitled to receive Income Support, housing benefit or a grant or loan from the social fund. Your social security or Jobcentre Plus office will advise you. As applies to Widow's Pension, widows who remarry, or live with a man as his wife, cease to receive Bereavement Allowance.

Widowed Parent's Allowance

This is paid to widowed parents with at least one child for whom they receive Child Benefit. The current value (2009/10) is £95.25 a week. The allowance is usually paid automatically. If for some reason, although eligible, you do not receive the money, you should inform your social security or Jobcentre Plus office.

Retirement pension

Once a widow reaches 60, she will normally receive a State pension based on her own and/or her late husband's contributions. If at the time of death the couple were already receiving the State retirement pension, the widow will continue to receive her share. An important point to remember is that a widow may be able to use her late husband's NI contributions to boost the amount she receives.

Other important points

Separate from the basic pension, a widow may also receive money from her late husband's occupational pension, whether contracted in or out of the State scheme. She may also get half of any of his graduated pension.

War widows and widowers

Until recently war widows who remarried or cohabited lost their War Widow's Pension, unless either the cohabitation ceased or they became single again as a result of the death of the new husband, divorce or legal separation, in which circumstances it was restored. After years of campaigning by many groups, at last the rules have been changed and war widows can now keep their pension for life. The new rules also include men, and war widowers equally can keep a late spouse's pension for life.

Part-timers

Thanks in large part to the sex discrimination legislation being extended to include access to pension schemes, many part-timers who were previously excluded can now join their employer's occupational pension scheme as of right – or may even be able to claim retrospective membership for the years they were 'unlawfully excluded'. Their claim can be backdated only to 1976 or, if later, to the start date of their employment and must be made (at the absolute latest) within six months of their leaving the job.

Part-timers who wish to claim must apply to an employment tribunal and, as a condition of receiving any backdated benefits due, must pay contributions in respect of those years. Although it is perhaps stating the obvious, successful appeals are not automatic, as the issue will be judged solely on grounds of sex discrimination (and not on exclusion for other reasons).

Pensions for women

Women who have worked all their adult lives and paid full Class 1 contributions should get a full basic State pension in their own right at the age of 60. The current amount is £95.25 a week. This rises every April.

Women who have worked for only part of their adult lives may not have enough contributions to get a full basic State pension on their own record. Instead, they may receive a reduced pension or one based on their husband's contributions, or one topping up the other. A wife entitled to a reduced pension on her own contributions can claim it at 60, regardless of whether or not her husband is receiving his pension.

Married women who have never worked are also entitled to a pension based on their husband's contributions. In money terms, the value is about 60 per cent of the level of basic pension to which the husband is entitled. There are several important conditions, however. First, a woman can receive a pension based on her husband's contributions only if he himself is in receipt of a basic pension. He will have to have reached 65 and must have retired. Additionally, the wife herself must be over 60 to qualify.

If a wife has had her 60th birthday but her husband has not yet reached 65 (or has decided to defer his retirement), she must wait until her husband retires to receive her share of the married couple's pension. An important point to note is that, since the introduction of independent taxation, a married woman is entitled to have her section of the joint pension offset against her own personal allowance instead of it being counted as part of her husband's taxable income. For many pensioner couples, this should have the happy result of reducing their tax liability.

If a wife who formerly worked is over 60 and retired but cannot yet get a basic pension on either her own or her husband's contributions, she may be able to qualify for an additional pension or graduated pension based on her own contributions. These are described a little further on; but first a word about two other important matters: reduced-rate contributions and Home Responsibilities Protection.

Reduced-rate contribution

Many women retiring today have paid a reduced rate of NIC, also known as 'the small stamp'. This option was given to working wives in 1948 and withdrawn in 1978, but women who had already chosen to pay the reduced rate were allowed to continue, provided they did not take more than a two-year break from employment after 1978. If you have never paid anything but reduced-rate contributions, you are not entitled to a basic pension in your own right but instead must rely on your husband's contributions for the married couple's pension.

Home Responsibilities Protection (HRP)

Men and women, whether single or married, who have been unable to work regularly because they have had to stay at home to care for children and/or a disabled or elderly person may be able to safeguard their pension by claiming Home Responsibilities Protection. This is a very important benefit, especially for the many single women in their 50s who are sacrificing their career to look after an elderly parent. This measure was introduced in 1978, and protection therefore applies only from this date. The person you are caring for must belong to one of the following categories:

- a child under 16 for whom you are getting Child Benefit;
- someone whom you are looking after regularly for at least 35 hours a week, who is in receipt of attendance allowance, constant attendance allowance or disability living allowance;
- someone – for example, an elderly person – for whom you have been caring at home and in consequence have been getting Income Support (or Supplementary Benefit in the past);
- a combination of the above situations.

A married woman or widow cannot get HRP for any tax year in which she was liable to pay only reduced-rate NIC. HRP can be given only for complete tax years (6 April to 5 April), so if you simply gave up work for a few weeks to help out you would be unlikely to qualify. Additionally, HRP cannot be used to reduce your total working life to below 20 years. To obtain a claim form, you should ask your pension centre for leaflet CF411.

Since 1978, anyone in receipt of Child Benefit, Supplementary Benefit or Income Support who is caring for someone in one of the eligible categories listed above is automatically credited with HRP. All other claimants should obtain leaflet CF411 from their pension centre.

There are concerns that up to 500,000 women over the age of 60 may be losing out on more than £1 billion in State pension entitlement through not receiving HRP. Because the HRP system reduces the number of qualifying years to receive a full State pension for women who have taken time off work to bring up children, this benefit should have been given automatically to women who were not working and who were receiving Child Benefit at any time after April 1978, when the system was introduced. Thousands of women are unaware of this and are not receiving full pensions because the government's system has failed to adjust their qualifying pension years automatically.

To get clarification, any woman over 60 or within four months of retirement should contact the Pension Service, Tel: 0845 606 0265 or 0845 300 0168; website: www.thepensionservice.gov.uk to find out whether her state pension is calculated with the benefit of HRP.

Graduated pension

This scheme operated between April 1961 and April 1975. Anyone earning over £9 a week and over age 18 at the time would probably have paid graduated contributions and be due a pension. You can only get a graduated pension based on your own personal contributions. However, the pension from the graduated scheme is likely to be small. Further, women were penalized because their pension was calculated at a less favourable rate than for men on account of their longer life expectancy.

Additional pension

The additional State pension scheme started with SERPS in 1978. As mentioned earlier, SERPS was discontinued by the government in April 2002 and has been replaced by a similar scheme called the State Second Pension (S2P). Women in contracted-out pension schemes are entitled either to a pension that is broadly equal to or better than its State equivalent, or to what are known as 'protected rights' (ie their and their employer's compulsory contributions together with their accumulated investment growth).

Useful reading

Pensions for Women – Your Guide (PM6) and *State Pensions for Parents and Carers – Your Guide* (PM9), obtainable from the Pensions Information order line, Tel: 0845 731 3233; website: www.thepensionservice.gov.uk.

Retiring Soon – What You Need to Do about Your Pension, free booklet available from the FSA Money Made Clear information line, Tel: 0845 606 1234; website: www. fsa.gov.uk/consumer.

4

Tax

As everyone knows, there are two certainties – death and taxes. So a chapter that provides information on taxes seems appropriate as, unless your earnings are very limited, you will almost certainly be paying Income Tax and possibly one or two other varieties of tax as well. Although over the years you may have been contributing many thousands of pounds to the Inland Revenue (now called HM Revenue & Customs or HMRC, for short), in practice you may have had very little direct contact with the tax system. The accounts department will have automatically deducted – and accounted for – the PAYE on your earnings as a salaried employee. If you were self-employed or had other money unconnected with your job, you may have had more dealings with your tax office.

Come retirement, even though for most people the issues are not particularly complex, a little basic knowledge can be invaluable. First, it will help you to calculate how much money (after deduction of tax) you will have available to spend: the equivalent, if you like, of your take-home pay. At a more sophisticated level, understanding the broad principles could help you save money by not paying more in taxation than you need.

The purpose of this chapter is not to give tax planning advice, apart from a few general points. Tax planning is a job for a specialist. Your tax adviser should be fully conversant with your financial affairs so that he or she can advise in the light of your own particular circumstances. Should you have significant assets, or if some of the recent Budget changes have implications for you, you should talk to your accountant. The aim here is simply to remind you of the basics and to draw your attention to some of the latest provisions that could have a bearing on your immediate or longer-term plans.

Income Tax

This is calculated on all (or nearly all) your income, after deduction of your personal allowance and, in the case of older married people, of the Married Couple's Allowance. The reason for saying 'nearly all' is that some income you may receive is tax-free: types of income on which you do not have to pay tax are listed a little further on.

Most income counts, however. You will be assessed for Income Tax on: your pension, interest you receive from most types of savings, dividends from investments, any earnings (even if these are only from casual work), plus rent from any lodgers if the amount you receive exceeds £4,250 a year. Many social security benefits are also taxable. The tax year runs from 6 April to the following 5 April, so the amount of tax you pay in any one year is calculated on the income you receive (or are deemed to have received) between these two dates.

The three different rates of Income Tax for 2009/10 are: the 10 per cent starting rate for savings, which applies to the first £2,440 of any savings income; the 20 per cent basic-rate tax for income up to £37,400; and the 40 per cent higher-rate tax, which is levied on all taxable income over £37,400.

Another change that affects many earners' take-home pay is the increase in National Insurance Contributions; the upper earnings limit for employees' Class 1 NIC and the Class 4 National Insurance upper profits limit, applicable to the self-employed, increased. Since 2009 these limits have been aligned to the upper limit for basic-rate Income Tax, making some people worse off.

Tax allowances

Personal allowance

You don't pay tax on every single penny of your money. You are allowed to retain a certain amount before Income Tax becomes applicable. This is known as your personal allowance. When calculating how much tax you will have to pay in any one year, first deduct from your total income the amount represented by your personal allowance. You should add any other tax allowance to which you may be entitled – see further on. You will not have to pay any Income Tax if your income does not exceed your personal allowance (or total of your allowances), and you may be able to claim a refund for any tax you have paid, or that has been deducted from payments made to you, during the year.

Calculating your personal allowance used to be fairly complicated, as there were all sorts of variations. These depended on whether individuals were married or single and whether only one partner, or both husband and wife, worked. Since the introduction of independent taxation the system has become easier to understand. Today everyone receives the same basic personal allowance. This is regardless of whether they are male, female, married or single. It does not matter where the income comes from, whether from earnings, an investment, a pension or another source.

The basic personal allowance (2009/10) is £6,475. People aged 65 to 74 are entitled to a higher personal allowance than the basic, by virtue of their age. For the year 2009/10 this is £9,490. For those over 75 this rises to £9,640. These allowances reduce where the income is above the income limit – by £1 for every £2 of income above the limit. People with incomes above a certain level do not receive any age allowance. However large your income, your personal allowance can never be reduced below the basic personal allowance.

NB: the extra allowance linked to age is normally given automatically. If you are not receiving it but believe you should be doing so, contact your local tax office by phone, or phone the HMRC general information line on 0845 900 0444. The HMRC website (www.hmrc.gov.uk) gives details. If you have been missing out, you may be able to claim back anything you have lost for up to six years and should receive a tax rebate. The amounts have been altered several times in recent years, so any rebate would only apply to allowances that would have been due to you at the time.

Married Couple's Allowance

Married Couple's Allowance has been abolished, except for older couples, where at least one of the partners was born before 6 April 1935 but is aged under 75. To be eligible, a couple must live together, as opposed to being separated.

As with the (age-related) personal allowance, couples whose income is below a set ceiling (the upper limit) are entitled to a higher allowance. This used to be known as Age-Related Married Couple's Allowance because it always applied only to couples where either husband or wife was aged at least 65. This is still the case, except that, for couples where neither partner has yet had a 75th birthday, income rather than age is now the only consideration. When either partner reaches 75, the allowance is increased but, as before, only couples whose income is below the upper limit receive any extra.

A further point to note is that, unlike the old basic Married Couple's Allowance, which could be shared equally between the spouses or transferred in whole to the wife, the age/income-related addition always goes to the husband. If the husband has insufficient income against which to use all of the age/income addition, he should enquire at the tax office about the possibility of transferring the remainder to his wife. In the case of civil partners, the allowance is based on the income of the higher earner.

The current (2009/10) Married Couple's Allowance, together with the income limits for the higher allowance, is as follows:

- The minimum Married Couple's Allowance is £2,670.
- When the husband or wife reaches 75, the allowance is increased to £6,965. In the 2009/10 tax year all Married Couple's Allowance claimants will

become 75 at some point during the year and will therefore be entitled to the higher amount of the allowance – for those aged 75 and over.

NB: three important points you should know:

1.   Married Couple's Allowance is restricted to 10 per cent tax relief.
2.   The increases based on age/income are normally given automatically. If couples are not receiving any extra but believe they should be, the husband should contact the local tax office, stating the ages of the couple. If there has been a mistake, he will be given a rebate.
3.   A widowed partner, where the couple at the time of death were entitled to Married Couple's Allowance, can claim any unused portion of the allowance in the year he or she became widowed.

Registered blind people can claim an allowance of £1,890 a year. If both husband and wife are registered as blind, they can each claim the allowance. It is called the Blind Person's Allowance. If you think you would be eligible, you should write to your local tax office with full relevant details of your situation. If you were entitled to receive the allowance earlier but for some reason missed out on doing so, you may be able to obtain a tax rebate.

Useful reading

For more detailed information about tax allowances, see the following HMRC leaflets obtainable free from any tax office (the general advice helpline is 0845 900 0444) or check the HMRC website (www.hmrc.gov.uk): IR 121, *Income Tax and Pensioners*; and *Rates and Allowances 2009/10*.

Same-sex partners

Same-sex couples who enter into a civil partnership by officially registering their relationship, from December 2005, are treated the same as married couples for tax purposes. As a result, they gain all the same tax advantages but also the same disadvantages. The most important is that only one property can qualify as their principal home for exemption from Capital Gains Tax. Against this, there is no CGT to pay on transfer of assets between the couple, and similarly any assets left in a will to each other are free of Inheritance Tax. Other major areas that stand to be affected are pension rights (other than the State scheme) and, though not specifically a tax issue, settlements between the couple in the event of a divorce.

Tax relief

Separate from any personal allowances, you can obtain tax relief on the following:

- a covenant for the benefit of a charity, or a donation under the Gift Aid scheme;
- contributions to occupational pensions, self-employed pension plans and other personal pensions;
- some maintenance payments, if you are divorced or separated and were aged 65 or older at 5 April 2000.

Mortgage interest relief

As many homeowners will know, mortgage interest relief was abolished on 6 April 2000. The only purpose for which relief is still available is in respect of loans secured on an older person's home to purchase a life annuity. However, to qualify the loan must have been taken out (or at least processed and confirmed in writing) by 9 March 1999. Borrowers in this situation can continue to benefit from the relief for the duration of their loan. As before, the relief remains at 10 per cent on the first £30,000 of the loan.

Maintenance payments

Tax relief for maintenance payments was also withdrawn on 6 April 2000. Individuals in receipt of maintenance payments are not affected and will continue to receive their money free of Income Tax. Those who had to pay tax under the pre-March 1988 rules now also receive their payments free of tax. Most individuals paying maintenance, however, face higher tax bills. This applies especially to those who set up arrangements before the March 1988 Budget. While previously they got tax relief at their highest rate, from 6 April 2000 when maintenance relief was withdrawn they no longer get any relief at all. An exception has been made in cases where one (or both) of the divorced or separated spouses was aged 65 or over at 5 April 2000. Those paying maintenance are still able to claim tax relief – but only at the 1999/2000 standard rate of 10 per cent.

Pension contributions

HMRC sets limits on the contributions that individuals can invest in their pension plan and on the pension benefits they can receive. Prior to April 2006, the rules differed between one type of scheme and another. These anomalies have now been swept away, as the government has brought all company and personal pensions under a single tax regime.

Among other important changes, the earnings cap is no longer a factor. Instead, individuals can now invest up to 100 per cent of annual earnings into their plan (or plans) with the benefit of tax relief up to a maximum figure – known as the annual allowance – of £255,000. Higher contributions are allowed but without any tax relief on the excess. If you have a stakeholder or personal pension, you can make contributions of up to £3,600 a year irrespective of your earnings (or even if you earn nothing at all). You pay the contributions net of basic-rate tax, and your pension provider will then reclaim the tax from HMRC (see 'Stakeholder pensions', page 56).

The annual allowance is not the only capped amount. There is also a lifetime limit of £1.8 million for total pension funds, including any fund growth. Funds in excess of the lifetime limit are subject to a 25 per cent recovery charge (ie tax) if taken as income, or 55 per cent if taken as a lump sum. The lifetime limit of £1.8 million will remain in place until 2015/16.

Fund protection

Individuals whose pension fund was already over the lifetime limit before 6 April 2006 – or anticipated to become so before they draw their pension – were able to protect their fund from the recovery charge, provided the fund was formally registered with HMRC within three years of 6 April 2006 (A-day), ie 5 April 2009.

Tax-free lump sum

A further major change concerns the tax-free lump sum. As opposed to a maximum of one and a half times final salary, which used to be the rule for members of company schemes, everyone (provided the scheme rules permit) is entitled to take up to 25 per cent of the value of their fund or 25 per cent of their lifetime limit, whichever is lower. Additional Voluntary Contributions (AVCs) and the opted-out benefits from the State Second Pension can count towards the lump sum instead of, as before, having to remain in the fund to provide pension income.

There is no longer any requirement for members of company schemes to wait until they retire before accessing their lump sum. Should they wish to do so, they can now take the money at any time from the age of 55. Members of final salary schemes cannot take their lump sum in isolation. There is now also greater flexibility for employees nearing retirement, who as well as taking their tax-free lump sum can also (provided their scheme rules allow) start drawing some pension income while still remaining at work part time.

Scheme rules

The fact that HMRC has changed the rules is unfortunately no guarantee that individuals will be able to take full advantage of all the new options that have become available. Their employer's pension scheme rules will also need to have been altered accordingly, which may not always be the case. Before making any definite plans, it is advisable to check first with whoever is responsible for the company pension scheme.

Pension Credit

Pension Credit is a means-tested State benefit for those over 60, giving certain pensioners extra money each week. It's made up of two elements – the 'Guarantee Credit' element and the 'Savings Credit' element. Pension Credit guarantees everyone aged 60 and over an income of at least £130.00 a week if you are single and £198.45 a week if you have a partner. Also, if you or your partner are 65 or over you may be rewarded for saving for your retirement, up to £20.40 a week if you are single; or £27.03 a week if you have a partner. You may get more Pension Credit if you have caring responsibilities, are severely disabled or have certain housing costs.

From 6 October 2008 some important changes have taken place to Pension Credit. From that date, if someone applies over the phone for Pension Credit and, at the same time, for housing and Council Tax benefits, the Pension Service will automatically send their claim information to the appropriate local authority. This does away with the need for another claim form to be completed and signed. Also claimants are now able to spend up to 13 weeks abroad (increased from four weeks) and still retain entitlement to Pension Credit. This brings the benefit into line with housing and Council Tax benefits.

Probably the most important change is that the backdating of pension credit claims is limited to three months, again bringing it into line with other benefits. Previously arrears were backdated for up to 12 months.

For further information, see Chapter 3, Pensions, or you can call the Pension Credit Helpline on 0800 99 1234, which will give you advice on whether your income and/or capital meet the necessary conditions for a successful claim. You can also look at the website: www.direct.gov.uk.

Tax-free income

Some income you may receive is entirely free of tax. It is not taxed at source. You do not have to deduct it from your income, as in the case of personal allowances. Nor do you have to go through the formality of claiming relief on it. If you receive any of the following, you can forget about the tax aspect altogether – at least as regards these particular items:

- Disability Living Allowance;
- industrial injuries disablement pension;
- Income Support (in some circumstances, such as when the recipient is also getting Jobseeker's Allowance, Income Support benefit will be taxable);
- housing benefit;
- Council Tax benefit;
- all pensions paid to war widows (plus any additions for children);
- pensions paid to victims of Nazism;

- certain disablement pensions from the armed forces, police, fire brigade and merchant navy;
- annuities paid to the holders of certain gallantry awards;
- the £10 Christmas bonus (paid to pensioners);
- National Savings Premium Bond prizes;
- SAYE bonuses;
- winnings on the football pools and on other forms of betting;
- rental income of up to £4,250 a year from letting out rooms in your home;
- the winter fuel payment (paid to pensioners);
- the extra £400 winter fuel payment paid to households with a resident aged 80 and over;
- income received from certain insurance policies (mortgage payment protection, permanent health insurance, creditor insurance for loans and utility bills, various approved long-term care policies) if the recipient is sick, disabled or unemployed at the time the benefits become payable;
- all income received from savings in an Individual Savings Account (ISA);
- all dividend income from investments in venture capital trusts (VCTs).

Other tax-free money

The following are not income, in the sense that they are more likely to be one-off rather than regular payments. However, as with the above list they are tax-free:

- virtually all gifts (in certain circumstances you could have to pay tax if the gift is above £3,000 or if, as may occasionally be the case, the money from the donor has not been previously taxed);
- a redundancy payment, or a golden handshake in lieu of notice, up to the value of £30,000;
- a lump sum commuted from a pension;
- a matured endowment policy;
- accumulated interest from a Tax Exempt Special Savings Account (TESSA) held for five years;
- dividends on investments held in a Personal Equity Plan (PEP);
- compensation money paid to people who were mis-sold personal pensions;
- compensation paid to those who were mis-sold free-standing AVCs (FSAVCs). To qualify for exemption from tax, the money must be paid as a lump sum as opposed to annual payments.

Income Tax on savings

Until fairly recently, all income from savings was taxed at a normal rate of 20 per cent and at 40 per cent for higher-rate taxpayers. Perversely, the 10 per cent starting rate of tax was not applicable to savings income such as bank and building society interest but instead applied only to earned and pension income. In consequence, many less well-off people, including in particular thousands of pensioners, were paying more tax than would otherwise have been due.

In the March 2000 Budget, the Chancellor extended the 10p starting rate of Income Tax to include savings income. This means that any income – whether from earnings, a pension or savings – now qualifies towards the 10p starting rate of tax. For 2007/08, this was on the first £2,230 of taxable income. From 2008/09 the 10 per cent starting rate has been abolished for earned and pensions income but does remain for savings income and capital gains. If you largely rely on your savings income and so believe you are among those who are or have been paying excess tax, you can reclaim this from HMRC. For advice on what to do, call the **Taxback Helpline** on 0845 077 6543. You might also find it useful to see 'Reclaiming tax overpaid', page 78. See the HMRC website: www.hmrc.gov.uk.

Income Tax on other investments

For most investments on which you are likely to receive dividends, basic-rate tax will already have been deducted before the money is paid to you. If you are a basic-rate taxpayer, the money you receive will be yours in its entirety and you will not have to worry about making deductions for tax. If you pay tax at the higher rate, you will have to pay some additional tax and should allow for this in your budgeting.

Exceptionally, there are one or two types of investment where the money is paid to you gross – without the basic-rate tax deducted. These include NS&I income bonds, capital bonds, the NS&I Investment Account – and all gilt interest. (People who prefer to receive gilt interest net can opt to do so.) As with higher-rate taxpayers, you will need to save sufficient money to pay the tax on the due date.

Avoiding paying excess tax on savings income

Banks and building societies automatically deduct the normal 20 per cent rate of tax from interest before it is paid to savers. As a result, most working people, except higher-rate taxpayers, can keep all their savings without having to worry about paying additional tax. While convenient for the majority, a problem is that some 4 million people on low incomes – including in particular many women and pensioners – are unwittingly paying more tax than they need. Those most affected are non-taxpayers (anyone whose taxable income is less than their allowances) who, although not liable for tax, are having it taken from their income before they receive the money.

Non-taxpayers can stop this happening quite simply by requesting their bank and/or building society to pay any interest owing to them gross, without deduction of tax at source. If applicable, all you need do is request form R85 from the institution in question or HMRC Enquiry Centre, which you will then need to complete. If you have more than one bank or building society account, you will need a separate form for each account. People who have filled in an R85 should automatically receive their interest gross. If your form was not completed in time for this to happen, you can reclaim the tax from your tax office after the end of the tax year in April.

Reclaiming tax overpaid

If you are a non-taxpayer and have not yet completed an R85 form (or forms), you are very likely to be eligible to claim a tax rebate. However, as stated earlier, this may also apply if you pay tax only at the 10 per cent starting rate or if, since becoming retired, most of your income comes from either taxed investments or bank or building society interest. If any of these circumstances apply and you believe that the probability is that you could be due a refund, the best advice is to ring the special **Taxback Helpline** on 0845 077 6543; they will send you a claim form and, if relevant, copies of form R85 for you to complete and give to your bank or building society.

If you had not realized that the tax could be deducted and so had not requested an R85 form or if, despite having given your bank or building society a completed form, it had forgotten to deduct the tax, you can ask the Taxback Helpline to send you form R40M, which once completed will enable your bank or building society to refund you any overpaid tax for up to six years.

Mistakes by HMRC

HMRC does sometimes make mistakes. Normally, if it has charged you insufficient tax and later discovers the error, it will send you a supplementary demand requesting the balance owing. However, under a provision known as the 'Official Error Concession', if the mistake was due to HMRC's failure 'to make proper and timely use' of information it received, it is possible that you may be excused the arrears. For this to be likely, you will need to convince HMRC that you could reasonably have believed that your tax affairs were in order. Additionally, HMRC itself will need to have been tardy in notifying you of the arrears: this will normally mean more than 12 months after the end of the tax year in which HMRC received the information indicating that more tax was due.

Undercharging is not the only type of error. It is equally possible that you may have been overcharged and either do not owe as much as has been stated or, not having spotted the mistake, have paid more than you needed to previously. In time HMRC may notice the error and send you a refund, but equally it may not. So if you have reason to think your tax bill looks wrong, check it carefully. Then, if you think there has been a mistake, write to your tax office explaining why you think the amount is too high. If a large sum is involved it could well be worth asking an accountant to help you.

As part of the Citizen's Charter, HMRC has appointed an independent Adjudicator to examine taxpayers' complaints about their dealings with HMRC and, if considered valid, to determine what action would be fair. Complaints appropriate to the Adjudicator are mainly limited to the way HMRC has handled someone's tax affairs, for example excessive delay, errors, discourtesy or how discretion has been exercised. In deciding fair treatment, the Adjudicator has power to recommend the waiving of a payment or even the award of compensation if, as a result of error by HMRC, the complainant had incurred professional fees or other expenses. Before approaching the Adjudicator, taxpayers are expected to have tried to resolve the matter, either with their local tax office or, should that fail, with the regional office.

HMRC is, however, getting tougher about mistakes where, for whatever reason, there is an understatement of the amount of tax due. Genuine mistakes will still be excused, but individuals may need to convince officials that they had not been careless in completing their returns, otherwise they could be at risk of incurring a penalty. More immediately, the deadline for filing paper self-assessment forms for the 2009/10 tax year is 31 October 2010. Those filing online will have until 31 January 2011.

For further information, see HMRC booklet Code of Practice 1, *Putting Things Right: How to Complain,* available from tax offices. Contact the Adjudicator's Office for information about referring a complaint. The Adjudicator acts as a fair and unbiased referee looking into complaints about HMRC, including the Tax Credit Office, the Valuation Office and the Office of the Public Guardian and the Insolvency Service. Contact the **Adjudicator's Office,** Tel: 0300 057 1111; website: www.adjudicatorsoffice.gov.uk.

Other useful organizations

The TaxPayers' Alliance has a campaign team of energetic volunteers committed to achieving a low-tax society. It has over 18,000 supporters and is regularly mentioned in the media. For further information contact the TaxPayers' Alliance, Tel: 0845 330 9554; e-mail: info@taxpayersalliance.com; website: www.tpa.typepad.com.

TaxHelp for Older People (TOP) is an independent free tax advice service for older people on low incomes who cannot afford to pay for professional advice. If your household income is less than £15,000 a year and you are a pensioner, you will qualify for free tax advice from TOP. This organization offers the service originally provided through the Low Incomes Tax Reform Group. For further information contact TOP, Tel: 0845 601 3321; e-mail: taxvol@taxvol.org.uk; website: www.taxvol.org.uk.

Tax Credits

There are two tax credits that could be of possible interest: the Working Tax Credit (WTC) and the Child Tax Credit (CTC). The amount of tax credits you get depends on how many children you have living with you, whether you work and how many hours you work, if you pay for childcare, if you or any child living with you has a disability, if you are aged 50-plus, and if you are coming off benefits.

Working Tax Credit

This is an earnings top-up given to low-income workers, including the self-employed. Eligibility is normally restricted to couples and single parents with a low income. In certain circumstances, including in particular households with three or more dependent children or where a member of the family has a disability, those with slightly higher incomes could still be eligible to apply. HMRC advises that the easiest way to check is to complete the form, listed under 'Tax credits', on its website (www.hmrc.gov.uk). For advice, call the Tax Credit Helpline (0845 300 3900) or check the website: www.direct.gov.uk.

To qualify, claimants must usually work for at least 30 hours a week. However, for those with a disability and/or dependent children, the minimum requirement is 16 hours a week. Working parents can receive up to 80 per cent of eligible childcare costs. All recipients receive the payment direct from HMRC into their bank, building society, Post Office or National Savings account either weekly or four-weekly.

Child Tax Credit

This is a cash payment given to all families with a low household income that have at least one child under 16, or under 20 if in full-time education. The amount of credit varies according to parental income but, at a minimum, is worth £545 a year to parents with income of up to £50,000. The credit is doubled for the first year of a new baby, extending entitlement to those with income of up to £66,000. Working parents can also claim extra towards childcare costs. The money, which is on top of Child Benefit, is paid direct to the main carer.

Need to claim

Payment is not automatic. In both cases – WTC and CTC – you need to complete an application form, obtainable from any Tax Enquiry Centre or by ringing the Tax Credit Helpline on 0845 300 3900 (for Northern Ireland, Tel: 0845 603 2000). The helplines are there to assist if help is required with any of the questions. See www.direct.gov.uk.

NB: CTC is one area where independent taxation could be said not to apply, as eligibility is based on the combined income of the parents.

Tax rebates

When you retire, you may be due for a tax rebate. If you are, this would normally be paid automatically, especially if you are getting a pension from your last employer. The matter could conceivably be overlooked, either if you are due to get a pension from an earlier employer (instead of from your last employer) or if you will be receiving only a State pension and not a company pension in addition.

In either case, you should ask your employer for a P45 form. Then either send it – care of your earlier employer – to the pension fund trustees or, in the event of your receiving only a State pension, to the tax office together with details of your age and the date you retired. Ask your employer for the address of the tax office to which you should write. If the repayment is made to you more than a year after the end of the year for which the repayment is due – and is more than £25 – HMRC will automatically pay you (tax-free) interest. HMRC calls this a 'repayment supplement'.

Post-war credits

Post-war credits are extra tax that people had to pay in addition to their Income Tax between April 1941 and April 1946. The extra tax was treated as a credit to be repaid after the war. People who paid credits were given certificates showing the amount actually paid. Repayment started in 1946, initially only to men aged 65 or over and to women aged 60 or over, but the conditions for claiming varied over the years until 1972, when it was announced that there would be a 'general release' and that all credits were to be repaid without any further restrictions. In 1972 people who could produce at least one of their post-war credit certificates were invited to claim. In cases where the original credit holder has died without claiming repayment and the post-war credit certificate is still available, repayment can be made to the next of kin or personal representative of the estate. Interest is payable on all claims at a composite rate of 38 per cent. The interest is exempt from Income Tax. All claims should be sent to the **Special Post-War Credit Claim Centre** at HM Revenue & Customs, HM Inspector of Taxes – PWC Centre V, Ty Glas, Llanishen, Cardiff CF4 5TX, Tel: 0845 300 3949.

Capital Gains Tax (CGT)

You may have to pay Capital Gains Tax if you make a profit (or, to use the proper term, 'gain') on the sale of a capital asset, for example stocks and shares, jewellery, any property that is not your main home, and other items of value. CGT applies only to the actual gain you make, so if you buy shares to the value of

£100,000 and sell them later for £125,000 the tax officer will be interested only in the £25,000 profit you have made.

Not all your gains are taxable. There is *an exemption limit of £10,100* (2009/10) a year so, if during the year your total gains amount to £14,500, tax will be levied only on £4,400. A very important point for married couples to know is that as a result of independent taxation each partner now enjoys his or her own annual exemption of £10,100 instead of, as before, their gains being aggregated (ie added together) for tax purposes. This means in effect that, provided both partners are taking advantage of their full exemption limit, a couple can make gains of £20,200 a year free of CGT. However, it is not possible to use the losses of one spouse to cover the gains of the other. Transfers between husband and wife remain tax-free, although any income arising from such a gift will of course be taxed. Income will normally be treated as the recipient's for tax purposes.

Gains made before April 2008 are taxed at the same rate as your income: 10 per cent where the gains fall below the starting-rate limit for Income Tax of £2,440; 20 per cent where they fall between the starting-rate and basic-rate limits for Income Tax, ie between £2,441 and £37,400; or at 40 per cent where they fall above the basic-rate limit for Income Tax, ie £37,401 and above. However, for gains made since April 2008, you are charged at a flat 18 per cent.

Taper relief was abolished in April 2008 when the Capital Gains Tax system was reformed. It was overhauled so that private equity firms would pay a fairer share of tax. The new single tax rate of 18 per cent applies across the board. However, a new entrepreneurs' relief will reduce the effective tax rate on some gains to 10 per cent.

Free of Capital Gains Tax

The following assets are not subject to CGT and do not count towards the gains you are allowed to make:

- your main home (but see the note below);
- your car;
- personal belongings up to the value of £6,000 each;
- proceeds of a life assurance policy (in most circumstances);
- profits on UK government stocks;
- National Savings certificates;
- SAYE contracts;
- building society mortgage cashbacks;
- futures and options in gilts and qualifying corporate bonds;
- Personal Equity Plan (PEP) schemes (now automatically ISAs);
- gains from assets held in an Individual Savings Account (ISA);
- Premium Bond winnings;
- Betting and lottery winnings and life insurance policies if you are the original owner;

- gifts to registered charities;
- small part-disposals of land (limited to 5 per cent of the total holding, with a maximum value of £20,000);
- gains on the disposal of qualifying shares in a Venture Capital Trust (VCT) or within the Enterprise Investment Scheme (EIS), provided these have been held for the necessary holding period (see below).

Enterprise Investment Scheme (EIS)

The EIS allows individuals investing in qualifying unquoted companies 20 per cent Income Tax relief on investments up to £500,000 and exemption from Capital Gains Tax on disposal of the shares, provided these have been held for at least three years. Losses qualify for Income Tax or CGT relief. A further advantage is that, whereas deferral relief has been withdrawn in respect of VCTs since 6 April 2004, those investing in an EIS can still defer any CGT liability, provided gains are invested in qualifying unquoted companies within three years. Also, an investor can become a paid director, provided he or she was not previously connected with the company at the time of the first investment. For further information, visit the HMRC website: www.hmrc.gov.uk.

Your home

Your main home is usually exempt from CGT. However, there are certain 'ifs and buts' that could be important. If you convert part of your home into an office or into self-contained accommodation on which you charge rent, the part of your home that is deemed to be a 'business' may be separately assessed – and CGT may be payable when you come to sell it. (CGT would not apply if you simply take in a lodger who is treated as family, in the sense of sharing your kitchen or bathroom.)

If you leave your home to someone else who later decides to sell it, then he or she may be liable for CGT when the property is sold (although only on the gain since the date of death). There may also be Inheritance Tax implications, so if you are thinking of leaving or giving your home to someone you are strongly advised to consult a solicitor or accountant. If you own two homes, only one of them is exempt from CGT, namely the one you designate as your 'main residence'.

Selling a family business

With taper relief having been abolished in April 2008, the CGT now payable if you are selling a family business is 18 per cent. One possible option is the CGT deferral relief allowable to investors in an EIS.

Investors – including entrepreneur owners or directors with gains arising from the sale of shares in their own companies – can defer paying CGT and in many cases can also obtain Income Tax relief at 20 per cent on investments of up to £500,000 a year, provided gains are reinvested in qualifying unquoted companies (including AIM and Ofex companies) within three years.

In recent years, some of the rules have been altered to create a more unified system of venture capital reliefs. The key changes that potential investors should note are:

- that the amount that can be invested is now £500,000 (previously £400,000);
- that the amount an individual may invest in shares issued in the first half of the tax year and qualifying for Income Tax relief for the previous year is now £50,000 (previously £25,000);
- that qualifying companies are limited to £7 million of gross assets before an investment (£8 million after an investment); and
- that companies with property-backed assets, such as farming and nursing homes, no longer qualify as eligible trading companies.

This is a very complex field, so before either retiring or selling shares you are strongly recommended to seek professional advice.

Useful reading

For further information about Capital Gains Tax, see booklet CGT1, *Capital Gains Tax: An Introduction*, available from any tax office. Consult the HMRC website: www.hmrc.gov.uk.

Inheritance Tax

Inheritance Tax (IHT) is the tax that is paid on your 'estate'. Broadly speaking this is everything you own at the time of your death, less any debts you have. It's sometimes payable on assets you may have given away during your lifetime. Assets include property, possessions, money and investments.

For the tax year 2009/10 Inheritance Tax applies if the value of your assets is above £325,000. It is only payable on the excess above this nil rate band. The threshold amount for married couples and civil partners is £650,000. For 2010/11 the threshold is £350,000 for individuals or £700,000 for married couples and civil partners. The value of estates over and above the allowance is taxed at 40 per cent.

Before any tax is calculated, there are a number of exemptions and other concessions that may be relevant. There is no immediate tax on lifetime gifts between individuals. The gifts become wholly exempt if the donor survives for seven years. When the donor dies, any gifts made within the previous seven years become chargeable and their value is added to that of the estate. The total is then taxed on the excess over £325,000. Chargeable gifts benefit first towards the £325,000 exemption, starting with the earliest gifts and continuing in the order in which they were given. Any unused balance of the £325,000 threshold goes towards the remaining estate.

The old rules on Inheritance Tax were that the value of anyone's estate above £325,000 was taxed at 40 per cent when that person died. The only notable exception with IHT was that married couples and civil partners could transfer unlimited assets between each other without being liable when one died. Under the new rules, the £325,000 threshold allows married couples or civil partners to transfer the unused element of their IHT-free allowance to their spouse or civil partner when they die. For many couples this effectively doubles the tax-free amount they can bequeath to their children. IHT will, however, still be levied at 40 per cent above £325,000 on the estate of anyone who is single or divorced when they die.

Gifts or money up to the value of £3,000 can also be given annually free of tax, regardless of the particular date they were given. Additionally, it is possible to make small gifts to any number of individuals free of tax, provided the amount to each does not exceed £250.

A previous loophole, whereby it was possible for an owner to dispose of assets such as houses, paintings or boats but continue to enjoy the benefit of them, no longer exists. Under the current rules, designed to tighten up on avoidance of IHT, people who continue to have some usage of the property they formerly owned but do not pay the market rent will be charged yearly Income Tax on the retained benefit.

As an alternative to the Income Tax charge, taxpayers can elect for IHT treatment on the relevant property in due course. The time limit for electing is the same as the self-assessment deadline for making a return for the tax year in which an individual is first liable for the pre-owned asset (POA) charge. Contact the **Probate/IHT Helpline** on 0845 302 0900.

While most ex-owners or their heirs will end up paying one way or another, the Chancellor has built in certain exclusions and exemptions, including preserving the important principle that transfers of property between spouses remain exempt from any tax. Tax will equally not be charged if the asset is sold for full market value or if, owing to a change in circumstance, an owner who had previously given away a property needs to reoccupy his or her former home.

Quite apart from IHT, Capital Gains Tax may have to be paid on any asset you left to a beneficiary, or as part of your estate, that is subsequently sold. HMRC treats such assets as having been acquired at the date of death and at their prevailing market value at the time. By the same token, CGT will have to be paid on any gain that has built up on an asset you gave away during your lifetime and that is subsequently sold.

Another important consideration that should not be overlooked is the need to make a will. The rules of intestacy are very rigid, and neglecting to make a proper will can have serious consequences for those whom you might wish to benefit. (For further information, see 'Making a will', page 390.) Likewise, if you have already written a will, it is strongly recommended that you have this checked by a professional adviser to ensure that you do not give money unnecessarily to HMRC. In view of the recent changes to IHT, check with your professional adviser or HMRC.

Tax treatment of trusts

Under the new rules for aligning the Inheritance Tax treatment for trusts, those who have set up or have an interest in 'accumulation & maintenance' trusts (A&Ms) and/or 'interest in possession' trusts (IIPs) that do not meet new IHT rules about their terms and the circumstances in which they were created are most affected. The new rules came into effect on 22 March 2006 for new trusts, additions of new assets to existing trusts, and other IHT-relevant events in relation to existing trusts. Transitional rules provided for a period of adjustment for certain existing trusts to 6 April 2008.

Discretionary trusts are assessed for IHT on their tenth anniversary and every 10 years thereafter. Distributions from the trust may also trigger an IHT charge. These rules apply to trusts created during the settler's lifetime and those created within the settler's will. Following proposals announced in the March 2006 Budget Statement, the same treatment will apply to funds gifted on or after 22 March 2006 into most IIP and A&M trusts.

This is a particularly complex area, and professional advice is recommended. Further information is available from the **Probate/IHT Helpline**, Tel: 0845 302 0900; website: www.hmcourts-service.gov.uk.

Independent taxation

The introduction of independent taxation in April 1990 affected nearly all married couples. As well as allowing married women privacy in their own financial affairs, another major gain was that many couples – especially retired people – became better off financially. In contrast to the old system, whereby a married woman's income was treated as belonging to her husband for taxation purposes, both husband and wife are now taxed independently on their own income. Each has his or her own personal allowance and rate band, and both independently pay their own tax and receive their own tax rebates. Moreover, independent taxation applies equally to the age-related additions, and both husband and wife are now eligible for their own higher tax allowance from the age of 65 (and a more generous allowance still after age 75).

A further important point for many couples is that independent taxation does not apply simply to Income Tax but applies equally to both Capital Gains Tax and Inheritance Tax. As a result, both husband and wife enjoy their own Capital Gains Tax exemption (£10,100 in the 2009/10 tax year) and their own exemption from IHT (£325,000 in the 2009/10 tax year). Property left to a surviving spouse remains, as before, free of Inheritance Tax.

Useful reading

Zurich Tax Handbook 2009–2010 available from Pearson: website: www.pearsoned. co.uk; Tel: 01279 623 928. Price £34.99 plus p&p.
HMRC leaflets that could be helpful, especially if you are interested in the possibility of becoming self-employed or starting your own business, include: SE1, *Thinking of Working for Yourself?* and IR56, *Employed or Self-Employed? A Guide to Employment Status for Tax and National Insurance*.

Self-assessment

If you are one of the 9 million people who need to complete a tax return, you will probably be all too familiar with self-assessment. The tax return forms are sent out in April, and the details you need to enter on the form you receive in April 2010 are those relating to the 2009/10 tax year.

Even if a taxpayer has never had a tax return, and so is unlikely to be directly affected by self-assessment unless his or her circumstances change, all taxpayers now have a legal obligation to keep records of all their different sources of income and capital gains. These include:

- details of earnings plus any bonus, expenses and benefits in kind received;
- bank and building society interest;
- dividend vouchers and/or other documentation showing gains from investments;
- pension payments, eg both State and occupational or private pensions;
- miscellaneous income, such as freelance earnings, maintenance payments and taxable social security benefits;
- payments against which tax relief can be claimed (eg charitable donations or contributions to a personal pension).

HMRC advises that taxpayers are obliged to keep these records for 22 months after the end of the tax year to which they relate.

If you are self-employed or a partner in a business, as well as the above list you also need to keep records of all your business earnings and expenses, together with sales invoices and receipts. All records (both personal and business) need to be kept for five years after the fixed filing date.

Those most likely to be affected by the self-assessment system include anyone who normally receives a tax return, higher-rate taxpayers, company directors, the self-employed and partners in a business. If your only income is from your salary, from which tax is deducted at source, you will not have to worry about self-assessment. If, however, you have other income that is not fully taxed under PAYE (eg possibly benefits in kind or expenses payments) or that is not fully taxed at source, you need to notify HMRC within six months of the end of the tax year, and you may need to fill in a tax return.

The same may be true when you retire. Even though you may not think of yourself as wealthy, if your financial affairs change, as they sometimes do on retirement (eg if you become self-employed or receive income that has not already been fully taxed), it is your responsibility to inform HMRC and, depending on the amount of money involved, you may need to complete a tax return. The cheering news, however, is that you could be among those receiving the new, much shorter form. In a drive to ease the administrative burden, many other individuals have recently been taken out of the system – and no longer need to complete a self-assessment form – owing to their no longer being liable to pay extra tax, as a result of their circumstances having changed. A further reason could be that the government has recently revised the guidelines, and higher-rate taxpayers will no longer automatically receive a self-assessment form if their affairs can be handled through the PAYE system.

A very important point to know for anyone who might be feeling worried is that *self-calculation is optional*. If you think the calculations are too complicated or that you might be at risk of making a mistake, HMRC will continue as before to do the sums for you. Until recently, taxpayers who wanted HMRC to calculate their tax liability for them had to file their return by an earlier date. Today, this is no longer an issue. Instead, what matters is whether you file online or submit a paper return. Paper returns must be filed by 31 October each year; the deadline for online filing is 31 January the following year.

For further information, see booklets SA/BK4, *Self-Assessment – A General Guide to Keeping Records*; SA/BK6, *Self-Assessment – Penalties for Late Tax Returns*; SA/BK7, *Self-Assessment – Surcharges for Late Payment of Tax* and SA/BK8, *Self-Assessment – Your Guide*, all obtainable free from any tax office. You can also call the **Self-Assessment Helpline** on 0845 900 0444; (website: www.direct.gov.uk) or contact HMRC (website: www.hmrc.gov.uk).

Retiring abroad

There are many examples of people who retired abroad in the expectation of being able to afford a higher standard of living and who returned home a few years later, thoroughly disillusioned. As with other important decisions, this is where it is essential to research your options thoroughly. It is crucial to investigate property prices, as well as the cost of health care. As anyone who has ever needed a doctor or dentist abroad knows, the term 'free health service' does not always mean what it says. While these and similar points are perhaps obvious, a vital question that is often overlooked is the taxation effects of living overseas. If you are thinking of retiring abroad, do look into the effect this will have on your finances before you go.

Taxation abroad

Tax rates vary from one country to another: a prime example is VAT, which varies considerably in Europe. Additionally, many countries levy taxes that don't apply in the UK. Wealth tax exists in quite a few parts of the world. Estate duty on property left by one spouse to another is also fairly widespread.

There are all sorts of property taxes, different from those in the UK, which – however described – are variously assessable as income or capital. Sometimes a special tax is imposed on foreign residents. Some countries charge income tax on an individual's worldwide income, without the exemptions that apply in the UK.

Even so-called 'tax havens' may fail to live up to their privileged reputation. While admittedly not actual taxation, all sorts of conditions are often imposed on foreigners, effectively excluding all but the super-rich. The terms may vary but could include any, or all, of the following: only property above a minimum (and pretty exorbitant) price may be purchased; you may have to produce evidence of a sky-high annual income; you may be required to invest in a local business; or you could be requested to deposit a sum with the government to cover you against repatriation costs, should the necessity arise.

Perhaps even more alarming, many hundreds of Britons in Spain have been landed with vast bills because, unbeknown to them, the developers from whom they purchased their home had taken out a mortgage against the property and then subsequently gone out of business, leaving the British owners with the debt plus interest and legal fees. Although new laws have been introduced in Spain to protect the buyer, it appears that these are not being applied as rigorously as they might.

Apart from the essential of getting first-class legal advice when buying property overseas, if you are thinking of retiring abroad the golden rule must be to investigate the situation thoroughly before you take an irrevocable step, such as selling your home in the UK. However, if many people blithely ignore the 'nasties' that may await them overseas, an even more common mistake is for people to misunderstand their UK tax liabilities after their departure.

Your UK tax position if you retire overseas

Many intending emigrants cheerfully imagine that, once they have settled themselves in a dream villa overseas, they are safely out of the clutches of the UK tax office. This is not so. You first have to acquire non-resident status. If you have severed all your ties, including selling your home, to take up a permanent job overseas, this is normally granted fairly quickly. But for most retirees, acquiring unconditional non-resident status can take up to three years. The purpose is to check that you are not just having a prolonged holiday but are actually living as a resident abroad. During the check period, HMRC may allow you conditional non-resident status and, if it is satisfied, full status will be granted retrospectively.

Rules

The rules for non-residency are pretty stringent. You are not allowed to spend more than 182 days in the UK in any one tax year, or to spend more than an average of 90 days per year in the UK over a maximum of four tax years. Even if you are not resident in the UK, some of your income may still be liable for UK taxation.

UK Income Tax

- All overseas income (provided it is not remitted to the UK) is exempt from UK tax liability.
- Income deriving from a UK source is, however, normally liable for UK tax. This includes any director's or consultant's fees you may still be receiving, as well as more obvious income such as rent from a property you still own.
- An exception may be made if the country in which you have taken up residency has a double tax agreement with the United Kingdom (see below). If this is the case, you may be taxed on the income in your new residence – and not in the UK.
- Additionally, interest paid on certain British government securities is not subject to tax.
- Non-residents may be able to arrange for their interest on a British bank deposit or building society account to be paid gross.
- Some former colonial pensions are also exempt.

Double tax agreement

A person who is a resident of a country with which the UK has a double taxation agreement may be entitled to exemption or partial relief from UK Income Tax on certain kinds of income from UK sources and may also be exempt from UK tax on the disposal of assets. The conditions of exemption or relief vary from agreement to agreement. It may be a condition of the relief that the income is subject to tax in the other country. *NB:* if, as sometimes happens, the foreign tax authority later makes an adjustment and the income ceases to be taxed in that country, you have an obligation under the self-assessment rules to notify HMRC.

Capital Gains Tax (CGT)

This is only charged if you are resident or ordinarily resident in the UK; so if you are in the position of being able to realize a gain, it is advisable to wait until you acquire non-resident status. However, to escape CGT, you must wait to dispose of any assets until after the tax year of your departure and must remain non-resident (and not ordinarily resident) in the UK for five full tax years after your departure. Different rules apply to gains made from the disposal of assets in a UK company; these are subject to normal CGT.

Inheritance Tax (IHT)

You escape tax only if:

- you were domiciled overseas for all of the immediate three years prior to death;
- you were resident overseas for more than three tax years in your final 20 years of life; and
- all your assets were overseas.

Even if you have been resident overseas for many years, if you do not have an overseas domicile you will have to pay IHT at the same rates as if you lived in the UK.

Domicile

Broadly speaking you are domiciled in the country in which you have your permanent home. Domicile is distinct from nationality or residence. A person may be resident in more than one country, but at any given time he or she can be domiciled in only one. If you are resident in a country and intend to spend the rest of your days there, it could be sensible to decide to change your domicile. If, however, you are resident but there is a chance that you might move, the country where you are living would not qualify as your domicile. This is a complicated area, where professional advice is recommended if you are contemplating a change.

UK pensions paid abroad

- Any queries about your pension should be addressed to the International Payments Office, **International Pensions Centre**, Tel: 0191 218 7777; website: www.thepensionservice.gov.uk.
- Technically your State pension could be subject to Income Tax, as it derives from the UK. In practice, if this is your only source of UK income, tax is unlikely to be charged.
- If you have an occupational pension, UK tax will normally be charged on the total of the two amounts.
- Both State and occupational pensions may be paid to you in any country. If you are planning to retire to Australia, Canada, New Zealand or South Africa, it would be advisable to check on the up-to-date position regarding

any annual increases you would expect to receive to your pension. Some people have found the level of their pension frozen at the date they left the UK, while others have been liable for unexpected tax overseas.

- If the country where you are living has a double tax agreement with the UK, as previously explained, your income may be taxed there – and not in the UK. The UK now has a double tax agreement with most countries. For further information, check the position with your local tax office.
- If your pension is taxed in the UK, you will be able to claim your personal allowance as an offset. A married man living with his wife may also be able to claim the Married Couple's Allowance, if by virtue of their age they would still be eligible to receive it (see 'Married Couple's Allowance', page 71).

Health care overseas

People retiring to another EU country before state retirement age can apply to **DWP Overseas Contributions** (Tel: 0845 915 4811; website: www.dwp.gov. uk/international/further-help-and-advice) for a form E106, which will entitle them to state health care in that country on the same basis as for local people. An E106 is valid only for a maximum of two and a half years, after which it is usually necessary to take out private insurance cover until State retirement age is reached. Thereafter, UK pensioners can request the **International Pensions Centre** at Newcastle (see under 'UK pensions paid abroad' above) for a form E121, entitling them and their dependants to state health care as provided by the country in which they are living.

Useful reading

Residents and Non Residents – Liability to Tax in the UK, (IR20) available from any tax office.
Leaflet SA29, *Your Social Security Insurance, Benefits and Health Care Rights in the European Community*, contains essential information about what to do if you retire to another EU country. It is available from any social security or Jobcentre Plus office (website: www.jobcentreplus.gov.uk).

5

Investment

Investment is a subject for everyone. One of your single most important aims must be to make your existing money work for you so you will be more comfortable in the years ahead. The younger you start planning the better. If you are already 65 or over, there is still plenty you can do.

You will read many articles on the subject of financial planning for retirement that concentrate on ways of boosting your immediate income. Although this would compensate for your loss of earnings, this could be misleading and short-sighted advice. A more critical consideration must be to safeguard your long-term security. Statistics show that an ever growing number of people live for 20 years or more after they retire. Your investment strategy must be aimed not just for your 60s and 70s but also for your 80s or even your 90s.

Inflation is another essential factor that must be taken into account. People on fixed incomes are the hardest hit when inflation rises. Currently many people are being drastically affected as a result of their savings being slashed in value. Even when inflation rates are low it takes its toll to an alarming extent. The good news is that there's plenty that can be done to make what money you have work hard for you, so it is worth spending some time reviewing all your options.

Sources of investable funds

You do not need to be in the director league to have money for investment. Possible sources of quite significant capital include:

- Commuted lump sum from your pension. There is now one set of rules for all types of pension scheme, with members allowed a maximum of 25 per cent of their pension fund or 25 per cent of their lifetime limit, whichever is lower. There is no tax to pay when you receive the money.

- Insurance policies designed to mature around your retirement. These are normally tax-free.
- Profits on your home, if you sell it and move to smaller, less expensive accommodation. Provided this is your main home, there is no capital gains tax to pay.
- Redundancy money, golden handshake or other farewell gift from your employer. You are allowed £30,000 redundancy money free of tax. The same is usually true of other severance pay up to £30,000, but there can be tax if, however worded, your employment contract indicates that these are deferred earnings.
- Sale of SAYE and other share option schemes. The tax rules vary according to the type of scheme, the date the options were acquired and how long the shares were held before disposal. Since the rules are liable to change with each Budget statement, for further information contact HMRC (website: www.hmrc.gov.uk).

General investment strategy

Investments differ in their aims, their tax treatment and the amount of risk involved. One or two categories are suitable only for the very rich, who can afford to take more significant risks. Others, such as certain types of National Savings, are really only suitable for those on a very low income.

These two groups apart, the aim for most people should be to acquire a balanced portfolio: in other words, a mix of investments variously designed to provide some income to supplement your pension and also some capital appreciation to maintain your standard of living in the long term.

Except for annuities, National Savings & Investments and property, which have sections to themselves, the different types of investment are listed by groups, as follows:

- variable interest accounts;
- fixed interest securities;
- equities;
- long-term lock-ups.

As a general strategy in the current economic climate, it is a good idea to mix and match, so that your investments should be spread across several groups.

Annuities

Definition

A normal life annuity is a very simple investment to understand. You pay a capital sum to an insurance company and in return are guaranteed a fixed income for life. The money is paid to you at fixed intervals and will remain exactly the same year in, year out. Payments are calculated according to life expectancy tables, and for this reason an annuity may not really be a suitable investment for anyone under 70. Other than your age, the key factor affecting the amount you will receive in payments is the level of interest rates at the time you buy: the higher these are, the more you will receive.

An annuity would probably give you more immediate income than any other form of investment. But whether you actually get good value depends on how long you live. When you die, your capital will be gone and there will be no more payments. So if you die a short while after signing the contract, it will represent very bad value indeed. On the other hand, if you live a very long time, you may more than recoup your original capital. As a precaution against early death, it is possible to take out a capital-protected annuity, an annuity that includes a guaranteed payment period, or an annuity that transfers to your partner for the duration of his or her life. Any of these options will reduce the annuity income you receive but could be worth considering if your primary concern is to give your partner (or other beneficiaries) added security.

The difference between the three choices is briefly as follows:

- *Capital-protected annuities* pay out any balance left from your original investment after deduction of the gross annuity payments paid to date.
- *Annuities with a guarantee period* are normal life annuities with the important difference that, if you die before the end of the guaranteed period, the payments for the remaining years (of the guaranteed period) will go to your partner or other beneficiary.
- *Annuities incorporating a spouse's benefit* pay out the annuity income to you during your lifetime and will then pass to your partner for the remainder of his or her life.

Tax

Income tax on optional annuities is relatively low, as part of the income is allowed as a return on capital that is not taxable. Pension-linked annuities are fully taxable.

How to obtain

You can buy an annuity either direct from an insurance company or via an intermediary, such as an independent financial adviser (IFA). But shop around, since as mentioned above the payments vary considerably. **To find an IFA,** consult the professional advice website: www.unbiased.co.uk. Choose the search service you need, tick your requirements and receive details of appropriate, qualified advisers close to your home or office.

Assessment

An annuity is safe, attractive if you live to a ripe old age, but highly vulnerable to inflation. It is a sacrifice of capital that might otherwise benefit successors.

National Savings & Investments (NS&I)

NS&I is one of the biggest savings institutions in the country. It is guaranteed by the government, and all investments are backed by HM Treasury. It is extremely easy to invest in NS&I products, as all you need do is go to the Post Office for information or telephone NS&I Customer Enquiries on 0845 964 5000 (all calls are charged at local rates) or visit the website: www.nsandi.com.

Most types of investment offered by NS&I are broadly similar to those provided by banks and other financial bodies. So rather than explain in detail the exact terms and conditions of, say, an NS&I Investment Account, it is easier to suggest that you pick up the relevant booklet at the Post Office counter, visit the NS&I website or ring Customer Enquiries (see above).

NS&I Savings Certificates, of which there are two types (fixed interest and inflation-beating), are free of tax. Although in most cases they do not pay a particularly high rate of interest, any investment that is tax-free is of potential interest, especially to higher-rate taxpayers. A long-standing feature of NS&I has been that non-taxpayers enjoyed the benefit of income receipts being paid gross, without deduction of tax. Since the abolition of composite rate tax, this now also applies to bank and building society interest. The one advantage, however, that NS&I still offers non-taxpayers is that there is no need for them to complete an HM Revenue & Customs (HMRC) form to receive their money in full, as this is automatic.

The main investments offered by National Savings & Investments are:

- *Easy Access Savings Account.* This is an easy way to build up your savings, with instant access to your money and the option to save regularly by standing order. You can invest between £100 and £2 million. The account offers variable, tiered rates of interest and allows instant access through the Post Office or cash machines.
- *Income Bonds.* These are worth considering if you are interested in earning monthly income and having easy access to your money. They pay fairly attractive, variable, tiered rates of interest, increasing with larger investments. Interest is taxable, but paid in full without deduction of tax at source. You can invest between £500 and £1 million. There is no set term for the investment.
- *Fixed Interest Savings Certificates.* These will earn you guaranteed and tax-free returns. They offer a moderate rate of interest. You can invest from £100 to £15,000 per issue. For maximum benefit, you must hold the certificates for five years.

- *Inflation-beating Savings Certificates*. These are worth considering if you want to make sure your investment grows ahead of inflation, tax-free. You can invest from £100 to £15,000 per issue. There is a fixed rate of interest, index-linked to the Retail Prices Index. No index-linking or interest will be earned on certificates cashed in within one year of purchase. Certificates must be retained for either three or five years. Interest is tax-free.
- *Children's Bonus Bonds*. These are for those who want to give a child a long-term tax-free investment. Bonds are sold in multiples of £25, and the maximum purchase per child is £3,000. The investment term is five years at a time until the 21st birthday. Interest rates are fixed for five years at a time plus a guaranteed bonus. These are tax-free for parents and children and need not be declared to HMRC.
- *Guaranteed Income Bonds*. These are worth considering if you want a monthly income with the certainty of knowing exactly what return you will get on your money without touching your capital investment. The income, which is paid monthly, is taxable and paid net. The minimum purchase is £500, and the maximum is £1 million. There is a choice of terms, currently one, three and five years. Interest rates are guaranteed for the length of the chosen term.
- *Guaranteed Growth Bonds*. These give a guaranteed return on your investment and offer a choice of fixed-rate terms. They are worth considering if you want to invest for a set term with the certainty of knowing exactly what return you will get on your money. The minimum purchase is £500; the maximum is £1 million. There is a choice of terms, currently one, three and five years. Interest rates are guaranteed for the length of the term chosen. Interest is taxable and paid net.

NS&I also offers cash ISAs, a direct ISA, Guaranteed Equity Bonds, an Investment Account and of course Premium Bonds, of which you can now hold up to £30,000 worth.

Complaints

If you have a complaint about any NS&I products, you should raise this with the Director of Savings. Should the matter not be resolved to your satisfaction you can contact the **Financial Ombudsman Service**, Tel: 0845 080 1800; website: www.financial-ombudsman.org.uk.

Variable interest accounts

People who rely on interest from their savings to provide them with extra income in their retirement will have been particularly affected when interest rates were slashed. Over the past few years, many savers have seen their incomes dwindle at an alarming rate, causing many older people to feel the pinch. This is not to say that variable interest accounts should necessarily be avoided (when interest rates are high, they provide a good home for one's money), but it is essential to understand how such accounts work – together with their advantages and drawbacks.

Over the past few years, most banks and building societies have introduced interest-bearing current accounts. Although an improvement on the standard current account, these do not qualify in anyone's language as a vehicle for investment and, as the banks themselves would be the first to agree, are not a suitable place for anyone to keep large savings for more than a short time. If you are tempted to switch to an interest-bearing current account, you should check very carefully what charges apply if you dip into overdraft.

A point to investigate is whether there is a fixed monthly or other charge. This can sometimes change at fairly short notice. You should check your monthly statement carefully and consider moving your account if you are dissatisfied. Banks and building societies frequently introduce new accounts with introductory bonuses, which are then slashed in value after a few months. Although this could equally apply to internet accounts, they could still be worth investigating as, generally speaking, they tend to offer more competitive rates.

Although keeping track may be fairly time-consuming, at least comparing the rates offered by different savings institutions has become very much easier, as all advertisements for savings products must now quote the annual equivalent rate (AER). Unlike the former variety of ways of expressing interest rates, the AER provides a true comparison taking into account the frequency of interest payments and whether or not interest is compounded.

Definition

Other than the interest-bearing current accounts described above, these are all savings accounts of one form or another, arranged with banks, building societies, the National Savings & Investments Bank, and some financial institutions that operate such accounts jointly with banks. The accounts include, among others, instant access accounts, high interest accounts and fixed-term savings accounts.

Your money collects interest while it is in the account, which may be automatically credited to your account or for which you may receive a regular cheque. Some institutions pay interest annually; others – on some or all of their accounts – will pay it monthly. If you have a preference, this is a point to check.

Although you may get a poor return on your money when interest rates drop, your savings will nearly always be safe, as you are not taking any kind of investment risk. Moreover, provided you deal with an authorized bank, up to £50,000 of your money will be 100 per cent protected under the **Financial Services Compensation Scheme**; see the website: www.fscs.org.uk; e-mail: enquiries@ fscs.org.uk, Tel: 020 7892 7300.

Access

Access to your money depends on the type of account you choose: you may have an ATM card and/or chequebook and withdraw your money when you want; you may have to give a week's notice or slightly longer; or, if you enter into a term account, you will have to leave your money deposited for the agreed specified period. In general, accounts where a slightly longer period of notice is required earn a better rate of interest.

Sum deposited

You can open a savings account with as little as £1. For certain types of account, the minimum investment could be anything from £500 to about £5,000. The terms tend to vary according to how keen the institutions are, at a given time, to attract small investors.

Tax

With the exception of cash ISAs which are tax-free, and of the National Savings & Investments Bank, where interest is paid gross, tax is deducted at source – so you can spend the money without worrying about the tax implications. However, you must enter the interest on your tax return and, if you are a higher-rate taxpayer, you will have additional liability.

Basic-rate taxpayers pay 20 per cent on their bank and building society interest. Higher-rate taxpayers pay 40 per cent. Non-taxpayers can arrange to have their interest paid in full by completing a certificate (R85, available from HMRC or the bank) that enables the financial institution to pay the interest gross. If you largely rely on your savings income and believe you are or have been paying excess tax, you can reclaim this from HMRC. For further information, see 'Income Tax on savings' (page 76) and 'Reclaiming tax overpaid' (page 78).

NB: there has been some rather disturbing news recently about cash ISA savers being badly let down by banks and building societies when they try to transfer their accounts. Because of poor administration, in some cases savers have not had access to their money for months. ISA rules prevent savers from switching their money between accounts themselves, because that would lose them the tax-free benefit. The trap is caused by a 10-year-old system in which ISA providers write each other cheques to move the money rather than using faster electronic transfers. Under the system, the provider holding your money has a month after receiving your transfer request to move your cash. If you are likely to be transferring your savings from one account to another, keep an eye on this potential hazard.

Choosing a savings account

There are two main areas of choice: the type of savings account and where to invest your money. The relative attractions of the different types of account and of the institutions themselves can vary according to the terms being offered at the time. Generally speaking, however, the basic points are as follows.

Instant access savings account

This attracts a relatively low rate of interest, but it is both easy to set up and very flexible, as you can add small or large savings when you like and can usually withdraw your money without any notice. It is a much better option than simply leaving your money in a current account and is an excellent temporary home for your cash if you are saving short-term for, say, a holiday. However, it is not recommended as a long-term savings plan.

High interest savings account

Your money earns a higher rate of interest than it would in an ordinary savings account. However, to open a high interest account you will need to deposit a minimum sum, which could be £500 to £1,000. Although you can always add to this amount, if your balance drops below the required minimum your money will immediately stop earning the higher interest rate. The terms often vary between one institution and another. There may be a minimum and/or maximum monthly sum you can pay into the account. Also, some accounts have a fixed term, at the end of which your money will no longer earn the more favourable rate of interest.

Fixed-term savings account

You deposit your money for an agreed period of time, which can vary from a few months to over a year. In return for this commitment, you will normally be paid a superior rate of interest. As with high interest accounts, there is a minimum investment: roughly £1,500 to £10,000. If you need to withdraw your money before the end of the agreed term, there are usually hefty penalties. Before entering into a term account, you need to be sure that you can afford to leave the money in the account. Additionally, you will need to take a view about interest rates: if they are generally low, your money may be better invested elsewhere.

Equity-linked savings account

This offers a potentially better rate of return, as the interest is calculated in line with the growth in the stock market. Should the market fall, you may lose the interest, but your capital should normally remain protected. The minimum investment varies from about £500 to £5,000 and, depending on the institution, the money may need to remain deposited for perhaps as much as five years. As with any investment, it is important to ensure that you fully understand all the terms and conditions – and, if anything is unclear, that you ask to have the point explained to you properly in simple language.

ISA savings

Information on ISAs and the changes introduced in 2009 can be found on page 108.

Information

For banks, enquire direct at your nearest high street branch. There will be leaflets available, describing the different accounts in detail, or if you have any questions you can ask to see your bank manager. You can also investigate the other banks to see whether they offer better terms. For building societies, enquire at any building society branch. There is such a wide range of these that it is advisable to look at a number of them, as the terms and conditions may vary quite widely.

The **Building Societies Association** offers a free range of helpful leaflets and information sheets, including: *Lost Savings? Taxation of Building Society Interest*; *Individual Savings Accounts and Building Societies*; and *The Child Trust Fund*. A list of members, giving head office addresses and telephone numbers, is also available. All leaflets can be ordered by calling the Consumer Helpline on 020 7520 5900, or by e-mail: information@bsa.org.uk; website: www.bsa. org.uk.

The safety of your investment

Investors are protected by the legislative framework in which societies operate and, in common with bank customers, their money (up to a maximum of £50,000) is protected under the **Financial Services Compensation Scheme (FSCS)**. Further details about the scheme are available from the FSCS, Tel: 020 7892 7300; e-mail: enquiries@fscs.org.uk; website: www.fscs.org.uk.

Complaints

If you have a complaint against a bank or building society, you can appeal to the **Financial Ombudsman Service (FOS)** to investigate the matter, provided the complaint has already been taken through the particular institution's own internal disputes procedure – or after eight weeks if the problem has not been resolved – and provided the matter is within the scope of the Ombudsman Scheme. Generally speaking, the FOS can investigate complaints about the way a bank or building society has handled some matter relating to its services to customers. Contact the Financial Ombudsman Service, Tel: 0845 080 1800; e-mail: complaint.info@financial-ombudsman.org.uk; website: www.financial-ombudsman.org.uk.

Fixed interest securities

In contrast to variable interest accounts, fixed interest securities offer a fixed rate of interest, which you are paid regardless of what happens to interest rates generally. If you buy when the fixed rate is high and interest rates fall, you will nevertheless continue to be paid interest at the high rate specified in the contract note. However, if interest rates rise above the level when you bought, you will not benefit from the increase. Generally these securities give high income but only modest, if any, capital appreciation. The list includes high interest gilts, permanent interest-bearing shares, local authority bonds and stock exchange loans, debentures and preference shares.

Gilt-edged securities

Definition

Usually known as 'gilts', these are stocks issued by the government, which guarantee both the interest payable and the repayment price, which is promised on a given date. The maturity date varies and can be anything from a few months to 20 years or longer. Accordingly, stocks are variously known as short-dated, medium-dated and long-dated. A further category is undated. Additionally, there are index-linked gilts. Prices for gilts are quoted per £100 of nominal stock. For example, a stock may be quoted as 10 per cent Treasury Stock 2015, 99½–100¼. In plain English, this means the following:

- 10 per cent represents the interest you will be paid. The rate is fixed and will not vary, whatever happens to interest rates generally. You will receive the interest payment twice-yearly, 5 per cent each time.
- You are buying Treasury Stock.
- The maturity date is 2015.
- To buy the stock, you will have to pay £100.25p (ie 100¼).
- If you want to sell the stock, the market price you will get is £99.50 (ie 99½).

In addition, when buying or selling, regard has to be given to the accrued interest that will have to be added to or subtracted from the price quoted. Gilts are complicated by the fact that you can either retain them until their maturity date, in which case the government will return the capital in full, or sell them on the London Stock Exchange at market value.

Index-linked gilts

While operating on the same broad principle, these are different in effect. They are designed to shield investors against inflation; they pay very low interest but are redeemable at a higher price than the initial purchase price, as their value is geared to the cost of living. They are most valuable when inflation is high but are even more sensitive than other gilts to optimum timing when buying or selling.

Tax

Gilt interest from whatever source is paid gross. Gross payment does not mean that you avoid paying tax, simply that you must allow for a future tax bill before spending the money. Recipients who prefer to receive the money net of tax can request for this to be arranged. A particular attraction of gilts is that no capital gains tax is charged on any profit you may have made, but equally no relief is allowed for any loss.

How to buy

You can buy gilts through banks, building societies, a stockbroker or a financial intermediary, or you can purchase them through **Computershare Investor Services**, website: www-uk.computershare.com, Tel: 0870 703 0143. In all cases, you will be charged commission. Prices of gilts are published every day in all the quality newspapers under the heading 'British Funds'. You may also find it helpful to refer to the section headed 'Bonds' (page 113).

Assessment

Gilts normally pay reasonably good interest and offer excellent security, in that they are backed by the government. You can sell at very short notice, and the stock is normally accepted by banks as security for loans, if you want to run an overdraft. However, gilts are not a game for amateurs as, if you buy or sell at the wrong time, you could lose money; and, if you hold your stock to redemption, inflation could take its toll on your original investment. Index-linked gilts, which overcome the inflation problem, are generally speaking a better investment for higher-rate taxpayers – not least because the interest paid is very low.

Gilt plans

This is a technique for linking the purchase of gilt-edged securities and with-profit life insurance policies to provide security of capital and income over a 10- to 20-year period. It is a popular investment for the commuted lump sum taken on retirement. These plans are normally obtainable from financial intermediaries, who should be authorized by the Financial Services Authority (FSA).

Permanent interest-bearing shares (PIBS)

These are a form of investment offered by some building societies to financial institutions and private investors, as a means of raising share capital. They have several features in common with gilts, as follows. They pay a fixed rate of interest that is set at the date of issue; this is likely to be on the high side when interest rates generally are low and on the low side when interest rates are high. The interest is usually paid twice-yearly and – again, similarly to gilts – there is no Stamp Duty to pay or Capital Gains Tax on profits. Despite the fact that PIBS are issued by building societies, they are very different from normal building society investments and have generally been rated as being in the medium- to high-risk category. Anyone thinking of investing their money should seek professional advice. To buy the shares, you will need to go to a stockbroker or financial adviser.

Equities

These are all stocks and shares, purchased in different ways and involving varying degrees of risk. They are designed to achieve capital appreciation as well as give you some regular income. Most allow you to get your money out within a week. In the past, equities were by and large considered suitable only for a privileged minority. Today, the number of shareholders is estimated to have soared to well over 15 million people. One reason is that equities can be excellent money-spinners. Another is that, over the last few years, investment has become very much easier, largely as a result of the increase in the number of internet and telephone share-dealing facilities.

As many will know to their cost from the recent market volatility, equities are always risky. But for those who believe in caution, the gamble can be substantially reduced by avoiding obviously speculative investments and by choosing a spread of investments, rather than putting all your eggs in one basket. Equities include ordinary shares, unit trusts, OEICs (see below), investment trusts and REITs (see page 00).

Unit trusts and OEICs

Definition

Unit trusts and OEICs (open-ended investment companies, a modern equivalent of unit trusts) offer the opportunity of investing collectively in a range of assets with other investors. Your money is pooled in a fund run by professional managers, who invest the capital in a wide range of assets including equities, bonds and cash. The advantages are that it is usually less risky than buying individual shares, it is simple to understand, you get professional management and there are no day-to-day decisions to make. Additionally, every fund is required by law to have a trustee (called a 'depository' in the case of OEICs) to protect investors' interests.

The minimum investment in some of the more popular funds can be as little as £25; in others, it can be as high as £10,000. There is often a front-end fee, and sometimes an exit fee, which varies from group to group and fund to fund.

Investors' contributions to the fund are divided into units (shares in OEICs) in proportion to the amount they have invested. As with ordinary shares, you can sell all or some of your investment by telling the fund manager that you wish to do so. The price you will receive is called the 'bid price'. The price at which you buy a unit is called the 'offer price'.

How to obtain

Units and shares can be purchased from banks, building societies, insurance companies, stockbrokers, specialist investment fund providers and independent financial advisers, directly from the management group and via the internet. Some firms advertise in the national press and financial magazines and also, increasingly, on the internet. Some have their own sales forces. Many of the larger firms may use all these methods. You may be asked to complete a form – stating how much you want to invest in which particular fund – and then return it to the company with your cheque. Alternatively, you may be able to deal over the telephone or internet.

For a list of unit trusts and OEICs, you can look in the *Financial Times*. You can also contact **Investment FactLine** Information Service (Tel: 020 7269 4639; website: www.investmentuk.org) to obtain a guide to investing called *Introducing Investment*, as well as various fact sheets on such topics as ISAs, ethical investment, unit trusts and tax. Tables comparing the performance of the various funds are published in specialist magazines or on websites such as *Money Management*, *Money Observer* and *What Investment*. With over 2,000 funds from which to choose, it is important to get independent professional advice. For further information see Chapter 6, Financial Advisers.

Tax

Units and shares invested through an ISA have special advantages (see 'Individual Savings Account (ISA)', page 108). Otherwise, the tax treatment is identical to that of ordinary shares (see the next section).

Assessment

Unit trusts and OEICs are an ideal method for smaller investors to buy stocks and shares: both less risky and easier. This applies especially to tracker funds, which have the added advantage that charges are normally very low. Some of the more specialist funds are also suitable for those with a significant investment portfolio.

Complaints

Complaints about unit trusts and OEICs are handled by the **Financial Ombudsman Service (FOS)**. It has power to order awards of up to £100,000.

Before approaching the FOS, you must first try to resolve the problem with the management company direct via its internal complaints procedure. If you remain dissatisfied, the company should advise you of your right to refer the matter to the FOS. Whether they inform you or not, contact the Financial Ombudsman Service, Tel: 0845 080 1800; e-mail: complaint.info@financial-ombudsman.org. uk; website: www.financial-ombudsman.org.uk.

Ordinary shares listed on the London Stock Exchange

Definition

Public companies issue shares as a way of raising money. When you buy shares and become a shareholder in a company, you own a small part of the business and are entitled to participate in its profits through a dividend, which is normally paid six-monthly. Dividends go up and down according to how well the company is doing, and it is possible that in a bad year no dividends at all will be paid. However, in good years, dividends can increase very substantially.

The money you invest is unsecured. This means that, quite apart from any dividends, your capital could be reduced in value – or if the company goes bankrupt you could lose the lot. Against this, if the company performs well you could substantially increase your wealth. The value of a company's shares is decided by the stock market. Thousands of large and small investors are taking a view on each company's prospects, and this creates the market price. The price of a share can fluctuate daily, and this will affect both how much you have to pay if you want to buy and how much you will make (or lose) if you want to sell. You could visit the **London Stock Exchange** website (www.londonstockexchange.com) to find a list of brokers in your area who would be willing to deal for you. Alternatively, you can go to the securities department of your bank or to one of the authorized share shops, which will place the order for you.

Whether you use a stockbroker, a share shop, a telephone share-dealing service or the internet, you will be charged both commission and Stamp Duty, which is currently 0.5 per cent. Unless you use a nominee account (see below), you will be issued with a share certificate that you or your financial adviser must keep, as you will have to produce it when you wish to sell all or part of your holding. It is likely, when approaching a stockbroker or other share-dealing service, that you will be asked to deposit money for your investment up front or advised that you should use a nominee account. This is because of the introduction of several new systems, designed to speed up – and stream-line – the share-dealing process.

There are three types of share, all quoted on the London Stock Exchange, that are potentially suitable for small investors. These are investment companies, REITs and convertible loan stocks. Other possibilities, but only for those who can afford more risky investments, are warrants and zero coupon loan stocks:

- *Investment companies* are companies that invest in the shares of other companies. They pool investors' money and so enable those with quite small amounts to spread the risk by gaining exposure to a wide portfolio of shares, run by a professional fund manager. There are over 300 different companies from which to choose. For a range of fact sheets on investment companies, contact the **Association of Investment Companies**, Tel: 020 7282 5555; e-mail: enquiries@theaic.co.uk; website: www.theaic.co.uk.
- *Real estate investment trusts (REITs)*. These are a fairly new type of fund, quoted on the London Stock Exchange, which, operating similarly to investment trusts, pool investors' money and invest it for them collectively in commercial and residential property. They offer individuals a cheap, simple and potentially less risky way of buying shares in a spread of properties, with the added attraction that the funds themselves are more tax-efficient, as both rental income and profits from sales are tax-free within the fund. Also, if wanted, REITs can be held within an ISA or Self-Invested Personal Pension (SIPP). There are numerous UK companies that have converted to REIT status. Stockbrokers and independent financial advisers are able to provide information and it is recommended that professional advice is taken before investing.
- *Convertible loan stocks* give you a fixed guaranteed income for a certain length of time and offer you the opportunity to convert them into ordinary shares. While capital appreciation prospects are lower, the advantage of convertible loans is that they usually provide significantly higher income than ordinary dividends. They are also allowable for ISAs.
- *Zero coupon loan stocks*. These stocks provide no income during their life but pay an enhanced capital sum on maturity. They would normally only be recommended for higher-rate taxpayers, and professional advice is strongly recommended.
- *Warrants* are issued by companies or investment trusts to existing shareholders either at launch or by way of an additional bonus. Each warrant carries the right of the shareholder to purchase additional shares at a predetermined price on specific dates in the future. Warrants command their own price on the stock market. They are a high-risk investment, and professional advice is essential.

Tax

All UK shares pay dividends net of 10 per cent Corporation Tax. Basic-rate and non-taxpayers have no further liability to income tax. Higher-rate taxpayers must pay further Income Tax at 22 per cent. Quite apart from Income Tax, if during the year you make profits by selling shares that in total exceed £10,100 (the Annual Exempt Amount for an individual in 2009/10) you will be liable for Capital Gains Tax, which is calculated at a flat rate of 18 per cent.

Assessment

Although dividend payments generally start low, in good companies they are likely to increase over the years and so provide a first-class hedge against inflation. The best equities are an excellent investment. In others, you can lose all your money. Good advice is critical, as this is a high-risk, high-reward market.

Individual Savings Account (ISA)

Definition

ISAs are the savings accounts that the government launched in April 1999 as a replacement for PEPs and TESSAs. They contain many of the same advantages in that all income and gains generated in the account are tax-free. There is a subscription limit. There are two types of ISA: cash ISAs and stocks and shares ISAs.

2009 changes

The annual subscription limit was increased for people over 50 from 6 October 2009 from £7,200 to £10,200, making it possible to invest a maximum of up to £5,100 in a cash ISA plus a further £5,100 in a stocks and shares ISA. The rest of the population have to wait until 6 April 2010 before these new limits apply. You can also now invest up to £10,200 in a stocks and shares ISA.

Tax

ISAs are completely free of all income tax and capital gains tax. You should be aware that a 20 per cent charge is levied on all interest accruing from non-invested money held in an ISA that is not specifically a cash ISA.

Assessment

ISAs offer a simple, flexible way of starting, or improving, a savings plan, although sadly they are no longer as attractive as they once were, and some readers may now find better homes for investing their money. While cash ISAs remain useful, as all interest is tax-free, stocks and shares ISAs – while still potentially worthwhile for higher-rate taxpayers – offer fewer advantages to basic-rate taxpayers as a result of the charges and the removal of the dividend tax credit.

Child Trust Funds

Child Trust Funds are designed to start every baby off with a savings plan to mature at the time of his or her 18th birthday. While clearly of no direct benefit to readers, they could be of interest to grandparents who would like to help grandchildren build up a nest egg for the future.

All children born since 1 September 2002 receive a voucher worth £250 to be invested in a fund until they reach 18. Children of less wealthy families are given £500. A further payment of £250 or £500 will be added at age 7. Family and friends are allowed to contribute up to a maximum of £1,200 a year into the fund. The money can be invested in cash, shares and bonds plus most FSA-approved schemes, and all growth in the fund is tax-free. The fund can then be rolled into ISAs once the child becomes 18. If the money is not invested after a year of receipt of the voucher, the money will be invested in a special 'stakeholder account'. There is no need to claim, as vouchers are sent automatically to every-one receiving Child Benefit.

Long-term lock-ups

Certain types of investment, mostly offered by insurance companies, provide fairly high guaranteed growth in exchange for your undertaking to leave a lump sum with them or to pay regular premiums for a fixed period, usually five years or longer. The list includes life assurance policies, investment bonds and some types of National Savings Certificates.

Life assurance policies

Definition

Life assurance can provide you with one of two main benefits: it can either provide your successors with money when you die or it can be used as a savings plan to provide you with a lump sum (or income) on a fixed date. In the past, it was very much an 'either or' situation: you chose whichever type of policy suited you and the insurance company paid out accordingly. In recent years, however, both types of scheme have become more flexible, and many policies allow you to incorporate features of the other. This can have great advantages from the point of view of enabling you to 'have your cake and eat it', but the result is that some of the definitions appear a bit contradictory. There are three basic types of life assurance: whole life policies, term policies and endowment policies:

- *Whole life policies* are designed to pay out on your death. In its most straight-forward form, the scheme works as follows: you pay a premium every year and, when you die, your beneficiaries receive the money. As with an ordi-nary household policy, the insurance holds good only if you continue the payments. If one year you did not pay and were to die, the policy could be void and your successors would receive nothing.

- *Term policies* involve a definite commitment. As opposed to paying premiums every year, you elect to make regular payments for an agreed period, for example until such time as your children have completed their education, say eight years. If you die during this period, your family will be paid the agreed sum in full. If you die after the end of the term (when you have stopped making payments), your family will normally receive nothing.
- *Endowment policies* are essentially savings plans. You sign a contract to pay regular premiums over a number of years and in exchange receive a lump sum on a specific date. Most endowment policies are written for periods varying from 10 to 25 years. Once you have committed yourself, you have to go on paying every year (as with term assurance). There are heavy penalties if, having paid for a number of years, you decide that you no longer wish to continue.

An important feature of endowment policies is that they are linked in with death cover. If you die before the policy matures, the remaining payments are excused and your successors will be paid a lump sum on your death. Endowment policies have long been a popular way of making extra financial provision for retirement. They combine the advantages of guaranteeing you a lump sum with a built-in life assurance provision. The amount of money you stand to receive, however, can vary hugely, depending on the charges and how generous a bonus the insurance company feels it can afford on the policy's maturity. Over the past few years, pay-outs have been considerably lower than their earlier projections might have suggested. Aim to compare at least three policies before choosing.

Options

Both whole life policies and endowment policies offer two basic options: with profits or without profits. Very briefly the difference is as follows:

- *Without profits.* This is sometimes known as 'guaranteed sum assured'. What it means is that the insurance company guarantees you a specific fixed sum (provided of course you meet the various terms and conditions). You know the amount in advance and this is the sum you – or your successors – will be paid.
- *With profits.* You are paid a guaranteed fixed sum plus an addition, based on the profits that the insurance company has made by investing your annual or monthly payments. The basic premiums are higher and, by definition, the profits element is not known in advance. If the insurance company has invested your money wisely, a 'with profits' policy provides a useful hedge against inflation. If its investment policy is mediocre, you could have paid higher premiums for very little extra return.
- *Unit linked.* This is a refinement of the 'with profits' policy, in that the investment element of the policy is linked in with a unit trust.

Other basics

Premiums can normally be paid monthly or annually, as you prefer. The size of premium varies enormously, depending on the type of policy you choose and the amount of cover you want. Also, of course, some insurance companies are more competitive than others. As a generalization, higher premiums tend to give better value, as relatively less of your contribution is swallowed up in administrative costs.

As a condition of insuring you, some policies require that you have a medical check. This is more likely to apply if very large sums are involved. More usually, all that is required is that you fill in and sign a declaration of health. It is very important that this should be completed honestly: if you make a claim on your policy and it is subsequently discovered that you gave misleading information, your policy could be declared void and the insurance company could refuse to pay.

Many insurance companies offer a better deal if you are a non-smoker. Some also offer more generous terms if you are teetotal. Women generally pay less than men of the same age because of their longer life expectancy.

How to obtain

Policies are usually available through banks, insurance companies, independent financial advisers (IFAs) and building societies. The biggest problem for most people is the sheer volume of choice. Another difficulty can be understanding the small print: terms and conditions that sound very similar may obscure important differences that could affect your benefit. An accountant could advise you, in general terms, whether you are being offered a good deal or otherwise. However, if it is a question of choosing a specific policy best suited to your requirements, it is usually advisable to consult an IFA. **For help in finding an IFA in your area**, search the website www.unbiased.co.uk, e-mail: contact@ifap.org.uk. See also Chapter 6, Financial Advisers.

Disclosure rules

Advisers selling financial products have to abide by a set of disclosure rules, requiring them to give clients certain essential information before a contract is signed. Although for a number of years the requirements have included the provision of both a 'key features' document (explaining the product, the risk factors, charges, benefits, surrender value if the policy is terminated early, tax treatment and salesperson's commission or remuneration) and a 'suitability letter' (explaining why a particular product or policy was recommended), the FSA recently decided to revamp the rules in order to provide consumers with clearer and more comprehensive information.

As a result, advisers must now give potential clients two 'key facts' documents: one entitled 'About our services', describing the range of services and the type of advice on offer; and a second entitled 'About the cost of our services', including among other information details of the advisers' own commission charges and – for comparison purposes – the average market rate. Importantly too, IFAs must offer clients the choice of paying fees or paying by commission.

The **Association of British Insurers (ABI)** has a number of useful information sheets on life insurance; Tel: 020 7600 3333; e-mail: info@abi.org.uk; website: www.abi.org.uk.

Tax

Under current legislation, the proceeds of a qualifying policy – whether taken as a lump sum or in regular income payments (as in the case of family income benefit) – are free of all tax.

If, as applies to many people, you have a life insurance policy written into a trust, there is a possibility that it could be hit by the new Inheritance Tax rules affecting trusts if the sum it is expected to pay out is above the (2010/11) £350,000 IHT threshold. The best advice is to check with a solicitor.

Assessment

Life assurance is normally a sensible investment, whether the aim is to provide death cover or the benefits of a lump sum to boost your retirement income. It has the merit of being very attractive from a tax angle, and additionally certain policies provide good capital appreciation – although a point to be aware of is that recent bonuses have tended to be considerably lower than their projected amount. However, you are locked into a long-term commitment. So, even more than in most areas, choosing the right policy is very important. Shop around, take advice and, above all, do not sign anything unless you are absolutely certain that you understand every last dot and comma.

Complaints

Complaints about life assurance products, including alleged mis-selling, are handled by the Financial Ombudsman Service (FOS). Before approaching the FOS, you first need to try to resolve a dispute with the company direct. For further information, contact the **Financial Ombudsman Service**, Tel: 0845 080 1800; e-mail: complaint.info@financial-ombudsman.org.uk; website: www. financial-ombudsman.org.uk.

Alternatives to surrendering a policy

As already mentioned, there are heavy penalties if you surrender an endowment policy before its maturity. Some people, however, either because they can no longer afford the payments or for some other reason, wish to terminate the agreement – regardless of any losses they may make or investment gains they may sacrifice.

Instead of simply surrendering the policy to the insurance company, people in this situation may be able to sell the policy for a sum that is higher than its surrender value. As a first step, you might usefully contact the **Association of Policy Market Makers**, Tel: 0845 011 9406; e-mail: valuations@apmm.org; website: www.apmm.org, which can put you in contact with a number of suitable firms.

For those looking for investment possibilities, second-hand policies could be worth investigating. Known as traded endowment policies (TEPs), they offer the combination of a low-risk investment with a good potential return. Owing to increased supply, there is currently a wide range of individual policies and a number of specialist funds managed by financial institutions. A full list of appropriate financial institutions and authorized dealers that buy and sell mid-term policies is obtainable from the Association of Policy Market Makers. It can also arrange for suitable policies to be valued by member firms, free of charge.

Bonds

You may have read that as you near retirement you should increasingly be moving your investments from equities into bonds. The reason for this advice is that, while bonds generally offer less opportunity for capital growth, they tend to be lower-risk, as they are less exposed to stock market volatility, and also have the advantage of producing a regular guaranteed income. Although this course of action is normally recommended as sensible, a particular problem owing to recent ups and downs in the stock market is that you could make a loss by selling some of your shares now, whereas possibly if you wait they might recover. A bigger problem is that there are different types of bonds, with varying degrees of risk, which it is important you should understand.

The three main types are government bonds (called gilt-edged securities or 'gilts'), corporate bonds and investment bonds. *Gilts,* which are explained earlier in the chapter (see page 102), are the least risky, as they are secured by the government, which guarantees both the interest payable and the return of your capital in full if you hold the stocks until their maturity. *Corporate bonds* are fairly similar except that, as opposed to lending your money to the government, you are lending it to a large company or taking out a debenture. The risk is higher because, although you would normally only be recommended to buy a corporate bond from a highly rated company, there is always the possibility that the company could fail and might not be able to make the payments promised. In general, the higher the guaranteed interest payments, the less totally secure the company in question.

Although gilts and corporate bonds are normally recommended for cautious investors, *investment bonds* (described below) are different in that they offer potentially much higher rewards but also carry a much higher degree of risk. Because even gilts can be influenced by timing and other factors, if you are thinking of buying bonds, expert advice is very strongly recommended.

Investment bonds

Definition

This is the method of investing a lump sum with an insurance company, in the hope of receiving a much larger sum back at a specific date – normally a few years later. All bonds offer life assurance cover as part of the deal. A particular feature of some bonds is that the managers have wide discretion to invest your money in almost any type of security. The risk/reward ratio is, therefore, very high.

While bonds can achieve significant capital appreciation, you can also lose a high percentage of your investment. An exception is guaranteed equity bonds, which, while linked to the performance of the FTSE 100 or other stock market index, will protect your capital if shares fall. However, while your capital should be returned in full at the end of the fixed term (usually five years), a point not always appreciated is that, should markets fall, far from making any return on your investment you will have lost money in real terms: first, because your capital will have fallen in value, once inflation is taken into account; second, because you will have lost out on any interest that your money could have earned had it been on deposit.

All bond proceeds are free of basic-rate tax, but higher-rate tax is payable. However, higher-rate taxpayers can withdraw up to 5 per cent of their initial investment each year and defer the higher-rate tax liability for 20 years or until the bond is cashed in full, whichever is earlier. Although there is no Capital Gains Tax on redemption of a bond (or on switching between funds), some Corporation Tax may be payable by the fund itself, which could affect its investment performance. Companies normally charge a front-end fee of around 5 per cent plus a small annual management fee, usually not related to performance.

Tax

Tax treatment is very complicated, as it is influenced by your marginal Income Tax rate in the year of encashment. For this reason, it is generally best to buy a bond when you are working and plan to cash it after retirement. *NB:* if you hold a policy with personal portfolio bonds, you should speak to your financial adviser or insurance company, as there have been some recent changes to the tax regulations. It appears likely that, despite the new 18 per cent CGT rate applicable since April 2008, some higher-rate taxpayers could still be hit by the (old) 40 per cent tax. They would be strongly advised to check their policy with an accountant.

Assessment

This investment is more likely to be attractive to the sophisticated investor with high earnings in the years before retirement.

Useful reading

Fair Shares by Simon Rose (Mercury). This is a layperson's guide to buying and selling stocks and shares.

Investor protection

Over the past few years, great strides have been made regarding investor protection. There is now a set of stringent rules on businesses offering investment services and also a powerful regulatory body, the Financial Services Authority (FSA), which is charged by Parliament with responsibility for ensuring that firms are 'fit and proper' to operate in the investment field and for monitoring their activities on an ongoing basis.

The main effects of these safeguards are as follows:

- Investment businesses (including accountants or solicitors giving investment advice) are not at liberty to operate without authorization or exemption from the FSA. Operating without such authorization or exemption is a criminal offence.
- Previously, under what was known as 'polarization', businesses providing advice on investment products either could operate as 'tied agents', limited to selling their own in-house products (or those of a single provider), or had to be independent financial advisers, advising on products across the whole market. The FSA recently took the view that this was too restrictive and, with the aim of providing consumers with greater choice, has now authorized a new category of adviser known as a 'multi-tied agent', able to offer the products from a chosen panel of providers.
- Whether tied, multi-tied or independent, advisers must give customers certain information before a contract is signed. Under the disclosure rules, this includes two 'key facts' documents – 'About our services' and 'About the cost of our services' – plus a 'suitability letter' explaining the rationale on which recommendations are based.
- Among other important details, the information must provide a breakdown of the charges (expressed in cash terms), describe the payment options (commission and/or fee) and, in the case of commission, must quote both the adviser's own commission and the average market rate.
- Investment businesses must adhere to a proper complaints procedure, with provision for customers to receive fair redress, where appropriate.
- Unsolicited visits and telephone calls to sell investments are for the most part banned. Where these are allowed for packaged products (such as unit trusts and life assurance), should a sale result the customer will have a 14-day cooling-off period (or a seven-day 'right to withdraw' period if the packaged product is held within an ISA and the sale follows advice from the firm).

The cooling-off period is to give the customer time to explore other options before deciding whether to cancel the contract or not.

A single regulatory authority

Finding out whether investment businesses are authorized or not and checking up on what information they are required to disclose has become very much easier in recent years. As a result of the Financial Services Markets Act 2000, all the former self-regulating organizations (including the PIA, IMRO and SFA) have now been merged under the Financial Services Authority, with the purpose of improving investor protection and of providing a single contact point for enquiries. You can contact the **FSA Money Made Clear** telephone helpline on 0300 500 5000; website: www.fsa.gov.uk.

A single Ombudsman scheme

The single statutory Financial Ombudsman Service (FOS), set up in December 2001, replaced the various former schemes that used to deal with complaints about financial services. It provides a 'one-stop shop' for dissatisfied consumers. The schemes concerned are: Banking Ombudsman, Building Societies Ombudsman, Insurance Ombudsman, Personal Insurance Arbitration Service, PIA Ombudsman, Investment Ombudsman, SFA Complaints Bureau (and Arbitration Schemes) and FSA Complaints Unit.

A welcome result of there being a single Ombudsman scheme is that the FOS covers complaints across almost the entire range of financial services and products – from banking services, endowment mortgages and personal pensions to household insurance and stocks and shares. The list equally includes unit trusts and OEICs, life assurance, FSAVCs and equity release schemes. A further advantage is that the FOS applies a single set of rules to all complaints. From April 2007 the Financial Ombudsman Service has also covered – for the first time – the consumer-credit activities of businesses with a consumer-credit licence issued by the Office of Fair Trading. Consumer-credit activities now covered by the Ombudsman range from debt consolidation and consumer hire to debt collecting and pawnbrokers.

Complaints

If you have a complaint against an authorized firm, in the first instance you should take it up with the firm concerned. You may be able to resolve the matter at this level, since all authorized firms are obliged to have a proper complaints-handling procedure.

The Financial Ombudsman Service advises that the best approach is to start by contacting the person you originally dealt with and, if you phone, to keep a written note of all telephone calls. If complaining by letter, it helps to set out the facts in logical order, to stick to what is relevant and to include important details such as customer policy or account numbers. You should also keep a copy of all letters, both for your own record purposes and as useful evidence should you need to take the matter further.

If you have gone through the firm's complaints procedure, or if after eight weeks you are still dissatisfied, you can approach the FOS, which will investigate the matter on your behalf and, if it finds your complaint is justified, may require the firm to pay compensation; depending on your losses, this could be up to £100,000. If you disagree with the Ombudsman's decision, this does not affect your right to go to court should you wish to do so.

For further information, contact the **Financial Ombudsman Service (FOS)**, Tel: 0845 080 1800; e-mail: complaint.info@financial-ombudsman.org.uk; website: www.financial-ombudsman.org.uk.

Warning

The existence of the FSA enables you to check on the credentials of anyone purporting to be a financial adviser or trying to persuade you to invest your money in an insurance policy, bond, unit or investment trust, equity, futures contract or similar. However, if either they or the organization they represent is not authorized by the FSA, you are very strongly recommended to leave well alone. You can check whether a firm is authorized by contacting the **FSA Money Made Clear** telephone helpline: 0300 500 5000; website: www.fsa.gov.uk.

Useful reading

Choosing a Financial Adviser – How Key Facts Can Help You and *Capital-at-Risk Products* (products where you could lose some of the money you invest) are available free from the FSA Money Made Clear telephone helpline: 0300 500 5000; website: www.fsa.gov.uk.

6

Financial advisers

If there is one golden rule when it comes to money matters, it must be: if in doubt, ask. Although most professional advisers are extremely sound, not everyone who proffers advice is qualified to do so. Before parting with your money, it is essential to ensure that you are dealing with a registered member of a recognized institution. Checking credentials has become much easier under the Financial Services Act.

Before making contact with a financial adviser it is generally a good idea to try to sort out your priorities. What are you looking for? Is it capital growth, or is your main objective to increase your income? If you have special plans, such as helping your grandchildren, or if you need several thousand pounds to improve your home, these should be thought through in advance. They could have a bearing on the advice you receive. A further reason for doing some pre-planning is that certain types of advisers – for example, insurance brokers – do not specifically charge you for their time. Other professional advisers, such as accountants and solicitors, charge their fees by the hour. Enjoying coffee in their office and musing aloud about the future delights of retirement may be a pleasant way of spending the afternoon, but it could be an expensive one.

Choosing an adviser

When choosing an adviser, there are usually four main considerations: respectability, suitability, price and convenience. Where your money is concerned, you cannot afford to take unnecessary risks. Establishing that an individual is a member of a recognized institution is a basic safeguard. But it is insufficient recommendation if you want to be assured of dealing with someone who will personally suit you. The principle applies as much with friends as with complete strangers. If you are thinking of using a particular adviser, do you already know him or her in a professional capacity? If not, you should certainly check on the adviser's reputation, ideally talking to some of his or her existing clients. No one who is any good will object to your asking for references. Most reputable professionals will be delighted to assist, as it means that the relationship will be founded on a basis of greater trust and confidence.

Accountants

Accountants are specialists in matters concerning taxation. If there is scope to do so, they can advise on ways of reducing your tax liability and can assess the various tax effects of the different types of investment you may be considering. They can also help you with the preparation of tax returns. Should you be considering becoming self-employed or starting your own business, they can assist you with some of the practicalities. These could range from registering for VAT to establishing a system of business accounts. Many accountants can also help with raising finance and offer support with the preparation of business plans. Additionally, they may be able to advise in a general way about pensions and your proposed investment strategy. Most accountants, however, do not claim to be experts in these fields. They may refer their clients to stockbrokers or other financial advisers for such specialized services.

If you need help in locating a suitable accountant, any of the following should be able to advise:

Association of Chartered Certified Accountants (ACCA). For enquiries, contact ACCA, Tel: 020 7059 5000; e-mail: info@accaglobal.com; website: www. accaglobal.com.
Institute of Chartered Accountants in England and Wales (ICAEW). If your enquiry is regarding membership or a specific member of the ICAEW, or to check if a firm is registered with the ICAEW, please call the ICAEW Membership Enquiry Line, Tel: 0906 614 0906 or e-mail members.registration@icaew.co.uk. Please note that, if you require confirmation of an ICAEW member in writing, a charge of £20 plus VAT will be implemented. For this service please e-mail the details to members.registration@icaew.co.uk (website: www.icaewfirms.co.uk).
Institute of Chartered Accountants of Scotland (ICAS). For enquiries regarding members' registration, contact ICAS, Tel: 0131 347 0100; e-mail: centralregistry@icas.org.uk; website: www.icas.org.uk.

Complaints

Anyone with a complaint against an accountancy firm can contact the Professional Conduct Department of the ICAEW (www.icaew.com).

Banks

Most people need no introduction to the clearing banks since, if they have a bank account, they are probably regularly bombarded with information on the latest products and services. Not all bank customers, however, realize what a comprehensive service their bank provides. In addition to the normal account facilities, all the major high street banks offer (either direct or through one of their specialized subsidiaries) a range of other advice and services. These include investment, insurance and tax-planning services, as well as how to draw up a will. Brief information follows on the main clearing banks, but there also are other more specialized banks such as Hoare's, Coutts and overseas banks that are all part of the UK clearing system and can offer a very good service. The contact details given are those of the head office:

Abbey (part of the Santander Group) offers a range of savings, mortgage, pension, current account, and medical and other insurance products plus loans for such items as home improvements, a car or money to finance a holiday. A broad range of savings accounts is available that includes branch-based, postal and internet instant access accounts, and fixed- and variable-rate savings bonds, including a retirement income bond for the over-55s. There is also a range of ISAs. Full details of all Abbey services can be obtained from any high street branch or by calling Abbey direct, Tel: 0800 555100; website: www.abbey.com.

Barclays Bank plc offers customers a range of accounts to suit a variety of personal savings requirements. Additionally, a number of financial planning services are available through Barclays Bank subsidiary companies. These include personal investment advice, investment management, stockbroking, unit trusts, personal taxation, wills and trusts. You can apply through your local branch of Barclays Bank, or call 08457 555 555; website: www.barclays.co.uk.

HSBC offers a comprehensive choice of financial products ranging from OEICs and ISAs to life assurance, which are selected according to a customer's requirements by a financial planning manager. HSBC Premier IFA offers investment management and estate planning services to clients who prefer to have a local specialist to look after their affairs on a regular basis. Clients typically have an income over £75,000 or liquid assets of over £100,000. Any HSBC branch can arrange a meeting if you would like to discuss these services, or phone 08457 404 404; website: www.hsbc.co.uk.

Lloyds TSB offers a wide range of financial services, including current and savings accounts, home insurance, investment management, and life assurance through Scottish Widows. As well as the classic account, which offers all the normal current account facilities, and the Gold Service, which among other facilities includes free travel insurance, there is Private Banking, which is a comprehensive wealth-management service tailored to individual requirements for customers with £250,000 or more of liquid assets. Details of all these services, as well as life assurance and investment products, are available at all Lloyds TSB branches, Tel: 0845 3 000 000; website: www.lloydstsb.com.

NatWest financial planning managers can advise on a wide range of banking and financial planning services for retirement, including investment funds and ISAs. To make an appointment, contact your local NatWest branch or call free on 0800 200 400; website: www.natwest.com.

RBS (Royal Bank of Scotland) offers a comprehensive range of current accounts and savings products. The Bank's Private Trust and Taxation Department offers free advice on making a will, although the usual legal fees are applicable if you proceed. Royal Scottish Assurance, the Royal Bank of Scotland's life assurance, pensions and investment company, offers a full financial planning service free of charge. Financial planning consultants can also recommend ISAs and unit trusts provided by the Royal Bank of Scotland unit trust managers. Further information is available from any branch of the bank, or phone 0808 100 0808; website: www. rbs.co.uk.

Other banking services. Several building societies converted to banks, including the Halifax (HBOS), Alliance & Leicester, Bristol & West and Bradford & Bingley. Full information about their services should be obtainable from your local branch or their respective websites.

Complaints

If you have a complaint about a banking matter, you must first try to resolve the issue with the bank or building society concerned. If you remain dissatisfied, you can contact the Financial Ombudsman Service (FOS). For further information, contact the **Financial Ombudsman Service (FOS),** Tel: 0845 080 1800; e-mail: complaint.info@financial-ombudsman.org.uk; website: www.financial-ombudsman.org.uk.

Independent financial advisers (IFAs)

IFAs can advise you across the whole spectrum of investment policies and products: endowment policies, personal pensions, life assurance, permanent health insurance, critical illness cover, unit trusts, ISAs and other forms of personal investment such as, for example, mortgages. Their job is to help you work out whether the type of policy you have in mind would be most suitable and where, depending on your circumstances and objectives, you could obtain best value for money. In other words, they act as your personal adviser and handle all the arrangements for you.

To be able to offer 'best advice', an IFA needs to try to ensure that you would not be at risk of over-committing yourself or taking some other risk that might jeopardize your security. He or she will, therefore, need an understanding of your existing financial circumstances (and future expectations) including, for example, your earnings, employment prospects and any other types of investment you might already have. In turn, you should also ask your adviser a number of questions including – as a first essential – by whom they are regulated. This should normally be the FSA but could be one of a small number of designated professional bodies, which themselves are answerable to the FSA. If you have any doubts, you can check via the **FSA's Central Register Money Made Clear** helpline on: 0300 500 5000; website: www.fsa.gov.uk.

Your adviser should provide you with two 'key facts' documents entitled 'About our Services' and 'About the Cost of our Services', plus a 'suitability letter' explaining all these points, but if for some reason you do not receive these or if there is anything you do not understand you should not hesitate to ask.

Under rules brought in by the FSA, advisers who want to call themselves 'independent' have to offer clients the option of paying by fee. This means of course that clients incur an upfront charge.

The following organizations provide information on locating local IFAs:

The **Institute of Financial Planning** will help you in your search for a certified financial planner by region, speciality or name. Call 0117 945 2470; e-mail: enquiries@financialplanning.org.uk; website: www.financialplanning.org.uk.

The **Personal Finance Society (PFS)** will also help you identify an adviser by postcode or specific financial need. Its website has a useful extra function in that it allows you to look for only chartered financial advisers. Once you have found an adviser, you can make sure that the adviser is approved by checking his or her credentials with the FSA, which is responsible for regulating the industry. Call the PFS on 020 8530 0852; e-mail: customer.serv@thepfs.org; website: www. thepfs.org.

Unbiased.Co.Uk – the professional advice website: www.unbiased.co.uk.

Insurance brokers

The insurance business covers a very wide range from straightforward policies – such as motor or household insurance – to the rather more complex areas, including life assurance and pensions.

Although many people think of brokers and IFAs as doing much the same job, IFAs specialize in advising on products and policies with some investment content, whereas brokers primarily deal with the more straightforward type of insurance, such as motor, medical, household and holiday insurance. Some brokers are also authorized to give investment advice. A broker should be able to help you choose the policies that are best suited to you, help you determine how much cover you require and explain any technical terms contained in the documents. He/she can also assist with any claims, remind you when renewals are necessary and advise you on keeping your cover up to date. An essential point to check before proceeding is that the firm the broker represents is regulated by the FSA.

A condition of registration is that a broker must deal with a multiplicity of insurers and therefore be in a position to offer a comprehensive choice of policies. The FSA disclosure rules require brokers to provide potential customers with a 'key facts' document. This should include the cost of the policy (but not commission), as well as a 'suitability' statement explaining the reasons for the recommendation. The information must also draw attention to any significant or unusual exemptions. Generally speaking, you are safer to use a larger brokerage with an established reputation. Also, before you take out a policy, it is advisable to consult several brokers in order to get a better feel for the market. **The British Insurance Brokers' Association** represents nearly 2,200 insurance broking businesses. It can put you in touch with a member broker in your area; Tel: 0870 950 1790; e-mail: enquiries@biba.org.uk; website: www.biba.org.uk.

Complaints

The **Association of British Insurers (ABI)** represents some 400 companies (as opposed to Lloyd's syndicates or brokers), providing all types of insurance from life assurance and pensions to household, motor and other forms of general insurance. About 90 per cent of the worldwide business done by British insurance companies is handled by members of the ABI. It publishes a wide range of information sheets, obtainable from the ABI, Tel: 020 7600 3333; e-mail: info@abi.org.uk; website: www.abi.org.uk.

Other pension advisers

If you have a query to do with your pension, there are some organizations that may be able to assist, discussed below.

Individuals in paid employment

If you are (or have been) in salaried employment and are a member of an occupational pension scheme, the normal person to ask is your company's personnel manager or pensions adviser – or, via him or her, the pension fund trustees. Alternatively, if you have a problem with your pension you could approach your trade union, since this is an area where most unions are particularly active and well informed.

If you are in need of specific help, a source to try could be the **Pensions Advisory Service**. It has a network of 500 professional advisers who can give free help and advice on all matters to do with any type of pension scheme. There is a local call rate helpline: 0845 601 2923; e-mail: enquiries@pensionsadvisoryservice.org.uk; website: www.pensionsadvisoryservice.org.uk.

As with most other financial sectors, there is also a Pensions Ombudsman. You would normally approach the Ombudsman if neither the pension scheme trustees nor the Pensions Advisory Service are able to solve your problem. Also, as with all Ombudsmen, the Pensions Ombudsman can only investigate matters that come within his orbit. These are: 1) complaints of maladministration by the trustees, managers or administrators of a pension scheme or by an employer; and 2) disputes of fact or law with the trustees, managers or an employer. You can contact the **Pensions Ombudsman** direct, Tel: 020 7630 2200; e-mail: enquiries@pensions-ombudsman.org.uk; website: www.pensions-ombudsman. org.uk. Unlike many of the other Ombudsman services, the Pensions Ombudsman has not become part of the single statutory Financial Ombudsman Service and will continue to remain as a separate scheme.

Another source of help is the Pension Tracing Service, which can provide individuals with contact details for a pension scheme with which they have lost touch. It is run by the Pension Service, part of the Department for Work and Pensions. As with the Ombudsman, there is no charge for the service. For further information, contact the **Pension Tracing Service,** Tel: 0845 600 2537. You can also fill in a tracing request form online by visiting the website: www.thepensionservice.gov.uk and following the links to the Pension Tracing Service.

Two other organizations that, although they do not advise on individual cases, are interested in matters of principle and broader issues affecting pensions, are:

National Association of Pension Funds, Tel: 020 7808 1300; e-mail: enquiries@napf.co.uk; website: www.napf.co.uk.
The Pensions Regulator, Tel: 0870 606 3636; e-mail: customersupport@ thepensionsregulator.gov.uk; website: www.thepensionsregulator.gov.uk.

Solicitors

Solicitors are professional advisers on subjects to do with the law or on matters that could have legal implications. They can assist with the purchase or rental of property, with drawing up a will, or if you are charged with a criminal offence or are sued in a civil matter. Additionally, their advice can be invaluable in vetting any important document before you sign it. If you do not have a solicitor (or if your solicitor does not have the knowledge to advise on, say, a business matter), often the best way of finding a suitable lawyer is through the recommendation of a friend or other professional adviser, such as an accountant. If you need a solicitor specifically for a business or professional matter, organizations such as Chambers of Commerce, small business associations, your professional institute or your trade union may be able to put you in touch with someone in your area who has relevant experience. Another solution is to contact the **Law Society,** Tel: 020 7242 1222; e-mail: contact@lawsociety.org.uk; website: www.lawsociety.org.uk.

A further resource of possible interest is **Solicitors for Independent Financial Advice (SIFA).** This is a network of law firms offering financial as well as legal services, with the aim of providing clients with a 'one-stop shop' when making important financial decisions. It maintains a nationwide register and will help source the best firm according to what advice is needed – such as investments, pension planning, wills or choosing a long-term care policy. For further information, contact SIFA, Tel: 01372 721172; e-mail: admin@sifa.co.uk; website: www. sifa.co.uk.

Community Legal Service (Legal Aid) funding

If you need a Community Legal Service (CLS) solicitor, or want to find out if you are eligible for Community Legal Service funding, the place to go is a solicitor's office or an advice centre. Ask for the leaflet *A Practical Guide to Community Legal Service Funding* by the Legal Services Commission. You can ask an adviser to go through this with you to help you work out whether you are eligible. If you have a low income or are in receipt of benefits and would welcome independent advice about tax credits, debt, employment or housing problems, you might usefully contact the Community Legal Advice helpline. As well as providing free information, help and advice, the Service lists solicitors and advice agencies that do CLS work. The **Community Legal Service** helpline is: 0845 345 4345; website: www. legalservices.gov.uk.

Complaints

All solicitors are required by the Law Society to have their own in-house complaints procedure. If you are unhappy about the service you have received, you should first try to resolve the matter with the firm through its complaints-handling partner. If you still feel aggrieved you can approach the Law Society's Legal Complaints Service (LCS), which is an independent arm of the Law Society responsible for handling complaints against solicitors.

If you believe you have a complaint of negligence, the LCS will help you either by putting you in touch with a solicitor specializing in negligence claims or by referring you to the solicitor's insurers. If it arranges an appointment for you with a negligence panellist, the panel solicitor will see you free of charge for up to an hour and advise you as to your best course of action. If you believe that you have been overcharged, you should ask to be sent the booklet *Can We Help?* This explains the procedure for getting your bill checked, the various time limits involved and the circumstances in which you might be successful in getting the fee reduced.

For practical assistance if you are having problems with your solicitor, you can ring the **Legal Complaints Service helpline,** Tel: 0845 608 6565; e-mail: enquiries@legalcomplaints.org.uk; website: www.legalcomplaints.org.uk.

If this has failed to resolve the problem, you can approach the Legal Services Ombudsman. You must try to do so within three months of the LCS's, or other professional body's, final decision or your complaint will risk being out of time and the Ombudsman will not be able to help you. Contact the **Legal Services**

Ombudsman, Tel: 0845 601 0794; e-mail: lso@olso.gsi.gov.uk; website: www. olso.org.

General queries

For queries of a more general nature, you should approach the **Law Society,** Tel: 020 7242 1222; e-mail: contact@lawsociety.org.uk; website: www.lawsociety. org.uk. If you live in Scotland or Northern Ireland, the LCS will not be able to help you. Instead you should contact the Law Society at the relevant address, as follows:

The Law Society of Scotland, Tel: 0131 226 7411; e-mail: lawscot@lawscot. org.uk; website: www.lawscot.org.uk.
The Law Society of Northern Ireland, Tel: 028 9023 1614; e-mail: info@ lawsoc-ni.org; website: www.lawsoc-ni.org.

Stockbrokers

Stockbrokers buy and sell shares quoted on the main market of the London Stock Exchange and on AIM, which trades mainly in the shares of young and growing companies. Investments can be made in British and international equities, bonds, investment trusts and gilts (government stocks). As well as trading for clients, stockbrokers can advise on the prospects of different companies, help individuals choose the best type of investment according to their financial situation, and also provide a wide range of other financial services including tax planning.

It is difficult to be specific about the cost of using a stockbroker. While some now charge fees in the same way as, say, a solicitor, generally stockbrokers make their living by charging commission on every transaction. You will need to enquire what the terms and conditions are before committing yourself, as these can vary quite considerably between one firm and another. A growing number of provincial stockbrokers are happy to deal for private investors with sums from about £5,000. Additionally, nearly all major stockbrokers now run unit trusts. Because through these they are investing collectively for their clients, they welcome quite modest investors with around £2,000.

There are several ways of finding a stockbroker: you can approach an individual through recommendation; you can check the **London Stock Exchange** website (www.londonstockexchange.com) for its 'Locate a broker' service. Alternatively there is the **Association of Private Client Investment Managers and Stockbrokers (APCIMS),** which provides a free directory of stockbrokers and investment managers, together with details of their services. APCIMS also has an online directory, which is searchable by region and type of service; Tel: 020 7448 7100; e-mail: info@apcims.co.uk; website: www.apcims.co.uk.

Complaints

If you have a complaint about a stockbroker or other member of the former Securities and Futures Authority (SFA), you should put this in writing to the compliance officer of the stockbroking firm involved. If the matter is not satisfactorily resolved, you can then contact the Financial Ombudsman Service (FOS), which will investigate your complaint and, if the Ombudsman considers this justified, can award compensation. For further information, contact the **Financial Ombudsman Service**, Tel: 0845 080 1800; e-mail: complaint.info@financial-ombudsman.org.uk; website: www.financial-ombudsman.org.uk.

A note of warning

Despite the safeguards of the Financial Services Act, when it comes to investment – or to financial advisers – there are no cast-iron guarantees. Under the investor protection legislation, all practitioners and/or the businesses they represent offering investment or similar services must be authorized by the FSA or, in certain cases, by a small number of Designated Professional Bodies that themselves are answerable to the FSA. A basic question, therefore, to ask anyone offering investment advice or products is: are you registered and by whom? The information is easy to check by telephoning the **FSA's Money Made Clear** helpline: 0300 500 5000, or searching the website (www.fsa.gov.uk). For further information, see 'Investor protection' at the end of Chapter 5, Investment.

Financial Ombudsman Service (FOS)

There is now a single contact point for dissatisfied customers, as the FOS covers complaints across almost the entire range of financial services, including consumer-credit activities (such as store cards, credit cards and hire purchase transactions). The service is free, and the FOS is empowered to award compensation of up to £100,000. However, before contacting the FOS, you must first try to resolve your complaint with the organization concerned. Also, the Ombudsman is powerless to act if legal proceedings have been started. For further information, contact the **Financial Ombudsman Service**, Tel: 0845 080 1800; e-mail: complaint.info@financial-ombudsman.org.uk; website: www.financial-ombudsman.org.uk.

Useful reading

Choosing a Financial Adviser – How key facts can help you, obtainable free from the FSA Money Made Clear helpline: 0300 500 5000; website: www.fsa.gov.uk.

7

Budget planner

It doesn't matter whether you are about to retire tomorrow or not for several years, completing the following Budget Planner (even if there are a great many gaps) is well worth the effort.

If retirement is imminent, then doing the arithmetic in as much detail as possible will not only reassure you but also help you plan your future life with greater confidence. You'll feel better knowing how you stand financially. Don't forget that even at this stage there are probably a number of options open to you. By examining the figures written down it will highlight the areas of greatest flexibility. One tip, offered by one of the retirement magazines, is to start living on your retirement income some six months before you retire. Not only will you see if your budget estimates are broadly correct, but since most people err on the cautious side when they first retire you will have the bonus of all the extra money you will have saved.

If retirement is still some years ahead, there will be more unknowns and more opportunities. When assessing the figures, you should take account of your future earnings. Perhaps you should also consider what steps you might be able to take under the pension rules to maximize your pension fund. You could also consider whether you should be putting money aside now in a savings plan and/ or making other investments. Imprecise as they will be, the Budget Planner estimates you have made in the various income and expenditure columns should indicate whether, unless you take action now, you could be at risk of having to make serious adjustments in your standard of living later on. To be on the safe side, assume an increase in inflation. Everyone should, if they possibly can, budget for a nest egg. This is to help cover the cost of any emergencies or special events – perhaps a family wedding – that may come along.

1. Possible savings when you retire

Item	Estimated monthly savings
National Insurance contributions	....
Pension payments	....
Travel expenses to work	....
Bought lunches	....
Incidentals at work, eg drinks with colleagues, collections for presents	....
Special work clothes	....
Concessionary travel	....
Free NHS prescriptions	....
Free eye tests	....
Mature drivers' insurance policy	....
Retired householders' insurance policy	....
Life assurance payments and/or possible endowment policy premiums	....
Other	....
TOTAL	....

NB: you should also take into account reduced running costs if you move to a smaller home; any expenses for dependent children that may cease; other costs, such as mortgage payments, that may end around the time you retire; and the fact that you may be in a lower tax bracket.

2. Possible extra outgoings when you retire

Items	Estimated monthly cost
Extra heating and lighting bills	....
Extra spending on hobbies and other entertainment	....
Replacement of company car	....
Private health care insurance	....
Longer, or more frequent, holidays	....
Life and permanent health insurance	....
Cost of substituting other perks, eg expense account lunches	....
Out-of-pocket expenses for voluntary work activity	....
Other	....
TOTAL	....

NB: looking ahead, you will need to make provision for any extra home comforts you might want and also, at some point, for having to pay other people to do some of the jobs that you normally manage yourself. If you intend to make regular donations to a charity or perhaps help with your grandchildren's education, these too should be included in the list. The same applies to any new private pension or savings plan that you might want to invest in to boost your long-term retirement income.

3. Expected sources of income on retirement

Many people have difficulty understanding the tax system, and you should certainly take professional advice if you are in any doubt at all. However, if you fill in your expected sources of income carefully below, it should give you a pretty good idea of your income after retirement and enable you to make at least provisional plans.

Remember too that you may have one or two capital sums to invest, such as:

- the commuted lump sum from your pension;
- money from an endowment policy;
- gains from the sale of company shares (SAYE or other share option scheme);
- profits from the sale of your home or other asset;
- money from an inheritance.

A. Income received before tax

Basic State Pension ....

State graduated pension ....

SERPS/State Second Pension ....

Occupational pension(s) ....

Stakeholder or personal pension ....

State benefits ....

Investments and savings plans paid
  gross, eg gilts, National Savings ....

Possible rental income ....

Casual or other pre-tax earnings ....

Total ....

Less: Personal tax allowance and possibly
  also married couple's allowance ....

Basic-rate tax ....

Total A ....

B. Income received after tax

Dividends (unit trusts, shares, etc) ....

Bank deposit account ....

Building society interest ....

Annuity income ....

Other (including earnings subject to PAYE) ....

Total B ....

Total A + Total B ....

Less: higher-rate tax (if any) ....

Plus: Other tax-free receipts, eg some state
benefits income from an ISA ....

Investment bond withdrawals, etc ....

Other ....

TOTAL NET INCOME ....

4. Unavoidable outgoings

Items	Estimated monthly cost
Food	....
Rent or mortgage repayments	....
Council tax	....
Repair and maintenance costs	....
Heating	....
Lighting and other energy	....
Telephone/mobile	....
Postage (including Christmas cards)	....
TV licence/Sky/digital subscription	....
Household insurance	....
Clothes	....
Laundry, cleaner's bills, shoe repair	....
Domestic cleaning products	....
Miscellaneous services, eg plumber and window cleaner	....
Car (including licence, petrol, etc)	....
Other transport	....
Regular savings and life assurance	....
HP and other loan repayments	....
Outgoings on health	....
Other	....
TOTAL	....

NB: before adding up the total, you should look at the 'Normal additional expenditure' list, as you may well want to juggle some of the items between the two.

5. Normal additional expenditure

Items	Estimated monthly cost
Gifts	....
Holidays	....
Newspapers/books/CDs/DVDs	....
Drink	....
Cigarettes/tobacco	....
Hairdressing	....
Toiletries/cosmetics	....
Entertainment (hobbies, outings, home entertaining, etc)	....
Miscellaneous subscriptions/membership fees	....
Charitable donations	....
Expenditure on pets	....
Garden purchases	....
Other	....
TOTAL	....

NB: for some items, such as holidays and gifts, you may tend to think in annual expenditure terms. However, for the purpose of comparing monthly income versus outgoings, it is probably easier if you itemize all the expenditure in the same fashion. Also, if you need to save for a special event such as your holiday, it helps if you get into the habit of putting so much aside every month (or even weekly).

8

Your home

Home sweet home is what matters to most people, especially as they grow older. One of the most important decisions to be taken as you approach retirement is whether you should make changes about where you live or to keep the status quo. To many people, one of the biggest attractions once they've finished work is the pleasure of being able to move home. No longer tied to an area within easy commuting distance they can indulge their long-held plans of living in a new area (possibly a new country). Although this could turn out to be everything they desire, without any real assessment of the pros and cons, some do regret having made a hasty decision. It is sensible at least to examine the various options. An obvious possibility is to stay where you are and perhaps adapt your present home to make it more suitable for your requirements. You might decide to move nearer to family or friends. Or, looking further ahead, you could consider buying or renting some form of purpose-built retirement accommodation.

Lots of people are conditioned to think of retirement as being a time for selling up and relocating. An all-too-common mistake is for people to retire to a place where they once spent an idyllic holiday, perhaps 15 or 20 years previously, without further investigation. Resorts that are glorious in midsummer can be bleak and damp in winter. They can also be pretty dull when the tourist season is over. Equally, many people sell their house and move somewhere smaller without sufficient thought. It may be that spending more time at home they will want more space, rather than less.

Although moving may be the right solution for some, especially if you want to realize some capital to boost your retirement income, there are plenty of ways of adapting a house to make it more convenient and labour-saving. Likewise, you may be able to cut the running costs, for example, with better insulation. Before you come to any definite decision, first ask yourself a few down-to-earth questions. What are your main priorities? Do you want to be closer to your family?

Would a smaller, more manageable home be easier for you to run – and less expensive? What about realizing some capital to provide you with extra money for your retirement? How about living in a specific town or village, which you know you like and where you have plenty of friends? Or does the security of being in accommodation that offers some of the facilities you may want as you become older, such as a resident caretaker and the option of having some of your meals catered for, appeal to you? Whatever choice you make is bound to have advantages and drawbacks; life is full of compromises. But it is important that you weigh up the pros and cons carefully so that you don't end up making a decision that – while attractive in the short term – you regret later on.

Staying put

With the property market less buoyant than it was, there is a huge rise in the number of householders opting to improve rather than move. If you're a home-owner who needs more space, it makes sound common sense to extend rather than sell up in the current climate. House prices are not likely to rise significantly in the foreseeable future, so many people's instinct is to sit tight. Instead of looking in estate agents' windows, it might be more sensible to seek the services of a reputable builder, plumber and electrician.

There may be plenty of arguments for moving, and there are probably just as many for staying where you are. Moving house can be a traumatic experience at the best of times, and even more so as you become older. Emotional ties are harder to break and precious possessions more painful to part with, as is usually necessary, especially if moving somewhere smaller.

Although ideally you may want to remain where you are, you may feel that your home is really too large or inconvenient for you to manage in the future. However, before you heave your last sigh of regret and put it on the market, it is worth considering whether there are ways of adapting it to provide what you want. If your house is too big, you might think about reusing the space in a better way. Would it be possible, for example, to turn a bedroom into a small upstairs study? Or perhaps you could convert a spare room into a separate workroom for hobbies and get rid of the clutter from the main living area? Have you thought about letting one or two rooms? As well as solving the problem of wasted space, it would also bring in some extra income.

Before embarking on any improvements, it is sensible to work out which ones will add the most value to your property. The loft conversion is a favourite, as it can add an extra bedroom and possibly even a bathroom. Building an extra room as an extension is the next most popular, followed by adding a conservatory, a new kitchen, central heating, bathrooms and new windows.

A few judicious home improvements carried out now could make the world of difference in terms of comfort and practicality. Many of us carry on for years with inefficient heating systems that could be improved relatively easily and cheaply.

Stairs need not necessarily be a problem, even when you are very much older, thanks to the many types of stair lifts now available. Even so, a few basic facilities installed on the ground floor could save your legs in years to come. Similarly, gardens can be replanned to suit changing requirements. Areas that now take hours to weed could be turned into extra lawn or a patio.

For some people, the problem is not so much the size or convenience of their home as the fact that they are unable to buy the freehold or extend the lease. They fear for their long-term security. But since the Leasehold Reform, Housing and Urban Development Act 1993 extended the right of enfranchisement to thousands of flat leaseholders, they now have the collective right to buy the freehold of their building and the individual right to extend their leases at a market price.

Among other requirements to enfranchise, your flat must be held under a lease that was originally granted for more than 21 years, and the eligible tenants of at least half of the flats in the block must also wish to buy the freehold. Before proceeding, you would be advised to obtain a professional valuation as a first step to establishing a fair price to which the landlord will be entitled. 'Fair price' is made up of the open market value of the building, half of any mortgage value that may be payable, plus possible compensation to the landlord for any severance or other losses. If you have a dwindling lease but do not wish to enfranchise, the more straightforward purchase of a 90-year lease extension might be a better option. For further information see leaflets *Collective Enfranchisement – Getting Started*; *Collective Enfranchisement – Valuation*; *Lease Extension – Getting Started* and *Lease Extension – Valuation*, obtainable free from LEASE at the address below.

If, as applies to many people, you want protection from a landlord but do not want to buy the freehold or extend your lease, you will be glad to know that leaseholders' rights have been strengthened over the last few years. Among other rights, where leaseholders believe that their service charges are unreasonable they can ask a leasehold valuation tribunal, rather than a court, to determine what charge is reasonable. This includes work that has been proposed but not yet started. Also, where there are serious problems with the management of a building, tenants can ask the tribunal to appoint a new manager. Importantly, leasehold valuation tribunals are less formal than a court and avoid the risk of potentially unknown costs being awarded, which can be the case with court proceedings. (Tribunals can award costs of up to £500 where they believe a person has acted abusively or otherwise unreasonably in connection with the proceedings.) For further information, obtain the booklet *Residential Long Leaseholders – Your Rights and Responsibilities* (ISBN 978 1409 809 593), available from Citizens Advice Bureau or from the Department for Communities and Local Government Publications Centre, Tel: 0300 123 1124; e-mail: contactus@communities.gov.uk; website: www.communities.gov.uk.

Additionally, the Commonhold and Leasehold Reform Act 2002 introduced a new right to take over the management of flats without having to prove fault on the part of the landlord, made buying the freehold or an extended lease of a flat easier, strengthened leaseholders' rights against unreasonable service charges, prevented landlords from taking any action for unpaid ground rent unless this has first been demanded in writing, made lease variations easier to obtain and provided further protection for the holding of leaseholders' monies. Furthermore, landlords are not able to commence forfeiture proceedings to obtain possession of the property unless they have first proved an alleged breach of the lease before a leasehold valuation tribunal. Where the breach relates to arrears, they must also have proved that the sum demanded is reasonable.

You could ask LEASE for copies of their leaflets *The Right to Manage* and *Service Charges and Other Issues*. For general advice on leasehold, including leaseholders' rights and responsibilities, contact the **Leasehold Advisory Service (LEASE)**, Tel: 020 7374 5380; e-mail: info@lease-advice.org; website: www.lease-advice. org. For advice on leasehold legislation and policy, consult the **Department for Communities and Local Government** website: www.communities.gov.uk; Tel: 020 7944 4400; e-mail: contactus@communities.gov.uk.

Moving to a new home

If you do decide to move, the sooner you start looking for your new home the better. There is no point in delaying the search until you retire and then rushing round expecting to find your dream house in a matter of weeks. With time to spare, you will have a far greater choice of properties and are less likely to indulge in any panic buying. While a smaller house will almost certainly be easier and cheaper to run, make sure that it is not so small that you are going to feel cramped. Remember that, when you and your partner are both at home, you may need more room to avoid getting on top of each other. Also, if your family lives in another part of the country, you may wish to have them and your grandchildren to stay. Conversely, beware of taking on commitments such as a huge garden. While this might be a great source of enjoyment when you are in your 60s, it could prove a burden as you become older.

If you are thinking of moving out of the neighbourhood, there are other factors to be taken into account such as access to shops and social activities, proximity to friends and relatives, availability of public transport and even health and social support services. While these may not seem particularly important now, they could become so in the future. Couples who retire to a seemingly 'idyllic' spot often return quite quickly. New friends are not always easy to make. So-called 'retirement areas' can mean that you are cut off from a normal cross-section of society, and health services are likely to be overtaxed. After a hard week's wheeling and dealing it is tempting to wax lyrical about exchanging the rat race for a life of rustic solitude. While retiring to the country can be glorious, city dwellers should, however, bear in mind some of the less attractive sides of rural living. Noise, for example low-flying aircraft and church bells, can be an unexpected irritant. If you are not used to it, living near a silage pit or farm can also be an unpleasant experience. Prices in village shops are often higher than in city super-markets, and bus services tend to be more infrequent.

Finally, would a small village or seaside resort offer sufficient scope to pursue your interests once the initial flurry of activity is over? Even if you think you know an area well, check it out properly before coming to a final decision. If possible take a self-catering let for a couple of months, preferably out of season when rents are low and the weather is bad. A good idea is to limit your daily spending to your likely retirement income rather than splurge as most of us do on holiday. This is even more pertinent if you are thinking of moving abroad, where additional difficulties can include learning the language, lower standards of health care and the danger of losing contact with your friends. Another problem for expatriates could be a change in the political climate, resulting perhaps on the one hand in your not being so welcome in your adopted country and, on the other, in a drop in the purchasing power of your pension. For more information on the financial implications of living overseas, see the section 'Retiring abroad', page 88.

Counting the cost

Moving house can be an expensive exercise but in the current economic climate, if you can afford to move, some good bargains can be had as desirable purchasers are not all that plentiful at present. It is estimated that the cost is between 5 and 10 per cent of the value of a new home, once you have totted up such extras as search fees, removal charges, insurance, Stamp Duty, VAT, legal fees and estate agents' commission. The current rate of Stamp Duty Land Tax (SDLT) or Stamp Duty for short (up to 31 December 2009) is 0 per cent on properties up to the value of £175,000. Properties purchased costing £175,001 to £250,000 will incur a rate of 1 per cent stamp duty. From £250,001 to £500,000 it is 3 per cent, rising to 4 per cent on properties costing over £500,001. (See Stop Press Section for changes for 2010.) To find out more about SDLT, including how you pay it and a link to the HM Revenue & Customs' Stamp Duty Land Tax calculator, consult the website: www.direct.gov.uk.

When buying a new home, especially an older property, it is essential to have a full building (structural) survey done before committing yourself. This will cost in the region of £500 for a small terraced house but is worth every penny. In particular, it will provide you with a comeback in law should things go wrong. A valuation report, while cheaper, is more superficial and may fail to detect flaws that could give you trouble and expense in the future.

If you are buying a newly built house, there are now a number of safeguards against defects. Most mortgagors will lend on new homes only if they have a National House Building Council (NHBC) warranty or its equivalent. The NHBC operates a 10-year *Buildmark* warranty and insurance scheme under which the builder is responsible for putting right defects during the first two years. It is designed to protect owners of newly built or newly converted residential housing if a problem does occur in a new home registered with NHBC. If the homeowner and builder do not agree on what needs to be done, NHBC can carry out a free independent resolution investigation and, if judged necessary, will instruct the builder to carry out repair works. If a problem becomes apparent after more than two years, the homeowner should contact NHBC, as the Buildmark covers a range of structural aspects as well as double glazing, plastering and staircases. For more information, contact **NHBC,** Tel: 0844 6331 000; e-mail: cssupport@ nhbc.co.uk; website: www.nhbc.co.uk.

Also helpful to home buyers, the Land Registry allows members of the public to seek information directly about the 20 million or so properties held on its register. The details can be accessed through Land Register Online or from one of its 24 local offices in England and Wales. Contact the **Land Registry,** Tel: 0844 8920 456; website: www.landregisteronline.gov.uk.

Another welcome change is that conveyancing is now more competitive, with banks, building societies, insurance companies and other bodies (as well of course as solicitors) offering these services.

Home information packs (HIPs)

The Home Information Pack (known as the HIP) is compulsory for most homes on the market in England and Wales. From 6 April 2009 important changes were made to HIPs, so that better information is available from the first day a property is put on the market. A HIP is a set of documents that provides the buyer of a property with key information on the property and must be provided by the seller or the seller's agent. It is a legal requirement to have a HIP and your property cannot be sold without one. The HIP lets buyers see important information about the property at the start of the process, free of charge. This means there is less chance of nasty surprises later on in the process. The HIP was designed to help reduce delays and extra expense to both buyer and seller. For further information consult the Directgov website: www.direct.gov.uk/en/HomeAnd Community/ BuyingAndSellingYourHome.

Bridging loans

Tempting as it may be to buy before you sell, unless you have the money available to finance the cost of two homes – including possibly two mortgages – you need to do your sums very carefully indeed. Bridging loans are a way of getting over the problem, but can be a very expensive option. As an alternative to bridging loans, some of the major institutional estate agents operate chain-breaking schemes and may offer to buy your property at a discount: normally around 10 or 12 per cent less than the market price. In some circumstances this could be worthwhile, but a lot of money is involved, so this is not a decision to be taken lightly.

Estate agents

Finding your dream house may prove harder than you think. The grapevine can be effective, so pass the word around about what you are looking for. The property advertisements, especially in local newspapers, may also be worth scanning. Additionally, you could contact a good estate agent in the area to which you want to move.

The **National Association of Estate Agents (NAEA)** runs a service called HomeLink, a network of Estate Agents working with like-minded professionals committed to making the moving experience straightforward by providing access to a professional, friendly property service. Your nearest member of HomeLink can get details of houses for sale from a HomeLink member in your target area. For names of member agents, call the HomeLink Hotline on 01926 417792; e-mail: homelink@naea.co.uk; website: www.naea.co.uk.

Some building societies, banks and insurance companies – including Halifax and Legal & General – have created large chains of estate agents, and many of these maintain systems for full exchange of information between their branches nationwide. All these, together with most other large groups as well as many independent estate agents, have introduced a Code of Practice and also formed a Property Ombudsman scheme to provide an independent review service for buyers or sellers of UK residential property in the event of a complaint. As with most Ombudsman schemes, action can be taken only against firms that are actually members of the scheme. The Property Ombudsman also cannot intervene in disputes over surveys of the property. Copies of the *Consumer Guide*, the Code of Practice and other information can be obtained by contacting **The Property Ombudsman,** Tel: 01722 333306; e-mail: admin@tpos.co.uk; website: www. tpos.co.uk.

A further welcome move to improve standards is the 1993 Property Misdescriptions Act, which prohibits estate agents and property developers from making misleading or inflated claims about a property, site or related matter. If you want to contact qualified local agents, the **Royal Institution of Chartered Surveyors (RICS)** contact centre can provide names and addresses of chartered surveyors who are estate agents. Call the contact centre on 0870 333 1600; or e-mail: contactrics@rics.org; website: www.rics.org.

If you are thinking of retiring abroad, you must be careful not to be caught unawares by unscrupulous property developers who have swindled hundreds of Britons, many of them retired people wishing to relocate to warmer climates such as in Mediterranean tourist resorts. In particular, don't be rushed into a purchase you may later regret by fast-talking salespeople, or make the mistake of putting down a deposit until you are as certain as you can be that you want to go ahead.

As well as all the obvious points such as water and electricity supply, it is essential to get the legal title and land rights thoroughly checked by an independent lawyer with specialist knowledge of the local property and planning laws. Otherwise you could be at risk of later discovering that the property you bought is not rightfully yours or, as recently happened to hundreds of homeowners in Spain, being informed that your home has been illegally built on greenbelt land and is due for demolition.

Removals

Transporting your worldly goods from A to B is an exhausting business. Professional help can remove many of the headaches if carried out by a reputable firm. Not only will they shift all the heavy furniture around for you, but they will also wrap your china and ornaments safely in packing cases that they provide as part of the service. Costs vary depending on the type and size of furniture, the distance over which it is being moved and other factors, including insurance and seasonal troughs and peaks. Obviously, valuable antiques will cost more to pack and transport than standard modern furniture. It pays to shop around and get at least three written quotes from different removal firms. Some may be able to help reduce costs by arranging part- or return loads. It is also worth asking whether the firm has a 'low-price day', as rates are often cheaper at the start of the week. Remember, however, that the cheapest quote is not necessarily the best. Find out exactly what you are paying for and whether the price includes packing and insurance.

A useful organization to contact is the **British Association of Removers**. It will send you a free leaflet advising you what to do when you move house and a list of approved removal firms that all work to a rigorous Code of Practice. Tel: 01923 699 480; e-mail: info@bar.co.uk; website: www.bar.co.uk.

Retirement housing and sheltered accommodation

The terms 'retirement housing' or 'sheltered accommodation' cover a wide variety of housing but generally mean property with a resident manager/caretaker, an emergency alarm system, optional meals, and some communal facilities such as living rooms, garden and laundry. Guest accommodation and visiting services such as hairdressers and chiropodists are sometimes also available. A number of companies offer extra care and nursing facilities in some of their developments. Designed to bridge the gap between the family home and residential care, such housing offers continued independence for the fit and active within a secure environment. Much of it is owned and run by local authorities, housing associations and charities. However, there are a number of well-designed, high-quality private developments of 'retirement homes' now on the market, for sale or rent, at prices to suit most pockets.

Many of the more attractive properties – and among the most expensive – are in converted country houses of architectural or historical merit, or in newly developed 'villages' and 'courtyard' schemes. As a general rule, you have to be over 55 when you buy property of this kind. While you may not wish to move into this type of accommodation just now, if the idea interests you in the long term it is worth planning ahead, as there are often very long waiting lists. Full details of the various types of sheltered accommodation, together with a price guide and some addresses, are given in Chapter 15, Caring for Elderly Parents.

Other options

Caravan or mobile home

Many retired people consider living in a caravan or mobile home that they keep either in a relative's garden or on an established site, possibly at the seaside or in the country. You may already own one as a holiday home that you are thinking of turning into more permanent accommodation. If you want to live in a caravan on your own or other private land, you should contact your local authority for information about any planning permission or site licensing requirements that may apply.

If, on the other hand, you want to keep it on an established site, there is a varied choice ranging from small fields with just a handful of mobile homes to large, warden-assisted parks with shopping and leisure facilities. Make absolutely sure, whichever you choose, that the site owner has all the necessary permissions. You should check this with the planning and environmental health department of the local authority. It should be noted that many site owners will not accept prospective residents' own mobile homes but require them to buy one from the site or from an outgoing resident. The rights of owners of residential mobile home sites and of residents who own their mobile home but rent their pitch from a site owner are set out in the Mobile Homes Act 1983.

Find out what conditions both the local authority and the site owner attach to any agreement (by law the site owner must provide a written statement setting out terms such as the services provided, charges and maintenance of the site). You should also check your statutory rights (which should be included in the written statement), in particular regarding security of tenure and resale. Under the Act, residents have the right to sell their unit to a person approved by the site owner, who will be entitled to up to 10 per cent commission on the sale price. In the event of a dispute, either party is free to go to court or, with the agreement of both sides, to arbitration. If following a sale the resident is unhappy with the terms of the written agreement, appeal to the court must be within six months of the written terms being received.

It should also be noted that ordinary caravans are not always suitable as long-term accommodation for the over-60s. They can be damp as well as cramped, and what may have been an enjoyable adventure on holiday may soon pall when it is your only option. Modern residential park homes, which are not all that different from bungalows, have the advantage of being more spacious and sturdier but, though usually cheaper than a house of equivalent size, are nevertheless a major expense. Moreover, the law regarding such purchases is complex, and legal advice is very strongly recommended before entering into a commitment to purchase a park home.

Two companies that specialize in new homes for sale on residential parks, ready for immediate occupation, are **Britannia Parks,** Tel: 01252 408 891; website: www.britanniaparks.com, and **Omar Homes,** Tel: 01842 810 673; website: www.omar.co.uk; e-mail: info@omar.co.uk,

If you do decide to go ahead with the plan, you might like to obtain a copy of *Mobile Homes – A Guide for Residents and Site Owners,* a free booklet available from your housing department or from the **Department for Communities and Local Government,** Tel: 0300 123 1124; e-mail: contactus@communities.gov.uk; website: www.communities.gov.uk.

Self-build

Over 25,000 people a year, including many in their 50s, are now building their own homes and, with typical cost savings estimated at between 25 and 40 per cent, the number has been growing. New building methods have been developed that defy the assumption that you need to be a fit young man to undertake such a project, and both women and elderly people have successfully become self-builders. No prior building experience is necessary, although this of course helps.

Further good news is that, in response to the demand, some building societies offer self-build mortgages to enable borrowers to finance the purchase of land plus construction costs. However, as with any mortgage, it is essential to make sure that you are not in danger of over-committing yourself. Not so long ago, hundreds of people lost their sites because, owing to falling land prices, the size of their loan exceeded the value of the property – and by law building societies cannot make secured loans that are more than 100 per cent of the valuation.

It is also as well to be aware that obtaining planning permission from local councils can often be a protracted business and could add to the cost if you have to submit new plans. Most self-builders work in groups and/or employ subcontractors for some of the more specialized work, but individuals who wish to build on their own can make arrangements with an architect or company that sells standard plans and building kits.

The **Centre for Alternative Technology** provides a free information and advice service on sustainable living and environmentally responsible building. Books on ecological building design and environmentally friendly products are available via mail order. Contact CAT on 01654 705980; website: www.cat.org.uk.

Making your home more practical

It is sensible to set about any home improvement plans earlier rather than later. For one thing, these are often easier to afford when you are still earning a regular salary. For another, any building work is tiresome, and most people find it easier to put up with the mess when they are not living among it 24 hours a day. Third, if you start early, you will enjoy the benefit that much sooner.

When embarking on changes a specific aim should be to make your home as economical, labour-saving and convenient as possible. Err on the side of simple systems rather than complex ones. You will be thankful you chose wisely as age increases. A reason for saying this is that many people become so involved with the add-ons or decorative aspects that they forget to think about some of the longer-term practicalities which, at next to no extra cost, could have been incorporated along with the other work.

Insulation

When you retire, you may be at home more during the day so are likely to be using your heating more intensively. One of the best ways of reducing those now alarmingly increasing utility bills is to get your house properly insulated. Heat escapes from a building in four main ways: through the roof, walls, floor, and loose-fitting doors and windows. Insulation not only can cut the heat loss dramatically but will usually more than pay for itself within four or five years.

Loft insulation

As much as 25 per cent of heat in a house escapes through the loft. The answer is to put a layer of insulating material, ideally 220 to 270 millimetres thick according to the material used, between and across the roof joists. You may be able to lay this yourself. The materials are readily available from builders' merchants. If you prefer to employ a specialist contractor, contact the **National Insulation Association** for a list of its members, Tel: 01525 383 313; e-mail: info@nationalinsulationassociation.org.uk; website: www.nationalinsulationassociation.org.uk. Your local Age Concern group or volunteer bureau may also be able to help.

Doors and windows

A further 25 per cent of heat escapes through single-glazed windows, half of which could be saved through double glazing. There are two main types: sealed units and secondary sashes (which can be removed in the summer). Compared with other forms of insulation, double glazing is expensive; however, it does have the advantage of reducing noise levels. As a result of building regulations that came into effect in April 2002, any replacement doors and windows installed after that date have to comply with strict thermal performance standards, and the work will need to be done by an installer who is registered under the FENSA scheme. To be on the safe side, contact the **Glass and Glazing Federation,** Tel: 0870 042 4255; e-mail: info@ggf.org.uk; website: www.ggf.co.uk.

Effective draught proofing saves heat loss as well as keeping out cold blasts of air. It is also relatively cheap and easy to install. Compression seals, mounted by a variety of methods and supplied in strip form, are the simplest and most cost-effective way to fill the gap between the fixed and moving edges of doors and windows. For draught proofing older sliding sash windows and doors, wiper seals, fixed with rustproof pins and screws, need to be used. For very loose-fitting frames, gap fillers that can be squeezed from a tube provide a more efficient seal between frame and surround, but this is normally work for a specialist. If you do fit draught seals, make sure you leave a space for a small amount of air to get through, or you may get problems with condensation. If the house is not well ventilated, you should put in a vapour check to slow down the leakage of moisture into the walls and ceiling. For advice on durable products and contractors, contact the **Draught Proofing Advisory Association,** Tel: 01428 654011; e-mail: dpaaassociation@aol.com; website: www.dpaa-association.org.uk.

Heat loss can also be considerably reduced through hanging heavy curtains (both lined and interlined) over windows and doors. Make sure all curtains cover the windowsill or rest on the floor. It is better to have them too long than too short.

Wall insulation

More heat is lost through the walls than perhaps anywhere else in the house: it can be as much as 50 per cent. If your house has cavity walls – and most houses built after 1930 do – then cavity wall insulation should be considered. This involves injecting mineral wool (rock wool or glass wool), polystyrene beads or foam into the cavity through holes drilled in the outside wall. It is work for a specialist and, depending on what grants are applicable, may be free or could cost upwards of £350. Against this, you could expect a typical saving of around 25 per cent off your heating bill each year, so in most cases the initial outlay should be recovered in under four years. Make sure that the firm you use is registered with a reputable organization, such as the British Standards Institution, or can show a current Agrément Certificate for the system and is approved by the British Board of Agrément (BBA). If a foam fill is used, the application should comply with British Standard BS 5617 and the material with BS 5618.

Solid wall insulation can be considerably more expensive, but well worthwhile, providing similar savings of around 25 per cent off your annual heating bill. Again, this is work for a specialist and involves applying an insulating material to the outside of the wall, plus rendering or cladding. Alternatively, an insulated thermal lining can be applied to the inside. Landlords who install wall insulation can offset up to £1,500 of the cost, per building, against Income Tax. This used only to apply to loft and cavity wall insulation but has now been extended to include solid wall insulation. The scope of the relief (officially known as the Landlord's Energy Saving Allowance) was further extended to include draught proofing and insulation for hot water systems. Floor insulation is included in the list of energy-saving items that qualify for the allowance. *NB:* the £1,500 cap, which previously applied to the building, now applies per property, so if there are two flats in the building, the £1,500 cap now applies to each one.

For further information and addresses of registered contractors, contact:

British Board of Agrément, Tel: 01923 665300; e-mail: contact@bba.star.co.uk; website: www.bbacerts.co.uk.

British Standards Institution, Tel: 020 8996 9001; e-mail: csservices@bsigroup.com; website: www.bsigroup.co.uk.

Cavity Insulation Guarantee Agency (CIGA), Tel: 01525 853300; e-mail: info@ciga.co.uk; website: www.ciga.co.uk.

Eurisol UK Ltd, Tel: 020 7935 8532; e-mail: info@eurisol.com; website: www.eurisol.com.

Insulated Render & Cladding Association Ltd (for solid or defective walls), Tel: 01428 654011; e-mail: incaassociation@aol.com; website: www.inca-ltd.org.uk.

National Insulation Association (for cavity wall and loft insulation, draught proofing and insulated thermal linings applied internally), Tel: 01525 383313; e-mail: info@nationalinsulationassociation.org.uk; website: www.nationalinsulationassociation.org.uk.

Floor insulation

Up to 15 per cent of heat loss can be saved through filling the cracks or gaps in the floorboards and skirting. If you can take up your floorboards, rock wool or glass wool rolls can be extremely effective when fixed underneath the joists. Filling spaces with papier mâché or plastic wool will also help, especially if a good felt or rubber underlay is then laid under the carpet. Be careful, however, that you do not block up the underfloor ventilation, which is necessary to protect floor timbers from dampness and rot. Solid concrete floors can be covered with cork tiles or carpet and felt or rubber underlay.

Hot water cylinder insulation

If your hot water cylinder has no insulation, it could be costing you several pounds a week in wasted heat. An insulating jacket around your hot water cylinder will cut wastage by three-quarters. Most hot water tanks now come ready supplied with insulation. If not, the jacket should be at least 80 millimetres thick and will cost from around £25. Jackets come in various sizes, so measure your cylinder before buying and look for one that conforms to BS 5615.

Grants

The Chancellor has announced grants of between £300 and £4,000 for pensioners installing insulation and central heating in their homes. Further details can be obtained from the government's website (www.direct.gov.uk) or from www.warmfront.co.uk; Tel: 0800 316 2805. The government-funded Warm Front Grant scheme provides grants for home insulation and heating measures and also gives energy-efficiency advice. The grants are mainly targeted at low-income householders – including people who are disabled, chronically sick or over 60 – who own or privately rent their home. It might also be worth enquiring at your local authority whether it provides any assistance with insulation and, if so, whether you would be likely to qualify for help. There are no guarantees, however, as any such grants – other than mandatory disabled facilities grants (see page 351) – are at the discretion of local authorities. For further information, contact the environmental health or housing department.

Heating

It may be possible to save money by using different fuels or by heating parts of your house off different systems. This could apply especially if some rooms are only occasionally used. Your local gas and electricity offices can advise on heating systems, running costs and energy conservation, as well as heating and hot water appliances. In particular, you might usefully enquire about Economy 7 electricity, which provides cheaper-rate supplies at night.

The **Solid Fuel Association** will also give free advice and information on all aspects of solid fuel heating, including appliances and installation. Contact the helpline on 0845 601 4406; e-mail: sfa@solidfuel.co.uk; website: www.solidfuel.co.uk.

You could consult the **Building Centre**. It has a very wide range of building products on display, with information officers on hand to give consumer guidance. Tel: 020 7692 4000; e-mail: reception@buildingcentre.co.uk; website: www.buildingcentre.co.uk.

Shopping note

Many people get rushed into expensive purchases on the promise of cheaper energy bills. A point to remember when comparing, say, gas with electricity is that fuel prices are volatile and relative cost advantages are not always maintained. If you have an otherwise adequate system, it could be a false economy to exchange it for the sake of a small saving in current heating costs.

Buying and installing heating equipment

When buying equipment, check that it has been approved by the appropriate standards approvals board. For electrical equipment, the letters to look for are BEAB (British Electro-technical Approvals Board) or CCA (CENELEC Certification Agreement), which is the European Union equivalent.

For gas appliances, look for the CE mark, which denotes that appliances meet the requirements of the Gas Appliance (Safety) Regulations Act 1995. Domestic solid fuel appliances should be approved by the Solid Fuel Appliances Approval Scheme; check the sales literature.

When looking for contractors to install your equipment, an important point to note is that new government legislation has come into force placing tighter controls on the standard of electrical and other installation work in households across England and Wales. It is now a legal requirement for electricians as well as kitchen, bathroom and gas installers to comply with Part P of the Building Regulations. You would therefore be well advised to check that any contractor you propose using is enrolled with the relevant inspection council or is a member of the relevant trade association.

Electricians should be approved by the **NICEIC**. All approved contractors are covered for technical work by the NICEIC Complaints Procedure and Guarantee of Standards Scheme and undertake to work to British Standard 7671. Any substandard work must be put right at no extra cost to the consumer. Names and addresses of local approved contractors can be found in the NICEIC Roll of Approved Contractors obtainable from NICEIC, Tel: 0870 013 0382; e-mail: enquiries@niceic.com; website: www.niceic.org.uk.

An alternative source for finding a reputable electrician is the **Electrical Contractors' Association**. Its members, all of whom have to be qualified, work to national wiring regulations and a published ECA Code of Fair Trading. There is also a work bond, which guarantees that, in the event of a contractor becoming insolvent, the work will be completed by another approved electrician at the originally quoted price, subject to the conditions of the scheme. Contact the ECA on 020 7313 4800; e-mail: info@eca.co.uk; website: www.eca.co.uk.

Gas appliances should only be installed by a Gas Safe Register registered installer (Gas Safe Register replaced CORGI as the gas registration body on 1 April 2009). Registration is compulsory by law. As a further safeguard, all registered gas installers carry a Gas Safe Register ID card with their photo, types of gas work they are competent to do, their employer's trading title and the Gas Safe Register logo. After a gas appliance has been installed, you should receive a safety certificate from the Gas Safe Register, proving that it has been installed by a professional. You should keep this safe, as you may need it should you want to sell your home in the future. To find a registered installer in your area, contact the **Gas Safe Register**, Tel: 0800 408 5500; website: www. gassaferegister.co.uk.

Additionally, members of the Heating and Ventilating Contractors' Association can advise on all types of central heating. All domestic installation work done by member companies is covered by a free three-year guarantee. For further information contact the **Heating and Ventilating Contractors' Association**, Tel: 020 7313 4900; e-mail: contact@hvca.org.uk; website: www. hvca.org.uk.

Tips for reducing your energy bills

Energy can be saved in lots of small ways. Taken together, they could amount to quite a large cut in your bills. You may find some of the following ideas worth considering:

- Set your central heating timer and thermostat to suit the weather. A saving of half an hour or one degree can be substantial. For example, reducing the temperature by 1 degree Celsius could cut your heating bills by up to 10 per cent.
- A separate thermostat on your hot water cylinder set at around 60 degrees Celsius will enable you to keep hot water for taps at a lower temperature than for the heating system.
- If you run your hot water off an immersion heater, have a time switch fitted attached to an Economy 7 meter so that the water is heated at the cheap rate overnight. An override switch will enable you to top up the heat during the day if necessary.
- Showers are more economical than baths, as well as being easier to use when you become older.
- Reflective foil sheets put behind your radiators help to reduce heat loss through the walls.
- Switch off, or reduce, the heating in rooms not being used, and close doors.
- Low-energy light bulbs can save several pounds a year.
- If you have an open fire, a vast amount of heat tends to be lost up the chimney. A wood-burning stove can help reduce heat loss as well as maximize the amount of heat you get from your wood or solid fuel in other ways. If you dislike the idea of losing the look of an open fire, there are now a number of appliances on the market that are open-fronted and fit flush with the fireplace opening. Contact your local office of the **Solid Fuel Association** for further information. If you decide to block up a fireplace, don't forget to fit an air vent to allow some ventilation.
- Some small cooking appliances can save energy in comparison with a full-sized cooker. An electric casserole or slow cooker uses only a fraction more energy than a light bulb and is economical for single households. Similarly, an electric frying pan or multi-cooker can be a sensible alternative for people living on their own. Pressure cookers and microwave ovens can save fuel and time.
- Defrosting fridges and freezers regularly reduces running costs.
- Finally, it is a good idea to get in the habit of reading your electricity and gas meters regularly. This will help you keep track of likely bills. British Gas customers can call the meter reading line, at any time 24 hours a day, for up-to-date readings. You should have your meter reading and account reference number to hand when you ring The number to call is printed clearly on your gas bill.

You might like to take advantage of one of the British Gas payment options that allows customers to spread their gas or electricity payments over the year in fixed monthly or quarterly instalments, based on an estimate of their annual consumption. Estimates are periodically adjusted up or down, depending on actual meter readings. Price reductions are offered to customers paying by monthly direct debit. For further details, contact **British Gas** (see your gas or electricity bill for the telephone number; website: www.britishgas.co.uk). Many other suppliers have similar budget plans.

Another useful organization to note is the **Energy Saving Trust**, a non-profit organization that provides free impartial advice tailored to suit individuals, including information on available grants. Contact number to call: 0800 512 012; website: www.energysavingtrust.org.uk.

Useful reading

A free fact sheet, *Help With Heating*, is available from Age Concern, Tel: 0800 009 966; website: www.ageconcern.org.uk.

Other useful addresses

Consumer Focus is the new statutory organization championing consumers' interests in England, Scotland, Wales and, for postal services, Northern Ireland. If you would like to make a consumer complaint, call 08454 04 05 06 or e-mail contact@consumerfocus.org.uk; website: www.consumerfocus.org.uk.

Improvement and repair

Building work is notoriously expensive, which can be a major deterrent to doing some of the alterations to your home that may be necessary. Before abandoning the idea, it is worth investigating whether you could take advantage of any assistance on offer. A bank loan may be the simplest way of raising funds for most repairs and improvements. Many banks and building societies are prepared to offer interest-only mortgages to older people to cover essential repairs and improvements.

If you are unlucky enough to discover dry rot or similar in your home, there is little you can do but try to ensure that the builder you employ does not do a botched job. Unfortunately, insurance cover does not usually extend to damage to your house caused by normal wear and tear, woodworm, rot, insects and vermin. If your house does need structural repairs, contact the Royal Institution of Chartered Surveyors (see 'Useful addresses', page 153). It will be able to advise you on your legal position as well as point you in the direction of reputable chartered surveyors.

Local authority assistance

The Regulatory Reform Order (RRO) gives local authorities greater discretionary powers to provide assistance – such as low-cost loans and grants -- to help with renovations, repairs and adaptations to the home, or to help someone move to more suitable accommodation if that is a better solution. The RRO replaces the previous legislation governing the renovation grant, common parts grant, HMO grant and home repair assistance and allows local authorities greater flexibility to determine their particular eligibility criteria, whether means-testing should be involved and the actual type of assistance available. Any assistance given, however, must be in accordance with the authority's published policy. For further information contact the environmental health or housing department of your local authority.

Disabled facilities grant (DFG)

This is designed to adapt or provide facilities for a home (including the common parts where applicable) to make it more suitable for occupation by a disabled person. It can cover a wide range of improvements to enable someone with a disability to manage more independently, including, for example, adaptations to make the accommodation safe for a disabled occupant, work to facilitate access either to the property itself or to the main rooms, the provision of suitable bathroom or kitchen facilities, the adaptation of heating or lighting controls, or improvement of the heating system. Provided the applicant is eligible, a mandatory grant of up to £30,000 may be available in England for all the above (local authorities may use their discretionary powers to provide additional assistance).

As with most other grants, there is a means test. The local authority will want to check that the proposed work is reasonable and practicable according to the age and condition of the property, and the local social services department will need to be satisfied that the work is necessary and appropriate to meet the individual's needs. The grant can be applied for either by the disabled person or by a joint owner or joint tenant or landlord on his or her behalf. For further information, contact the environmental health or housing department of your local authority. See also the leaflet *Disabled Facilities Grant*, obtainable from DCLG Publications Department, Tel: 0300 123 1124; e-mail: contactus@communities. gov.uk; website: www.communities.gov.uk.

Do not start work until approval has been given to your grant application, as you will not be eligible for a grant once work has started.

Community care grant

Income Support recipients may be able to obtain a community care grant from the Social Fund to help with repairs. For further information, see leaflet GL18, *Help from the Social Fund*, obtainable from any social security office.

Other help for disabled people

Your local authority may be able to help with the provision of certain special facilities such as a stair lift, telephone installations or a ramp to replace steps. Apply to your local social services department and, if you encounter any difficulties, ask for further help from your local disability group or Age Concern group.

Useful addresses

APHC Ltd (Association of Plumbing and Heating Contractors Ltd) maintains a national register of licensed members and can put you in touch with a reputable local engineer. All are carefully vetted every year to ensure they are working to the highest standards. Tel: 024 7647 0626; e-mail: switchboard@competentpersons scheme.co.uk; website: www.competentpersonsscheme.co.uk.

Association of Building Engineers can supply names of qualified building engineers/surveyors. Tel: 0845 1261 058; e-mail: building.engineers@abe.org.uk; website: www.abe.org.uk.

Association of Master Upholsterers & Soft Furnishers Ltd has a list of over 500 approved members throughout the country that specialize in all forms of upholstery including curtains and soft furnishings. Names of those operating in your area can be obtained from the Association. Tel: 029 2077 8918; website: www.upholsterers.co.uk.

The Building Centre has displays of building products, heating appliances, bathroom and kitchen equipment and other exhibits and can give guidance on building problems. It has manufacturers' lists and other free literature you can take away, and there is also a well-stocked bookshop covering all aspects of building and home improvement. It is open Monday to Friday, 9.30 am to 6 pm; Saturday, 10 am to 2 pm. Tel: 020 7692 4000; website: www.buildingcentre.co.uk.

Federation of Master Builders (FMB): lists of members are available from regional offices. A warranty scheme, which insures work in progress and gives up to 10 years' guarantee on completion of work, is available from some of its members. Tel: 020 7242 7583; website: www.fmb.org.uk.

Guild of Master Craftsmen can supply names of all types of specialist craftspeople including, for example, carpenters, joiners, ceramic workers and restorers. Tel: 01273 478449; e-mail: theguild@thegmcgroup.com; website: www.guildmc.com.

Institute of Plumbing and Heating Engineering can provide a list of professional plumbers. Tel: 01708 472791; e-mail: info@ciphe.org.uk; website: www.ciphe.org.uk.

Property Care Association has remedial treatment companies throughout the UK and can recommend reputable damp proofing companies in your area, as well as independent consultants, freelance surveyors and members specializing in cellar and basement conversions. Tel: 0870 1216 737; e-mail: pca@property-care.org; website: www.propertycare.org.

Royal Institute of British Architects (RIBA) has a free Clients' Service, which, however small your building project, will recommend up to three suitable architects. It can also supply you with useful leaflets giving advice on working with an architect. Tel: 020 7580 5533; e-mail: info@inst.riba.org; website: www.architecture.com.

Royal Institution of Chartered Surveyors (RICS) will nominate qualified surveyors in your area, who can be recognized by the initials MRICS or FRICS after their name. It also publishes a number of useful leaflets. Tel: 0870 3331 600; e-mail: contactrics@rics.org; website: www.rics.org.

The Scottish and Northern Ireland Plumbing Employers' Federation (SNIPEF) is the national trade association for all types of firms involved in plumbing and domestic heating in Scotland and Northern Ireland. It has over 800 member firms and operates a Code of Fair Trading, independent complaints scheme and guarantee-of-work scheme. Lists of local members are available on request. Tel: 0131 225 2255; e-mail: info@snipef.org; website: www.snipef.org.

Useful reading

Older Home Owners – Financial Help with Repairs and Adaptations, free fact sheet, is available from Age Concern; Tel: 0800 009 966; website: www.ageconcern.org.uk.

Home improvement agencies (HIAs)

Home improvement agencies (sometimes known as 'staying put' or 'care and repair' agencies) work with older or disabled people to help them remain in their own homes by providing advice and assistance on repairs, improvements and adaptations. They also advise on the availability of funding and welfare benefits, obtain prices, recommend reliable builders and inspect the completed job. For information about your nearest HIA, contact **Foundations,** Tel: 01457 891 909; e-mail: foundations@cel.co.uk. You can search the website for a directory of local home improvement agencies: www.foundations.uk.com. Your local authority or Citizens Advice Bureau will also know about local schemes.

Another possibility is to contact **Anchor Trust,** which has 'staying put' agencies across England. Tel: 0845 140 2020; website: www.anchor.org.uk.

Safety in the home

Accidents in the home account for 40 per cent of all fatal accidents, resulting in nearly 5,000 deaths a year. Seventy per cent of these victims are over retirement age, and nearly 80 per cent of deaths are caused by falls. A further 3 million people need medical treatment. The vast majority of accidents are caused by carelessness or by obvious danger spots in the home that for the most part could very easily be made safer. Tragically, it is all too often the little things that we keep meaning to attend to but never quite get round to that are the ones that prove fatal.

Steps and stairs should be well lit, with light switches at both the top and the bottom. Frayed carpet is notoriously easy to trip on. On staircases especially, defective carpet should be repaired or replaced as soon as possible. All stairs should have a handrail along the wall to provide extra support – on both sides, if the stairs are very steep. It is also a good idea to have a white line painted on the edge of steps that are difficult to see – for instance in the garden or leading up to the front door.

It may be stating the obvious to say that climbing on chairs and tables is dangerous – and yet we all do it. You should keep proper steps, preferably with a handrail, to do high jobs in the house such as hanging curtains or reaching cupboards.

Floors can be another danger zone. Rugs and mats can slip on polished floors and should always be laid on some form of non-slip backing material. Stockinged feet are slippery on all but carpeted floors, and new shoes should always have the soles scratched before you wear them. Remember also that spilt water or talcum powder on tiled or linoleum floors is a number one cause of accidents.

The *bathroom* is particularly hazardous for falls. Sensible precautionary measures include using a suction-type bath mat and putting handrails on the bath or alongside the shower. For older people who have difficulty getting in and out of the bath, a bath seat can be helpful. Soap on a rope is safer in a shower, as it is less likely to slither out of your hands and make the floor slippery. Regardless of age, you should make sure that all medicines are clearly labelled. Throw away any prescribed drugs left over from a previous illness.

Fires can all too easily start in the home. If you have an open fire, you should always use a fireguard and sparkguard at night. The chimney should be regularly swept at least once a year, maybe more if you have a wood-burning stove. Never place a clothes horse near an open fire or heater, and be careful of flammable objects that could fall from the mantelpiece. Upholstered furniture is a particular fire hazard, especially when polyurethane foam has been used in its manufacture. If buying new furniture, make sure that it carries a red triangle label, indicating that it is resistant to smouldering cigarettes. Furniture that also passes the match ignition test carries a green label. Since March 1989, the use of polyurethane foam in furniture manufacture has been banned, and 'combustion modified foam' that has passed the BS 5852 test now has to be used instead.

Portable heaters should be kept away from furniture and curtains and positioned where you cannot trip over them. Paraffin heaters should be handled particularly carefully and should never be filled while alight. Avoid leaving paraffin where it will be exposed to heat, including sunlight. If possible, it should be kept in a metal container outside the house.

Gas appliances should be serviced regularly by British Gas or other Gas Safe Register registered installers. You should also ensure that there is adequate ventilation when using heaters. Never block up air vents: carbon monoxide fumes can kill.

If you smell gas or notice anything you suspect could be dangerous, stop using the appliance immediately, open the doors and windows and call the National Grid 24-hour emergency line free: 0800 111 999.

More than one in three fires in the home are caused by accidents with *cookers*. Chip pans are a particular hazard: only fill the pan one-third full with oil and always dry the chips before putting them in the fat or, better still, use oven-ready chips that you just pop into the oven to cook. Pan handles should be turned away from the heat and positioned so you cannot knock them off the stove. If called to the door or telephone, always take the pan off the ring and turn off the heat before you leave the kitchen. Cigarettes left smouldering in an ashtray could be dangerous if the ashtray is full. Smoking in bed is a potential killer!

Faulty electric wiring is another frequent cause of fires, as are overloaded power points. The wiring in your home should be checked every five years and you should avoid using too many appliances off a single plug. Ask an electrician's advice about what is the maximum safe number. Use only plugs that conform to the British Standard 1363. It is a good idea to get into the habit of pulling the plug out of the wall socket when you have finished using an appliance, whether TV or toaster.

All electrical equipment should be regularly checked for wear and tear, and frayed or damaged flexes immediately replaced. Wherever possible, have electric sockets moved to waist height to avoid unnecessary bending whenever you want to turn on the switch. In particular, *electric blankets* should be routinely overhauled and checked in accordance with the manufacturer's instructions. It is dangerous to use both a hot water bottle and electric blanket – and never use an underblanket as an overblanket.

Electrical appliances are an increasing feature of labour-saving *gardening* but can be dangerous unless treated with respect. They should never be used when it is raining. Moreover, gardeners should always wear rubber-soled shoes or boots, and avoid floppy clothing that could get caught in the equipment.

As a general precaution, keep *fire extinguishers* readily accessible. Make sure they are regularly maintained and in good working order. Portable extinguishers should conform to BS EN 3 or BS 6165. Any extinguishers made before 1996 should conform to BS 5423, which preceded BS EN 3. Many insurance companies now recommend that you install a smoke alarm, which should conform to BS 5446–1:2000 or BS EN 14604:2005, as an effective and cheap early warning device. Prices start from about £10.

Useful reading

Your Safety, Fire, Keep Out the Cold and *Your Security* are free from the Information Resources Team, Help the Aged, Tel: 020 7278 1114; e-mail: info@helptheaged. org.uk; website: www.helptheaged.org.uk.

Home security

Nine out of 10 burglaries are spontaneous and take less than 10 minutes. However, there is much you can do to protect yourself. The crime prevention officer at your local police station will advise you how to improve your security arrangements. He or she will also tell you whether there is a Neighbourhood Watch scheme and how you join it. This is a free service that the police are happy to provide.

The most vulnerable access points are doors and windows. Simple precautions such as fitting adequate locks and bolts can do much to deter the average burglar. Prices for a good door lock are about £60 to £80 plus VAT, and prices for window locks are about £15 to £20 plus VAT per window. Doors should have secure bolts or a five-lever mortise lock strengthened by metal plates on both sides, a door chain and a spyhole in the front door. Additionally, you might consider outside lights (ideally with an infrared sensor) to illuminate night-time visitors and an entry phone system requiring callers to identify themselves before you open the door.

Windows should also be properly secured with key-operated locks. The best advice is to fit locks that secure them when partially open. Install rack bolts or surface-mounted security press bolts on French windows, and draw your curtains at night so potential intruders cannot see in. Louvre windows are especially vulnerable because the slats can easily be removed. A solution is to glue them in place with an epoxy resin and to fit a special louvre lock. An agile thief can get through any space larger than a human head, so even small windows such as skylights need properly fitted locks. Both double glazing and venetian blinds act as a further deterrent. If you are particularly worried, you could also have bars fitted to the windows or install old-fashioned internal shutters that can be closed at night. Alternatively, many DIY shops sell decorative wrought-iron security grilles.

An obvious point is to ensure that the house is securely locked whenever you go out, even for five minutes. If you lose your keys, you should change the locks without delay. Insist that official callers such as meter readers show their identity cards before you allow them inside. If you are going away, even for only a couple of days, remember to cancel the milk and the newspapers. You might also like to take advantage of the **Royal Mail's Keepsafe** service. It will store your mail while you are away and so avoid it piling up and alerting potential burglars to your absence. There is a charge for the service, which (for 2009) varies from £8.95 for up to 17 days to £29.40 for 66 days. A week's notice is necessary. Application forms are obtainable from the post office or by calling the Royal Mail Enquiry Line: 0845 7777 888; website: www.royalmail.com/redirections.

If your home will be unoccupied for any length of time, it is sensible to ask the local police to put it on their unattended premises register. Finally, consider a time switch (cost around £15) that will turn the lights on and off when you are away and can be used to switch on the heating before your return.

If you want to know of a reputable locksmith, you should contact the **Master Locksmiths Association**, which can either give you the name of an approved locksmith in your area over the telephone or send you a list of its members, classified county by county. Tel: 01327 262255; e-mail: enquiries@locksmiths.co.uk; website: www.locksmiths.co.uk.

Useful reading

The Home Office issues a couple of useful booklets, *Your Practical Guide to Crime Prevention* and *How to Beat the Bogus Caller*. They are available free from your local police station or telephone the Home Office publications line on 0870 2414 680.

Burglar alarms and safes

More elaborate precautions such as a burglar alarm are among the best ways of protecting your home. Although alarms are expensive – they cost from about £450 to well in excess of £1,000 for sophisticated systems – they could be worth every penny. In the event of a break-in, you can summon help or ask the police to do what they can if you are away.

Many insurance companies will recommend suitable contractors to install burglar alarm equipment. Alternatively, contact the **National Security Inspectorate**, which will send a free list of approved contractors in your locality that install burglar alarm systems to, among other, British and European standards. There are 700 recognized firms and some 1,000 branches. The National Security Inspectorate will also investigate technical complaints. Tel: 0845 006 3003; e-mail: nsi@nsi.org.uk; website: www.nsi.org.uk.

If you keep valuables or money in the house, you should think about buying a concealed wall or floor safe. If you are going away, it is a good idea to inform your neighbours so that if your alarm goes off they will know something is wrong. Burglar alarms have an unfortunate habit of ringing for no good reason (a mouse or cat can trigger the mechanism), and many people ignore them as a result. It is advisable to give your neighbours a key so that they can turn off and reset the alarm should the occasion arise.

Insurance discounts

According to recent research, seven out of 10 householders are underinsured, some of them unknowingly but some intentionally to keep premiums lower. This could be dangerous because in the event of a mishap they could end up seriously out of pocket. With recent increases in premiums, many readers may feel that this is hardly the moment to be discussing any reassessment of their policy. However, there are two good reasons why this could be sensible. First is because the number of burglaries has risen, so the risks are greater. But, more particularly, you may be able to obtain better value than you are getting at present. A number of insurance companies now give discounts on house contents premiums if proper security precautions have been installed. These include Cornhill Direct, Royal & Sun Alliance and Direct Line.

Some insurance companies approach the problem differently and arrange discounts for their policyholders with manufacturers of security devices. If you would welcome independent advice on choosing a policy, you might usefully contact the **Institute of Insurance Brokers (IIB)** for details of local IIB brokers; Tel: 01933 410003; e-mail: inst.ins.brokers@iib-uk.com; website: www.iib-uk. com. See also the section headed 'Insurance', below.

Personal safety

Older people who live on their own can be particularly at risk. A number of personal alarms are now available that are highly effective and can generally give you peace of mind. A sensible precaution is to carry a 'screamer alarm', sometimes known as a 'personal attack button'. These are readily available in department stores, electrical shops and alarm companies.

Age Concern Aid-Call provides a service that enables anyone living alone to call for help simply by pressing a button. The subscriber has a small radio transmitter, worn as a pendant or like a watch, which contacts a 24-hour monitoring centre. The centre alerts a list of nominated relatives and friends, or the emergency services, that something is wrong. There are several ways of paying for Aid-Call based on installation, monitoring and rental. The firm operates a nationwide service and will arrange a demonstration through its head office. For a brochure, contact Age Concern Aid-Call, Tel: 0800 77 22 66; e-mail: info@ aidcall-alarms.co.uk; website: www.aidcall.co.uk.

A telephone can also increase your sense of security. Some families come to an arrangement whereby they ring their older relatives at regular times to check that all is well. Older people feel particularly vulnerable to mugging. While the dangers are often exaggerated, it must be sensible to take all normal precautions. The police are of the view that many muggings could be avoided if you are alert, think ahead and try to radiate confidence.

Insurance

As you near retirement, it is sensible to reassess your building and home contents policy. If the insurance was originally arranged through your building society, it may cease when your mortgage is paid off. In this case it will be essential for you to arrange new cover directly. Similarly, when buying for cash – for instance when moving to a smaller house – it will be up to you to organize the insurance and to calculate the rebuilding value of your home. It is advisable to get a qualified valuer to do this for you.

Over the last 15 years the value of your home may have doubled or more, and the chances are that the cost of replacing the fabric of your house, were it to burn down, would be significantly greater than the amount for which it is currently insured. Remember, you must insure for the full rebuilding cost: market value may be inadequate. Your policy should also provide money to meet architects' or surveyors' fees, as well as alternative accommodation for you and your family if your home were completely destroyed.

If you are planning to move into accommodation that has been converted from one large house into several flats or maisonettes, check with the landlord or managing agent that the insurance on the structure of the total building is adequate. All too many people have found themselves homeless because each tenant insured only his or her own flat and the collective policies were not sufficient to replace the common parts.

If when buying a new property you decide to take out a new mortgage, contrary to what many people believe you are under no obligation to insure your home with the particular company suggested by your building society. It is not being recommended here that you should necessarily go elsewhere: the point is that, as with all insurance, policies vary and some are more competitive than others.

In 2007 and subsequently, many people have been affected by serious flooding. About 2 million people live under threat of flooding in the UK – about one in 10 homes – and over 270,000 are at risk. It is highly advisable to check whether you live in a high-risk area and if so take steps to protect your property. This could cut your insurance premium by 10 per cent. According to the Association of British Insurers it can cost up to £40,000 to protect your home fully from flood damage. Further information on flood-risk areas can be obtained by calling **Floodline** on 0845 988 118; e-mail: enquiries@environment-agency.gov.uk; website: www.environment-agency.gov.uk.

Many people are woefully underinsured with regard to the contents of their home. Insurance that simply covers the purchase price is normally grossly insufficient. Instead, you should assess the replacement cost and make sure you have a 'new for old' or 'replacement as new' policy. Most insurance companies offer an automatic inflation-proofing option for both building and contents policies. While it is obviously prudent to take advantage of this, many people unthinkingly sign on the dotted line, quite forgetting to cancel items such as furniture or jewellery that they may have given away or sold – and so are encumbered with higher charges than necessary. Equally, many forget to add new valuables they have bought or received as presents. In particular, do check that you are adequately covered for any home improvements you may have added, such as a new kitchen or garage, conservatory, extra bathroom, swimming pool or other luxury.

Where antiques and jewellery are concerned, simple inflation-proofing may not be enough. Values can rise and fall disproportionately to inflation and depend on current market trends. For a professional valuation, contact either the **British Antique Dealers' Association (BADA)**, Tel: 020 7589 4128; website: www.bada.org; or **LAPADA (the Association of Art & Antiques**

Dealers), Tel: 020 7823 3511; website: www.lapada.org, for the name of a specialist. Photographs of particularly valuable items can help in the assessment of premiums and settlement of claims, as well as give the police a greater chance of recovering them in the case of theft. Property marking, for example with an ultraviolet marker, is another useful ploy, as it will help the police trace your possessions should any be stolen.

The **Association of British Insurers** will send you information sheets on various aspects of household insurance and loss prevention, including *Buildings Insurance for Home Owners* and *Home Contents Insurance,* which describe what policies you need and advise on how to ensure you have the correct amount of cover. Contact the ABI on 020 7600 3333; e-mail: info@abi.org.uk; website: www.abi. org.uk.

The **British Insurance Brokers' Association** can provide you with a list of registered insurance brokers in your area. Contact the Consumers' helpline, Tel: 0870 9501 790; e-mail: enquiries@biba.org.uk; website: www.biba.org.uk.

Some insurance companies offer home and contents policies for older people (age 50 and over) at substantially reduced rates. The rationale behind such schemes is that older people are less likely to leave their homes empty on a regular basis (ie 9 to 5) and are therefore less liable to be burgled. In some cases, policies are geared to the fact that many retired people have either sold or given away many of their more valuable possessions and therefore need to insure their homes only up to a relatively low sum. Such policies are arranged through **Age Concern Insurance Services**, Tel: 0800 1692 700; website: www.ageconcern.org.uk; **Saga Services Ltd**, Tel: 0800 0688 412; website: www.saga.co.uk; and **Help the Aged Insurance**, Tel: 0800 413 180; website: www.helptheaged.org.uk.

An increasing number of insurance companies, including Legal & General, offer generous no-claims discounts. Another type of discount-linked policy that is becoming more popular is one that carries an excess, whereby the householder pays the first chunk of any claim, say the first £100 or £250. Savings on premiums can be quite appreciable, so it is certainly worth asking your insurance company what terms they offer. If these are not very attractive, it could pay you to shop around for a better deal.

Raising money on your home

The problem for many retired people is that they are 'asset rich, cash poor', with their main asset being their home. As a result, many retired owner-occupiers have substantial amounts of money tied up in their homes while they struggle to make ends meet on reduced incomes. One way round the dilemma is to sell up and move somewhere smaller in order to provide extra income. For those who prefer to stay put, however, there are a number of schemes that enable people to unlock capital without having to move. Generally known as 'equity release plans', these usually fall into one of three categories: reversion schemes, lifetime mortgages and home income plans. While all have their attractions, no such scheme is without its drawbacks, so it is essential to make sure that you fully understand all the financial implications – including how the plan may affect your estate – before entering into any agreement.

A crucial point to check is that any plan you are considering carries an absolute guarantee of your being able to remain in your home for as long as you need or want to do so. In the past, many elderly people tragically lost their homes as a result of ill-advised and dangerous schemes. Today it is extremely unlikely that you would be offered a high-risk plan, because in October 2004 all lifetime mortgages and home income plans came under the regulation of the FSA. Where your home is concerned you simply cannot afford to take any chances. Since April 2007, reversion schemes have also come under the regulation of the FSA.

Home reversion schemes

Home reversion schemes work as follows. You sell the ownership of all or part of your home to the reversion company for an agreed sum of money and additionally retain the right to live in the property for the rest of your life or until the plan comes to an end owing to the need for long-term care. You will not be charged any interest payments, and normally the setting-up costs are fairly low. However, the downside is that the money you receive from the sale will be substantially less than the current market value of your home. The price paid will reflect the fact that it could be a great many years before the reversion company can realize its investment. The longer you live, the more value you will get from the scheme. If your life expectancy is not that great, a particular point to query is whether there are any benefit guarantees in the event of early death. Home reversion plans are offered by:

Aviva Equity Release (formerly Norwich Union), Tel: 0800 015 4015; www. aviva.co.uk.
Bridgewater Equity Release Ltd, Tel: 0808 1001 065; www.bridgewaterequity release.co.uk.
Hodge Equity Release, Tel: 0800 7314 076; e-mail: info@hodgelifetime.com; www.hodgelifetime.com.
Home & Capital, Tel: 0800 253 657; e-mail: enquiries@homecapital.co.uk; www.homecapital.co.uk.
In Retirement Services, Tel: 0800 70 75 80; www.inretirementservices.co.uk.
Key Retirement Solutions, Tel: 0800 531 6027; www.keyrs.co.uk.
LV=, Tel: 0870 6090 616; www.lv.com.
Partnership Home Loans, Tel: 0845 1087 240; www.partnershiphomeloans. co.uk.
Retirement Plus Ltd, Tel: 0845 8508 510; e-mail: customerservices@retirement-plus.co.uk; www.retirement-plus.co.uk.

Lifetime mortgages

Lifetime mortgages (sometimes known as 'roll-up loans') advance you a sum of money or regular income or an initial sum plus drawdown facility, on which you pay no interest during your lifetime. Instead, the interest payments are added to the original loan at compound rates and are repaid from your estate on death. While attractive in that recipients can spend the money safe in the knowledge that they will not have to make any repayments, the disadvantage is that compound interest can very quickly mount up, leaving little or nothing for their heirs to inherit. To reduce the risk, particular points to check are, first, that the interest is fixed rather than variable and, even more important, that the plan includes a guarantee that there is no danger to your estate of negative equity. Roll-up loans are offered by:

Aviva Equity Release (formerly Norwich Union), Tel: 0800 015 4015; www. aviva.co.uk.
Hodge Equity Release, Tel: 0800 7314 076; e-mail: info@hodgelifetime.com; www.hodgelifetime.com.
Home & Capital, Tel: 0800 253 657; e-mail: enquiries@homecapital.co.uk; www.homecapital.co.uk.
Just Retirement Ltd, Tel: 01737 233296; e-mail: ifasupport@justretirement. com; www.justretirement.com.
LV=, Tel: 0870 6090 616; www.lv.com.

Home income plans

Home income plans work on the basis of a mortgage arrangement whereby the loan is used to purchase an annuity to provide a guaranteed income for life. The mortgage interest is fixed and is deducted from the annuity payment before you receive your share. While popular at one time, such plans have largely fallen out of favour owing to the abolition of mortgage interest relief and worsening annuity rates. Few people would derive much value and they should really be considered only by those well into their mid-80s. Home income plans are offered by the following companies:

Hodge Equity Release, Tel: 0800 7314 076; e-mail: info@hodgelifetime.com; www.hodgelifetime.com.
Home & Capital, Tel: 0800 253 657; e-mail: enquiries@homecapital.co.uk; www.homecapital.co.uk.
LV=, Tel: 0870 6090 616; www.lv.com.

Cashing in on the value of your home while continuing to live there for the remainder of your life has attractive advantages, especially if the priority is to generate additional income or to provide you with a lump sum. However, expert advice is essential and you should also consult an independent financial adviser (IFA) with expertise in equity release schemes. A welcome safeguard is that the Financial Services Authority, which regulates lifetime mortgages, extended its powers to include home reversion schemes from April 2007.

Using your home to earn money

Rather than move, many people whose home has become too large are tempted by the idea of taking in tenants. For some it is an ideal plan, for others a disaster. At best, it could provide you with extra income and the possibility of pleasant company. At worst, you could be involved in a lengthy legal battle to regain possession of your property. Before you either rush off to put a card in the newsagent's window or reject the idea out of hand, it is helpful to understand the different options, together with your various rights and responsibilities.

There are three broad choices: taking in paying guests or lodgers, letting part of your home as self-contained accommodation, or renting the whole house for a specified period of time. In all cases for your own protection it is essential to have a written agreement and to take up bank references, unless the let is a strictly temporary one where the money is paid in advance. Otherwise, rent should be collected quarterly and you should arrange a hefty deposit to cover any damage. An important point to be aware of is that there is now a set of strict rules concerning the treatment of deposits, with the risk of large fines for landlords and agents who fail to abide by them.

In a move to encourage more people to let out rooms in their home, the government allows you to earn up to £4,250 a year free of tax. Any excess rental income you receive over £4,250 will be assessed for tax in the normal way. For further information, see leaflet IR 87, *Letting a Room in Your Home*, available from any tax office. If you have a mortgage or are a tenant yourself (even with a very long lease), check with your building society or landlord that you are entitled to sublet.

Paying guests or lodgers

This is the most informal arrangement, and will normally be either a casual holiday-type bed-and-breakfast let or a lodger who might be with you for a couple of years. In either case, the visitor will be sharing part of your home, the accommodation will be fully furnished, and you will be providing at least one full meal a day and possibly also basic cleaning services.

There are few legal formalities involved in these types of lettings, and rent is entirely a matter for friendly agreement. As a resident owner you are also in a very strong position if you want your lodger to leave. Lodging arrangements can easily be ended, as your lodger has no legal rights to stay after the agreed period. A wise precaution is to check with your insurance company that your home contents policy will not be affected, since some insurers restrict cover to households with lodgers. Also, unless you make arrangements to the contrary, you should inform your lodger that his or her possessions are not covered by your policy.

NB: if, as opposed to a lodger or the occasional summer paying guest, you offer regular B&B accommodation, you could be liable to pay Business Rates. Although this is not new, it appears that in recent years the Valuation Office Agency has been enforcing the regulation more strictly against people running B&B establishments.

Holiday lets

It is a good idea to register with your tourist information centre and to contact the environmental health office at your local council for any help and advice.

Useful reading

Want to Rent a Room? housing leaflet, available from local libraries, housing advice centres and Citizens Advice Bureau.
The Complete Guide to Letting Property by Liz Hodgkinson, published by Kogan Page, £10.99 (website: www.koganpage.com).

Letting rooms in your home

You could convert a basement or part of your house into a self-contained flat and let this either furnished or unfurnished. Alternatively, you could let a single room or rooms. As a general rule, provided you continue to live in the house your tenant(s) have little security of tenure and equally do not have the right to appeal against the rent. Whether you are letting part of the house as a flat or simply a room to a lodger, you would be advised to check your home contents policy with your insurance company. For more details, see the housing booklet *Letting Rooms in Your Home – A Guide for Resident Landlords* available from The Department for Communities and Local Government, Tel: 020 7944 4400, e-mail: contactus@communities.gov.uk; website: www.communities.gov.uk/publications/housing.

As a resident landlord, you have a guaranteed right to repossession of your property. If the letting is for a fixed term (eg six months or a year), the let will automatically cease at the end of that fixed period. If the arrangement is on a more ad hoc basis with no specified leaving date, it may be legally necessary to give at least four weeks' notice in writing. The position over notices to quit will vary according to circumstances. For further information, see the housing booklet *Notice that You Must Leave* (see Useful reading, below). Should you encounter any difficulties, it is possible that you may need to apply to the courts for an eviction order.

Tax note

If you subsequently sell your home, you may not be able to claim exemption from Capital Gains Tax on the increase in value of a flat if it is entirely self-contained. It is therefore a good idea to retain some means of access to the main house or flat, but take legal advice as to what will qualify.

Renting out your home on a temporary basis

If you are thinking of spending the winter in the sun or are considering buying a retirement home that you will not occupy for a year or two, you might be tempted by the idea of letting the whole house. In spite of the changes in the Housing Act 1996, there are plenty of horror stories of owners who could not regain possession of their own property when they wished to return.

For your protection, you need to understand the assured shorthold tenancy rules. Unless notified in advance that you need the property back sooner (there are very few grounds on which you can make this notification) or unless earlier possession is sought because of the tenant's behaviour, your tenant has the right to stay for at least six months and must be given two months' notice before you want the tenancy to end.

It is strongly advisable to ask a solicitor or letting agent to help you draw up the agreement. Although this provides for greater protection, you will probably still require a court possession order if your tenant will not leave after you have given the required amount of notice. The accelerated possession procedure may help in some cases to speed up the process.

In most circumstances, by far the safest solution if possible is to let your property to a company rather than to private individuals, since company tenants do not have the same security of tenure. However, it is important that the contract should make clear that your let is for residential, not business, purposes. Before entering into any agreement, you might find it useful to obtain a copy of the booklet *Assured and Assured Shorthold Tenancies – A Guide for Landlords*, available from your local housing department, or from DCLG, Tel: 020 7944 4400; e-mail: contactus@communities.gov.uk; website: www.communities.gov.uk. (*NB:* the leaflet is about letting to individuals, not companies.)

Holiday lets

Buying a future retirement home in the country and renting it out as a holiday home in the summer months is another option worth considering. As well as providing you with a weekend cottage at other times of the year and the chance to establish yourself and make friends in the area, it can prove a useful and profitable investment.

As long as certain conditions are met, income from furnished holiday lettings enjoys most – but not all – of the benefits that there would be if it were taxed as trading income rather than as investment income. In practical terms, this means that you can claim 25 per cent writing-down capital allowances on such items as carpets, curtains and furniture as well as fixtures and fittings, thereby reducing the initial cost of equipping the house. This allowance is being reduced to 10 per cent, which will hit property owners badly. Alternatively, you can claim an annual 10 per cent wear and tear allowance. The running expenses of a holiday home, including maintenance, advertising, insurance cover and Council Tax (or Business Rates – see below), are all largely allowable for tax, excluding that element that relates to your own occupation of the property. Since independent taxation was introduced, married couples should consider whether the property be held in the husband's name or the wife's name, or owned jointly. A solicitor or accountant will be able to advise you.

To qualify as furnished holiday accommodation, the property must be situated in the UK, be let on a commercial basis, be available for holiday letting for at least 140 days during the tax year and be actually let for at least 70 days. Moreover, for at least seven months a year, not necessarily continuous, the property must not normally be occupied by the same tenant for more than 31 consecutive days. This still leaves you with plenty of time to enjoy the property yourself.

The usual word of warning, however: there is always the danger that you might create an assured tenancy, so do take professional advice on drawing up the letting agreement. Similarly, if you decide to use one of the holiday rental agents to market your property, get a solicitor to check any contract you enter into with the company. **RICS (Royal Institution of Chartered Surveyors)**, Tel: 0870 3331 600; website: www.rics.org, has a useful set of guidelines for managing agents called *Code of Practice for Management of Residential Property*.

A further point to note is that tax inspectors are taking a tougher line as to what is 'commercial', and loss-making ventures are being threatened with withdrawal of their tax advantages. To safeguard yourself, it is important to draw up a broad business plan before you start and to make a real effort to satisfy the minimum letting requirements. In particular, you should be aware that HMRC has been targeting landlords in the belief that many have been failing to declare their rental income or have over-calculated the amount of tax relief to which they are entitled. Even for innocent mistakes, the likely penalty is the same sum as the amount of tax due – so, if you owe £1,000, it could cost you £2,000.

Tenants' deposits

The Tenancy Deposit Scheme came into force in April 2007 and affects all landlords who let out property under an assured shorthold tenancy. Its purpose is variously to ensure tenants get back the amount owing to them, to make any disputes about the deposit easier to resolve and to encourage tenants to look after the property during the agreed term of their let. The big difference as a result of this new law is that, instead of simply holding the deposit until all or part of it is due to be returned, landlords or agents must now protect it under an approved scheme. Failure to do so within 14 days of receiving the money could result in the landlord being forced to pay the tenant three times the deposit amount.

Landlords and agents have a choice of three approved scheme providers, two of which are insurance-based schemes: Tenancy Deposit Solutions Ltd and the Tenancy Deposit Scheme, and one, the Deposit Protection Service, that provides what is known as 'custodial deposit protection'. With insurance-based schemes, landlords keep the deposit but pay the scheme to insure against their failing to repay the tenant any money due to him or her. The custodial service is free but requires the landlord to put the deposit into the scheme at the start of the tenancy, where it is held until such time as any money is due to be repaid.

In the event of a dispute over the return of the deposit, the custodial scheme will continue to hold the disputed amount until the Alternative Dispute Resolution Service (ADR) or the courts decide what is fair. With insurance-based schemes, the disputed amount must be handed over to the scheme for safekeeping until the amount is resolved by the scheme's ADR service. Both types of ADR service are free to the landlord.

The telephone numbers of the three schemes are **The Deposit Protection Service**: 0870 7071 707; **Tenancy Deposit Solutions Ltd**: 0871 7030 055; and the **Tenancy Deposit Scheme**: 0845 2267 837, or for further information, visit the government website at www.direct.gov.uk/en/Tenancydeposit.

Finally, property that is rented 'commercially' (ie for 140 days or more a year) is normally liable for Business Rates, instead of the Council Tax you would otherwise pay. This could be more expensive, even though partially allowable against tax.

Useful reading

Housing booklets *Letting Rooms in Your Home* and *Notice that You Must Leave*, available from local authority housing departments or DCLG, Tel: 020 7944 4400; e-mail: contactus@communities.gov.uk; website: www.communities.gov.uk.

Benefits and taxes

Housing Benefit

Provided you have no more than £16,000 in savings, you may be able to get help with your rent from your local council. You may qualify for Housing Benefit whether you are a council or private tenant or live in a hotel or hostel. Housing Benefit is fairly complicated and the following outline is intended only as a very general guide. For more detailed advice about your own particular circumstances, contact your local authority or your Citizens Advice Bureau or Age Concern group.

The amount of benefit you get depends on five factors: the number of people in your household; your eligible rent (up to a prescribed maximum); your capital or savings; your income; and your 'applicable amount', which is the amount of money the government considers you need for basic living expenses. These are defined roughly as follows.

Eligible rent

This includes rent and some service charges related to the accommodation but excludes meals, water rates and, as a rule, fuel costs. An amount will generally also be deducted for any adult 'non-dependant' (including an elderly relative) living in your household, based on a reasonable contribution on their part towards housing costs. This does not apply to commercial boarders or sub-tenants – but any income from a boarder or sub-tenant will be taken into account.

Capital

Any capital or savings up to £6,000 will be disregarded and will not affect your entitlement to benefit. People with savings or capital between £6,000 and £16,000 will receive some benefit, but this will be on a sliding scale, with every £500 (or part of £500) over £6,000 assessed as being equivalent to an extra £1 a week of their income. (See the paragraph below starting 'If your income is less than your applicable amount…'.) This is called 'tariff income'. If you have savings of more than £16,000, you will not be eligible for Housing Benefit at all. 'Capital' generally includes all savings, bonds, stocks and shares and property other than your own home and personal possessions. The capital limits are the same for a couple as for a single person.

Income

Income includes earnings, social security benefits, pension income and any other money you have coming in after tax and National Insurance Contributions have been paid. While most income counts when calculating your entitlement to Housing Benefit (NB: a couple's income is added together), some income may be ignored, for example: all Disability Living Allowance and Attendance Allowance; the first £5 of earnings (single person), £10 of earnings (couple) or £20 of earnings if your 'applicable amount' includes a disability premium or carer's premium; and a £25 disregard for lone parents. War pensions are also ignored in part.

Applicable amount

Your 'applicable amount' will generally be the same as any benefit to cover weekly living expenses you would be eligible for and consists of: your personal allowance, and personal allowances for any younger children (normally those for whom you are receiving Child Benefit), plus any premiums (ie additional amounts for pensioners, the disabled and so on) to which you might be entitled. Details of allowances and premium rates are contained in leaflet GL 23 from any housing benefit office.

If your income is less than your applicable amount you will receive maximum Housing Benefit towards your eligible rent (less any non-dependant deduction). You may be eligible for Income Support if your capital is less than £8,000, or less than £16,000 if you are aged 60 or over. If your income is equal to your applicable amount you will also receive maximum Housing Benefit. If your income is higher than your applicable amount, a taper adjustment will be made and maximum Housing Benefit will be reduced by 65 per cent of the difference between your income and your applicable amount. If this leaves you with Housing Benefit of less than 50p a week, it is not paid.

How to claim

If you think you are eligible for benefit (see leaflets GL16 and GL17 available from any Housing Benefit office), ask your council for an application form. It should let you know within 14 days of receiving your completed application whether you are entitled to benefit, and will inform you of the amount. See websites: www.dwp.gov.uk and www.direct.gov.uk.

Special accommodation

If you live in a mobile home or houseboat, you may be able to claim benefit for site fees or mooring charges. If you live in a private nursing or residential care home you will not normally be able to get Housing Benefit to help with the cost. However, you may be able to get help towards both the accommodation part of your fees and your living expenses through Income Support or possibly under the Community Care arrangements. If you make a claim for Income Support you can claim Housing Benefit and Council Tax Benefit at the same time. A claim form for these is included inside the Income Support claim form. When completed, the form is returned to your local authority.

Useful reading

Leaflet RR 2, *A Guide to Housing Benefit and Council Tax Benefit*, free from your council.
Housing Benefit and Council Tax Benefit, free fact sheet from Age Concern, Tel: 0800 009 966; website: www.ageconcern.org.uk.

Council Tax

Council Tax is based on the value of the dwelling in which you live (the property element) and also consists of a personal element – with discounts and exemptions applying to certain groups of people.

The property element

Most domestic properties are liable for Council Tax, including rented property, mobile homes and houseboats. The value of the property is assessed according to a banding system, with eight different bands (A to H). The banding of each property is determined by the government's Valuation Office Agency based on prices applying at 1 April 1991, except for Wales, where revaluation took effect in April 2003. Small extensions or other improvements made after this date do not affect the valuation until the property changes hands. New homes in England and Scotland are banded as if they had already been built and sold on 1 April 1991, in order to be consistent. The planned Council Tax revaluation in England, due to take place in 2007, was postponed.

Notification of the band is shown on the bill when it is sent out in April. If you think there has been a misunderstanding about the valuation (or your liability to pay the full amount) you may have the right of appeal (see 'Appeals', page 173).

Liability

Not everyone pays Council Tax. The bill is normally sent to the resident owner or joint owners of the property or, in the case of rented accommodation, to the tenant or joint tenants. Married couples and people with a shared legal interest in the property are jointly liable for the bill, unless they are students or severely mentally impaired. In some cases, for example in hostels or multi-occupied property, a non-resident landlord or owner will be liable but may pass on a share of the bill to the tenants or residents, which would probably be included as part of the rental charge.

The personal element

The valuation of each dwelling assumes that two adults will be resident. The charge does not increase if there are more adults. However if, as in many homes, there is a single adult, your Council Tax bill will be reduced by 25 per cent. Certain people are disregarded when determining the number of residents in a household. There are also a number of other special discounts or exemptions, as follows:

- People who are severely mentally impaired are disregarded or, if they are the sole occupant of the dwelling, qualify for an exemption.
- Disabled people whose homes require adaptation may have their bill reduced to a lower band.
- People on Income Support should normally have nothing to pay, as their bill will be met in full by Council Tax Benefit.
- Disabled people on higher-rate Attendance Allowance need not count a full-time carer as an additional resident and therefore may continue to qualify for

the 25 per cent single (adult) householder discount. Exceptions are spouses or partners and parents of a disabled child under 18 who would normally be living with the disabled person and whose presence therefore would not be adding to the Council Tax.

● Young people over 18 but still at school are not counted when assessing the number of adults in a house.
● Students living in halls of residence, student hostels or similar are exempted; those living with a parent or other non-student adult are eligible for the 25 per cent personal discount.
● Service personnel living in barracks or married quarters will not receive any bill for Council Tax.

Discounts and exemptions applying to property

Certain property is either exempt from Council Tax or is eligible for a discount.

Discounts. Until April 2004, there was a standard 50 per cent discount on second homes and long-term empty property (except in Wales, where councils could charge the full amount on second homes if they wished). However, you can no longer count on this as, in England, councils now have the power to charge owners of second homes up to 90 per cent of the standard rate, and owners of long-term empty property up to 100 per cent.

Exemptions. The most common cases of exemptions include:

● Property that has been unoccupied and unfurnished for less than six months.
● The home of a deceased person; the exemption lasts until six months after the grant of probate.
● A home that is empty because the occupier is absent in order to care for someone else.
● The home of a person who is or would be exempted from Council Tax because of moving to a residential home, hospital care or similar.
● Empty properties in need of major repairs or undergoing structural alteration can be exempt from Council Tax for an initial period of six months, but this can be extended for a further six months. After 12 months, the standard 50 (or possibly full 100) per cent charge for empty properties will apply.
● Granny flats that are part of another private domestic dwelling may be exempt, but this depends on access and other conditions. To check, contact your local Valuation Office.

Business-cum-domestic property

Business-cum-domestic property is rated according to usage, with the business section assessed for Business Rates and the domestic section for Council Tax. For example, where there is a flat over a shop, the value of the shop will not be included in the valuation for Council Tax. Likewise, a room in a house used for business purposes will be subject to Business Rates and not to Council Tax.

Appeals

If you become the new person responsible for paying the Council Tax (eg because you have recently moved or because someone else paid the tax before) on a property that you feel has been wrongly banded, you have six months to appeal and can request that the valuation be reconsidered. Otherwise, there are only three other circumstances in which you can appeal: 1) if there has been a material increase or reduction in the property's value; 2) if you start, or stop, using part of the property for business or the balance between domestic and business use changes; 3) if either of the latter two apply and the listing officer has altered the Council Tax list without giving you a chance to put your side.

If you have grounds for appeal, you should take up the matter with the Valuation Office (see local telephone directory). If the matter is not resolved, you can then appeal to an independent valuation tribunal. For advice and further information, contact your local Citizens Advice Bureau.

Useful reading

Council Tax: A Guide to Your Bill and *Council Tax: A Guide to Valuation, Banding and Appeals*, obtainable free from any council office or from DCLG Free Literature, Tel: 020 7944 4400; e-mail: contactus@communities.gov.uk; website: www. communities.gov.uk.

Council Tax Benefit

If you cannot afford your Council Tax because you have a low income, you may be able to obtain Council Tax Benefit. The help is more generous than many people realize. For example, people on Pension Credit (Guarantee Credit) are entitled to rebates of up to 100 per cent. Even if you are not receiving any other social security benefit, you may still qualify for some Council Tax Benefit. The amount you get depends on your income, savings, personal circumstances, who else lives in your home (in particular whether they would be counted as 'non-dependants') and your net Council Tax bill (ie after any deductions that apply to your home). If you are not sure whether your income is low enough to entitle you to Council Tax Benefit, it is worth claiming, as you could be pleasantly surprised.

If you disagree with your council's decision, you can ask for this to be looked at again (a revision) or you can appeal to an independent appeal tribunal, administered by the Appeals Service. If you are still dissatisfied, you may apply for leave to appeal to the Social Security Commissioners, but only on a point of law. If you want a revision, you should get on with the matter as soon as possible, as if you delay your request may be out of time.

Apart from Council Tax Benefit for yourself, you may also be able to get help with your Council Tax if you share your home with someone who is on a low income. This is known as 'Second Adult Rebate' or 'Alternative Maximum Council Tax Benefit'. For further information, ask your local council for leaflet GL 17, *Help with Your Council Tax*. As well as the English version, this is available in 11 other languages.

Useful organizations

The following should be able to provide general advice about housing and help with housing problems:

- local authority housing departments;
- housing advice or housing aid centres;
- Citizens Advice Bureau;
- local authority social service departments if your problem is linked to disability;
- welfare rights centres if your problem, for example, concerns a landlord who does not keep the property properly maintained;
- leasehold valuation tribunals if there are serious problems with the management of the building;
- local councillors and MPs.

Other organizations that provide a helpful service are:

CHAS Central London. CHAS serves anyone in acute housing need regardless of race or religion. It provides free information, advice and advocacy on housing, homelessness, debt and welfare benefits issues. Tel: 020 7723 5928; e-mail: advice@chascl.org.uk; website: www.chascl.org.uk.

The Federation of Private Residents' Associations Ltd (FPRA) is a federation of associations of long leaseholders and tenants in private blocks of flats. It advises on setting up residents' associations and provides legal and other advice to its member associations. It issues quarterly newsletters and information sheets, publishes a pack on how to form a tenants' or residents' association (price £15 including postage and packing) and acts as a pressure group seeking to influence legislation regarding leasehold and management of flats in the private sector. FPRA also gives advice on buying the freehold and on management of collectively owned blocks of flats. Tel: 0871 2003 324; e-mail: info@fpra.org.uk; website: www.fpra.org.uk.

Shelter. The National Campaign for Homeless People, Shelter, provides advice to over 100,000 badly housed and homeless people every year through a national network of housing aid centres and a free 24-hour housing helpline: Tel: 0808 8004 444; e-mail: info@shelter.org.uk; website: www.shelter.org.uk.

9

Leisure activities

Now that retirement is approaching (or has already arrived), are you looking forward to all the free time you will have? Some people who take their retirement seriously will have made lists of all the things they are going to do, once the daily commute or work routine has ceased. Depending on your sphere of interest, there are more opportunities than time available to pursue hobbies, travel to new places, take up sport activities or do some volunteering. Most people over 60 wonder how they ever found time to go to work. The over-55s are a growth industry; current statistics show that there are far fewer under-16-year-olds in comparison. As a result the choice of leisure pursuits is enormous. No wonder that there are endless opportunities for almost every kind of leisure activity. The only problem is likely to be fitting everything in.

This chapter deals with spare-time activities, sport and holidays, but all are interrelated. Many holidays, for example, involve special interest groups and tours, while other hobbies and pastimes involve short courses or visits to places of interest. Additionally there are volunteering opportunities for retired people who wish to make a valuable contribution within their own community or beyond. You might consider visiting the elderly in their own homes, driving patients to hospital, running a holiday play scheme, helping out at your local Citizens Advice Bureau or becoming a Samaritan. Other ideas that might appeal are conservation work or playing a more active role in local politics. Whatever amount of time you have available, there is bound to be something suitable on offer. Most organizations offer special concessionary rates to people of retirement age, as do a number of theatres and other places of entertainment. Given the immense variety of tantalizing options available, it's not surprising that many retired people find they have never been so busy in their lives.

What hobbies do you have? When you are not working, what do you enjoy doing as a leisure activity? Now that retirement is approaching, or has already arrived, are you looking forward to studying for a degree or trying your hand at an entirely new pastime? The good news is that the choice is enormous. You can do anything from basket-weaving to bridge, archery to amateur dramatics. You can join a music-making group, a Scrabble club or a film society, or become a beekeeper. If you are interested in heritage, there are any number of historic homes and beautiful gardens to visit, as well as museums, art galleries, abbeys and castles. Additionally, almost every locality now has excellent sports facilities and there is scope for complete novices to take up bowls, golf, badminton, croquet and many others. Similarly, there are dancing and keep fit classes, railway enthusiasts' clubs and groups devoted to researching their local history.

This chapter should be read in conjunction with Chapter 14, Holidays, as many of the organizations listed there – such as the Field Studies Council – would be equally relevant here. However, to avoid repetition, most are described only once. Those that appear in Chapter 14 either tend in the main to offer residential courses or would probably involve most people in spending a few days away from home to take advantage of the facilities. While every effort at the time of writing has been made to ensure that any prices that are included are correct, these cannot be guaranteed. For safety it is best to consult the website of the relevant organizations or e-mail them for their latest information.. The reason for mentioning this is that most organizations alter their charges from time to time and, since there is no set date when this happens, it is impossible to keep completely up to date. Whatever prices are quoted are the latest figures given by the particular organization.

Adult education

Have you ever longed to take a degree, learn about computing, study philosophy or do a course in archaeology? Opportunities for education abound, and there are scores of other subjects easily available to everyone, regardless of age or previous qualifications.

Adult education institutes

There is an adult education institute (AEI) in most areas of the country. Classes normally start in September and run through the academic year. Many AEIs allow concessionary fees for students over 60. Despite some recent cutbacks, the choice of subjects is still enormous; at one institute alone we counted over 50 options, ranging from Indian history, video production and creative writing to self-defence, calligraphy, dressmaking and drama. Ask at your local library for details. For courses in London, consult Floodlight; the helpline number is 0800 100 900; website: www.london.floodlight.co.uk. The following website gives further information: www.careersadvice.direct.gov.uk. Other organizations are as follows:

National Adult School Organisation (NASO) promotes 'Conversation with a Purpose' through friendly discussion groups, meeting at places and times to suit the members. They follow either the NASO Handbook programme, topics of their own choice or a mixture of the two. Social activities and weekend conferences are organized regionally. For information about your nearest group contact NASO's General Secretary, Tel: 0116 253 8333; e-mail: GenSec@naso.org.uk; website: www.naso.org.uk.

National Extension College (NEC) was set up over 40 years ago as a not-for-profit organization to help people of all ages fit learning into their lives. Many of NEC's most able students are retired and are returning to study after many years. There is a choice of over 100 courses, including GCSE and A-level studies, personal development, childcare, bookkeeping, creative writing, arts, modern languages, counselling and many others. A student adviser can offer guidance on any aspect of your study plans and help you make an appropriate choice. Contact the NEC, Tel: 0800 3892 839; e-mail: info@nec.ac.uk; website: www.nec.ac.uk.

Open and Distance Learning Quality Council (ODLQC) provides home study, distance learning, online or e-learning and other open learning or flexible learning courses. Its list includes colleges that teach your chosen subject, plus general advice on open and distance learning courses. The choice of subjects is enormous and, as well as academic and business subjects, includes such options as art, creative writing, graphology, needlework and sailing. Contact ODLQC, Tel: 020 7612 7090; e-mail: info@odlqc.org.uk; website: www.odlqc.org.uk.

Open University (OU). Why not take a degree or other qualification through the Open University? Students are all ages (the oldest OU graduate was 92), most courses require no academic qualifications and there is a wide range of subjects from which to choose. Courses normally involve a mix of correspondence work, online learning, audio- and videotapes, and contact with local tutors. Some courses have a residential school. You can study at your own speed: on average people take up to six or eight years to get a degree. However, there is no long-term commitment and, if you wish, you can sign on just for one course.

The Open University also offers a range of short courses that are designed to give you a flavour of OU study if you want to try out a subject before committing yourself to a longer course. These can be a week's full-time residential course (with some part-time study before and after) or a part-time course lasting between eight and 20 weeks. As well as being interesting in their own right, they can count towards an Open University degree, if you wish to continue. Fees range from around £125 for a short course to in excess of £500 for a standard nine-month course. Individuals who would have difficulty in paying may be eligible for financial support. There are also special allowances (DSAs) available to students who might be prevented from studying because of a disability, to help with the extra costs of services and facilities. For more information on the OU, Tel: 0845 300 60 90; website: www.open.ac.uk.

University extra-mural departments – non-degree and short courses

Many universities have a department of extra-mural studies that arranges courses for adults, sometimes in the evening or during vacation periods; here are a few:

Birkbeck, University of London, Faculty of Lifelong Learning, offers over 1,000 part-time courses in a range of subjects, including literature and drama, music, philosophy, history, sociology and psychology. Classes normally meet once a week, and students are required to do reading and written work. Fees vary according to the length of the course, and many offer concessions to those whose main source of income is a State pension or government benefit. Contact Birkbeck on 0845 6010 174; e-mail: info@bbk.ac.uk; website: www.bbk.ac.uk. For other universities, enquire locally.

Third Age Trust, U3A (The University of the Third Age) is a self-help movement for people no longer in full-time employment, offering a wide range of educational, creative and leisure activities. It operates through a national network of local U3As, each of which determines its own courses and social programmes according to the interests of its members. There is also a national magazine, *U3A News*, which is published four times a year. For a brochure, together with a list of names and addresses of all local U3As, Tel: 020 8466 6139; e-mail: national.office@u3a.org.uk; website: www.u3a.org.uk.

Workers' Educational Association (WEA) is the UK's largest voluntary sector provider of adult learning. Founded over 100 years ago, its members come from all walks of life and share a belief in the value of education and lifelong learning for all adults, regardless of circumstance. It offers a wide range of courses, including education for retirement. Currently there are over 19,000 members. For further information contact the National Membership Department, WEA, Tel: 020 7426 3450; e-mail: membership@wea.org.uk; website: www.wea.org.uk.

Animals

If you are an animal lover, you may already know about such events as sheepdog trials and gymkhanas, and the many wildlife sanctuaries around the country. Our list is effectively limited to 'the birds and the bees', with just a couple of extra suggestions for fun:

British Beekeepers' Association runs correspondence courses and practical demonstrations and will be glad to put you in touch with one of the 60 local organizations. Tel: 024 7669 6679; website: www.britishbee.org.uk.

Our Dogs Publishing has information if you would enjoy showing a dog. The weekly newspaper *Our Dogs* gives details of local shows, rule and registration changes and also news and addresses of canine and breed societies all over the country. There is an Our Dogs diary, which contains feeding and other hints, advice about the Kennel Club and much other useful information. Contact Our Dogs on 0870 7316 503; e-mail: subs@ourdogs.co.uk; website: www.ourdogs. co.uk.

Wildfowl & Wetlands Trust (WWT) works to conserve threatened wetland birds and their habitats. In addition to Slimbridge, there are visitor centres in Lancashire, Sussex, Tyne and Wear, the Cambridgeshire/Norfolk border, London, Dumfriesshire, South Wales and Northern Ireland. Membership gives you free entry to all WWT centres plus a quarterly magazine. There is wheelchair access to all centres and grounds and many hides. For further information contact WWT on 01453 891900; e-mail: enquiries@wwt.org.uk; website: www.wwt.org.uk. See also 'Animals' in Chapter 12 (page 267).

Arts

Enjoyment of the arts is not confined to London. Whether you are interested in active participation or just appreciating the performance of others, there is an exhilarating choice of events, including theatre, music, exhibitions, film-making and so on. Many entertainments offer concessionary prices to retired people.

Regional Arts Council offices

For first-hand information about what is going on in your area, contact your regional Arts Council office (see the national website – www.artscouncil.org.uk, or telephone 0845 300 6200; e-mail: enquiries@artscouncil.org.uk). Most areas arrange an immensely varied programme with musical events, drama, arts and craft exhibitions and sometimes more unusual functions, offering something of interest to just about everyone. Many regional Arts Councils produce regular newsletters with details of arts information in their area:

Arts Council England, East. Area covered: Bedfordshire, Cambridgeshire, Essex, Hertfordshire, Norfolk, Suffolk, and the unitary authorities of Luton, Peterborough, Southend-on-Sea and Thurrock.

Arts Council England, East Midlands. Area covered: Derbyshire, Leicestershire, Lincolnshire (excluding North and North East Lincolnshire), Northamptonshire, Nottinghamshire, and the unitary authorities of Derby, Leicester, Nottingham and Rutland.

Arts Council England, London. Area covered: Greater London.

Arts Council England, North East. Area covered: Durham, Northumberland, the metropolitan authorities of Gateshead, Newcastle-upon-Tyne, North Tyneside, South Tyneside and Sunderland, and the unitary authorities of Darlington, Hartlepool, Middlesbrough, Redcar and Cleveland, and Stockton-on-Tees.

Arts Council England, North West. Area covered: Cheshire, Cumbria, Lancashire, the metropolitan authorities of Bolton, Bury, Knowsley, Liverpool, Manchester, Oldham, Rochdale, St Helens, Salford, Sefton, Stockport, Tameside, Trafford, Wigan and Wirral, and the unitary authorities of Blackburn with Darwen, Blackpool, Halton and Warrington.

Arts Council England, South East. Area covered: Buckinghamshire, East Sussex, Hampshire, Isle of Wight, Kent, Oxfordshire, Surrey, West Sussex, and the unitary authorities of Bracknell Forest, Brighton and Hove, Medway Towns, Milton Keynes, Portsmouth, Reading, Slough, Southampton, West Berkshire, Windsor and Maidenhead, and Wokingham.

Arts Council England, South West. Area covered: Cornwall, Devon, Dorset, Gloucestershire, Somerset, Wiltshire, and the unitary authorities of Bath and North East Somerset, Bournemouth, Bristol, North Somerset, Plymouth, Poole, South Gloucestershire, Swindon and Torbay.

Arts Council England, West Midlands. Area covered: Shropshire, Staffordshire, Warwickshire, Worcestershire, the metropolitan authorities of Birmingham, Coventry, Dudley, Sandwell, Solihull, Walsall and Wolverhampton, and the unitary authorities of Herefordshire, Stoke-on-Trent, Telford and Wrekin.

Arts Council England, Yorkshire. Area covered: North Yorkshire, the metropolitan authorities of Barnsley, Bradford, Calderdale, Doncaster, Kirklees, Leeds, Rotherham, Sheffield and Wakefield, and the unitary authorities of East Riding of Yorkshire, Kingston upon Hull, North East Lincolnshire, North Lincolnshire and York.

For those who wish to join in with amateur arts activities, public libraries keep lists of choirs, drama clubs, painting clubs and similar in their locality.

Films

The cinema is hugely popular as an art form. If the only films showing in your area are the latest releases, you might think of joining a film society or perhaps taking a trip to the National Film Theatre to view some of the great performances of the past or to see some of the excellent foreign films that are rarely shown outside London. Here are some other ideas:

British Federation of Film Societies (BFFS) – Cinema for All. BFFS is the national organization for the development, support and representation of film societies (of which there are over 300) throughout the UK. Most offer reduced rates for senior citizens. Contact details can be obtained from BFFS. If, as a growing number of people are, you are interested in forming a local film society with a group of friends and neighbours, contact the BFFS Central Office for information on equipment, money and how to get started. Tel: 0114 221 0314; e-mail: info@bffs.org.uk; website: www.bffs.org.uk.

BFI Southbank shows some 2,000 films a year at the BFI's three cinemas. Contact the Box Office booking line, Tel: 020 7928 3232.

British Film Institute (BFI) membership, from £20 annually, is available from the BFI. Tel: 020 7815 1374; website: www.bfi.org.uk.

Music and ballet

The scope ranges from becoming a Friend and supporting one of the famous 'Houses' such as Covent Garden to music-making in your own right. If you live close enough to take advantage of the 'perks', subscribing as a Friend allows you a number of very attractive advantages, including in all cases priority for bookings:

Friends of Covent Garden. Friends receive regular mailings of news and information, and free copies of the magazine *About the House*, plus opportunities to attend talks, recitals, study days, master classes and some 'open' rehearsals of ballet and opera. For further details contact the Royal Opera House, Tel: 020 7212 9268; e-mail: friends@roh.org.uk; website: www.royalopera.org.

Friends of English National Opera (ENO). As a Friend of ENO, you have the opportunity to apply for tickets for dress rehearsals and to gain an insight into the creation of opera through a variety of special lunchtime and evening events. You also receive advance programme information. For further information and full details contact ENO on 0871 2715 577; e-mail: friends@eno.org; website: www.eno.org.

Friends of Sadler's Wells. Sadler's Wells has an ever-changing programme of ballet, opera and contemporary dance. Friends receive discounts and free ticket offers. For further details contact Sadler's Wells, Tel: 020 7863 8134; e-mail: membership@sadlerswells.com; website: www.sadlerswells.com.

Music-making

Just about every style of music is catered for, from bell-ringing to recorder playing. There is even an orchestra for retired people. Here are some contacts:

Handbell Ringers of Great Britain. The Society, which was formed in 1967, promotes the art of handbell tune ringing and supports handbell, handchime and belleplate players. Concerts, rallies, seminars and workshops are organized. General enquiries should be made through the national secretary (e-mail: sandra@hrgb.org.uk; website: www.hrgb.org.uk).

Making Music, The National Federation of Music Societies can provide you with addresses of some 2,000 affiliated choral societies, orchestras and music societies throughout the country. Most charge a nominal membership fee, and standards range from the semi-professional to the unashamedly amateur. For further details contact Making Music, Tel: 020 7422 8280; e-mail: info@making music.org.uk; website: www.makingmusic.org.uk.

National Association of Choirs. Choirs come in all shapes and sizes, are sometimes informal and sometimes fully functioning societies. Provided you can sing in tune, are keen to learn and the conductor is tolerant, you can really enjoy the emotional satisfaction to be found in group singing as well as gaining the benefit of regular aerobic exercise for lungs and abdominal muscles. Singing is good for you and more fun than jogging. The Association will put you in contact with an amateur choir in your area; Tel: 0844 504 2000; website: www.nationalassociationofchoirs.org.uk.

Society of Recorder Players. The Society has groups in many areas where members play together regularly. The branches welcome players of all standards and ages but do not provide tuition for beginners. There is an annual festival with massed playing, competitions and concerts. For details contact the Membership Secretary, Tel: 01706 853312; e-mail: memsec@srp.org.uk; website: www.srp.org.uk.

Poetry

Poetry used to be a minority interest. However, largely thanks to both the media and the Poetry Society, there has been an increase in enthusiasm about poetry and poetry readings in clubs, pubs and other places of entertainment. Your library should be able to tell you about any special local events.

Poetry Society. Membership of the Society is open to anyone who enjoys reading, listening to or writing poetry. The Society runs a poetry criticism service where, for an agreed fee, you can have your work assessed. Each year the Society organizes a national poetry competition with a first prize of £5,000. Additionally, members receive the Society's quarterly magazines *Poetry Review* and *Poetry News*. For further details, contact the Poetry Society on: 020 7420 9880; e-mail: info@ poetrysociety.org.uk; website: www.poetrysociety.org.uk.

Television and radio audiences

If you would like to be part of the invited studio audience for a BBC radio or television programme you can apply to **BBC Radio and Television Studio Audiences,** Tel: 0370 9011 227; website: www.bbc.co.uk/tickets. Ticket information for programmes outside London should normally be obtainable from the programme direct or via the local BBC studio/office.

For independent television channels, information can be obtained by contacting:

Channel 4 Viewers Enquiries, Tel: 0845 0760 191; website: www.channel4. com.

ITV Viewer Enquiries, Tel: 0844 8814 150; e-mail: bookings@lostintv.com; websites: www.itv.com, www.itvlocal.com.

Ulster TV, Tel: 028 9032 8122; website: www.ulstertv.com.

Theatre

Details of current and forthcoming productions, as well as theatre reviews, are contained in the newspapers. Preview performances are usually cheaper, and there are often concessionary tickets for matinees. Listed here are some theatres and organizations that offer special facilities of interest, including priority booking and reduced price tickets. Also included is an association for enthusiasts of amateur dramatics:

Barbican Centre. The Barbican Centre combines two theatres, a concert hall, two art galleries, three cinemas and a library. There are frequent free live musical events in the foyers, free exhibitions and restaurant facilities. Reduced tickets for senior citizens are available for many concerts and theatre performances and are also given for the art gallery and cinema. Members receive a monthly guide and enjoy advance information and special offers for theatre, music and other events. Contact the Barbican Centre on 0845 1216 823; e-mail: tickets@barbican.org.uk; website: www.barbican.org.uk.

National Theatre. The National Theatre offers backstage tours, talks by theatre professionals, live foyer music before performances, free exhibitions and restaurant facilities, as well as its three theatres. There are group price reductions, and pensioners can also buy midweek matinee tickets at concessionary prices. The National Theatre has a mailing list membership (£10 a year for senior citizens) that provides advance information, priority booking and exclusive special offers. For details, contact the National Theatre, Tel: 020 7452 3500, 10 am to 6 pm, Monday to Friday; e-mail: advance@nationaltheatre.org.uk; website: www. nationaltheatre.org.uk.

Scottish Community Drama Association aims to develop amateur drama in the community by offering clubs and societies advice, encouragement and practical help. Membership gives access to the Association's libraries, training courses and script discounts. The Association also runs playwriting competitions and can put you in touch with local dramatic societies. Members receive regular copies of the house magazine. Contact the Association, Tel: 0131 557 5552; e-mail: headquarters@scda.org.uk; website: www.scda.org.uk.

Society of London Theatre (SOLT). Senior citizens can get substantial reductions for midweek matinee performances at many West End theatres. They can also receive concessionary prices for evening performances or weekend matinees on a standby basis with all listings showing the symbol 'S' in the *London Theatre Guide*. Standby tickets are available approximately an hour before the performance begins. Concessions are subject to availability, and it is always wise to check with the box office to make sure there are tickets before setting off for a performance. When buying tickets on a concessionary basis, you will need to present proof of your senior citizen status at the box office, for example using a travel pass or pension book.

The Society presents the annual Laurence Olivier Awards. Members of the general public serve on the judging panels. If you would like to be considered for the theatre, opera or dance panel, write to the Awards Office, enclosing a stamped addressed envelope, for application forms (available in the autumn). Members of the panels receive two complimentary tickets for all proposed productions during the judging period. Theatre tokens, which are welcome at over 235 theatres nationwide including all London West End theatres, are available by calling **Tokenline** on 0870 1648 800 or by e-mail: enquiries@theatretokens.com; website www.theatretokens.com.

Also extremely useful is the Society's *Disabled Access Guide to London West End Theatres*, which provides information about special facilities, access for wheelchairs, transport advice and price concessions for disabled theatregoers; it is available free from SOLT, Tel: 020 7557 6700; e-mail: enquiries@solttma.co.uk; website: www.officiallondontheatre.co.uk.

Theatre groups are for any age and include play readings, theatre visits and their own productions – depending on the objects of each society. Sufficiently static to avoid expending too much energy – but intellectually and emotionally lively. If you don't belong to a group, but would like to: check the website: www.uktheatre.tv.

TKTS, run by the Society of London Theatres, is a booth, located in Leicester Square, selling tickets to many West End theatres at half-price on the day of the performance. It is open to personal callers only, Monday to Saturday from 10 am to 7 pm, and on Sundays from 12 noon to 3 pm. In the case of matinees, it is open for ticket sales until half an hour before starting time. There is a service charge of £2.50 per ticket. See the website: www.officiallondontheatre.co.uk.

Visual arts

If you enjoy attending exhibitions and lectures, membership of some of the arts societies offers you a number of delightful privileges:

Art Fund. The Art Fund raises money to help museums, galleries and historic houses buy works of art to enrich their collections. The benefits of membership include: free entrance to over 200 museums and galleries; half-price admission to major exhibitions; a countrywide programme of lectures, concerts, private views and other special events, including visits to houses not normally open to the public; and *Art Quarterly* magazine plus an illustrated review of the year's acquisitions. There are also art tours at home and abroad led by experts. For further information, contact the Art Fund on 0870 8482 003; e-mail: members@artfund. org; website: www.artfund.org.

Contemporary Art Society. The aim of the Society is to promote the collecting of contemporary art and to acquire works by living artists for gift to public galleries. Members can take part in an extensive programme of events including visits to artists' studios and private collections, previews and parties at special exhibitions, and trips outside London and overseas. All events are free. Contact the

Society on 020 7831 1243; e-mail: cas@contempart.org.uk; website: www. contempart.org.uk.

National Association of Decorative & Fine Arts Societies (NADFAS). Member societies of NADFAS have programmes of monthly lectures and museum and gallery visits, as well as guided tours of historic houses. Events are usually held in the daytime (although some take place in the evening), and some societies may be able to help with transport. Many societies have volunteer groups working in museums, libraries and historic houses, and there are also church-recording groups that make detailed records of the interiors of churches. Details of your local society are available from NADFAS. Membership of a local society gives access to nationally run study courses, a quarterly magazine and reduced entry to some galleries plus the opportunity to join day events and tours organized both in the UK and abroad. Contact NADFAS, Tel: 020 7430 0730; e-mail: enquiries@nadfas.org.uk; website: www.nadfas.org.uk.

Royal Academy of Arts. Senior citizens enjoy reduced entrance charges to all exhibitions, including the big annual Summer Exhibition. You can become a Friend of the Royal Academy, which gives you free admission to all exhibitions with an adult guest and up to four family children under 16. Friends may also use the Friends' Rooms to meet for coffee and attend exhibition previews. For further information contact the Royal Academy on 020 7300 5664; e-mail: friend.enquiries@royalacademy.org.uk; website: www.royalacademy.org.uk.

Tate Britain and **Tate Modern**. London now boasts two magnificent Tate galleries: Tate Britain at Millbank, which houses the most important collection of British art from 1500 to the present day; and Tate Modern, on the site of the Bankside Power Station at Southwark, which contains international 20th- and 21st-century art, including works by Giacometti, Picasso and Warhol. There are free weekly lectures and guided tours every day, except Sunday, and also special tours for disabled people by prior arrangement. Tate members enjoy free admission to all exhibitions, receipt of *Tate Magazine* and access to the Members' Room, including those at Tate Liverpool and Tate St Ives. For further information, contact the Tate on 020 7887 8888; e-mail: members@tate.org.uk; website: www.tate.org.uk.

Painting as a hobby

If you are interested in improving your own painting technique rather than simply viewing the works of great masters, art courses are available at your local adult education institute. See 'Adult education' at the beginning of this chapter. Your library may have details of painting groups and societies in your area.

Crafts

The vast majority of suggestions are contained in Chapter 14, Holidays, variously under 'Arts and crafts' and 'Special interest holidays', the reason being that most of the organizations concerned make a feature of arranging residential courses or of organizing, for example, painting holidays. However, if you are interested in a particular form of craftwork and want information or advice, many of the societies and others listed in Chapter 14 should be able to help you. Here are a few additional possibilities:

Basketmakers' Association promotes better standards of design and technique in the art of basketmaking, chair seating and allied crafts. It arranges day schools, residential courses, demonstrations and exhibitions. There is a quarterly newsletter. Contact the Association, Tel: 0845 2011 936; website: www.basketassoc.org.

Crafts Council runs an information centre and reference library that can give advice on almost everything you could possibly want to know: different craft courses throughout the country, addresses of craft guilds and societies, and fact sheets on business practice for craftspeople, as well as details of craft fairs and markets, galleries, shops and other outlets for work. Additionally, the Crafts Council has a slide and video library, publishes a bi-monthly magazine, *Crafts*, and maintains an index of craftspeople and the national register of makers. For further information contact the Crafts Council, Tel: 020 7806 2500; website: www.craftscouncil.org.uk.

Open College of the Arts (OCA), which is affiliated to the Open University, offers home study courses for those wishing to acquire or improve skills or gain a higher education qualification. Courses offered include creative digital arts, sculpture, textiles, art and design, creative writing and photography. Course books are supplied, and students have professional tutorial support from artists, writers and designers. Courses cost from around £450. For further information and a free *Guide to Courses*, contact the Open College on 0800 7312 116; e-mail: enquiries@oca-uk.com; website: www.oca-uk.com.

Dance/keep fit

Clubs, classes and groups exist in all parts of the country, variously offering ballroom, old time, Scottish, folk, ballet, disco dancing and others. Additionally, there are music and relaxation classes, aerobics and more gentle keep fit sessions. Many of the relaxation and keep fit classes in particular cater for all standards, and some are specially designed for older people to tone up muscles and improve their circulation while making friends in an agreeable atmosphere. Best advice is to contact your adult education or sports centre. Alternatively, the library may help you to find out what is available in your area. Listed here are some of the national organizations that can advise you and put you in touch with local groups (there are also some extra names in Chapter 13, Health, 'Keeping fit'):

British Dance Council. The Council, which is the governing body of ballroom dancing in Great Britain, can put you in touch with recognized dance schools in your area. Contact the Secretary on 020 8545 0085; e-mail: secretary@british-dance-council.org; website: www.british-dance-council.org.

CCPR, One Voice for Sport and Recreation. The CCPR represents over 270 governing and representative bodies in the sport and recreation sectors. For more information contact the CCPR, Tel: 020 7976 3900; e-mail: info@ccpr.org.uk; website: www.ccpr.org.uk.

English Folk Dance and Song Society. There are some 590 clubs around the country that organize both regular and special events. In addition to ordinary folk dancing, programmes may include country dancing, Morris dancing, 'knees up', clog workshops, musician band sessions, sea shanties, lectures and concerts. Membership includes journals and use of the library. Contact the Society for details of your nearest group, Tel: 020 7485 2206; e-mail: info@efdss.org; website: www.efdss.org.

Imperial Society of Teachers of Dancing. Throughout the UK there are some 7,000 teachers offering instruction in virtually all forms of dancing. Many organize classes and events particularly for older people. The Society has lists of teachers in each geographic area. There is no standard charge, but dance classes and social dancing tend to be inexpensive activities. For further details contact the Society, Tel: 020 7377 1577; e-mail: membership@istd.org; website: www.istd.org.

Keep Fit Association (KFA). The Association offers 'Fitness through Movement, Exercise and Dance' classes, suitable for all ages and abilities. KFA teachers have special training in working with older people. Almost all adult education centres run classes in the daytime; many have special classes for keeping fit in retirement. (See also 'Extend', in Chapter 13, Health.) For more information, contact the Association, Tel: 01403 266000; e-mail: kfa@emdp.org; website: www.keepfit.org.uk.

Royal Scottish Country Dance Society has members from 16 to 80-plus in its many branches and groups all over the world. It publishes books, CDs and DVDs and holds an annual summer school at St Andrew's University. The branches offer instruction at all levels, and members join in dance events. Information about your local branch or group can be obtained by contacting the Society on 0131 225 3854; e-mail: info@rscds.org; website: www.rscds.org.

Games

Many local areas have their own bridge, chess, whist, dominoes, Scrabble and other groups that meet together regularly in a club, hall, pub or other social venue to enjoy friendly games. Competitions are organized and, certainly in the case of bridge and chess, district and county teams are usually taken very seriously. Your library should know about any clubs or regular group meetings. Alternatively, you can contact the national organizations listed below:

English Bridge Union has details of over 1,000 affiliated bridge clubs throughout England. Members receive a wide range of services including a free diary, discounts on cards and other bridge items and six magazines a year, which among other features of interest contain details of tournaments and bridge holidays at home and abroad. For further information, Tel: 01296 317200; e-mail: postmaster@ebu.co.uk; website: www.ebu.co.uk.

English Chess Federation can provide information about chess clubs and tournaments throughout England. Contact the Federation, Tel: 01424 775222; e-mail: office@englishchess.org.uk; website: www.englishchess.org.uk.

Scrabble Clubs UK. There are over 300 Scrabble clubs up and down the country. Some have their own premises and are highly competitive. Others meet in halls or members' houses for a friendly game. Many of them are involved in charitable work, such as raising money for people with disabilities or visiting the housebound. Many competitions are held, including a National Scrabble Championship and a big tournament for clubs. For details of your nearest Scrabble club, e-mail: evan.simpson@absp.org.uk; website: www.absp.org.uk.

Gardens and gardening

Courses, gardens to visit, special help for people with disabilities, and how to run a gardening association; these and other interests are all catered for by the organizations listed:

English Gardening School teaches all aspects of gardening. Courses ranging in length from a day to an academic year are held in the lecture room of the historic Chelsea Physic Garden, a centre for the study of horticulture for over 300 years. Topics include among others: garden design, container gardening, pruning roses, the mixed border and botanical illustration. For further information contact the School on 020 7352 4347; e-mail: info@egs.dircon.co.uk; website: www.english-gardeningschool.co.uk.

Gardening for Disabled Trust and Garden Club provides practical and financial help to disabled people who want to garden actively. The Garden Club publishes a quarterly newsletter, gives answers to horticultural questions and encourages gardeners with disabilities to meet. Contact the Secretary via the website: www.gardeningfordisabledtrust.org.uk.

Garden Organic is Europe's largest organic gardening organization. It encourages environmentally friendly gardening, and its centre is open to visitors throughout the year. One of the major attractions is the vegetable kingdom, which is a fully interactive visitor centre. Individuals can help by experimenting in their own gardens and joining a network of countrywide local groups. Members receive a quarterly magazine, a sales catalogue with discounts, and gardening advice. For further information contact Garden Organic, Tel: 024 7630 3517; e-mail: enquiry@gardenorganic.org.uk; website: www.gardenorganic.org.uk.

National Gardens Scheme covers some 3,500, mostly privately owned, gardens that open to the public a few days a year to raise money for a variety of nursing, caring and gardening charities including Macmillan Cancer Relief, Marie Curie Cancer Care and the Queen's Nursing Institute. Tea is often available, as are plants for sale. For further information contact the Scheme on 01483 211535; e-mail: ngs@ngs.org.uk; website: www.ngs.org.uk.

National Society of Allotment & Leisure Gardeners Ltd. The Society encourages all forms of horticultural education and the forming of local allotment and gardening associations. It also acts as a national voice for allotment and leisure gardeners. Membership gives you access to free help and advice, and the right to attend the annual meeting, plus receipt of the Society's bulletin. There is also a seeds scheme, offering special prices. Leaflets are available on growing vegetables, how to form a gardening association and the running of flower shows. For further information contact the Society, Tel: 01536 266576; e-mail: natsoc@nsalg.org.uk; website: www.nsalg.org.uk.

Royal Horticultural Society. Members enjoy free entry to over 130 gardens across Britain and privileged entry and reduced-rate ticket discounts to RHS flower shows, including both Chelsea and Hampton Court Palace. They also receive a monthly copy of *The Garden* magazine and a free gardening advice service. For further information, contact the Society, Tel: 0845 0621 111; e-mail: membership@rhs.org.uk; website: www.rhs.org.uk.

Scotland's Gardens Scheme supports retired Queen's Nurses, the Gardens Fund of the National Trust for Scotland and other charities through 360 gardens that are open to the public either on one day only or on a regular basis. The booklet giving opening times is widely available, or contact the Scheme, Tel: 0131 226 3714; e-mail: info@sgsgardens.co.uk; website: www.gardensofscotland.org.

Thrive is a small national charity that uses gardening to change lives. It champions the benefits of gardening, carries out research and offers training and practical solutions so that anyone with a disability can take part in, benefit from and enjoy gardening. It will give advice about special tools and where these can be obtained. Thrive also runs garden projects based in Battersea Park, London SW11 and Beech Hill, near Reading, Berkshire. Contact Thrive, Tel: 0118 988 5688; website: www.thrive.org.uk.

History

People with an interest in the past have a truly glorious choice of activities to sample. You can visit historic monuments, including ancient castles and stately homes, in all parts of the country; explore the City of London; study genealogy; research the history of your local area; and attend lectures and receptions. Here are some suggestions:

Age Exchange features exhibitions recording the lifestyles of the 1920s and 1930s. There are also publications depicting the period for visitors to enjoy plus a year-round programme of activities including, for example, reminiscence through the arts, music and drama. The Centre is open Monday to Friday from 10 am to 5 pm, and on Saturday from 10 am to 4 pm. Admission is free. There is a small charge for group bookings. The Centre is fully equipped for disabled access and has a café serving light refreshments. Contact the Centre, Tel: 020 8318 9105; e-mail: administrator@age-exchange.org.uk; website: www.age-exchange.org.uk.

Architectural Heritage Society of Scotland promotes the protection of Scottish architecture and encourages the study of Scottish buildings, their furniture and fittings, urban design and designed landscapes. There are six regional groups, covering all of Scotland, which arrange regular events including talks, visits and study trips. Members can also join case panels to assess listed building and conservation area consent applications and planning applications. Contact the Society, Tel: 0131 557 0019; e-mail: administrator@ahss.org.uk; website: www.ahss.org.uk.

British Association for Local History exists to promote the study of local history. It will give advice and invite you to conferences and courses. Typical topics include introductory days at the Public Record Office, computers in local history and writing about your local area. Membership includes copies of both the *Local Historian* and *Local History News*. Contact the Association, Tel: 01283 585947; e-mail: info@balh.co.uk; website: www.balh.co.uk.

City of London Information Centre acts as a tourist office for the area, giving advice and guidance. Among the many attractions, all of which are open to the public at varying times, are: St Paul's Cathedral, the Guildhall (open most of the year, Monday to Saturday, from 10 am to 4 pm, free), Dr Johnson's House, the Monument, the Barbican, the Central Criminal Court and several museums. Additionally, there are interesting examples of London's architecture. Many of the 43 churches give organ recitals and, in the summer, you can enjoy open-air concerts. The Centre offers lots of free leaflets, including the monthly events list. Contact the Centre, Tel: 020 7332 1456; e-mail: pro@cityoflondon.gov.uk; website: www.cityoflondon.gov.uk.

English Heritage manages over 400 historic attractions throughout England. Members receive a colour handbook with map. They enjoy free admission to all English Heritage properties and are sent a quarterly magazine publicizing events and developments of conservation interest. *The English Heritage Visitors' Handbook* indicates which sites have access for wheelchairs. Contact English Heritage, Tel: 0870 3331 182; e-mail: members@english-heritage.org.uk; website: www.english-heritage.org.uk.

Federation of Family History Societies is an umbrella organization for more than 200 societies throughout the world (160 in the UK) that provide assistance if you are interested in tracing your ancestors. You can be put in touch with your local society and obtain useful guidelines on how to get started. Contact the

Federation, Tel: 01455 203133; e-mail: info@ffhs.org.uk; website: www.ffhs.org.
uk.

Friends of Historic Scotland. Membership gives you free access to 330 of Scotland's historic buildings and ancient monuments, a free directory of the sites and a quarterly magazine to keep you up to date with new activities. Contact Friends of Historic Scotland, Tel: 0131 668 8999; website: www.stately-homes.com.

Garden History Society is concerned with the study, enjoyment and conservation of historic parks and gardens. It organizes visits and lectures for members. An annual summer conference and foreign tours are also arranged. A journal, *Garden History*, is published twice a year, and there are also regular newsletters. Contact the Society, Tel: 020 7608 2409; e-mail: enquiries@gardenhistory society.org; website: www.gardenhistorysociety.org.

Georgian Group. The Group exists to preserve Georgian buildings and to stimulate public knowledge and appreciation of Georgian architecture and town planning. Activities include day visits and long weekends to buildings and gardens, private views of exhibitions and a programme of evening lectures in London. The Georgian Group also publishes advisory leaflets and holds study days on the history and conservation of Georgian buildings. Contact the Group, Tel: 0871 7502 936; e-mail: tina@georgiangroup.org.uk; website: www.georgiangroup.org.uk.

Historic Houses Association (HHA). Friends of the HHA enjoy access to nearly 300 HHA-member houses and gardens in England, Scotland and Wales and receive the quarterly magazine *Historic House*, as well as invitations to lectures, concerts, receptions and other events. Contact the HHA, Tel: 01462 896688; e-mail: hhafriends@hall-mccartney.co.uk; website: www.hha.org.uk.

Historical Association. The Association brings together people of all ages and backgrounds who share an interest in and love for the past. Members receive the *Historian* (a fully illustrated quarterly magazine) and may join in a wide variety of activities such as lectures, outings, conferences and tours both at home and abroad conducted by expert lecturers. There are over 50 local branches nationwide offering a programme of social events and monthly talks by top historians. The Association also publishes a number of very useful historical pamphlets. Tel: 020 7735 3901; e-mail: enquiry@history.org.uk; website: www.history.org.uk.

Monumental Brass Society encourages the preservation and appreciation of monumental brasses. Members attend four meetings with lectures and discussions and receive three bulletins, the annual *Transactions*, and an invitation to the annual excursion and study day. There are many brass-rubbing centres around the country where facilities are provided for the craft. Contact the membership secretary, e-mail: rmwillatts@tiscali.co.uk; website: www.mbs-brasses.co.uk.

National Trust. The National Trust exists to protect historic buildings and areas of great natural beauty in England, Wales and Northern Ireland. Membership gives you free entry to the Trust's many properties and to those of the National Trust for Scotland. You also receive three mailings with an annual handbook, magazines and details of activities in your own region. Thousands of special events are arranged each year, including guided house tours, pop and classical concerts, children's events and adult education activities. The Trust publishes a free annual booklet on facilities for visitors with disabilities; those requiring the help of a companion will be charged admission as normal, but their companion will be admitted free of charge on request. The booklet is available from the membership department on receipt of a stamped addressed adhesive label (minimum postage). Contact the National Trust, Tel: 0844 8001 895; e-mail: enquiries@thenationaltrust.org.uk; website: www.nationaltrust.org.uk.

National Trust for Scotland. The National Trust for Scotland cares for over 100 properties and 183,000 acres of countryside. Members also enjoy free admission to any of the National Trust properties in England, Wales and Northern Ireland. Contact the National Trust for Scotland, Tel: 0844 4932 100; e-mail: information@nts.org.uk; website: www.nts.org.uk.

Northern Ireland Tourist Board. There is a free information bulletin, *Visitor Attractions*, listing historic sites and other places of interest. Many sites are free, and others offer reduced rates for pensioners. An *Events* leaflet describes a selection of the most important, interesting or new events in Northern Ireland each year, such as music festivals, sporting occasions, agricultural shows and art exhibitions. Accommodation offers – including hotel breaks, self-catering holidays, guest houses and bed-and-breakfasts – are listed in the *Short Breaks* brochure, which offers year-round deals throughout Northern Ireland. Contact the Board, Tel: 028 9023 1221; e-mail: info@nitb.com; website: www.discovernorthernireland.com.

Oral History Society. The Society offers support and advice to groups and individuals around the country who record the memories of older people for projects in community history, schools, reminiscence groups and historical research. It publishes twice-yearly journals and runs regular workshops and conferences. It welcomes the help of older people in all these activities. Contact the membership secretary, Tel: 020 7412 7405; e-mail: rob.perks@bl.uk; website: www.ohs.org.uk.

Society of Genealogists. The Society promotes the study of genealogy and heraldry. Lectures are arranged throughout the year, and there is also a variety of courses, including day and weekend seminars. Members have access to the library and also receive a quarterly magazine. Non-members may use the library on payment of hourly, half-daily or daily fees. Contact the Society, Tel: 020 7251 8799; e-mail: membership@sog.org.uk; website: www.sog.org.uk.

Victorian Society. The Victorian Society campaigns to preserve fine Victorian and Edwardian buildings. It organizes walks, tours, lectures and conferences through its national office and eight regional groups. Contact the Society, Tel: 020 8994 1019; e-mail: admin@victoriansociety.org.uk; website: www.victorian-society.org.uk.

Museums

Most museums organize free lectures, guided tours and sometimes slide shows on aspects of their collection or special exhibitions. As with art galleries and theatres, an increasing trend is to form a group of 'Friends', who pay a membership subscription to support the museum and in return enjoy certain advantages, such as access to private views, visits to places of interest, receptions and other social activities:

British Association of Friends of Museums (BAFM) is an umbrella organization that acts as a national forum for Friends and volunteers who support museums around the UK. It shares news, provides advice on good practice, holds regional meetings and also produces a number of publications, including a *Handbook* on setting up and running a Friends organization. Many museums offer the opportunity, through membership of a Friends group, of rewarding voluntary activity. If you like the idea, enquire locally or contact the Association to discover what scope exists in your area via e-mail: admin@bafm.org.uk; website: www. bafm.org.uk.

British Museum Friends. Members enjoy free entry to exhibitions and evening openings as well as information about lectures, study days and 'visits behind the scenes'. A mailing including the events programme and the *British Museum Magazine* is sent three times a year. Contact British Museum Friends, Tel: 020 7323 8195; e-mail: friends@britishmuseum.org; website: www.britishmuseum.org.

Friends of the Fitzwilliam Museum receive regular mailings with information about museum events, including exhibitions, concerts, lectures and parties. There are visits to other museums and historic houses in the Cambridge area and throughout the UK, and trips to overseas cities are also arranged. Another attractive way of meeting other Friends is to become a voluntary helper at the Museum. For membership details contact the Friends of the Fitzwilliam Museum, Tel: 01223 332900; e-mail: fitzmuseum-friends@lists.cam.ac.uk; website: www.fitzmuseum.cam.ac.uk.

Friends of the National Maritime Museum. The Museum complex, housed in Greenwich Park, comprises the largest maritime museum in the world, Wren's Royal Observatory and Inigo Jones's Queen's House. Friends enjoy free entry to the buildings and exhibitions as well as private views, lectures, astronomy and art clubs, sailing trips (for all abilities), visits to exhibitions and places of interest both in Britain and abroad, and a regular glossy magazine. There are reciprocal free entry arrangements with many other maritime organizations. Contact Friends of the National Maritime Museum, Tel: 020 8312 6678; e-mail: membership@nmm.ac.uk; website: www.nmm.ac.uk.

Friends of the V&A (Victoria and Albert Museum). Members enjoy free admission to V&A exhibitions, members' previews, a programme of events and a free subscription to *V&A Magazine*. Contact the V&A, Tel: 020 7942 2271; e-mail: membership@vam.ac.uk; website: www.vam.ac.uk.

Membership of the National Museums of Scotland. Members receive regular mailings and the *Explorer* magazine, invitations to lectures and other events, and free admission to exhibitions and some sites. There is also a UK and overseas travel programme. Contact the National Museums of Scotland, Tel: 0131 247 4191; e-mail: membership@nms.ac.uk; website: www.nms.ac.uk.

Nature and conservation

Many conservation organizations are very keen to recruit volunteers and are, therefore, listed in Chapter 12, Voluntary Work, rather than here. By the same token, many of those concerned with field studies arrange courses and other special activity interests that, because there is usually a residential content, seem more appropriate in Chapter 14, Holidays. The potential list is enormous. To give you a taste of what is on offer, this is a truncated list ranging from canals to ecology:

Amenity organizations. If you are interested in conservation and the environment, you might like to join your local amenity society. You should be able to contact it through your public library, or for a comprehensive list consult the website: www.handbooks.btcv.org.uk.

Civic Trust is an environmental charity concerned about the quality of urban living that acts as an umbrella organization for a network of 850 local societies. The Trust coordinates heritage open days and publishes a quarterly newsletter, with articles on planning, conservation and transport issues. Contact the Trust, Tel: 020 7539 7900; website: www.civictrust.org.uk.

Epping Forest Field Centre. This Field Studies Council day centre promotes 'bringing environmental understanding to all' through a wide-ranging programme of courses that take place both during the week and on many weekends of the year. Facilities include wheelchair access and a specially designed wheelchair path into the forest. Contact the Centre, Tel: 020 8502 8500; e-mail: enquiries. ef@field-studies-council.org; website: www.field-studies-council.org.

Forestry Commission. For details of walks and trails, forest drives, picnic places, wildlife watching and visitor centres, contact your local Forestry Commission office or the public enquiries service, Tel: 0845 3673 787; website: www.forestry. gov.uk.

Scottish Inland Waterways Association. The Association coordinates the activities of local canal preservation societies and will put you in touch with your nearest group. Contact the Association, Tel: 0131 229 8796; e-mail: secretary@ siwa.org.uk; website: www.siwa.org.uk.

Wildlife Trusts. There are 47 local Wildlife Trusts caring for 2,500 nature reserves and campaigning for the future of our threatened wildlife. If you would be interested in visiting the reserves, participating in some of the activities such as guided walks, or joining a work party – which could mean taking part in anything from scrub bashing to otter surveys – contact your local trust. Membership includes receipt of a magazine and events programmes. For further information, contact the Wildlife Trusts, Tel: 01636 677711; e-mail: enquiry@ wildlifetrusts.org; website: www.wildlifetrusts.org.

Public library service

Britain's public library service is among the best in the world. It issues about 600 million books free a year, lends CDs and DVDs and is a source of an enormous amount of information about both local and national activities. Additionally, the reference sections contain newspapers and periodicals as well as a wide selection of reference books that might cover any subject from flower arranging to genealogy.

Many libraries have a mobile service that takes books into villages and/or to senior citizens' clubs, day centres and clinics for elderly and infirm people. Some libraries also have volunteer library visitors who deliver books and materials to housebound people. Among the many facilities on offer, large print books are available at most libraries, as are musical scores, leaflets on state benefits, consumer information and details of local community activities. The majority of libraries now have access to computer databases and can provide specialized information from Europe and North America. Some also hold the International Genealogical Index, with information on microfiche. Additionally, all libraries act as a source of information. If the information you require is not available in the library itself, the trained staff will normally do their best to tell you where you might find it. There is an excellent online public library service if you are interested in searching on the internet.

Sciences and other related subjects

If astronomy fascinates you or you would like to understand more about meteorology (who wouldn't, given our uncertain climate!) there are several societies and associations that would welcome you as a member:

British Astronomical Association. The Association is open to all people interested in astronomy. Members' work is coordinated in such sections as Sun, Moon, terrestrial planets, meteors, Jupiter, asteroids, historical, telescope making and so on. The Association holds meetings both in London and elsewhere and lends instruments to members. Contact the Association, Tel: 020 7734 4145; e-mail: office@britastro.org; website: www.britastro.org.

Geologists' Association. The Association organizes lectures, field excursions and monthly meetings at Burlington House, and members also receive a quarterly magazine. Subscription rates vary. Contact the Association, Tel: 020 7434 9298; e-mail: geol.assoc@btinternet.com; website: www.geologists.org.uk.

Royal Meteorological Society. The Society, which includes among its membership both amateurs and professionals, exists to advance meteorological science. Members and others may attend scientific meetings and receive the monthly magazine *Weather*. Contact the Society, Tel: 0118 956 8500; e-mail: info@rmets.org; website: www.rmets.org.

Special interests

Whether your special enthusiasm is stamp collecting or model flying, most of the associations listed organize events, answer queries and can put you in contact with kindred spirits:

British Association of Numismatic Societies (BANS) is an umbrella organization that helps to coordinate the activities of some 50 local clubs for those interested in the study or collection of coins, medals or similar. It organizes two conferences a year, maintains a slide library and will be able to put you in touch with your nearest group. Contact the Association, Tel: 0161 275 2643; e-mail: phyllis.stoddart@manchester.ac.uk; website: www.coinclubs.freeserve.co.uk.

British Jigsaw Puzzle Library. This is a lending library with puzzles usually exchanged by post. The puzzles are wooden and have no guide pictures. They vary in difficulty, style and size, and the library tries to suit each member. Postal charges are extra. Contact the Library, Tel: 01227 742222; e-mail: jigsawinfo@aol.com; website: www.britishjigsawpuzzlelibrary.co.uk.

British Model Flying Association (BMFA) is responsible nationally for all types of model flying, now the world's most popular aviation sport. It organizes competitions and fun-fly meetings, provides advice and guidelines on model flying, and can put you in touch with clubs in your area from its list of over 700 clubs. Many older members specialize in indoor free-flight or radio-controlled flying. Membership includes third-party liability insurance cover. Contact the Association, Tel: 0116 244 0028; e-mail: admin@bmfa.org; website: www.bmfa.org.

Miniature Armoured Fighting Vehicle Association (MAFVA) is an international society that provides advice and information on tanks and other military vehicles and equipment, issues a bi-monthly magazine, *Tankette*, and can put you in touch with a local branch or overseas members with similar interests. There are meetings, displays and competitions. Contact the Association, Tel: 01477 535 373; e-mail: mafvahg@aol.com; website: www.mafva.net.

National Association of Flower Arrangement Societies (NAFAS). NAFAS can put you in touch with local clubs and classes, but it is now also able to offer individual affiliated membership through a yearly subscription. The Association was formed 49 years ago and has a membership of over 70,000 members. The structure of the membership was formed through members belonging to one of the existing clubs within the 21 existing geographical areas of NAFAS. Lifestyles have changed, and a number of people who would benefit from membership are unable to commit to club membership but are still interested in the work of NAFAS and floral art and design. The yearly subscription includes four issues of the *Flower Arranger* magazine, two newsletters, details of NAFAS events, information on the National Show, and details of NAFAS courses in floral art and design, including a home study course. For further information contact the Association, Tel: 020 7247 5567; e-mail: flowers@nafas.org. uk; website: www.nafas.org.uk.

National Philatelic Society. If you are interested in stamp collecting, you might like to join the National Philatelic Society. As a member, you can buy and sell stamps through the Society's auctions or postal packet scheme. Members also receive invitations to monthly Saturday afternoon meetings, get a free bi-monthly magazine, *Stamp Lover*, and can borrow books from the Society's extensive library. For further information, contact the Society, Tel: 020 7239 2571; e-mail: nps@ukphilately.org.uk; website: www.ukphilately.org.uk.

Railway Correspondence and Travel Society. The Society is among the leading railway enthusiast groups, with nearly 4,000 members all over the country. Members receive the monthly magazine, the *Railway Observer*, which includes information on the Society's fixtures. There are regular meetings at about 30 centres, and the Society has a library with a postal loan facility. Contact the Society on e-mail: renewals@rcts.org; website: www.rcts.org.uk. *Railway Modeller* is a magazine for railway enthusiasts. It lists railway preservation events and gives information about local railway societies – including how to contact them.

Sport

Retirement is no reason for giving up sport. On the contrary, it is an ideal time to get fit. Facilities abound and, unlike people with a 9-to-5 job, you enjoy the great advantage of being able to book outside peak hours. To find out about opportunities in your area, contact your local authority recreational department or your sports or leisure centre.

Angling

Angling Trades Association. The Association promotes the interests of anglers and angling, including educational and environmental concerns. It can advise on where to find qualified tuition, local tackle dealers and similar information, as well as supply a number of useful leaflets. Contact the Association, Tel: 024 7641 4999; e-mail: ata@sportsandplay.com; website: www.anglingtradesassociation.com.

Archery

Grand National Archery Society (GNAS). The Society is the governing body for archery in the UK. It will put you in touch with your nearest club, of which there are over 1,000 around the country. Most clubs provide coaching at all levels, including beginners' courses (covered by public liability insurance) for which they supply all equipment. The GNAS organizes a full calendar of events and says many archers are still actively competing in their 70s, as the handicap system covers all abilities and enables disabled people to compete on equal terms. Contact the Society, Tel: 01952 677888; website: www.gnas.org.

Badminton

Badminton England is the sport's governing body in England. Many categories of membership are available, from supporters, through club and county players to the World Class squad. Most sports and leisure centres have badminton courts and give instruction, as do many adult education institutes. If you need advice, call Badminton England for a local contact, Tel: 01908 268400; e-mail: enquiries@badmintonengland.co.uk; website: www.badmintonengland.co.uk.

Bowling

Over the past years, bowling has been growing in popularity. Your local authority may provide facilities. Alternatively contact:

English Bowling Association. There are 2,600 local clubs, many of which provide instruction for beginners by qualified coaches. Some clubs have reduced rates for senior citizens. A national competition for 55-plus singles and pairs is organized through clubs each year. If you decide to take up bowls, you are advised not to buy your equipment without advice from the club coach. Contact the Association, Tel: 01903 820222; e-mail: enquiries@bowlsengland.com; website: www.bowlsengland.com.
English Indoor Bowling Association and **The English Women's Bowling Association** have now merged into one association named the English Indoor Bowling Association Limited. Details of the new association can be found on the website: www.eiba.co.uk.

Clay pigeon shooting

Clay Pigeon Shooting Association (CPSA). The CPSA is an association of individual shooters and a federation of clubs. As a member you have public liability insurance of £5 million, your scores are recorded in the national averages and you can compete in national events. The Association produces its own magazine, *Pull!*, which is distributed free of charge to all members. There are other specialist booklets available on most aspects of clay pigeon shooting. Contact the Association, Tel: 01483 485400; e-mail: info@cpsa.co.uk; website: www.cpsa.co.uk.

Cricket

Brit Oval is home to the Surrey County Cricket Club and one of the main venues for international and county cricket. Club membership entitles you to a number of benefits, including free or reduced price tickets for the Members' Pavilion to watch international matches as well as county events. Contact the Brit Oval, Tel: 08712 461100; e-mail: enquiries@surreycricket.com; website: www.surreycricket.com.

England and Wales Cricket Board (ECB). If you want to play, watch or help at cricket matches, contact your local club or contact the ECB. It can put you in touch with your county cricket board, and it also organizes an over-50 County Cricket Championship. Tel: 020 7432 1200; e-mail: feedback@ecb.co.uk; website: www.ecb.co.uk.

Lord's Cricket Ground. You can enjoy a conducted tour of Lord's that includes the Long Room, the futuristic Media Centre and the MCC Museum, where the Ashes urn is on display. There are three tours per day during the summer at 10 am, 12 noon and 2 pm. From November to March there are two tours per day at 12 noon and 2 pm. These times are subject to variation, and you are advised to check before making a special visit. Senior citizens can attend County Championship matches and the National League matches for half-price. There are no concessions, however, for major matches, and early booking for these events is recommended. Contact Lord's, Tel: 020 7616 8500; e-mail: reception@mcc.org; website: www.lords.org.

Croquet

Croquet Association. A growing number of local authorities as well as clubs now offer facilities for croquet enthusiasts. The Croquet Association runs coaching courses and can advise you about clubs, events, purchase of equipment and other information. Contact the Association, Tel: 01242 242318; e-mail: caoffice@croquet.org.uk; website: www.croquet.org.uk.

Cycling

CTC (Cyclists' Touring Club) is the largest national cycling organization. It offers members free third-party insurance, free legal aid, colour magazines, organized cycling holidays and introductions to 200 local cycling groups. There is also a veterans' section. Contact CTC, Tel: 0844 7368 451; e-mail: membership@ctc.org.uk; website: www.ctc.org.uk.

Darts

British Darts Organisation. Opportunities for playing darts can be found almost anywhere in clubs, pubs and sports centres. Contact the Organisation, Tel: 020 8883 5544; e-mail: britishdarts@btconnect.com; website: www.bdodarts.com.

Golf

English Golf Union is one of the largest sports governing bodies in England, looking after the interests of over 1,900 golf clubs and 740,000 members. It is a not-for-profit organization run for the benefit of the game and its players. Contact the Union, Tel: 01526 354500; e-mail: info@englishgolfunion.org; website: www.englishgolfunion.org.
Golfing Union of Ireland, Tel: 00 353 1 505 4000; e-mail: information@gui.ie; website: www.gui.ie.
Scottish Golf Union, Tel: 01334 466477; e-mail: sgu@scottishgolfunion.org; website: www.scottishgolfunion.org.
Welsh Golfing Union, Tel: 01633 436040; e-mail: office@golfunionwales.org; website: www.golfunionwales.org.

National Golf Unions can provide information about municipal courses and private clubs, of which there are some 1,700 in England alone. Additionally many adult education institutes and sports centres run classes for beginners.

Swimming

Amateur Swimming Association (ASA). Coaching and 'learn to swim' classes are arranged by many authorities, which also make the pool available at various times of the week for older people who prefer to swim quietly and unhindered. The Association offers an award scheme to encourage greater proficiency in swimming and as an incentive to swim regularly for fitness and health. If you are already a fitness swimmer, you might like to join **Swimfit**, which gives members access to training programmes and stroke technique tips. For further details contact the ASA, Tel: 0871 2000 928; e-mail: customerservices@swimming.org; website: www.sportcentric.com.

Table tennis

English Table Tennis Association. Table tennis can be enjoyed by people of all ages and all levels of competence. It is played in community halls, church halls, clubs and many sports centres. Contact the Association, Tel: 01424 722525; website: www.englishtabletennis.org.uk.
Veterans English Table Tennis Society (VETTS) holds regional and national championships including singles and doubles events for over-40s, over-50s, over-60s and over-70s. These attract increasing numbers of men and women who

enjoy playing socially and competitively well into their retirement. For further information on VETTS contact the Membership Secretary, Tel: 01462 671191; e-mail: valmurdoch@advance-internet.com; website: www.vetts.org.uk.

Tennis

Lawn Tennis Association (LTA) facilities have been greatly improving, and your local authority recreation department should be able to inform you. The LTA can give you information about anything to do with tennis, from advice on choosing a racket to obtaining tickets for major tournaments. Contact the LTA, Tel: 020 8487 7000; e-mail: membership@lta.org.uk; website: www.lta.org.uk.

Vets Tennis GB promotes competitions for older players in various age groups from 35 to 80 years. Its website lists affiliated clubs, gives the results of its national championships (indoor, clay and grass courts) and also provides details of club, county and international events. Contact Vets Tennis GB, Tel: 07774 264169; e-mail: vw@vetstennisgb.org; website: www.vetstennisgb.org.

Veteran rowing

Amateur Rowing Association (ARA). Veteran rowing as a sport is fast growing in popularity. Enthusiasts range in age from 31 to well past 80. For those who enjoy a competitive edge, there are special races and regattas, with types of boat including eights, fours and pairs, as well as single, double and quadruple sculling. Touring rowing is also on the increase, and additionally there is plenty of scope for those who simply want the exercise and a pleasant afternoon afloat. Nearly all clubs welcome novice veterans, both male and female, and usually the only qualification required is the ability to swim. Coaching is provided. For information about clubs in your locality, contact the ARA, Tel: 020 8237 6700; e-mail: info@ara-rowing.org; website: www.ara-rowing.org.

Walking

Ramblers' Association. Rambling can be anything from a gentle stroll to an action-packed weekend trek with stout boots and a rucksack. The Ramblers' Association provides a comprehensive information service on all aspects of walking and can advise on where to walk, clothing and equipment and organized walking holidays. There are 450 local groups throughout the country that between them organize hundreds of walks a week. Contact the Association, Tel: 020 7339 8500; e-mail: ramblers@ramblers.org.uk; website: www.ramblers.org.uk.

Windsurfing

Seavets, which is affiliated to the Royal Yachting Association, aims to encourage the not-so-young of all abilities to enjoy the challenge of windsurfing. Events are organized throughout the country from March to October, providing recreational windsurfing and racing for enthusiasts aged 35-plus. Average membership age is 63. Additionally, Seavets raises money every year for the charity Research into Ageing, which funds research into the disabilities of old age. For more information, e-mail the membership secretary: paulfet@aol.com; website: www.seavets. co.uk.

Yachting

Royal Yachting Association (RYA). There are 2,200 clubs affiliated to the RYA and more than 1,500 recognized training centres. The Association also provides comprehensive information services for boat owners and can give advice on everything from moorings to foreign cruising procedure. Contact the RYA, Tel: 0845 3450 400; e-mail: member.services@rya.org.uk; website: www.rya.org.uk.

Women's organizations

Although today women can participate in almost any activity on equal terms with men, women's clubs and organizations continue to enjoy enormous popularity. Among the best known are Women's Institutes, the Mothers' Union and Townswomen's Guilds:

Mothers' Union (MU). The Mothers' Union is a Christian organization, with over 3.6 million members in 77 countries, which promotes the well-being of families through practical work, policy and prayer. Membership is open to all baptized Christians who support the charity's objectives. Members can be involved in a wide range of projects within their local community as well as with a worldwide fellowship network. Contact the MU, Tel: 020 7222 5533; e-mail: mu@themothersunion.org; website: www.themothersunion.org.

National Association of Women's Clubs. There are 212 clubs with a membership of 7,250 throughout the country. They are open to women of all ages and interests. Each club is self-governing, choosing its own meeting times and programme. Typical activities include crafts, drama, keep fit and talks from guest speakers covering a wide variety of subjects. There are outings to theatres and exhibitions and visits to places of interest, and some clubs arrange holiday groups in Great Britain and abroad. Many do voluntary service in their communities for the sick and elderly. Contact the Association, Tel: 020 7837 1434; website: www.nawc.org.uk.

National Federation of Women's Institutes (NFWI). The WI is the largest national organization for women, with nearly 215,000 members and 7,100 local WIs in England and Wales. Through its community ties and wide-ranging activities, it offers women both friendship and the opportunity to develop their skills and talents. The WI has its own residential college, Denman College, and also publishes a monthly magazine, *WI Life*. Contact the NFWI, Tel: 020 7371 9300; e-mail: hq@nfwi.org.uk; website: www.womens-institute.co.uk.

National Women's Register (NWR) is an organization of 400 groups of 'lively minded women' who meet informally in members' homes to enjoy challenging discussions. The groups choose their own topics and many also arrange a varied programme of social activities. Contact NWR, Tel: 0845 4500 287; website: www.nwr.org.uk.

Scottish Women's Rural Institutes (SWRI). This is the Scottish counterpart of the Women's Institute movement. It has about 25,000 members of all ages who enjoy social, recreational and educational activities. There are talks and demonstrations, classes in arts and crafts, and discussions on matters of public interest. You can be put in touch with your local institute via the headquarters office. Contact the SWRI, Tel: 0131 225 1724; e-mail: swri@swri.demon.co.uk; website: www.swri.org.uk. If you live in Northern Ireland, contact the **Federation of Women's Institutes of Northern Ireland,** Tel: 028 9030 1506/ 028 9060 1781; website: www.wini.org.uk.

Townswomen's Guilds is an organization committed to advancing the social awareness of all women, irrespective of race, creed or political affiliation. It has around 43,000 members in 1,100 Guilds across the UK who meet to exchange ideas, learn new skills and take part in a wide range of activities. Contact Townswomen's Guilds, Tel: 0121 326 0400; e-mail: tghg@townswomen.org.uk; website: www.townswomen.org.uk.

For people with disabilities

There are fewer activities from which disabled people are now debarred through lack of suitable facilities. This is evident from many of the suggestions listed earlier in the chapter. This section therefore deals only with one topic not covered elsewhere, namely enjoyment of books, which for many blind or partially sighted people can be a special problem:

Calibre Audio Library is a free lending library of over 7,000 recorded books on ordinary standard cassettes. Many titles are also available on MP3 disks. These are available to anyone who cannot read printed books because of poor sight or other physical difficulty. An official form is required certifying 'inability to read printed books in the normal way' – a photocopy of the Blind Registration is acceptable. Books include fiction and non-fiction and cover the full range of classifications. Members use their own listening devices. For further information contact Calibre, Tel: 01296 432339; website: www.calibre.org.uk.

Listening Books provides a postal audio-book library service to anyone with an illness or disability that makes it impossible or difficult to hold a book, turn pages or read in the usual way. Contact Listening Books, Tel: 020 7407 9417; e-mail: info@listening-books.org.uk; website: www.listening-books.org.uk.

The National Library for the Blind and **RNIB Talking Book Service** have now merged. They operate a lending library service of audio-books for anyone who is registered as blind or whose vision is such that they cannot easily read standard print. Application should be made to the local authority social services department or direct to Customer Services. The subscription rate for the service is normally paid by local authorities. The books, which are unabridged, are professionally recorded and allow easy navigation for readers. There are thousands of titles from which to choose. There is also a Braille library containing fiction and non-fiction titles, music scores and tactile maps. For further information contact the RNIB, Tel: 0845 7626 843; e-mail: cservices@rnib.org.uk; website: www.rnib.org.uk.

Public transport

One of the big gains of reaching retirement age is the availability of cheap travel. Local authorities are now required to offer men, as well as women, concessionary bus fares from the age of 60 instead of men having to wait till 65 before being able to benefit. Even better, since April 2008, bus travel is free out of peak hours, anywhere in the country. Coaches very often have special rates for older people, and Senior Railcards, available to men and women over 60, offer wonderful savings. Details of these are given in Chapter 14, Holidays.

10

Starting your own business

Have you ever thought of running your own business? Maybe after years of working for someone else the idea of continuing to work is not high on your list of priorities. For some people, running a small business can be one of the most satisfying retirement occupations.

The top three reasons over-55s decide to continue to work are: they have a specialist area of knowledge or expertise they have gained over a number of years of working experience and are keen to continue to use it (rather than lose it). Second, they have been longing to have an opportunity to do something different – possibly related to a lifelong interest that has been kept firmly on the back burner due to restrictions of time while they were employed. Third, they want to do something useful and regard working as a vocational thing rather than being profit-driven so are prepared to keep remuneration levels low.

There are hundreds of success stories of those who took the plunge at 55-plus to build a company that provided involvement, fun and income, plus a legacy for their children. To encourage you still further, according to the latest Annual Vocational Rich List (published by City & Guilds) all those featured are entrepreneurs and entirely self-made. They achieved huge success without any of the traditional prestige qualifications that are regarded as necessary for success. Whether you graduated from Oxbridge or the University of Life, nothing should stop you from accumulating wealth if you are hungry for success. Some people may have served time as apprentices or taken vocational training, but all have one thing in common: they approach their work with a hands-on style. The average age of those in the top 25 is 61, and some of them are still working in the fields in which they started. Whether or not you intend to make it to the ranks of the super-rich, building an empire does take time and effort.

For every success story, however, there is a failure, and your money could disappear fast if you set up in big-company style. Small business is all about keeping costs down, handling the finances intelligently and doing it yourself until you have a positive cash flow and are making profits. If you are married, your partner's attitude is a crucial one. Even if not directly involved, he or she will have to accept (at least) the loss of a room in the house being used as an office. There will be the added distractions of out-of-hours phone calls and suddenly cancelled social engagements. If you have a skill to offer, the drive to sell it and the health to support your ambition, this chapter will give you the information you need to set up or buy into a small concern and join the ranks of other successful entrepreneurs.

It is an exciting prospect but it is not advisable to make things too complicated in the beginning. Best advice is to keep things small and simple in the early days. This will leave you time to get on with the work you obviously want to do – whether that is acting in a consultancy capacity, or doing something you love (and get paid for it) such as gardening or sewing. Plenty of time for bureaucracy and paperwork later. Here is some straightforward and simple advice about getting started if you are thinking of going self-employed.

Legal structure of the business

If you are thinking of starting a business, you have three main choices as to the legal form it can take. You can operate as a sole trader, a partnership or a limited company.

Sole trader

This is the simplest form of trading, with virtually no start-up expenses and minimal bureaucracy involved. If you trade under your own name then, apart from informing HM Revenue & Customs (HMRC), there are no legal formalities. If you use another name, you must indicate on documents such as letterheads that you are the owner. Even if you employ others, you will be treated as self-employed for both tax and National Insurance purposes and will be liable to pay personal Income Tax on your profits, after deducting allowable expenses. You will also be required to pay National Insurance Contributions on your earnings.

In April 2008 HMRC introduced an improved main tax return for self-assessment including fewer self-employment pages for businesses with a turnover of less than £30,000. They are now able to submit a three-line statement showing income, expenses and profit. Proper records will nevertheless need to be kept in the event of a query or investigation by the tax office.

The main disadvantage of operating as a sole trader – and it is a major one – is that it carries unlimited liability, so you are personally liable for all business debts. Should the business fail, your own assets as well as your business ones would be at the disposal of your creditors – and, if the worst came to the worst, you could be made personally bankrupt.

Partnership

A partnership is a business with two or more proprietors. It is similar to a sole trader in that it can be formed without any legal formalities or documentation other than informing HMRC. To avoid any possible future misunderstanding, however, it is advisable to have a formal partnership agreement drawn up at the outset, covering such points as distribution of profits (equal or unequal shares), voting rights, control of the bank account and arrangements for admitting new partners. While it is a simple matter to form a partnership, it can be very irksome to settle the affairs of one that has gone wrong. A few legal expenses at the beginning could prove a worthwhile investment.

As with sole traders, partners are treated as self-employed for both tax and National Insurance purposes. Profits are divided and taxed as the personal income of individual partners. However, if one partner fails to pay his or her share the other partners will be called upon to meet the shortfall. Similarly, each partner carries unlimited liability for all the debts of the business.

An exception to this rule – although rare today – is that of a limited partnership. This has to be registered at Companies House and at least one partner has to incur unlimited liability. The limited partners (sometimes known as 'sleeping partners') cannot take part in the running of the business in any way, and their liability is limited to their share of the partnership capital. Accounts need to be prepared at least once a year, but they do not need to be published.

Limited company

A limited company is a legal entity in its own right. As the name implies, liability for the company's debts in the event of insolvency is limited to the amount invested in the business by each shareholder. As a director of a limited company, you will be treated for tax and National Insurance purposes as an employee of the business, paying Income Tax under the PAYE system. Corporation Tax will also be payable on the profits of the company.

The main disadvantage of a limited company is the bureaucracy. Although the government claims to have been reducing the amount of red tape for small firms, there are still many legal requirements that must be fulfilled, both before and after trading starts. A limited company must be registered by Companies House (or, in Scotland, by the Registrar of Companies for Scotland): this involves the filing of both a Memorandum of Association and the Articles of Association (see below). The company's accounts have to be audited once a year by a firm of qualified accountants, and a set, showing among other details a profit and loss account, must be filed annually with Companies House, together with basic information about the company and its directors, all of which are open to public inspection.

NB: small companies can take advantage of an abbreviated form of accounts for filing provided they can meet two of the following criteria: 1) fewer than 50 employees; 2) turnover of less than £5.6 million; and 3) a balance sheet total of less than £2.8 million. These exemption thresholds (ie £5.6 million and £2.8 million) apply to financial years ending on or after 30 January 2004.

Registering a limited company

Although you can register a limited company yourself, it is advisable to get a professional accountant, solicitor or company registration agent to do it for you. Charges vary considerably but are likely to start from around £80.

To register a limited company, you need to fill in Form 10, Notification of First Directors and Secretary and Location of Registered Office, and Form 12, Declaration of Compliance. These must be sent to the Registrar of Companies together with the Memorandum of Association (stating the company's name, registered office, share capital and nature and scope of the business arrangements, including the extent of liability) and the Articles of Association (stating the internal rules of the company). All the necessary forms can be obtained either from law stationers or from Companies House in Cardiff. Specimen memoranda and articles can only be obtained from law stationers.

There are two scale rates: the normal service, which costs £20 to register (plus an additional £30 per year, or £15 for filing electronically, payable when the annual returns are sent in for public display); and the same-day incorporation service, which costs £50. To take advantage of the same-day service, it is necessary to present the completed documents at Companies House by 3 pm. If you use the standard service, registering a new company will take five working days from the receipt of correct documents at Companies House.

'Off the shelf'

Another possibility, if you are not too fussy about the company name, is to buy a previously registered company 'off the shelf' from a company registration agent. This will cost, on average, about £150 for all the documentation, including the company books. There will be a further charge of around £75 should you decide to change the name and a charge of around £25 to change the Articles of Association. If you simply need to change the name, which is not a difficult matter, you could do it direct with the Registrar. The cost in this case will be £10. Forms, guidance notes and other information are available from Companies House (see the website). Get in touch with the **Companies House Contact Centre**, Tel: 0870 3333 636; e-mail: enquiries@companies-house.gov.uk; website: www.companieshouse.gov.uk.

Co-operative enterprise

This is another possible form of business structure. Co-operatives are basically owned and controlled by the workers according to international co-operative principles – for instance, all members have equal voting rights irrespective of financial involvement, profits are distributed in proportion to members' participation in the activities of the business, and all workers qualify for membership after a suitable probationary period. Co-operatives provide their members with limited liability, by registering either as limited companies (requiring a minimum of two founder members) or as industrial and provident societies (requiring a minimum of three founder members).

Most new workers' co-operatives adopt model rules for registration. There are a number of different models available from the three national support bodies: Co-operatives UK, Wales Co-operative Centre Ltd and Employee Ownership Scotland Ltd. Registration will usually cost £300 to £400 if model rules are used. Alternatively, Co-operatives UK provides a 'tailor-made' service where a group has special requirements, costing from £550. In addition, some areas of the country are now served by local Co-operative Development Agencies that can advise and assist on the establishment of a new co-operative venture; some of these also have loan funds available to provide start-up capital.

For more information, contact:

Co-operatives UK, Tel: 0161 246 2900; e-mail: info@cooperatives-uk.coop; website: www.cooperatives-uk.coop.
Wales Co-operative Centre Ltd, Tel: 029 2055 4955; website: www.walescoop.com.
Employee Ownership Scotland Ltd, Tel: 0141 304 5465; e-mail: eos@sol. co.uk; website: www.uk.coop/eos.

Business names

It is no longer necessary to register a business name. However, where a sole trader uses a business name that is different from his or her real name, or where a partnership trades under a name that differs from those of all the partners, or a limited company trades other than under its full corporate name, then certain legal requirements have to be met. All business stationery – including letterheads, order forms, invoices and receipts – must contain the real name(s) of the sole trader, partner or company, together with the official address of the business. These details must also be prominently displayed on all business premises. Failure to do so is a criminal offence, punishable by a fine.

There are also certain regulations governing the words that may be used in a business or company name 'without justification'. Prohibited words include those considered offensive or those that imply connection with the Crown, the government or a local authority, for instance 'British', 'National' and 'European'.

Other prohibited categories are titles like 'Society' and 'Institute' that suggest a representative status, or words that imply a specific function such as insurance or banking. In all such cases, approval must be sought from the appropriate government department or governing body that the use of such words is justified. For more information see *Company Names* (GBF 2) and *Business Names* (GBF 3), available from Companies House, Tel: 0870 3333 636; e-mail: enquiries@companies-house.gov.uk; website: www.companieshouse.gov.uk.

Domain names

Now that businesses rely heavily on the internet, an important first step – should you be considering setting up a new business in retirement – is what domain name to have and how to register it. There are two basic steps for getting your website online. Registering or reserving the domain name is the first. For those of you who are unfamiliar with this process, the domain name makes up the address of your website, and can end with .co.uk, .com, .net, .org, .info, .us, .biz, etc. This name, once registered, will require a web host. The web host is the 'nuts and bolts' of your website, because this is where you design and publish your web pages, add and improve them and operate your site.

Depending on what sort of business you are running it may be important to you to be found easily and quickly in the major search engines (such as Yahoo, Google, etc). If so, you should try to register a name that contains key words as to what you do, rather than your company name. Use a company name that includes a word that your target audience would be likely to use when they start searching. You can still list your company name on your web pages. It is, however, essential that the domain name includes your 'search-friendly' key words if you want customers to find you easily.

Top tips on choosing the best domain name include: don't make it too long or complicated, and it needs to be easy to remember (for you and your customers). Use hyphens if your name is long; it makes it easier to understand, and it looks better. It is very important to protect your name by registering multiple extensions (such as .net, .org, etc). This prevents people from copying your name. It doesn't mean you have to have multiple websites, but by reserving them it stops people infringing your territory or copying your name and ideas. Your business could become valuable, and this step will prevent predatory competitors from encroaching.

Reserving a domain name is easy and remarkably low-cost. It doesn't matter where you register your domain. Every registrar provides similar services. You should take steps, when registering, to protect your privacy. This means keeping your domain name private, which will stop your information (name, e-mail address, etc) from becoming part of the global internet database. It is also essential for preventing loads of spam from reaching your e-mail box. This tip is highly recommended, as it comes from many people who wish it had been available when they first created their sites.

A huge number of companies offer domain name registration and ongoing support. Search 'domain names and how to register them' on Google and you will find over 18 million offers of advice. Best suggestion: ask friends who are already 'web savvy', or small business owners who you know operate their business using a website. Don't ignore help that is right in front of your nose: young friends or relatives, especially the grandchildren, will know more than you ever will about this subject. They may even prove keen to help and can design your website if you want.

As with all new things, take advice and think carefully before committing yourself. But if you are going to be taken seriously in business, having a website is essential.

Alternative ways of getting started

Rather than start a new business, you could buy into one that is already established, or consider franchising.

Buying a business

Buying an established business can be an attractive route to becoming your own boss, as it eliminates many of the problems of start-up. The enterprise is likely to come equipped with stock, suppliers, an order book, premises and possibly employees. It is also likely to have debtors and creditors.

Take professional advice before buying any business, even one from friends. In particular, you should consider why the business is being sold. It may be for perfectly respectable reasons – for instance, a change of circumstances such as retirement. But equally, it may be that the market is saturated, that the rent is about to go sky-high or that major competition has opened up nearby.

The value of the company's assets will be reflected in its purchase price, as will the 'goodwill' (or reputation) that it has established. For more information, contact the agents specializing in small businesses, **Christie & Co**, Tel: 020 7227 0700; e-mail: enquiries@christie.com; website: www.christie.com.

Before parting with your money, make sure that the assets are actually owned by the business and get the stock professionally valued. You should also ensure that the debts are collectable and that the same credit terms will apply from existing suppliers. Get an accountant to look at the figures for the last three years and have a chartered surveyor check the premises. It is also advisable to ask a solicitor to vet any legal documents, including staff contracts: you may automatically inherit existing employees. See the DTI booklet *Employment Rights on the Transfer of an Undertaking*, available from Jobcentre Plus; see the website: www. jobcentreplus.gov.uk or from the Department for Business, Enterprise and Regulatory Reform, website: www.berr.gov.uk.

Franchising

Franchising has become an increasingly popular form of business, with attractions for both franchisor and franchisee. The franchisor gains in that an ambitious group is able to expand very quickly. The advantage to the franchisee is that there are normally fewer risks than starting a business from scratch.

A franchisee buys into an established business and builds up his or her own enterprise under its wing. In return for the investment plus regular royalty payments, he or she acquires the right to sell the franchisor's products or services within a specified geographic area and enjoys the benefits of its reputation, buying power and marketing expertise. Examples of recent award-winning franchises include Autosmart International, TaxAssist Accountants and Domino's Pizza.

As a franchisee you are effectively your own boss. You finance the business, employ the staff and retain the profits after the franchisor has had its cut. You are usually expected to maintain certain standards and conform to the broad corporate approach of the organization. In return, the franchisor should train you in the business, provide management support and give you access to a wide range of back-up services.

Cost

The amount of capital needed to buy a franchise varies enormously according to the type of business, and can be anywhere between £3,000 and £500,000 or more. The franchisee is normally liable to pay an initial fee, covering both the entry cost and the initial support services provided by the franchisor, such as advice about location and market research. Advice should be taken as to whether the fee will be partially or wholly allowable for tax purposes. The franchisee is also normally liable to pay recurring fees or royalties, which are usually based on a percentage of gross sales (typically 10 per cent), exclusive of VAT. Sometimes, where the franchisor supplies its own exclusive products, it may derive its income from the usual mark-up on the sale of products to you.

Length of agreement

The length of the agreement will depend both on the type of business involved and on the front-end fee. Agreements can run from three to 20 years, with five years being average. Many franchisors include an option to renew the agreement, which should be treated as a valuable asset.

Raising the finance

Franchising has now built up a good track record with a relatively low rate of business failures, so raising the money for a franchising venture is rarely a major difficulty. Most of the leading high street banks operate specialist franchise loan sections. Franchisors may also be able to help in raising the money and can sometimes arrange more advantageous terms through their connections with financial institutions.

The **British Franchise Association** (BFA) represents 'the responsible face' of franchising, and its members have to conform to a stringent code of practice. The BFA publishes a *Franchisee Guide* (approximately £30), which provides comprehensive advice on buying a franchise, together with a list of BFA member franchisors and affiliated advisers. It is well worth visiting one of the five annual British Franchise Exhibitions, where you can see and compare the various franchise options on offer.

A good franchisor will provide a great deal of invaluable help. However, some franchisors are very casual in their approach, lacking in competence, or even downright unethical. Points to look out for include overpricing of exclusive stock and lack of back-up services. Make careful enquiries before committing any money: as basic information, you should ask for a bank reference together with a copy of the previous year's accounts. Also check with the BFA whether the franchisor in question is a member and talk to some of the other franchisees to find out what their experience has been. Before signing, seek advice from an accountant or solicitor. For more information, contact the British Franchise Association on: 01865 379 892; website: www.thebfa.org.

Developing an invention

If you have a clever idea that you would like to market, you should ensure that your intellectual property is protected. For information about patenting an invention and much more, contact the **UK Intellectual Property Office**, Tel: 0845 9500 505; e-mail: enquiries@ipo.gov.uk; website: www.ipo.gov.uk.

Taxation

Taxation arrangements vary considerably according to whether you are operating as a sole trader, partnership or limited company. As you will know, tax rates, bands and allowances are revised annually and take effect at the beginning of the financial year in April. Figures quoted in this section apply to the 2009/10 financial year.

Sole trader or partnership

As soon as you start work on your own account, you should inform your local Inspector of Taxes. To do so, you should obtain form CWF1 from your local tax office (see website www.hmrc.gov.uk and search using the local tax office locator) and return it, when completed, together with your form P45, which your employer will have given you when you left.

Income Tax

As a sole trader or member of a partnership, you are treated as self-employed for tax purposes. Profits are aggregated with any other personal income and are taxed at the normal rates of Income Tax. From April 2009, the basic rate of 20 per cent applies to the first £37,400 of taxable income, with all income in excess of this subject to the higher rate of 40 per cent.

Not all your income is taxable. In common with everyone else, you get a personal tax allowance (currently £6,475); and if you qualify for the married couple's allowance you will also receive the minimum £2,670 allowance (or more if the husband's income is below the income threshold).

Additionally, as a self-employed person (Schedule D), you are allowed certain other reliefs. As a general guideline, the following expenses and allowances are tax deductible:

- *Business expenses.* These must be incurred 'wholly and exclusively' for the purposes of the trade. Professional publications will probably qualify; however, your 'wages', National Insurance Contributions and any business entertaining will not. Bad debts are usually allowable. Certain expenses incurred in advance of getting the business started are also permitted, for example necessary travelling, printing costs and telephoning. You can claim up to 40 pence on every mile up to 10,000 on private cars and then 25 pence for every mile after that.

- *Partially allowable expenses.* These mainly apply if you are working from home. They include such items as that part of your rent, heating, lighting and telephone usage that you devote to business purposes, and also possibly some of the running expenses on your car, if you use your car for your business. Remember that your business equipment and premises are capital items. These cannot be counted as an expense. Instead they must be categorized under fixed assets and writing-down allowances are calculated at the year end, to reduce your profits (see below).

- *Spouse's wages.* If you employ your partner in the business, his or her pay (provided this is reasonable) qualifies as a legitimate expense, in the same way as any other employee's, but must of course be accounted for through the PAYE system.

- *Pension contributions.* Since the new rules came into force in April 2006, everyone is free to invest up to 100 per cent of annual earnings into a pension plan with the benefit of tax relief, up to a maximum figure (known as the 'annual allowance') of £255,000. There is also a lifetime limit of £1.8 million for total pension funds including fund growth.

- *Capital allowances.* April 2008 heralded a major overhaul of the capital allowances regime. There is a new annual investment allowance for the first £50,000 of expenditure (except on certain items such as cars), and the writing-down allowance for plant and machinery in the general pool is reduced from 25 to 20 per cent. The rate of writing-down allowances on long-life assets expenditure increases from 6 to 10 per cent. The rate of writing-down allowances on certain features integral to a building is set at 10 per cent (previously these may have qualified for plant and machinery allowances at 25 per cent).
- *Research and development.* There are generous reliefs available if you can meet the stringent qualifying conditions. Best advice is to check with an accountant.
- *Interest on loans.* Tax relief is given on money borrowed to invest in a small firm, in most normal circumstances.
- *Tax losses.* Any tax losses in the first four years may enable you to recover PAYE from your last three years in employment. A tax loss made by the business can also be set against any other income the proprietor may have.

Because of these reliefs, being a sole trader or partner can offer substantial tax advantages. As a result, HMRC has become increasingly strict about the definition of self-employed. If you work as a consultant or freelance and most of your income derives from one employer, your Inspector of Taxes may argue that you are an employee of that firm – and not a self-employed person. For more information, see leaflet IR 56 *Employed or Self-Employed? A Guide to Employment Status for Tax and National Insurance* on the website: www.hmrc.gov.uk.

Capital Gains Tax (CGT)

From 6 April 2008 CGT is charged at an 18 per cent flat rate for all individuals, personal representatives and trustees. Additionally, existing entitlements to taper relief and indexation allowance were lost from that date. Some relief has been given in the form of the new entrepreneurs' relief, which allows the first £1 million of lifetime gains to be taxed at an effective rate of 10 per cent. This is less significant for taxpayers making very large gains or serial entrepreneurs. Since the introduction of independent taxation, in the case of a married couple both husband and wife are taxed independently on their capital gains and each enjoys his or her own separate annual exemption. Tax may not be payable if the proceeds are reinvested within three years in another business (or business assets). Assets bought the previous year might also qualify. This is normally referred to as 'roll-over relief'.

Another valuable relief allows trading losses to be offset against Capital Gains Tax. Proprietors of unincorporated businesses who make a loss (and do not have enough income in the year to offset that loss in full) can make a claim to set the unused loss against capital gains of the same year – with any excess of loss carried forward against capital gains of the following years. If the owners want to give part of their business (or its assets) to their family, CGT need not be payable until a sale to a third party occurs. This is called 'hold-over relief'.

When calculating your likely gains, you should be aware that the definition of business assets has been tightened up by HMRC and, for a business relief to apply, the assets must be solely relevant to the business and not include, for example, unrelated property or other investments.

In all cases mentioned above, it would be sensible to ask an accountant for advice before deciding on a particular course of action.

Inheritance Tax

Most small family-owned businesses can be passed on to the next generation free of Inheritance Tax. Although in recent years tax planning has become much easier for small business owners, you would nevertheless be strongly advised to speak to an accountant.

Preparation of accounts

Since self-assessment, sole traders and partners are no longer required to submit accounts to HMRC. Very small businesses – that is, those with a turnover of less than £30,000 – are required to submit only a three-line account on their tax return to provide HMRC with the following information:

- details of their total takings;
- details of their expenses;
- their profits.

Larger businesses will need to provide more detail, with accounts normally in two parts, in line with HMRC's standard format: a trading account and profit and loss account, which provide a summary of the year's trading transactions; and the balance sheet, which shows the assets and liabilities of the business at the end of the year.

The accounts of a sole trader, partnership or limited company with a turnover of less than £5.6 million do not have to be audited by an independent qualified accountant, provided it has either fewer than 50 employees or a balance sheet total of less than £2.8 million. However, whether you draw up the accounts yourself or engage professional help, full and accurate records must be kept from the start. While not essential, there is a very strong argument for having a qualified accountant to help you, since his or her advice is likely to prove invaluable on a whole range of matters.

Making a tax return

As an employee, you will have had Income Tax deducted from your gross pay automatically under the PAYE system. When you become self-employed, you become responsible for the payment of tax and are required by law to make a true return of your income each year.

Self-assessment

As an employer, self-assessment might both affect you personally and also affect some of your employees and/or co-directors. People who work for (or with) you who receive a tax return will require certain information from you – mainly about PAYE, benefits in kind and expenses payments. Details are contained in *Self-Assessment: What It Will Mean for Employers*, obtainable free from tax offices, Tel: 0845 9000 444; website: www.hmrc.gov.uk.

There is no obligation on anyone to work out their tax liability themselves, as self-calculation is optional. However, regardless of whether you opt for self-calculation, both in your own capacity and as an employer, you need to be aware of the requirements (including the need to keep records of all your sources of income and capital gains for at least 22 months, or five years and 10 months in the case of a business).

If you intend to file your tax return online you have a slightly longer deadline, 31 January. Paper returns must be filed by 31 October. If you submit your return online, the calculation will be made automatically. The dates are important, as there is an automatic penalty of £100 if your tax return arrives after 31 January. For further information, see booklets SA/BK4, SA/BK6, SA/BK7 and SA/BK8, all obtainable free from any tax office. You can also call the Self-Assessment helpline on: 0845 9000 444, or see the website: www.hmrc.gov.uk.

Useful reading

For more information about the tax position of sole traders and partnerships, see HMRC booklet SE/1 *Thinking of Working for Yourself?* obtainable by phoning 0845 9000 444 or see the website: www.hmrc.gov.uk. Other publications include: *A Guide to Working for Yourself* by Jonathan Reuvid and Godfrey Golzen (£12.99), *Start Up and Run Your Own Business* by Jonathan Reuvid (£12.99) and *Starting a Successful Business* by Michael Morris (£12.99), all published by Kogan Page (website: www.koganpage.com).

Limited company

HMRC will be automatically notified when a limited company is formed, and will contact the directors in due course. However, to avoid delays it is sensible for you to contact HMRC as soon as the company is incorporated.

Corporation Tax

A company pays Corporation Tax on its taxable profits. The main rate is 28 per cent for the 2009/10 tax year. The small companies' rate is 21 per cent for the 2009/10 tax year.

The main rate of Corporation Tax applies to companies with taxable profits over £1.5 million. The small companies' rate applies to businesses with taxable profits of £300,000 or less. There is marginal relief due if the profits are between £300,001 and £1.5 million. Profits paid out in dividends will equally be subject to the minimum 21 per cent tax (2009/10).

If you are a director of a limited company, the business will pay your salary (which will be subject to PAYE) out of its trading income. Allowable expenses, similar to those for sole traders and partnerships, are also deductible before Corporation Tax is charged. Directors' expenses may, however, be disallowed, in whole or in part, if HMRC takes the view that these benefited directors personally – as opposed to being a legitimate business expense. Such expenses may be taxed as a personal benefit.

Relief for losses

If your company makes a loss, the directors cannot offset this against their personal taxable income. The losses can, however, be offset against both future and past profits made by the company, with trading losses carried back for up to one year.

Relief for pre-trading expenditure

The period for tax relief for expenditure incurred before the start of trading is seven years.

Preparation of accounts

Limited companies are required to file annual accounts within 10 months of their year-end. These accounts will normally form the basis of HMRC's tax assessment. As stated earlier, however, small companies can take advantage of an abbreviated form of accounts for filing provided they can meet two of the following criteria: 1) fewer than 50 employees; 2) turnover of less than £5.6 million; 3) a balance sheet total of less than £2.8 million.

Capital Gains Tax

When a company sells an asset such as a building at a profit, it will pay Corporation Tax on the chargeable gain. If the company itself is subsequently sold, the shareholders will have CGT at the flat rate of 18 per cent to pay on the gain realized from the sale of the shares.

Venture capital relief

Many entrepreneurs wishing to defer paying tax on gains arising from the sale of shares in their own companies used to think in terms of reinvestment relief.

Reinvestment relief, as such, has been abolished and is now merged with the *Enterprise Investment Scheme (EIS)* to create a unified system of venture capital reliefs. Consult your tax adviser or accountant about this.

Tax offset

If your company makes a trading loss, this can be used as an offset against profits made on the sale of assets, provided the sale takes place in the same or the previous year.

Inheritance Tax

Since 1992 most small family-owned businesses have been taken out of the Inheritance Tax net and can be passed on to the next generation free of tax. There are certain cases, however, where IHT could still be a factor; these are where the controlling shares are in a fully quoted company, and where certain assets are owned by partners or by controlling shareholders and are used in their respective businesses. In such cases, there is tax relief of 50 per cent. Although IHT planning has now become much easier for small business owners, you would nevertheless be strongly advised to speak to an accountant.

Recent tax rule changes

If, as many individuals do, you are thinking of setting up a limited company, charging your clients fees for your services and paying yourself a dividend at the end of the year according to what the company can afford, you should be aware that HMRC has tightened up the rules in order to clamp down on what it sees as the avoidance of PAYE and Class 1 National Insurance Contributions. Whereas previously there was a considerable advantage for owner-managers – especially those with taxable profits of £50,000 or less – to pay themselves in dividends, in lieu of salary, today profits distributed in dividends are subject to a minimum 21 per cent tax.

Although nothing to do with Corporation Tax as such, a further unwelcome change, which will affect married couples who jointly run a business, is that dividends paid out of the business will be taxed according to each partner's ownership of the shares. This means, in practice, that the partner with the majority shareholding can no longer reduce the joint tax bill by arranging most of the dividends to be paid to a spouse in a lower tax bracket.

If you are thinking of operating in an independent capacity – as opposed to becoming a bona fide employee – it would be sensible to discuss the tax implications with an accountant before determining whether you should operate as self-employed, sole trader, partnership or limited company.

Value Added Tax (VAT)

VAT is imposed on most business transactions. The legal structure of the enterprise does not in general affect the issue.

Registration

Registration is required if your annual 'taxable turnover' exceeds the £68,000 threshold (2009/10) in any period of 12 months or less, or if you expect it to exceed the threshold in a future period of 30 days. 'Taxable turnover' applies to the gross turnover of goods or services that are made or supplied by the business. You have 30 days to notify HMRC if you become liable to register. Businesses may deregister from VAT, if they so choose, if their taxable turnover falls below £66,000.

Charging and paying VAT

You collect VAT from your customers by including it in, or adding it to, the price you charge (output tax). Similarly, you will be charged VAT by your suppliers on the goods and services you buy (input tax). When you receive a VAT return, your input tax is subtracted from your output tax and the difference is paid to HMRC. If the input tax is greater than the output tax, you can claim a refund on the difference.

Small businesses with a taxable turnover of up to £150,000 can opt to take advantage of a flat-rate scheme for calculating their VAT liability. Instead of keeping detailed records of the VAT charged on every purchase and sale, they can calculate the amount due by applying a flat-rate percentage to their total turnover.

Businesses with an annual turnover of less than £1.35 million can opt to submit a VAT return once a year instead of quarterly. A condition is that they must make monthly payments by direct debit, based on estimates agreed with HMRC, with a balancing adjustment made when the annual return is submitted. Businesses will be able to take advantage of this scheme until their taxable turnover reaches £1.6 million.

Businesses with an annual turnover of less than £1.35 million can opt for cash accounting for VAT, enabling them to delay paying the VAT on their sales to HMRC until they have actually received payment for them. However, you cannot issue invoices in advance of supply or for sales where payment is not due for more than six months after the date of the invoice. The scheme should help the cash flow of small firms with tardy customers and provide automatic VAT relief for bad debts. Bad debts can be written off for the purpose of claiming VAT relief after six months. A debtor no longer has to be declared formally insolvent for relief to be allowed. Businesses can use this scheme until their taxable turnover reaches £1.6 million.

Taxable supplies and exempt supplies

Most transactions are liable to VAT at either the standard rate (currently 17.5 per cent) or the zero rate (nil). Zero-rated supplies include most food (but not catering), books and newspapers, sales of new dwellings, young children's clothing and footwear, protective boots and helmets meeting EC safety standards, export of goods, dispensing of prescriptions and the supply of many aids for disabled people, mobile homes and houseboats, water and sewage services. Zero-rated suppliers have to complete and return a VAT form, even though they are not liable to pay this tax.

Exempt supplies include insurance, betting, gaming and lotteries, provision of credit, certain education and training, services of doctors and other medical specialists, and certain supplies by undertakers. If all the supplies you make are exempt from VAT, you will not be required to register for VAT but you will not be able to reclaim the VAT you pay on goods and services for your business. If some of the supplies are exempt, you would probably still need to be registered. Your accountant should be able to advise, or check with your local HMRC office.

Below the VAT registration limit

If you are not registered for VAT, any expenditure you incur that includes a charge for VAT should be entered in your records, inclusive of VAT. Even if you do not have to register at present, you may have to do so in the future if your taxable turnover increases. There could be an argument for early registration, as you would be able to offset the VAT the business has to pay to its suppliers. Another advantage is that VAT usually helps in establishing well-kept accounts. For more information, see VAT notice 700/1, *Should I Be Registered for VAT?* from the HMRC website: www.hmrc.gov.uk.

How to register

Fill in form VAT 1 (or the Welsh equivalent, form VAT 20). If the business to be registered is a partnership you will also need form VAT 2. If you have acquired a business as a going concern you may be able to have the registration number of the previous owner reallocated to you. For more details, see VAT leaflet 700/9, *Selling or Transferring a Business as a Going Concern*, from the HMRC website: www. hmrc.gov.uk.

NB: it is important that you notify HMRC within the 30-day limit once you are liable to be registered. Should you forget to do so, you may have to account for tax that you have not collected, together with penalties for late registration. You should start keeping VAT records and charging VAT to your customers from the date of your registration, which will be notified to you on the certificate of VAT registration that will be sent to you after your registration application has been processed and approved by HMRC. You will have to account for VAT from this date, whether or not you have included VAT in your prices.

Helpful reforms

The government has tried to make VAT simpler and less onerous for business. In the event of a bad debt, firms are no longer required to notify their debtors in writing that they are claiming relief. Even more welcome, businesses with turnover up to £150,000 that are late with their VAT payments can expect to be offered help and advice rather than get an automatic fine. For further information, contact **HM Revenue & Customs National Advice Service**, Tel: 0845 0109 000; website: www.hmrc.gov.uk.

Benefits in kind

The rules affecting benefits in kind apply to all directors and to employees earning £8,500 or more a year (including the value of benefits in kind). Any tax payable is deducted via the PAYE system. A particular item of interest to many smaller businesses is company cars. Other possible items that you may need to check are company computers and mobile phones loaned to employees for their private use.

Computers and mobile phones

The rules concerning the loan of computers and mobile phones to employees for private use have recently been revised. Both (other than computers where the annual benefit exceeded £500) used to be tax-exempt. This exemption has been removed for computers, with the result that the benefit is now liable for tax and National Insurance in the same way as other benefits in kind. While mobile phones still largely escape the tax, there is now a limit on the number of mobile phones that employers can loan to employees, tax-free, for private use. The figure is one per employee, and the benefit is no longer extended to the employee's family or members of the household. In both cases, where the equipment is solely provided for business purposes, no tax and National Insurance are due.

Useful reading

HMRC booklet 480, *Expenses and Benefits Tax Guide*, see website: www.hmrc.gov. uk.

National Insurance

As with tax, your liability for National Insurance Contributions will depend on whether you are self-employed (sole trader or partner) or whether you are a director of a limited company.

Self-employed

If you are self-employed, you will have to pay flat-rate Class 2 contributions – currently £2.40 a week – unless:

- you are over 65 (men) or 60 (women) (even if you have not retired from work);
- you are entitled to pay married women's or widow's reduced-rate Class 1 contributions;
- you have been granted 'a certificate of exception' because your earnings are likely to be less than £5,075 a year.

You must register to pay Class 2 contributions within three months of becoming self-employed or you risk incurring a £100 penalty.

If your annual taxable profits or profit share are above £5,715, you will also have to pay Class 4 contributions of 8 per cent on profits between £5,715 and £43,875, plus 1 per cent on profits above this amount, unless you are in one of the following categories:

- not resident for income tax purposes in the UK;
- trustee, executor or administrator of wills and settlements (there are, however, exceptions);
- sleeping partner, taking a profit and supplying capital, but not active in the business.

How to pay

Class 2 contributions can be paid either by direct debit from your bank or by the quarterly billing system that has replaced the traditional NI stamps. If you prefer quarterly billing, the National Insurance Contributions Office should automatically advise you of the amount owing for the previous quarter, which is payable through banks or at all post offices via Girobank. Class 4 contributions are normally assessed and collected by HMRC, together with PAYE or Schedule D income tax. As they will be paid retrospectively, remember to keep the necessary cash ready and not spend it as part of your monthly salary.

Husband and wife

As with independent taxation, husband and wife are assessed separately for Class 4 contributions. Further information about Schedule D tax assessments and related Class 4 National Insurance contributions can be obtained from your local Inspector of Taxes. For help on deferment or refund of Class 4 contributions, contact the **National Insurance Contributions Office**, Deferment Group, HM Revenue & Customs, website: www.hmrc.gov.uk.

Double income

If you are self-employed but also receive a salary you may have to pay NIC on both incomes. If too much has been deducted in total you can reclaim the excess or ask for a reduction of Class 2 and/or Class 4 contributions.

Useful reading

Leaflet CA 04, *Class 2 and Class 3 National Insurance Contributions: Direct Debit – The Easier Way to Pay*, available at all HMRC offices, website: www.hmrc.gov.uk.

Limited company

If you trade as a limited company, the company will pay employer's Class 1 contributions and you will suffer the same deductions from your salary as any other employee. If you control the company, you will in effect be paying both the employer and the employee's share of NIC on your own account. If you are a director of several companies, you may be liable for multiple NI contributions. See leaflet CA 44, *National Insurance for Company Directors*, available from HMRC offices, website: www.hmrc.gov.uk.

National Insurance benefits

Different classes of contributions qualify you for different types of benefit.
   Class 2 Contributions count for:

- incapacity benefit;
- basic retirement pension;
- bereavement benefits;
- basic maternity benefit.

Class 1 Contributions entitle you to all the above and additionally to the Jobseeker's Allowance, should the need ever arise. They also count towards the additional State pension.

Class 3 Contributions. These may be paid voluntarily to help you qualify for, or improve your entitlement to, certain benefits. A flat rate of £8.10 a week is payable. See leaflet CA 5603, *To Pay Voluntary National Insurance Contributions*, available from any HMRC office, website: www.hmrc.gov.uk.

Pensions

Sole traders and partners are self-employed for pension, as well as tax, purposes and must make their own arrangements, which might variously be a personal pension, SIPP or stakeholder pension. Directors of limited companies are treated as employees and may be included in their company's pension scheme or may run their own self-administered pension schemes. See Chapter 3 for more detail.

Your responsibilities as an employer

Should you consider employing staff, you will immediately increase the complexity of your business. Sole traders who need to take on staff would be sensible to take advice before doing so on what roles and responsibilities this will involve. Many people starting a business wisely limit recruitment to the minimum in the early days, until they are sure that they can afford the cost of having permanent staff. Once you become an employer, you take on responsibilities. As well as paying the salaries, you will have to account for PAYE, keep National Insurance records and conform to the multiple requirements of employment legislation. While this may sound rather daunting, two recent measures should hopefully reduce much of the complexity. First, the Contributions Agency has been transferred to HMRC, with the advantage that employers now need to go through only a single organization to sort out tax and National Insurance matters. Second, the government provides a service, staffed by new business advisers, to help small businesses employing staff for the first time get to grips with the tax and National Insurance systems. For telephone advice or to arrange a visit by an adviser, ring the **New Employer Helpline**, Tel: 0845 6070 143; website: www.hmrc.gov.uk.

If you are still worried or don't want the bother of doing the paperwork yourself, your bank and possibly your accountant are likely to offer a full payroll service, which will cost you money but will take the burden off your shoulders. Here is some brief information on the main points you should consider.

PAYE

If you employ someone in your business (including your spouse) you are responsible for deducting Income Tax under the PAYE arrangements and accounting for it to the Collector of Taxes. You will be provided with tax tables and working sheets. The tax office will then notify you of the various PAYE tax codes in respect of your employees and explain how to use the tax table to work out the deductions. If an employee does not have an existing P45, you should ask him or her to complete a starting certificate, form P46, obtainable from the tax office.

An individual is liable for tax after deduction of his or her personal allowance and various reliefs. If your business has fewer than 50 employees, you could save £250 in tax by filing your PAYE return online. If you have any queries or need advice, call the **HMRC Online Services Helpdesk**, Tel: 0845 6055 999; website: www.hmrc.gov.uk.

Working Tax Credit. If you employ any low-income members of staff, they may be entitled to an earnings top-up known as Working Tax Credit. All recipients receive the money direct from HMRC.

Personnel records

Many businesses find it useful to keep personnel records, covering such information as National Insurance numbers, tax codes, merit appraisal reports and so on. You should contact the Information Commissioner for advice about your obligations under the Data Protection Act. Contact the **Information Commissioner**, Tel: 0845 6306 060; website: www.ico.gov.uk.

Employment legislation

As an employer, you have certain legal obligations in respect of your staff. The most important cover such issues as health and safety at work, terms and conditions of employment and the provision of employee rights including, for example, parental leave, trade union activity and protection against unfair dismissal. Very small firms are exempt from some of the more onerous requirements and the government is taking steps to reduce more of the red tape. However, it is important that you understand in general terms what legislation could affect you.

Minimum wage

There are now three levels of minimum wage. For all workers under the age of 18 who are no longer of compulsory school age, the minimum hourly rate from 1 October 2008 is £3.53; for those aged 18 to 21, the minimum is £4.77; and for those aged 22 and above, the minimum is £5.73 an hour.

Health and safety at work

The Health and Safety at Work Act applies to everyone in a business, whether employer, employee or self-employed. It also protects the general public who may be affected by your business activity. The Health and Safety Executive publishes a number of useful free leaflets and also has a public enquiry point that is open between 8 am and 6 pm. Ring the **HSE Information Line**: 0845 3450 055 or consult HSE's website: www.hse.gov.uk.

Discrimination

An employer – however small the business – may not discriminate against someone on the grounds of sex, race, disability, religion, marital status, sexual orientation or, since October 2006, age. This applies to all aspects of employment, including training, promotion, recruitment, company benefits and facilities.

In particular, following the 1995 Disability Discrimination Act, there is a duty to make any necessary changes – known as 'reasonable adjustments' – to the workplace and employment arrangements, so that a disabled person is not at any substantial disadvantage. Until recently, companies with fewer than 15 employees were exempt from this requirement, but now even the smallest companies are required to comply with the legislation.

As stated above, the new age discrimination legislation now equally makes it illegal for employers to discriminate against older candidates or employees on account of age. Provided individuals are still physically and mentally capable of doing their job, an employer can no longer force them to retire before the 'default' retirement age of 65. Employers now also have a duty to consider requests by employees to postpone their retirement and need to give those they wish to retire at 65 at least six months' notice of their decision in writing.

On 1 October 2007 the new Equality and Human Rights Commission opened, working to eliminate discrimination, reduce inequality, protect human rights and build good relations within society. The previous commissions – the Equal Opportunities Commission, the Commission for Racial Equality and the Disability Rights Commission – have been incorporated into this new organization, which is a non-departmental public body. This means it is accountable for its public funds but independent of government. For more information, contact the **Equality and Human Rights Commission** helplines: England: 0845 6046 610; Wales: 0845 6048 810; Scotland: 0845 6045 510; or consult the website: www.equalityhumanrights.com.

Contract of employment

A contract of employment is an agreement entered into between an employer and an employee under which they have certain mutual obligations. It comes into being as soon as an employee starts work, when it is taken that he or she accepts the job on the terms offered. Within two months of the job starting, the employer must normally give the employee a written statement highlighting the key terms and conditions of the job, together with a general description of the duties.

Entitlement to a written statement applies to all staff, including part-timers and employees working on fixed-term contracts. By law, they are required to be treated no less favourably than comparable full-timers or permanent employees in respect of their terms and conditions of employment, including access to training, holiday entitlement and benefits.

Useful guidance documents prepared by the **Department for Business, Enterprise and Regulatory Reform** include *Written Statement of Employment Particulars, Contracts of Employment* and *Individual Rights of Employees* and are available from the BERR website: www.berr.gov.uk. For further information and advice consult your local Citizens Advice Bureau or your solicitor, or ring the **Acas** helpline on 0845 7474 747; website: www.acas.org.uk.

Disputes

If you find yourself with a potential dispute on your hands, it is sensible to approach Acas, which operates an effective information and advisory service for employers and employees on a variety of workplace problems, including employment legislation and employment relations. Contact Acas, Tel: 0845 7474 747; website: www.acas.org.uk.

Acas also has a wide range of publications, giving practical guidance on employment matters, from writing a contract of employment to the latest employment legislation, obtainable by calling the Acas Publications Orderline, Tel: 08702 429090; website: www.acas.org.uk.

Trading regulations

Trading regulations laying down your obligations to your customers are contained in various Acts of Parliament, such as the Fair Trading Act, Trade Descriptions Act, Sale of Goods Act, Consumer Credit Act, Enterprise Act and Consumer Protection Act. For free advisory literature, contact the **Office of Fair Trading,** Tel: 0845 4040 506; website: www.oft.gov.uk. Solicitors are also qualified to advise on such matters.

Licences

Certain types of business require a licence or permit to trade; these include pubs, off-licences, nursing agencies, pet shops, kennels, mini-cabs or buses, driving instructors, betting shops, auction sale rooms, cinemas, hairdressers, street traders and, in some cases, travel agents and tour operators. You will also require a licence to import certain goods. Your local authority planning office will advise you whether you require a licence, and in many cases your council will be the licensing authority.

The Consumer Credit Act 1974 also imposes a licensing requirement on various types of business that offer credit and hire facilities. The Act is administered by the Office of Fair Trading, which publishes a helpful booklet, *Do You Need a Credit Licence?* Tel: 0845 4040 506; website: www.oft.gov.uk.

Permissions

Depending on the nature of your business, other permissions may also need to be obtained, including those of the police, the environmental health department, licensing authorities and the fire prevention officer. In particular, there are special requirements concerning the sale of food and safety measures for hotels and guest houses. Your local authority will advise you on what is necessary.

Working from home

Many people quietly 'set up shop' from home and there are no questions asked. There could, however, be trouble if in consequence of the business there is an increase in traffic, noise, smells or other inconvenience caused to neighbours. Even more likely, unless you own the freehold of your home, you could have problems with your landlord if the tenancy agreement states that the accommodation is for domestic use only. If you simply use your home as a telephone base, this will probably not be an issue, but if you have a stream of callers and a van parked outside, you could be accused of violating the lease. You may have to pay Business Rates (in addition to your Council Tax) on that part of your home you use as business premises.

Another possible downside of working from home is that this could have Capital Gains Tax implications should you ever want to sell the property. As working out the various financial pros and cons has become rather a complex matter, before taking any decision you would be advised to take professional advice.

Insurance

Insurance is more than just a wise precaution. It is essential if you employ staff, have business premises or use your car regularly for commercial purposes. Many insurance companies now offer 'package insurance' for small businesses that covers most of the main contingencies in a single policy. This usually works out cheaper than buying a collection of individual policies. If you buy a package, check that it contains whichever of the following are relevant to your needs:

- *Employers' liability.* This is compulsory if you employ staff. It provides indemnity against liability for death or bodily injury to employees and subcontractors, arising in connection with the business. Exceptionally, companies that employ only the owner of the business are not obliged to buy employers' liability insurance.
- *Product and public liability.* This insures the business and its products against claims by customers or the public. It could also cover legal expenses and the cost of complying with enforcements or judgements.
- *Professional indemnity.* This is now essential for all businesses offering investment advice in whatever form. It is also highly recommended for doctors, architects, consultants and other professionals who might be sued personally – or whose business might be sued – if a client suffered a mishap, loss or other damage in consequence of advice or services received. With the recent growth in litigation, many professional bodies are recommending that cover should continue after retirement in the event of an individual – or his or her estate – being sued for work done some years previously.

- *Material damage risk.* This covers against fire or other risk to the property, damage to equipment and theft. You can also be insured against loss of money or goods in transit.
- *Loss of profits or business interruption risk.* This insures the business against loss of profits in the event of your having to cease or curtail trading for a time, owing to material damage. The two policies are normally linked. It should also cover the risk of breakdown of a key item of machinery.
- *Motor risks.* This is compulsory for all motor vehicles.
- *Life assurance.* This is essential should you wish to provide for your own family or key employees' families or to ensure that funds are available to pay off any debts or to enable the business to continue in the event of your death.
- *Permanent health insurance.* Otherwise known as 'income protection', it provides insurance against long-term loss of income as a result of severe illness or disability. Most income protection plans are pretty flexible and can be tailored to individual needs.
- *Key person insurance.* This applies to the loss of a key person through prolonged illness as well as death. In small companies where the success or failure of the business is dependent upon the skills of two or three key executives, key person insurance is increasingly being written into investment deals as part of the necessary security demanded by banks, financial institutions and private investors. Remember however that, whereas life insurance benefits your family, key person insurance benefits only the company.
- *Jury service insurance.* Businesspeople cannot seek automatic exemption from jury service even though prolonged absence from work could severely disrupt their business. Insuring against the risk of being called for jury service is therefore worth considering.

Insurance when working from home

If you are self-employed, you may need to extend your existing private policies to cover your commercial activities. A fire at home could destroy business products as well as your domestic possessions. Likewise, your motor insurance may not be sufficient for business purposes, if the loss of your car could cause serious interruption to your trading. You should discuss these points with your insurance company or a broker.

Insurance brokers

To find an insurance broker, contact the **British Insurance Brokers' Association**, Tel: 0870 9501 790; e-mail: enquiries@biba.org.uk; website: www.biba.org.uk.

Useful reading

The Association of British Insurers publishes a useful free booklet, *Insurance Advice for Small Businesses*. Contact the Association, Tel: 020 7600 3333; e-mail: info@abi.org.uk; website: www.abi.org.uk.

Marketing

Unless you were employed in sales or marketing, you may suspect that this is likely to be a weak point in your business plan. The essence of good marketing is very simple: find out what the customer wants and then try to supply it. This is far easier than designing a product or service and hoping that buyers will come flocking to your door. The points you need to consider are:

- what kinds of individuals (or companies) are likely to be your customers, including their age group and sex;
- whether you are competing with existing suppliers or are offering a genuinely new concept (including, for example, a delivery service that other local shopkeepers do not supply);
- whether the market is expanding or contracting, with particular emphasis on how many potential customers live close by;
- finally, how you can inform the potential market that your new product or service is available.

This sort of preliminary thinking is essential. The organizations outlined below may be able to help you formulate a realistic marketing plan.

Your local library will probably have trade directories and *Yellow Pages*, from which you can research the competition. It may also have copies of trade magazines relevant to the industry you plan to enter.

Your local council will have information on the population and demographic profile of the area and will be able to give you details of any development plans that could affect customer potential. Your local Enterprise Agency and Business Link exist to help small businesses and should be able to offer valuable marketing advice. Approved Chambers of Commerce should be able to offer practical advice and training in marketing techniques and may be able to assist with useful contacts. There is also a wealth of information and sources of help available from the internet.

National organizations that offer help include the following:

The Chartered Institute of Marketing runs courses for non-members who need general marketing advice; Tel: 01628 427500; e-mail: info@cim.co.uk; website: www.cim.co.uk.

The Chartered Management Institute runs an extensive management information centre, which non-members can visit with the agreement of the Institute; Tel: 01536 204222; e-mail: enquiries@managers.org.uk; website: www.managers.org.uk.

The Market Research Society (MRS) can supply you with a copy of *The Research Buyer's Guide*, £80 (plus postage and packing), which contains details of companies that could mount a research exercise on your behalf. Costs range from £2,000 upwards depending on what is required. Tel: 020 7490 4911; e-mail: info@mrs.org.uk; website: www.mrs.org.uk.

The Office for National Statistics holds information on many aspects of the economy, including sales by UK manufacturers; Tel: 0845 6013 034; e-mail: info@statistics.gov.uk; website: www.statistics.gov.uk.

Promotion

Once you have assessed where your market lies, you have to decide how to promote yourself. Methods of advertising your product or service might include:

- direct mailshots and leaflet drops;
- advertising in specialist publications or local newspapers with a potentially high readership among your target market;
- a good website design that is user-friendly;
- exhibitions and local displays at functions such as school prize-givings, agricultural shows or local sporting events;
- telephone sales, perhaps with the help of a small team;
- editorial coverage in the press, on local radio programmes or on TV.

You are likely to succeed better with any of these techniques if you discuss your plans with a professional consultancy. The names of local practitioners should be available from:

The Chartered Institute of Marketing, Tel: 01628 427500; e-mail: info@cim.co.uk; website: www.cim.co.uk.

The Chartered Institute of Public Relations, Tel: 020 7766 3333; e-mail: info@cipr.co.uk; website: www.cipr.co.uk.

Public Relations Consultants Association Ltd, Tel: 020 7233 6026; e-mail: pressoffice@prca.org.uk; website: www.prca.org.uk.

Competitors

It is useful to know who your competitors are and what they are doing. One way is to get copies of their annual reports, which are available from Companies

House. If you can quote the company registration number this will help; all companies should have this listed on their letterhead. Contact **Companies House**, Tel: 0870 3333 636; e-mail: enquiries@companies-house.gov.uk; website: www.companieshouse.gov.uk.

It is also sensible to attend trade shows of the industries within which you are planning to compete. For a list of major UK trade shows, check the website: www.exhibitions.co.uk.

Exports

UK Trade & Investment, the government organization dedicated to building UK business success in Europe and elsewhere, offers comprehensive information, advice and practical assistance to help British exporters compete successfully. Assistance ranges from doing the groundwork for market research through to establishing a presence in the market. Contact UK Trade & Investment, Tel: 020 7215 8000; website: www.uktradeinvest.gov.uk.

The Institute of Export (IOE) offers technical help and advice on international trading matters and provides education and training through its short course programme. Fees and membership subscription details are available on request. Contact the IOE, Tel: 01733 404400; e-mail: Institute@export.org.uk; website: www.export.org.uk.

Your local **Chamber of Commerce** should have information on some of the problems you might encounter, and your **bank** will also have up-to-date information on the market conditions in most overseas countries, which it should supply free of charge.

Raising finance

Before you approach anyone for money, you must have a proper business plan. This means that you are bound to spend some time researching your business ideas and producing a realistic projection of cash flow needs. Your business plan should be brief and to the point but must contain the following items:

- a clear statement of what product or service you plan to offer;
- sales and marketing projections, based if possible on some research or knowledge of the market;
- your initial investment plus ongoing cash flow requirements;
- basic information concerning premises, staff, equipment and development plans;
- profit and loss projections, showing when you expect the business to start making money.

It is a good idea to ask an accountant to vet your business plan. Some high street banks offer the same service for a fixed fee and may also offer other help, such as a period of free banking. The different types of finance now available to small businesses through traditional sources such as banks and other institutions are more extensive than most people realize.

Advice and training

Small business is very well served when it comes to general help and training. A number of organizations offer free advice and low-cost consultancy, as well as a variety of training schemes, ranging from general information on setting up and developing a business to more specialized courses.

Business Links

A network of Business Links exists throughout England to provide small businesses with access to the full range of advisory and support services in their area. They can provide help and guidance across a wide range of topics, including business planning, financial management, employment issues, marketing and e-commerce. For further information, contact **Business Link**, Tel: 0845 6009 006; website: www.businesslink.gov.uk.

Adult education centres

Short courses in specific business skills are run by business schools and colleges of higher and further education. Various trade and professional associations also run courses. Further information is available from www.learndirect.co.uk and www.direct.gov.uk.

Regional agencies

These organizations are designed to assist the development of industrial activity in their areas, and all have small business divisions that will be only too glad to offer any assistance they can. Consult the website: www.berr.gov.uk. In addition:

Scottish Enterprise. Scottish Enterprise operates through a network of 12 Local Enterprise Companies in lowland Scotland, offering a wide range of services to start-up and expanding businesses. For your nearest regional office contact Scottish Enterprise, Tel: 0845 6078 787; website: www.scottish-enterprise.com.
Highlands and Islands Enterprise (HIE). The HIE network covers the northern and western parts of Scotland, as well as the Scottish islands. It offers a free

counselling service to small firms and to those considering setting up in these areas. Financial assistance may be given to meet start-up and training expenses. Contact HIE, Tel: 01463 234171; website: www.hie.co.uk.

Non-government sources of advice and training

Many enterprise agencies, Chambers of Commerce, business institutes and small business clubs, scattered around the country, provide counselling services, together with, in some cases, more formal training.

Lawyers for Your Business is a legal advisory service set up by the Law Society with the aim of encouraging smaller businesses to seek the advice of a solicitor at an early stage in the hope of avoiding future problems. Applicants are offered an initial free half-hour consultation at which they can discuss – and may often resolve – any queries. Further consultations, if these are required, are charged at normal rates. Contact Lawyers for Your Business, Tel: 020 7405 9075; website: www.lawsociety.org.

Trade associations

Virtually all industries have a trade association that provides advice and other services to members. If you are considering purchasing or starting a business in a particular trade sector, ask at your local library for the name and address of the relevant trade body or search on the internet. Examples are the National Federation of Retail Newsagents, the British Institute of Interior Design, the Institute of Employment Consultants and the Booksellers Association.

The following are the key organizations representing small business interests. Some act as pressure groups and conduct research as well as provide a service to their members:

Federation of Small Businesses, Tel: 01253 336000; e-mail: membership@fsb. org.uk; website: www.fsb.org.uk.
Forum of Private Business, Tel: 0845 1301 722; e-mail: info@fpb.org; website: www.fpb.org.
Institute of Directors, Tel: 020 7451 3188; e-mail: enquiries@iod.com; website: www.iod.com.
CBI, Tel: 020 7379 7400; website: www.cbi.com.

Useful reading

The No-Nonsense Guide to Government Rules and Regulations for Setting up Your Business, available from the Business Links website: www.businesslink.gov.uk or the

Department for Business, Enterprise and Regulatory Reform Order Line, Tel: 0845 0150 010; website: www.berr.gov.uk.

An extensive list of books is available for small and start-up businesses published by Kogan Page; Tel: 020 7278 0433; website: www.koganpage.com.

11

Looking for paid work

Far from thinking of putting your feet up when you retire from your present job, perhaps you would like (or feel it would be prudent) to continue working in some form of paid employment. If so, the encouraging news is that prospects are improving all the time, as more and more employers are actively seeking to recruit older people. Think about some of the options available before rushing into a job straight away. Here are a few basic things to consider.

In an ideal world, instead of seeking a new job, would you rather remain in your existing one? You may find that, contrary to past practice, your employer is willing to keep you on beyond the organization's normal retirement age. This could be for several reasons. Since the age discrimination legislation came into effect, it has become illegal to require employees to leave on account of age without good reason (at least until age 65). Also, thanks to a recent change in the pension rules, people in occupational schemes are no longer prevented from drawing their pension benefits while continuing to work for their existing employer.

If you have already left or are shortly about to do so, what is your main motive in wanting to work? Is it the wish to supplement your income? Is it for the companionship? Do you fear boredom if you don't work? Or do you enjoy the mental stimulation you derive from working? Some people admit they like having a sense of purpose, which is why they wish to continue to work. Others have a lurking suspicion that, if they don't have a job, their friends and social acquaintances will be less interested in them.

Whatever your reason for wanting to continue actively working, it should be a valid one and something you've thought through and talked about with family and friends. The answer may well be a combination of factors, but you should at least try to pinpoint your priorities to avoid drifting into a job that does not suit your lifestyle. There are too many stories of people whose prime reason for seeking work was to get out of the house to make new friends, who then took on a solitary occupation working from home. Likewise, there are numerous cases of people whose real purpose was financial but who somehow signed on instead for unpaid voluntary work.

Another fundamental consideration is how much work to do. Have a serious think about how many hours per week you would like to work. Is it a full working week, Monday to Friday? Or would just a couple of half-days be sufficient? While on the subject of time, is working a long-term goal? Or do you just envisage it as a pleasant occupation to fill in the next year or so?

What about distance? Would you be prepared to commute? If not, perhaps you are aiming for a job that is strictly local. Was there anything – for example, the requirement to take part of your holiday at specified times – that you particularly disliked about your previous employment? If so, make sure that it is something you keep in mind and avoid a similar situation occurring in the future.

One very important point to bear in mind is what you are going to do. Are you planning to seek an opening in a similar field, where your experience and contacts would come in useful? Or do you want to do something entirely different? If you want a complete change, would you be willing to do a training course?

There is also the economics of the whole matter. It may sound stupid when you have been working most of your life, but factors such as your age, your total weekly earnings, your pension and other income, as well, of course, as any out-of-pocket expenses you incur could mean that at the end of the day the sums look rather different from what you had supposed.

Financial considerations

Since the abolition of the earnings rule, no matter what age you are or how much you earn there is no longer any forfeit to your State pension, although of course you may have to pay tax on your additional income. If you are working close to a full-time week and/or have enough money to live on, there could still be an advantage in asking the DWP to defer your pension, as this will entitle you to a bigger pension in the future. Each year of deferral earns an increment of about 10.4 per cent of the pension. Another advantage is that, if you choose to defer your pension by at least a year, you will have the option of taking the money as a taxable lump sum instead of in higher weekly pension payments.

Decisions concerning your occupational pension

These could also arise, particularly if you are looking not so much for a retirement job as for a last big move before you retire. Most (though not all) pension schemes apply actuarial reductions for early retirement, and joining a new pension scheme in late middle age, though not impossible, can present difficulties or impose certain limitations, not least because many employers are revising their pension schemes, with rather less generous benefits for new members.

National Insurance (NI)

NI is another consideration. Unless you are over state retirement age or have earnings of £110 a week or less (2009/10), in which case you can forget about NIC, you will be liable for the normal Class 1 contributions. If, as many early retirees do, you work for two or more different employers, you will have to pay Class 1 in respect of each.

If you obtain work through an agency (eg catering, nursing or exhibition work), you are usually regarded as an employee of the agency for NI purposes, and the agency is responsible for the payment of Class 1 contributions on your behalf. However, this does not apply if you do the work from home, are not subject to anyone's direct supervision, or are in the entertainment business.

If you are over retirement age and have a job, the only requirement is that you obtain an exemption card to give to your employer; see form CF 384 (Certificate of Exception). If you do freelance or other assignment work (unless virtually all your earnings come from one employer, in which case HM Revenue & Customs (HMRC) would argue that you are an employee of the organization), you are officially considered to be self-employed for both NI and taxation purposes (see Chapter 10, Starting Your Own Business). For further information, you might find it helpful to read leaflet IR 56, *Employed or Self-Employed? A Guide to Employment Status for Tax and National Insurance*, available from any tax office.

Tax rules

NB: HMRC has tightened up the rules in order to clamp down on what it sees as the avoidance of PAYE and Class 1 NIC in respect of the provision of services, including for example consultancy and contract work. Those most likely to be affected are individuals who: 1) offer their services via small limited companies; 2) work over a period of time for a sole organization; or 3) work for a client or clients who have the right to control and supervise how the work is performed, as opposed to leaving the initiative to the individual concerned. If you are thinking of operating in an independent capacity – as opposed to becoming a bona fide employee – it would be sensible to discuss the tax implications with an accountant before determining whether you should operate as self-employed, sole trader, partnership or limited company.

Jobseeker's Allowance (JSA)

You can claim JSA provided you:

- are under State pension age;
- are unemployed or working on average less than 16 hours a week;
- have paid, or have been treated as having paid, sufficient National Insurance Contributions; or
- have a low income.

To qualify, however, you must be capable of, available for and actively seeking work, and must enter into a jobseeker's agreement with your local Jobcentre. The essence of the agreement is an action programme aimed at maximizing your chances of finding a job. You will receive help and advice, and there is also a fortnightly Jobsearch review to give you and your adviser an opportunity to assess your progress and to discuss any potential openings that might be suitable.

Claimants are not allowed to turn down a job offered to them via their Jobcentre without good reason. Lower pay would not normally be accepted as a reason although, that said, there is a 'permitted period' up to a maximum of 13 weeks when individuals may be allowed to restrict their job search to openings that take advantage of their skills, experience and reasonable salary expectations. A particularly welcome feature of JSA is that it makes it more worthwhile for recipients to do part-time work. For further information about JSA and other benefits, contact your local Jobcentre or **Jobcentre Plus** office on 0800 055 66 88 or see the website: www.jobcentreplus.gov.uk.

Working Tax Credit

If you have a job but are not earning very much, you may be able to boost your income by claiming Working Tax Credit. In certain circumstances, including in particular households with three or more dependent children or where a member of the family has a disability, those with slightly higher incomes could still be eligible to apply. HMRC advises that the easiest way to check is to complete the form listed under 'Tax credits' on its website. To qualify, you would usually be expected to work at least 30 hours a week. However, those with a disability and/or dependent children are required to work only 16 hours. All recipients now receive the payment direct from HMRC. Application forms are obtainable by ringing the **HMRC Helpline.** Its advisers will be pleased to give assistance, if needed, with any of the questions; Tel: 0845 300 39 00; website: www.hmrc.gov.uk.

Redundancy

If you have just been made redundant, or fear this is a possibility, see the information in Chapter 2, Money in General (page 9).

Special measures to assist disabled people to work

If you can't work because of illness or disability which started before 27 October 2008, you may be able to get Incapacity Benefit. This is a weekly payment for people who become incapable of work while under State Pension age. For details on eligibility go to the website: www.direct.gov.uk or look at www.jobcentreplus.gov.uk.

New Deal 50-plus Programme

The government has extended the New Deal for help in getting a job to include people aged 50-plus. It is applicable to individuals who have been in receipt of JSA, Income Support, Incapacity Benefit, Severe Disablement Allowance or Pension Credit for at least the last six months and who need practical help to get started again, in either a self-employed capacity or paid work. You might also be eligible if you have been in receipt of a combination of the above benefits for six months or more or if you have been getting NI credits, Carer's Allowance or Bereavement Allowance. There is no upper age limit, and the New Deal 50-plus Programme is also available if your partner has been receiving an increase in benefits for you for at least six months.

The package offered consists of practical one-to-one support from a personal adviser, including help in preparing a curriculum vitae (CV) and writing job application letters, and help for individuals to update their existing skills or gain new ones for the job they are doing. Low earners may also be eligible to receive the Working Tax Credit to make returning to work financially viable.

For further information, contact any **Jobcentre Plus** offices or Tel: 0845 606 0234; website: www.jobcentreplus.gov.uk.

Age discrimination

The age discrimination legislation came into force in October 2006, making it illegal for employers to discriminate against older candidates on account of age, as regards recruitment, training and promotion. In particular, provided individuals are still physically and mentally capable of doing their job, an employer can no longer oblige them to retire before a 'default' retirement age of 65. Employers also now have a duty to consider requests by employees who want to postpone their retirement and will need to give those they want to retire at 65 at least six months' written notice of their decision.

Assessing your abilities

Some people know exactly what they want to do. They have planned their action campaign for months, done their research, prepared a CV and followed up selective openings, and are just waiting for their present employment to come to an end before embarking on a new career. But, for most of us, it is not like that. Having merrily announced our intention to find a job, there comes a moment of truth when the big question is: what?

Knowing what you have to offer is an essential first step. Make a list of everything you have done, in both your formal career and ordinary life, including your outside interests, such as local politics, Rotary, hobbies, voluntary work and even jobs around the home – decorating, gardening, carpentry or cooking. In particular, consider any practical or other skills, knowledge or contacts that you have acquired through these activities that may now prove useful, for example public speaking, fundraising, committee work, conference organization, production know-how, computer knowledge or fluency in a foreign language. As a result of writing everything down, most people find that they have far more to offer than they originally realized.

Add your personal attributes and any special assets you can offer an employer. The list might include health, organizing ability, a good telephone manner, communication skills, the ability to work well with other people, use of a car and willingness to do flexible hours. Maturity can also be a positive asset. Many employers prefer older people as being more reliable and less likely to be preoccupied with family and social demands. Also, in many small firms in particular, a senior person's accumulated experience is often rated as especially valuable.

If you look at yourself afresh in this fashion, you may get a clearer idea of the sort of job that would suit you. Although it's sensible to keep a fairly open mind and not limit your applications too narrowly, the worst mistake you can make is to answer scores of advertisements indiscriminately – and end up with a sack load of rejections, which always make depressing reading. Of course, offers do sometimes turn up out of the blue, and in some cases in a field that it would never have occurred to you to enter. But as a general rule when job hunting, it helps to know at least in broad terms what you are seeking before you start.

Many people find this extraordinarily difficult. After years of working in one occupation, it takes quite a leap in imagination to picture yourself in another role – even if it is in the same or a related area. If you intend to do something completely different, it will be harder still, as your knowledge of what the job entails will probably be second-hand. Also, quite apart from the question of what you would enjoy, in many parts of the country the issue may be more a matter of what is available.

Talking to other people helps. Friends, family, work colleagues or business acquaintances may have useful information and moreover will quite likely be able to appraise your abilities more objectively than you can yourself. It could also be sensible to consult outside experts who specialize in adult career counselling and whose advice may be more realistic than that of friends in the context of the current job scene.

Job counselling

This is usually a mixture of helping you to identify your talents in a vocational sense combined with practical advice on successful job-hunting techniques. Counsellors can assist with such essentials as writing a CV, preparing for an interview and locating job vacancies. They can also advise you of suitable training courses. Counselling is offered both by government agencies and by private firms.

Jobcentre Plus

Jobcentre Plus brings together the former Benefits Agency and Employment Service to provide a one-stop shop where jobseekers can get help and advice about work and training opportunities and also about any benefits for which they might be eligible. Jobcentre Plus provides a network of offices and telephone contact centres. For further information, contact your local Jobcentre or Jobcentre Plus office, Tel: 0845 606 0234; website: www.jobcentreplus.gov.uk. There is a list of job vacancies (around 400,000 at any time) available through Jobcentre Plus, together with information about JSA and other relevant benefits.

Travel to interview scheme

This provides financial assistance in meeting travel costs to long-distance inter-views. The scheme is available to people who have been unemployed and are receiving JSA or help with NI Contributions.

Private counselling

Job counselling has become a growth industry in the private sector. Some people find it extremely helpful, others an expensive waste of time. The best advice is to obtain brochures from a variety of agencies and study the literature carefully to see exactly what you are being offered. You could ask for a list of former clients and then speak to one or two of them direct, to find out whether they found the service useful.

Career Counselling Services

One organization that may help is Career Counselling Services. Individual career counselling ranges over two to five sessions and covers motivation, values and key strengths to identify the work/life balance that would best suit the client. Fees for three sessions are around £500. A service to help with job hunting is also available. Contact the Career Counselling Services on 020 3178 5261; website: www.career-counselling-services.co.uk.

When looking on the internet, key in the words 'Career' or 'Vocational' in your search engine.

Training opportunities

Knowing what you want to do is one thing, but before starting a new job you may want to brush up existing skills or possibly acquire new ones. Most professional bodies have a full programme of training events, ranging from one-day seminars to proper courses lasting a week or longer. Additionally, adult education institutes run a vast range of courses or, if you are still in your present job, a more practical solution might be to investigate open and flexible learning, which you can do from home.

Open and flexible learning

Open and flexible learning is successfully helping to provide a greater range and flexibility of vocational education and training opportunities for individuals of all ages. In particular, it is designed to increase the scope for participants to learn at a time, place and pace best suited to their own particular circumstances.

The following organizations offer advice and an excellent range of courses: **Learn Direct**, Tel: 0800 101 901; website: www.learndirect.co.uk and **Home Learning Courses**, Tel: 0800 138 77 80; website: www.homelearningcourses. com.

AgeWorks – Wise Owls can help you if you are over 45 and looking for employment and are currently unwaged and living in certain London boroughs. For further information, Tel: 020 7923 7771; e-mail: recruitment@wiseowls.co. uk; website: www.wiseowls.co.uk.

IT skills

If you are considering a change in direction, maybe some new qualifications would help. Certainly IT skills are in great demand in many jobs. If you don't have much IT experience or specialist knowledge, it is important to have the skills that employers want. **SkillsTrain** is the UK's largest specialist home learning college and has a proven blended learning programme that helps you achieve industry-recognized qualifications. It will help anyone who feels his or her IT skills need updating or enhancing; more importantly, you don't need any previous experience and age is no barrier. You can learn from home at your own pace with full support. To maintain a pleasant work/life balance, the training is designed to fit around the busiest schedule. For further information contact SkillsTrain on 0800 181 076; website: www.skillstrainuk.com.

Help with finding a job

The ideal is to find a job for your retirement while you are still at work. Quite apart from it being more difficult for people to summon the energy to start looking around after a period of being idle, employers tend to give preference to those they see as being busy and involved, rather than those whom they suspect of having got out of the habit of the normal disciplines of work. However, whether you leave it a while or start hunting well in advance, this will not affect the approach you probably adopt. The only extra tip, if you have been retired for some time, is to consider doing some voluntary work, or a short course, so you have a convincing answer to the inevitable question: what have you been doing?

There are four basic ways of finding a job: through contacts, by following up advertisements, by applying to an agency for suitable introductions, or by direct approaches to suitable employers. As with most other things, the more ways you try, the better your chances of success.

Make sure all your friends and acquaintances know that you are in the market for work – and include on the list your present employer. Some firms actually encourage consultancy links with former executives, or at least are prepared to respond to a good idea. A greater number are more than happy to take on previous employees over a rush period or during the holiday season.

Another obvious move, if you are a member of a professional institute, is to inform it of your availability. Many institutes keep a register of members wanting work and, encouragingly, receive a fair number of enquiries from firms seeking qualified people for projects, part-time or temporary work, or sometimes even permanent employment.

A further source of very useful contacts is your local Chamber of Commerce, the CBI or the Institute of Directors. Likewise, if you are a member of a Rotary Club, it can only be useful to spread the word; and the same applies to, say, a golf club, political association where you are active, any committee you sit on or any other group with which you are involved. Often the most unlikely person turns out to be the one who helps you most.

If you intend to follow up advertisements, selectivity is the name of the game. Rather than write around to all and sundry, limit your applications to those that sound genuinely promising. You will save yourself a lot of stationery and postage, not to mention disappointments when another 'sorry' letter arrives or you fail to hear anything at all. As well as national and local newspapers, remember that the trade press often offers the best bet of all.

Agencies will invariably have more applicants than vacancies, except where skill shortages exist. However, most of them clearly place a fair number of people (or they would be out of business). When applying, please note that enthusiasm counts. People who simply register their name and then sit back and wait tend to be forgotten. The best advice is to telephone frequently to enquire what opportunities have arrived. If you live close by, pop into the office from time to time. Being on the spot at the right time is nine-tenths of success. A selection of agencies that specialize in appointments for people aged 50-plus is listed at the end of this chapter.

A direct approach to likely employers is another option. Study the business press and talk to your colleagues for ideas of firms that might be interested in employing someone with your abilities. Always find out who the appropriate person is to whom you should be writing – a properly addressed letter is far more likely to get noticed than one merely marked 'For the attention of the Personnel Manager'.

Regardless of whether you use contacts, advertisements or agencies – or preferably all three – a prime requirement will be to have a well-presented CV.

CV writing

This is your personal sales document. It should contain:

- your name;
- your address;
- your telephone number;
- your age (optional);
- brief details of your education;
- a summary of your work experience including dates, employers, job titles and outline of responsibilities;
- other achievements;
- key outside interests.

Ideally your CV should not be longer than two pages of A4, and it must be typed. There are a number of firms that specialize in providing assistance with the writing of CVs: look in the national press for advertisements or search on the internet. While some CVs are highly professional, a common fault tends to be that they are overlong. This can definitely be counterproductive.

An all-purpose CV can also put off employers. Wherever possible, you should try to gear your CV specifically to the job on offer, emphasizing those elements of your experience and skills that are relevant. If you are thinking of using a specialist service, check the price first, as charges can be on the hefty side. As with other purchases, you should do a bit of price comparison before making a decision. The price will normally include a batch of immaculately typed copies of your CV, ready for you to distribute.

A far cheaper option is to take advantage of the government work preparation courses, which are run by Jobcentre staff or other agencies on the government's behalf to assist those who have been out of work for six months or more (people with disabilities can apply as soon as they wish). As part of the service, help is given with CV preparation, and free facilities are provided, including telephone, computer and photocopying equipment. Contact your **Jobcentre** for details: Tel: 0845 606 0234; website: www.jobcentreplus.gov.uk.

Interview technique

If you have worked for the same employer for a number of years, your interview skills are liable to be a little rusty. It is a good idea to list all the questions you expect to be asked (including those you hope won't be brought up) and then get a good friend to rehearse you in your answers. In addition to questions about your previous job, be prepared for some or all of the following: what you have done since leaving employment; why, if you are now seeking a job, you retired earlier than you might have done; whether your health is good – this may take the form of a polite enquiry as to whether you would not find the hours or travelling too much of a strain; why you are particularly interested in working for this particular employer; and, given the job requirements, what you think you have of special value to offer. You may also be asked what you know about the organization. If you know little to nothing about the company, perhaps you should do a bit of research. Why not read up about the organization via its website?

Obvious mistakes to avoid are claiming skills or knowledge that you do not possess; it is amazing how many people do this and then get found out later. Giving the impression that you have a series of stock answers to problems is not likely to impress prospective employers. Criticizing your former employer or, by contrast, drawing comparisons that could be interpreted as being faintly disparaging of the organization where you are attending for interview is also not advisable.

Possibly the most difficult subject of all to come up may be the question: how much money would you expect? Unfortunately most jobs for retired people – including early retirees – pay less than their previous employment. This is starting to improve since the age discrimination legislation came into effect, but you may have to take a reality check and strike a balance between what you want and the risk of pricing yourself out of the market.

Useful reading

Preparing the Perfect CV (5th edn), *Preparing the Perfect Job Application* (5th edn), and *Successful Interview Skills* (5th edn), all by Rebecca Corfield and published by Kogan Page (website: www.koganpage.com).

Part-time openings

Another reason why the pay may appear low is that the work is part time. For some people, of course, this is the ideal arrangement. Others may regard it as second best. However, do not sniff at part-time work if the opportunity is available. It is a way back into the market, and many part-time or temporary assignments develop into full-time jobs in due course. This is especially true in small firms, which may of necessity be cautious about recruitment while the business is in the early development stage.

Additionally, far-reaching changes have been happening in the job market, with temporary, or project-based, professional and executive assignments becoming increasingly common. For example, freelance accountants are in growing demand, as are supply teachers, call centre staff and personnel specialists with particular knowledge of, say, pensions or performance pay. Corporate governance, regulation and risk assessment are other areas of major growth where people with relevant expertise are being actively sought. Proficient temporary secretaries are again high on the 'wanted list'. Likewise, there are a growing number of part-time and other openings for older people to work in supermarkets, chain stores, hotels, conference centres and other outlets connected with the tourist industry.

It is estimated that over a fifth of all new jobs are now on a contract basis, the average being for six months or a year. While the downside is an obvious lack of security for younger people seeking permanent employment, mature candidates have everything to gain. First, there is greater turnover of jobs – so more vacancies. Second, the stock excuses for not employing older applicants are now patently nonsensical. These used to revolve around the fact that older employees would not 'develop' with the company and that it wasn't worth training them for just a short time. Denying older employees access to relevant training on account of their age is fortunately now illegal under the age discrimination legislation.

Part-time or freelance work can to all intents and purposes become a full-time occupation in its own right. Ask retired businesspeople who have taken on half a dozen such appointments. They are more than likely to tell you that they are working harder than they have ever done in their life.

Employment ideas

Going the established routes (agencies and so forth), while obviously recommended, may not suffice. Many of the best jobs are never advertised. This is either because people obtain them through personal recommendation or because (and this is becoming more frequent) individuals have been partially instrumental in creating their own opportunities. One clear-cut way of doing so is to use a bit of initiative when spreading the word of your availability, by actually suggesting work you could usefully perform. Consultancy is very much a case in point.

Consultancy

Many retired executives make a good income by hiring themselves back to their former employer in a consultancy guise. As opposed to being paid a regular salary and working full time, they undertake specific projects for which they are paid a fee. This may be structured as a lump sum, for example £5,000 for devising and helping implement a merit appraisal scheme, or, as many consultants do, they may negotiate a day-rate. Consultancy, by definition, is not limited to a single client. By using your contacts judiciously plus a bit of marketing initiative, it is quite possible to build up a steady list of assignments on the basis of your particular expertise. Marketing skills are always in demand, as is knowledge of website design, accountancy, HR issues and, increasingly today, public relations experience. Small firms are often a good bet for consultants, as they cannot afford to employ specialists full time and normally buy in expertise as and when it is required.

Many established consultancies retain a list of associates – a sort of freelance register – whom they call on, on an 'as needed' basis, to handle suitable assignments. If you are serious about consulting, an organization called the Institute of Business Consulting (IBC) offers plenty of guidance, including details of the standards required to qualify for membership. The IBC, which has several thousand members and over 20 branches nationwide, has contact with all business advice centres, enterprise agencies and similar organizations seeking business-people qualified to advise small, start-up and medium-sized businesses. A Code of Conduct and professional standards of competence and personal development have been established, and substantial business experience is a prerequisite of membership. Further details are available from the **Institute of Business Consulting**, Tel: 020 7497 0580; e-mail: ibc@ibconsulting.org.uk; website: www.ibconsulting.org.uk.

Interim management

Interim management represents a huge growth area in recruitment over the past few years. The term covers an enormously wide range, from a temporary manager engaged to cover in an emergency to someone taken on to handle a specific job such as the closure of a plant. In essence it is an outside specialist recruited short term to implement a particular assignment – for example, a marketing campaign or the installation of a new computer system.

The growth is largely due to two factors. One is the downsizing of personnel by large organizations. The second is the requirement of many small companies for specialist skills that they cannot afford to employ full time. Either way, what it means is an upsurge in temporary job opportunities for experienced managers and/or those with particular expertise to offer. Many of the best jobs go to those who have recently taken early retirement or been made redundant.

Most of the organizations that specialize in such placements have more candidates on their books than vacancies but all agree that this is a growing industry with opportunities set to increase. As in consultancy, fees vary enormously. While the going rate for senior people is upwards of £750 a day, some managers command double or even more. However, as with any temporary or freelance situation, there will inevitably be days when you will not be working. Don't forget that, in contrast to a permanent job, very few interim assignments offer the normal executive perks. Typical assignments last between six and nine months and may be full time or simply involve one or two days' work a week.

Contact the **Interim Management Association**, Tel: 020 7009 2195; website: www.interimmanagement.uk.com, which can put you in touch with its accredited members in a location suitable to you.

Openings via a company or other reference

Just as your company could turn out to be your best customer for consultancy services, it could also open other doors. If you are still a couple of years off retirement, you could broach the subject with your employer about seconding you to an enterprise agency or charity, where you would be helping small businesses or a worthwhile voluntary organization in your local community. Secondment can be part time for a few hours a week or full time for anything from a few weeks to two years. It can also often lead to a new career.

Normally only larger employers are willing to consider the idea since, as a rule, the company will continue to pay your salary and other benefits during the period of secondment. If you work for a smaller firm it could still be worth discussing the suggestion, as employers benefit from the favourable publicity the company attracts by being seen to support the local community.

Business in the Community can provide information on secondment opportunities for both employers and individuals. Contact Business in the Community, Tel: 020 7566 8850; e-mail: information@bitc.org.uk; website: www.bitc.org.uk.

Public appointments

Opportunities regularly arise for individuals to be appointed to a wide range of public bodies, such as tribunals, commissions and consumer consultative councils. Many appointments are to local and regional bodies throughout the country. Some are paid but many offer an opportunity to contribute to the community and gain valuable experience of working in the public sector on a part-time, expenses-only basis.

These opportunities are now advertised on a website that provides a single source of information about public appointments vacancies at local and regional levels across England as well as those with a national remit. You can search the site by subject area, government department and location to find vacancies that are of interest to you. You can view detailed information about each vacancy and how to apply. See www.publicappts-vacs.gov.uk or www.direct.gov.uk.

Non-executive directorships

Many retiring executives see this as the ideal. The problem, whichever way you look at it, is either that more executives want appointments than there are directorships available or that not enough companies have yet recognized the merits of having outside directors on their board. Such appointments carry heavy demands made more onerous by recent legislation. If you are able and committed and have the necessary experience, you could contact the following:

First Flight (Placements) Ltd provides non-executive directors, non-investing non-execs and chairmen/women to start-up, early stage and mature companies.

Tel: 01797 270 920; e-mail: info@ffplacements.co.uk; website: www.nonexecu
tivedirector.co.uk.
NER (Non-Executive Register) places candidates for FTSE 250 and Fortune
500 companies wishing to strengthen their boards. Tel: 01525 862 234; e-mail:
info@ner.co.uk; website; www.nonexecutive.com.

Market research

In addition to the normal consultancy openings in marketing, there is also scope
for those with knowledge of market research techniques. The work covers a very
broad spectrum, from street or telephone interviewing to data processing, designing questionnaires, statistical analysis and sample group selection. Some market
research agencies employ researchers and analysts on a freelance basis. However,
as with other fields, supply exceeds demand, so there is a certain amount of luck
involved, as well of course as ability, in finding regular work. For a list of market
research companies, see *The Research Buyer's Guide*, obtainable from the **Market
Research Society (MRS)**, Tel: 020 7490 4911; e-mail: info@mrs.org.uk;
website: www.marketresearch.org.uk.

Survey interviewing

No experience is necessary to become a freelance interviewer for the **National
Centre for Social Research (NatCen)**. It recruits people nationwide to ask
members of the public for their views on such topics as education, health,
housing and similar. Applicants need to have the use of a car and landline telephone and have good IT skills. There are three days' paid training at the start. For
further information, contact NatCen, Tel: 020 7250 1866; e-mail: info@natcen.
ac.uk; website: www.natcen.ac.uk.

Paid work for charities

Although charities rely to a very large extent on voluntary workers, most charitable organizations of any size have a number of paid appointments. Other than
particular specialists that some charities may require for their work, the majority of openings are for general managers or administrators, fundraisers and
those with financial skills. Secretarial vacancies also occur from time to time.
Salaries have been improving but in general are still considerably below the
commercial market rate. A further point is that, unlike the situation in the
corporate world, managers cannot expect to find a battery of support staff and
must be willing to turn their hand to almost everything – as well as handling
meetings, building up good media relations and sustaining the enthusiasm of
volunteers and paid staff alike.

It is essential therefore that anyone thinking of applying for a job in a charity
must be in sympathy with its aims and style. Agencies specializing in charity

recruitment advise that it is a good idea to do a stint as a volunteer before seeking a paid appointment, as not only will this provide useful experience but will help you to decide whether you would find the work satisfying. Most national newspapers such as the *Guardian*, the *Independent*, *The Times* and the *Sunday Times* carry charity job advertisements, or you could register with one of the following:

CharityJob.co.uk helps candidates, charities and agencies in their search to find work or personnel or place people. Tel: 020 8939 8430; e-mail: info@charityjob. co.uk; website: www.charityjob.co.uk.

CF Appointments helps charities and not-for-profit organizations fill their key jobs – for example, chief executive, finance director and fundraiser – and also finds trustees who are unpaid. Tel: 020 7220 0180; e-mail: enquiries@cfappoint ment.com; website: www.cfappointments.com.

CR Search and Selection charity recruitment professionals, specializes in recruiting senior and middle managers for charities and other not-for-profit organizations. CR also helps charities to find trustees who can offer skills and experience on a voluntary basis. Tel: 020 7833 0770; e-mail: info@crsearchand selection.com; website: www.crsearch.co.uk.

Sales

Almost every commercial firm in the country needs good sales staff, so if you have authority, charm and persuasiveness to win extra orders, you will be in high demand.

Many people who have never thought of sales could be excellent in the job because of their specialist knowledge in a particular field combined with their enthusiasm for the subject. Educational and children's book publishers, for example, are often keen to recruit ex-teachers to market their books to schools and libraries. There is an almost insatiable demand for people to sell advertising space, and if you are an avid reader of a particular publication, for example a specialist motoring or gardening magazine, you might find the work fun and be very successful.

Additionally, many firms employ demonstrators in shops or at exhibitions for special promotions. The work is usually temporary or freelance by definition, and while pay is normally good the big drawback is that you could be standing on your feet for long periods of the day. The big 'beware' is firms that pay on a commission-only basis: far from merely earning a pittance, you could end up distinctly out of pocket.

If the idea of selling appeals, either study the newspaper advertisements or, better still, approach firms direct that you reckon could make genuine use of your special knowledge. If the idea makes you quail, the likelihood is that selling is not for you. If it fires you with enthusiasm, you could actually find yourself making more money in your retirement than ever before.

Sales distributor

Some companies employ softer-sell methods, using self-employed distributor agents who call on their neighbours with a catalogue or arrange parties at which it is possible to buy a range of merchandise. Betterware, which recruits several thousand distributors a year (including many retirees), says the essence is building up friendly relationships, noting down orders and delivering the goods a few days later. There is no financial outlay, the hours are totally flexible and most agents can reckon on earning about £50 to £200 a week, depending on the number of hours they work. The minimum requirement is 10 hours a week.

Other big-name companies that use freelance distributors include Avon and Kleeneze and, while their terms and conditions all vary slightly (eg some encourage distributors to purchase samples or charge them a nominal amount for catalogues), all have frequent openings for both permanent and temporary work.

For further information, contact the companies direct; or you can obtain a list of all member companies together with their advice sheet, listing points to check before signing on as a distributor, by contacting the **Direct Selling Association**, Tel: 020 7497 1234; e-mail: info@dsa.org.uk; website: www.dsa.org.uk.

Tourist guide

An extrovert personality is one of the qualities needed for tourist guide work. Happily age is no longer a factor – there is a growing number of tourist guides well into their 60s and older. However, fitness is essential, as it is a job that requires bags of stamina as well as a real liking for people.

You must also be prepared to put in some fairly concentrated study. While there are various possible qualifications (some easier than others), training for the coveted Blue Badge takes 15 months, and the exam itself is considered to be equivalent in standard to a first degree. Even the Blue Badge is no guarantee of steady work, as openings are largely seasonal, most tourist guides are self-employed and the field is highly competitive. Perhaps not surprisingly, opportunities are greatest in London, especially for those with fluency in one or more foreign languages. If, despite the challenges, you would like to know more, contact the **Guild of Registered Tourist Guides**, Tel: 020 7403 1115; e-mail: guild@blue-badge.org.uk; website: www.blue-badge-guides.com.

Another possibility is to sign on as a lecturer with one of the growing number of travel companies offering special interest holidays. To be eligible you need real expertise in a subject, the ability to make it interesting and an easy manner with people. Pay is usually fairly minimal, although you may receive tips – plus of course the bonus of a free holiday. While the number of openings is fairly limited, people who get on the circuit could end up lecturing on tours around India or running painting classes in Italy. Chapter 14, Holidays, gives names of operators that make a feature of special interest programmes. The travel pages of most newspapers should also give you plenty of ideas.

Other tourist work

You might like to consider courier work. Holiday firms are increasingly looking to recruit people in their 50s and early 60s because they are finding that their clients often prefer having more mature people in charge. Some jobs take you overseas, others not. Either way, it is demanding work that calls for a calm, unflappable personality.

If you live in a popular tourist area, there is a whole variety of seasonal work, including jobs in hotels, restaurants, shops and local places of interest. Depending on the locality, the list might also include jobs as deckchair attendants, play leaders for children, caravan site staff, extra coach drivers and many others.

Teaching and training skills

If you have been a teacher at any stage of your career, there are a number of part-time possibilities.

Coaching

With examinations becoming more competitive, demand has been increasing for ex-teachers with knowledge of the public examination system to coach young-sters in preparation for A and AS levels, GCSE and common entrance. Contact local schools, search the internet or contact a specialist educational consultancy. Gabbitas Educational Consultants provides a wide range of recruitment and consultancy services to independent schools in Great Britain and to English-speaking schools overseas. It also maintains an extensive register of teachers seeking appointments, as well as a register for tutors. For further information contact **Gabbitas Educational Consultants,** Tel: 020 7734 0161; e-mail: consultants@gabbitas.co.uk; website: www.gabbitasrecruitment.com.

Specialist subjects

Teachers are in demand for mathematics, physics, chemistry, technology and modern languages. People with relevant work experience and qualifications may be able to teach or give tuition in these subjects. A formal teaching qualification is, however, required to teach in state-maintained schools. The **Training and Development Agency for Schools** has a range of publications about entry into teaching. Contact: 020 7023 8000; e-mail: corporatecomms@tda.gov.uk; website: www.tda.gov.uk.

English as a foreign language

Over the past decade there has been a mini-explosion of new schools teaching English to foreign students. These tend to be concentrated in London and the major academic cities such as Oxford, Cambridge, Bath and York. Good English-language schools require teachers to have an initial qualification in teaching English to those who have a different first language. The following websites give information about how to do this: www.global-english.com; www.intesolinternational.com; www.tefl.net; and www.direct.gov.uk.

Working in developing countries

There are various opportunities for suitably qualified people to work in the developing countries of Africa, Asia, the Caribbean and the Pacific on a semi-voluntary basis. Skills most in demand include civil engineering, mechanical engineering, water engineering, architecture, urban, rural and regional planning, agriculture, forestry, medicine, teaching English as a foreign language, maths and physics training, and economics. All air fares, accommodation costs and insurance are usually covered by the organizing agency, and pay is limited to a 'living allowance' based on local levels. As a general rule, there is an upper age limit of 65 (VSO accepts volunteers up to 75), and you must be willing to work for a minimum of two years. The following are the major agencies involved in this kind of work (fuller details are contained in Chapter 12, Voluntary Work):

International Service, Tel: 01904 64 77 99; e-mail: is@internationalservice.org.uk; website: www.internationalservice.org.uk.
Progressio, Tel: 020 7354 0883; e-mail: enquiries@progressio.org.uk; website: www.progressio.org.uk.
Skillshare International, Tel: 0116 254 1862; e-mail: info@skillshare.org; website: www.skillshare.org.
Voluntary Service Overseas (VSO), Tel: 020 8780 7500; e-mail: enquiry@vso.org.uk; website: www.vso.org.uk.

Publishing

Publishers are increasingly using freelance staff with appropriate experience for proofreading, copy-editing, design, typography, indexing and similar work as well as for writing specialist copy. For a list of firms that could be interested, *The Bookseller* (www.thebookseller.com) has classified advertisements, useful for advertising your own skills as well as for finding work.

Freelance journalism

This is a highly competitive field with limited scope and one for professionals. The best bet if you remain undaunted is to approach specialist magazines direct, to find out exactly what the publication wants, including number of words and so on.

Caring for other people

There are a number of opportunities for paid work in this field. Mature women or couples are often preferred. If you are considering working with vulnerable people (young or old), you will be required to have a full Criminal Records Bureau (CRB) check with enhanced disclosure. This applies to many jobs these days, both paid and unpaid. It is to protect those who need to rely on other people and ensure that no one unsuitable is appointed to a position of trust who is likely to abuse it. These checks are extremely thorough and can take several weeks or even months to process. Please be patient and as accurate as possible when asked to provide information by prospective employers, charities or not-for-profit organizations. For further information about CRB checks and why they are required, see the **Criminal Records Bureau** website: www.crb.gov.uk.

Home support schemes for elderly people

An increasing number of local authorities run schemes whereby an elderly person either lives with a family as an ordinary member of the household, receiving whatever care and special assistance are necessary, or receives daytime support at a neighbour's or in his or her own home. Enormous trouble is taken by social workers in matching families with their guest. Pay varies from area to area but is paid by the hour for daytime support and weekly for every elderly person cared for on a live-in basis.

Ask at your social services department whether there is an adult placement scheme to which you could contribute, or contact the **NAAPS (National Association of Adult Placement Services)** on 0151 227 3499; website: www. naaps.co.uk.

Domestic work

A number of private domestic agencies specialize in finding temporary or permanent companions, housekeepers and extra-care help for elderly and disabled people or for those who are convalescent. Many of these jobs are particularly suitable for retired people or couples and, with ever-growing demand especially for carers, finding work is probably easier than it has ever been. Pay rates vary depending on which part of the country you live in and the number of hours involved. Agencies worth contacting include:

Anchor Care, Tel: 0845 140 2020; website: www.anchor.org.uk.
Consultus Care & Nursing Agency Ltd, Tel: 01732 355 231; e-mail: office@ consultuscare.com; website: www.consultuscare.com.
Country Cousins, Tel: 0845 601 4003; e-mail: info@country-cousins.co.uk; website: www.country-cousins.co.uk.

Universal Aunts Ltd, Tel: 020 7738 8937; e-mail: aunts@universalaunts.co.uk; website: www.universalaunts.co.uk.

Check on the internet for other agencies – search under 'Domestic', 'Employment' or 'Care Agencies' or look in *The Lady* magazine, published every Wednesday.

Home helps

Local authorities sometimes have vacancies for home helps, to assist disabled or elderly people in their own home by giving a hand with the cleaning, light cooking and other chores. Ask at your local social services department.

Childminding

If you already look after a grandchild during the day, you might consider caring for an additional couple of youngsters. You will need to be registered with the local social services department, which will explain all the requirements, including details of any basic training – such as first aid – that you may first need to do.

Nursing

Qualified nurses are in great demand in most parts of the country and stand a good chance of finding work at their local hospital or through one of the many nursing agencies. Family planning clinics could also be worth approaching. Those with suitable experience, although not necessarily a formal nursing qualification, could apply to become a care support worker for the charity Crossroads, which provides regular short-term relief for carers of sick or disabled people in their own homes. For information on local schemes, contact **Crossroads**, Tel: 0845 4500 350; website: www.crossroads.org.uk.

Homesitting

This means taking care of someone else's home while they are away on holiday or business trips. Mature, responsible people, usually non-smokers with no children or pets, are in demand for this type of work. It is more like a paid holiday, and you get paid every week (extra if care of pets is involved), depending on the responsibilities and on the size of the house or flat. Food and travelling expenses are normally also paid. It is useful to have your own car. Firms specializing in this type of work include:

Absentia, Tel: 01279 777 049; e-mail: theteam@home-and-pets.co.uk; website: www.home-and-pets.co.uk.
Homesitters Ltd, Tel: 01296 630 730; website: www.homesitters.co.uk.
Universal Aunts Ltd, Tel: 020 7738 8937; e-mail: aunts@universalaunts.co.uk; website: www.universalaunts.co.uk.

Cashing in on your home interests

Cooking, gardening, home decorating, dressmaking and DIY skills can all be turned into modest money-spinners.

Cooking

Scope includes catering other people's dinner parties, selling home-made goodies to local shops and cooking for directors' lunches. Other than top-class culinary skills, requirements are a large deep freeze, a car (you will normally be required to do all the necessary shopping) and plenty of stamina. Notify your friends, advertise your services through the local newspapers, Chamber of Commerce or local business clubs or, if you are really serious about it, enrol with one of the specialist catering agencies.

Gardening

Small shopkeepers and florists sometimes purchase flowers or plants direct from local gardeners, in preference to going to the market. Alternatively, you might consider dried flower arrangements or herbs, for which there has been a growing demand. However, before spending any money, check around to find out what the sales possibilities are. If you are willing to tend someone else's garden, the likelihood is that you will be inundated with enquiries. Spread the word among friends and acquaintances and in local shops and the pub.

Dressmaking and home decorating

If you are happy to do alterations, the chances are that you could be kept busy from dawn to dusk. Many shops are desperate for people who sew. Likewise, many individuals and families would love to know of someone who could alter clothes, as well as dress-make properly. Perhaps to a slightly lesser extent, the same goes for curtains, chair covers and other soft furnishings. Often a good move is to approach firms selling materials for the home, which might be only too glad to put work out to you. Alternatively, put up a card in newsagents' shops or run a small advertisement in the local paper.

DIY

Competition is more intense, as many small builders offer this service. However, elderly people often require small jobs, as do those who do not have someone capable of DIY available. Advice for getting your services known is the same as for gardening.

Pubs and paying guests

Many people dream of running a pub in their retirement – and many people live to regret it. A less strenuous option that others may prefer is offering bed-and-breakfast accommodation in their own home.

Running a pub

Running a pub is more a way of life than a job, and one that requires a great deal of stamina. Anything less like a quiet retirement would be hard to imagine. You are on your feet for most of the day, the hours are long and when you are not pulling pints or preparing bar snacks you will be dealing with the paperwork plus all the other day-to-day business requirements.

You can either buy your own 'free house' outright or become the tenant or lessee of a brewery or pub-owning company. Prices vary according to the length of lease, location and so on but, as a rough guide, you would need at least £5,000 to get started as a tenant, around £60,000 for a leasehold and between £200,000 and £1.5 million – or even more – for a 'free house'. On top of all this, as with any other business you will need to budget for operating capital.

Tenancy packages vary and may include the range of products you sell as well as repairs and decorations. As a self-employed businessperson, a tenant or lease-holder has responsibility for the hiring and firing of any staff, and compliance with the fire regulations and the other laws of the land. As a licensee, he or she is also required to know and enforce the licensing laws.

If you are over 50, some experience of self-employment or the leisure industry is vital in order to be considered for a tenancy or long-term lease, and even then you may need to convince the company that you are not making the mistake of imagining that running a pub is a congenial way of easing into retirement. The **British Institute of Innkeeping (BII)** advises that, if you are thinking of running a pub, you should try working in one first and only then, if after a fair trial you are still enthusiastic, begin looking at the options seriously. Information on train-ing courses and qualifications can be obtained from the BII; Tel: 01276 684 449; e-mail: reception@bii.org; website: www.bii.org.

Bed-and-breakfast

Tourist areas, in particular, offer scope for taking in bed-and-breakfast visitors. However, unless you want to make a regular business of it, it is advisable to limit the number of guests to a maximum of five; otherwise you will be subject to stringent fire regulation precautions requiring special doors and other expensive paraphernalia. To be on the safe side, contact the local environmental health officer (see the telephone directory or enquire at the town hall), who will advise you of anything necessary you should do. You should also register with your local tourist information centre. See the section 'Letting rooms in your home' in Chapter 8, Your Home.

Agencies and other useful organizations

Job hunting through agencies is very much a question of luck. People can be on an agency's books for months and months and not be sent to a single interview. Someone else can walk through the door and within 48 hours be fixed up with an ideal job. Applicants normally greatly exceed vacancies, and the majority of jobs, especially for the over-60s, tend to be on the modest side: clerical, security work, gardening, domestic services and similar. However, more challenging opportunities are sometimes registered, and one or two of the organizations listed below specialize in executive appointments. Retired accountants in particular are almost always in demand, as are individuals with fundraising skills.

A positive attitude – with agencies as well as with prospective employers – unquestionably helps. While you may be asked to state your date of birth (in which case it is usually better to be honest), there is no need to volunteer the information unless requested, least of all at the start of an interview.

Equally, there is no need to limit your applications to agencies that specialize in placing older candidates. If you are serious about finding work, you need to cast your net as widely as possible, so keep an eye on the local papers for other agencies in your area or search the internet. Depending on what you are looking for, several of the following organizations may be able to help.

Jobcentres

It is easy to forget the obvious. Jobcentres have changed their image considerably over the last few years and now carry a wide range of vacancies for all levels of ability. In particular, many small firms use them for recruitment in preference to the more expensive private employment agencies. There are around 1,000 Jobcentres and Jobcentre Plus offices throughout Great Britain, which between them are notified of over 60,000 jobs a week. They also act as a gateway to many of the training courses and advisory services. See the website: www.jobcentre plus.gov.uk.

Others you could contact are:

The Corps offers full- or part-time employment across a wide range of occupations, including security guards, concierges, receptionists, post-room staff, and commissionaires who provide an usher service at corporate functions and sporting events. All applicants are invited to an interview and are required to provide well-documented references. Contact the Corps on 0800 028 6303; e-mail: info@corpssecurity.co.uk; website: www.the-corps.co.uk.

Executive Stand-By Ltd specializes in placing executives of proven competence in management or similar posts in industry, commerce and voluntary organizations. These are mainly temporary or part-time but can lead to permanent positions. There are also occasional openings abroad. Contact Executive Stand-By Ltd on 01244 323 600; e-mail: executives@btconnect.com; website: www.esbpeople.co.uk.

Extend runs recreational exercise-to-music classes for the over-60s and for people with disabilities of all ages. The organization is constantly looking for potential group teachers. Training courses last approximately 12 days spread over several weeks and cost about £500. There are written and practical assessments on completion. At the present time, eight training teams operate in different parts of the UK. Contact Extend on 01582 832 760; e-mail: admin@extend.org.uk; website: www.extend.org.uk.

Manpower UK is a major supplier of temporary, contract and permanent staff. Skills in particular demand include secretarial and clerical experience, driving and assembly or manufacturing, and finance and accountancy. One of the fastest-growing areas of demand is for Telephone call centre staff. Contact Manpower UK on 01895 205 200; e-mail: enquiries@manpower.co.uk; website: www.manpower.co.uk.

Officers' Association. The Association provides a job-finding service for managerial, professional and senior technical people who are either leaving the armed services or who, having served as officers, are currently unemployed. A wide range of vacancies is handled in all sectors. Contact the Association on 0845 873 7144; e-mail: info@officersassociation.org.uk; website: www.officersassociation.org.uk.

Resourcing Solutions – Parity specializes in all types of IT contract and permanent work, with openings nationwide for, among others, senior project managers, analysts, programmers and network and software engineers. Contact Parity on 0845 873 0790; e-mail: marketing@parity.net; website: www.parity.net.

Quality Assurance Design Services caters for both permanent and contract (part- and full-time) personnel, specializing in the engineering, technical and construction sectors. Assignments cover both the UK and overseas. Contact Quality Assurance Design Services on 01244 323 100; e-mail: busy@qads.co.uk; website: www.qads.co.uk.

Wrinklies Direct is a network of recruitment agencies around the country that specialize in finding work for older people. Vacancies handled vary across a very broad range and could be anything from night-portering to a senior management job. To be put in touch with your nearest local agency, call the central number: 0845 260 1117; e-mail: info@wrinklies.org; website: www.wrinklies.org.

Local job-finding agencies

A number of selective recruitment agencies, concentrating on the over-40s or over-50s, have recently been springing up in different parts of the country to assist unemployed people in their middle years back into work. Most concentrate on fairly local vacancies – with the range of jobs very much a question of what is needed in the area. Enquire at your library or Jobcentre for any useful names and addresses. Your local Chamber of Commerce may also have information, and you can search the internet.

12

Voluntary work

If the idea of working as a volunteer interests you, and you have some spare time now that you are approaching retirement or are recently retired, this could be one of the most satisfying things you've ever done. There are probably as many different kinds of voluntary work that need to be done as there are organizations that need your help. The range of tasks and the variety of groups are both enormous. Perhaps this is one reason why some people simply steer clear of the whole area, fearing that the commitment may get out of control and that they may find themselves involved to a greater extent than they wish. Though this may be true in a few cases, there are probably many thousands more who, starting in a small way, find themselves caught up in the enthusiasm for their cause. They soon find they are immensely rewarded by the contribution they feel able to make and by the new friends this has brought them. Very broadly, voluntary help falls into four main categories: clerical and administrative, fundraising, committee work, and direct work with the public.

Clerical

Any active group is likely to need basic administrative help, from typing and stuffing envelopes to answering the telephone and organizing committees. This may involve a day or so a week or simply occasional assistance at peak times. Many smaller charities in particular would also greatly welcome hearing from individuals with IT expertise to assist with setting up a database, website design and similar.

Fundraising

Every voluntary organization needs more money, and their ingenuity in raising it seems boundless. Events are many and varied, but sponsored fundraisers are growing in popularity, and negotiating contributions from local or national busi-nesses may test anyone's diplomatic skills.

Committee work

This can cover anything from very occasional help to virtually full-time commit-ment as branch treasurer or secretary. People with business skills or financial or legal backgrounds are likely to be especially valuable, and those whose skills include minute taking are always in demand.

Direct work

Driving, delivering 'meals on wheels', doing counselling work, visiting the house-bound, working in a charity shop, helping with a playgroup, giving the mother of a sick child a chance to get out of the house for an hour or so: the list is endless and the value of the work incalculable.

While certain qualifications and experience – financial, legal, nursing and social work – have particular value in some circumstances, there is also a multitude of interesting and useful jobs for those without special training or with relatively ordinary abilities like driving or computer skills. Similarly, the time commitment can be varied to suit both helper and organization. It is far better to give just one morning a month and be reliable than to promise more time than you can spare and end up always being late or having to cancel at the last minute. Equally, as with a paid job, before you start you should be absolutely clear about all the terms and conditions:

- What sort of work is involved?
- Who will be working with you?
- What is expected?
- When will you be needed?
- Are expenses paid? What for? How much? (See 'Tax note' below.)

If you straighten all this out in the beginning there will be less chance of any misunderstandings, and you will find that voluntary work is not only very rewarding in its own right but also allows you to make a real contribution to the community.

As mentioned in Chapter 11, Looking for Paid Work, if you are considering working with vulnerable people (young or old) you will be required to have a full Criminal Records Bureau (CRB) check with enhanced disclosure. This applies to many jobs these days, both paid and unpaid. It is to protect those who rely on other people from anyone unsuitable being appointed to a position of trust who is likely to abuse it. These checks are extremely thorough and can take several weeks or even months to process. Please be patient and as accurate as possible when asked to provide information by prospective employers, charities or not-for-profit organizations. For further information about CRB checks and why they are required, see the **Criminal Records Bureau** website: www.crb.gov.uk.

Tax note

Volunteer drivers who receive a motor mileage allowance and who make a small profit, in that the allowance exceeds their actual incurred expenses (ie petrol and maintenance), are taxed on any profit they make. For further information, see leaflet IR 122, *Guidance – Volunteer Drivers Available* from HMRC; see website: www.hmrc.gov.uk.

Choosing the right voluntary work

It is one thing to decide that you would like to do some kind of voluntary work and quite another to discover what is available in your area and what particular outlet would suit you. For this reason we have included a list of organizations, arranged in broad categories of interest, indicating the types of activities for which they are seeking volunteers. But no such list can be complete – there are literally thousands of voluntary groups, national and local, which need help in some way or other. For further information on needs and opportunities in this sector there are several other major sources to which you can turn:

REACH finds voluntary, part-time opportunities for experienced managers and professional people of all ages who would like to use their skills working for a voluntary organization. Out-of-pocket expenses are paid, and the service, which is free, is available throughout the UK. Many openings are waiting to be filled, so there is a good chance of finding one that makes real use of your skills, as well as giving you the opportunity of acquiring new ones. Contact REACH, Tel: 020 7582 6543; e-mail: mail@reachskills.org.uk; website: www.reachskills.org.uk.

Volunteer centres. Most towns have a body of this kind that seeks to match up volunteers with local organizations seeking help.

Volunteering England can help you find out about volunteering opportunities anywhere in England by putting you in touch with a local organization. Tel: 0845 305 6979. e-mail: volunteering@volunteeringengland.org; website: www.volunteering.org.uk.

Volunteer Development Scotland can help you find out about volunteering opportunities anywhere in Scotland by putting you in touch with a local organization. Tel: 01786 479 593; e-mail: vds@vds.org.uk; website: www.vds.org.uk.

Wales Council for Voluntary Action. This is the umbrella body for voluntary activity in Wales. If you are interested in volunteering, it would be glad to put you in contact with an organization that would welcome your help. Tel: 0800 288 8329; e-mail: help@wcva.org.uk; website: www.wcva.org.uk.

General

The scope of the work of the British Red Cross, WRVS and Citizens Advice Bureau is so broad that they almost justify a category to themselves:

British Red Cross. The Red Cross is the world's largest humanitarian organization. It needs volunteer help from men and women for first aid, staffing medical loan depots, fire victim support, emergency response and vital community services. Training is always provided. Contact information and details of local branches are available from National Headquarters, Tel: 0844 871 1111; e-mail: information@redcross.org.uk; website: www.redcross.org.uk.

WRVS works in partnership with many organizations, including local authorities and hospitals, to cover a wide range of needs in the community. It particularly welcomes offers of help from men and women with time during the working day. Activities are wide-ranging but include meals on wheels, home support for older people, providing transport in rural areas, helping in hospital shops and assisting with catering and welfare services in emergencies. No special qualifications are required, as training is given. Contact WRVS, Tel: 0845 601 4670; website: www.wrvs.org.uk.

Citizens Advice Bureau. Founded in 1939, the charity has continued giving invaluable help and advice for 70 years. Throughout the country, it deals with millions of enquiries a year and has thousands of volunteers working from over 4,000 locations. The work involves interviewing and advising clients on a wide range of questions, including welfare benefits and legal rights. No formal qualifications are required, and training is given. As well as general advisers, the CAB is also looking for volunteers to assist with IT, social policy work and general administrative support. Language skills are also urgently needed to help local people for whom English is a second language. Contact the Volunteer Recruitment line on 0845 126 4264; website: www.citizensadvice.org.uk.

Community Service Volunteers (CSV) operates a UK-wide programme called the Retired and Senior Volunteer Programme (RSVP) for people aged 50 and over who want to be involved in their community. Each local group plans its own activities, which include befriending frail older people, helping children with reading and numeracy in schools, and working with health centres on primary care projects. For further details, contact RSVP on 020 7643 1385; e-mail: information@csv.org.uk; website: www.csv.org.uk.

Toc H has branches in all parts of the country involved in a wide range of good neighbour schemes within their local community. Volunteers are needed for such activities as hospital visiting, giving a day out to children in inner cities and providing a helping hand to people with disabilities. There is no special commitment – just whatever time you can spare. For further information contact Toc H on 01296 331 099; e-mail: info@toch.org.uk; website: www.tochparticipation.co.uk.

Animals

The Cinnamon Trust. The Cinnamon Trust is a registered charity that seeks to relieve the problems of elderly pet owners who, owing to illness or some other emergency, are temporarily unable to care for their pets. It also offers a long-term haven to animals whose owners have died and who had registered their pets with the Trust. Animal lovers throughout the country assist in a voluntary capacity, either by fostering a pet in their own home or by helping out on a daily basis, for example walking a dog, feeding it, cleaning out a bird cage or similar. Likewise, long-term homes are required for pets that have lost their owners. For further details contact the Trust on 01736 757 900; e-mail: admin@cinnamon.org.uk; website: www.cinnamon.org.uk.

Pet Fostering Service Scotland. The service provides short-term foster care for the pets of elderly people who, owing to some emergency such as going into hospital, are temporarily unable to manage. Volunteers may either look after a pet in their own home until the owner is able to take it back or provide some other caring service, such as walking a dog. Food, cat litter and any vet's fees that may be incurred are paid for by the owner. If you live in Scotland, have a love of pets and would like to help out in a crisis, contact the service on 0131 499 4393; e-mail: info@pfss.org.uk; website: www.pfss.org.uk.

Pets As Therapy (PAT) is a national charity that originated the PAT visiting scheme to give those in hospitals, care homes and other establishments the important contact with animals that many may miss. It is essential that the dogs and cats are well behaved and fully vaccinated. At present, there are around 4,000 volunteers throughout the country making regular visits. For further information contact PAT on 01844 345 445; e-mail: reception@petsastherapy.org; website: www.petsastherapy.org.

The Royal Society for the Prevention of Cruelty to Animals (RSPCA) works to promote kindness and to prevent cruelty to animals. Operating through its team of inspectors, it is concerned with the welfare of all animals and with education of the general public by campaigning in the media and through its range of promotional material. It also works for the cause of animal welfare abroad. Volunteers are needed to help with fundraising at local level. Contact the RSPCA; Tel: 0300 1234 555; website: www.rspca.org.uk.

The Wildfowl & Wetlands Trust (WWT) works to conserve threatened wetland birds and their habitats. As well as Slimbridge, there are visitor centres in Lancashire, Sussex, Tyne and Wear, the Cambridgeshire/Norfolk border, London, Dumfriesshire, South Wales and Northern Ireland. All have a network of volunteers who give valuable help, variously attending the information desk, dealing with visitor enquiries, conducting guided tours and assisting staff with administrative work. There is no minimum commitment, but most volunteers come in for a few hours or one day a week. For further information contact the WWT, Tel: 01453 891 900; e-mail: enquiries@wwt.org.uk; website: www.wwt.org.uk.

Bereavement

Cruse Bereavement Care, which has 150 branches throughout the UK, is the national organization for people who have been bereaved. It provides support, information and advice. Volunteers are needed in the branches to help with all these services. For further information, contact Cruse Bereavement Care on 020 8939 9530; e-mail: info@cruse.org.uk; website: www.crusebereavementcare. org.uk.

Children and young people

Action for Sick Children is a charity that supports sick children and their families and advocates that health services be planned to cater for their special needs. Local branches give practical help to parents and professionals in the hospitals. Work is organized through local branches that can be contacted through the head office. Although different branches may operate slightly different schemes, most will welcome voluntary help, for example help with surveys, help with fundraising for more parents' and children's facilities in hospital, and administrative assistance at the branches. Contact Action for Sick Children on 01663 763 004; website: www.actionforsickchildren.org.

Barnardo's provides services for children who face disability or disadvantage. Projects throughout the country include work with families, day care centres, community projects, playgroups, play buses and holiday schemes. Two major areas require help; the first is fundraising. Thousands of people work as voluntary fundraisers for Barnardo's. Activities may include helping in a charity shop or with local flag days and events. Write to the National Volunteer Development Manager, who will pass on your application to your regional branch. The second major area is the childcare programme. This could involve helping a child with reading or befriending a young person with a disability, to give the parent a much-needed break. For further information and a list of national and regional offices phone Barnardo's on 020 8550 8822, e-mail the information officer: dorothy.howes@barnardos.org.uk; website: www.barnardos.org.uk.

Children's Society runs projects for highly vulnerable children and young people in England, including children at risk on the streets, young refugees, disabled children and those in trouble with the law. Every local branch would be grateful for more fundraisers. There are also charity shops throughout the country that need volunteers. Contact the London headquarters on 0845 3001 128; e-mail: supporteraction@childrenssociety.org.uk; website: www.childrenssociety.org.uk.

Save the Children UK fights for children in the UK and around the world who suffer from poverty, disease, injustice and violence, working with them to find long-term answers to their problems. Volunteers are very much welcomed to assist with fundraising, campaigning, working in a shop or becoming involved in a specialist assignment, which could be anything from promoting an initiative in schools to helping out at the head office. For further information contact Save the Children UK on 020 7012 6400; e-mail: supporter.care@savethechildren.org.uk; website: www.savethechildren.org.uk.

Scout Association provides an enjoyable programme of activities for young people aged 6 to 20. Volunteers are needed in many roles, for example as leaders running weekly meetings or as commissioners overseeing several different groups. Other openings include becoming administrators or fellowship members who, among other aspects of the Association's work, help with managing the property, organize fundraising, contribute to training (eg vehicle maintenance, map reading and first aid) and edit newsletters. Contact the Association, Tel: 0845 300 1818; e-mail: info.centre@scout.org.uk; website: www.scouts.org.uk.

Sea Cadet Corps. This is a youth organization that offers boys and girls aged 10 to 18 challenging new experiences and adventure. Emphasis is placed on waterborne activities, with encouragement given to those who wish to pursue a career at sea. Units exist throughout the UK and welcome volunteer help either as administrators or as specialist instructors. Contact national headquarters on 020 7654 7000; e-mail: info@ms-sc.org; website: www.ms-sc.org.

Volunteer Reading Help (VRH) recruits and trains volunteers to work with children who find reading difficult. The volunteers then work in a primary school with the same children every week, helping them to improve their literacy skills and increase their confidence. No formal qualifications are needed, but you would be asked to give up to three hours a week during term-time for at least a year. For further information, contact the National Office on 020 7729 4087; e-mail: info@vrh.org.uk; website: www.vrh.org.uk.

Conservation

Architectural Heritage Society of Scotland promotes the study and protection of Scottish architecture. As well as enjoying events such as talks and visits, members can join case panels, for which volunteers are always needed. The work involves visiting and assessing listed buildings and conservation and planning applications. Contact the Society, Tel: 0131 557 0019; e-mail: administrator@ahss.org.uk; website: www.ahss.org.uk.

British Trust for Conservation Volunteers (BTCV) plays a leading role in encouraging volunteers from both town and country to improve the environment. Over 500 working holidays are organized nationally, and over 1,600 local groups run community projects at weekends and during the week. Typical projects include planting trees, cleaning ponds, restoring footpaths, protecting valuable habitats for wildlife, creating urban nature areas and assisting with woodland management. Not all of them involve heavy work, but a reasonable degree of fitness is required. Volunteers are also needed to help the local offices with administration, fundraising and publicity. Contact BTCV, Tel: 01302 388 883; e-mail: information@btcv.org.uk; website: www2.btcv.org.uk.

Campaign to Protect Rural England (CPRE) works to protect and enhance the countryside. Volunteers act as local watchdogs within CPRE's county branches, assessing and reporting unsightly development projects and threats to the environment, and sometimes representing CPRE at enquiries. There is also a need for help with fundraising, which is carried out by local groups. Contact CPRE on 020 7981 2800; e-mail: info@cpre.org.uk; website: www.cpre.org.uk.

Friends of the Earth is one of the leading environmental pressure organizations in the UK, aiming to conserve and protect the resources of the planet. Over 200 groups run local campaigns and fundraising projects. These can be contacted through the London office, which can also use help with the administration and with answering enquiries. Travel and lunch expenses are reimbursed. Contact Friends of the Earth on 020 7490 1555, or fill in the e-mail contact form on its website: www.foe.co.uk.

Greenpeace is an international environmental pressure group that campaigns to protect the natural environment. Volunteers are needed both to help in the London office and also for campaigning by local groups across the country. Contact Greenpeace on 020 7865 8100; e-mail: info@uk.greenpeace.org; website: www.greenpeace.org.uk.

Ramblers' Association aims to encourage walking, to defend and improve access to the outdoors and to protect the beauty of the countryside throughout the UK. Nearly all the work is carried out by volunteers, who keep an eye on footpaths, check maps of access areas, campaign on countryside matters, compile guidebooks, organize walks, help with administration and perform many other tasks. The time involved is whatever you can manage. Contact the Association on 020 7339 8500; e-mail: ramblers@ramblers.org.uk; website: www.ramblers.org.uk.

Royal Society for the Protection of Birds (RSPB) works to secure a healthy environment for birds and wildlife. It has over a million members and a network of over 180 nature reserves around the UK. Volunteers have a valuable contribution to make and are regularly needed to undertake biological surveys, help with management work on nature reserves, assist visitors and young people, and carry out administrative tasks in offices around the country. Volunteer opportunities range from a few days to a few weeks. No particular expertise is required nor, if you would like to help, is it necessary to become a member. For more information about volunteering, contact the RSPB on 01767 680 551; e-mail contact can be made via the enquiry form on its website: www.rspb.org.uk.

The elderly

The Abbeyfield Society. Local volunteers perform a number of roles to help support older people in family-style residential homes. The aim is to achieve a friendly atmosphere and to support the independence of each resident. There are also registered residential care houses for older people who need a high degree of support. Voluntary help needed may vary from befriending residents or gardening to committee work or organizing fundraising events. Contact the Society on 01727 857 536; e-mail: post@abbeyfield.com; website: www.abbeyfield.com.

Age Concern. The aim of Age Concern is to promote the welfare of older people. It does this by campaigning on their behalf and by organizing services to meet their needs. Local groups, using volunteer helpers, operate all over the country, and services can include day care, lunch clubs, home visiting, over-60s clubs and, in some areas, specialist services for physically and mentally frail elderly people. Fundraising activities in all their variety are also organized locally. For further information contact the Age Concern Information Line on 0800 00 99 66.

Age Concern England, Tel: 020 8765 7200; e-mail: supporterservices@ace. org.uk; website: www.ageconcern.org.uk.

Age Concern Wales, Tel: 029 2043 1555; e-mail: enquiries@accymru.org.uk; website: www.accymru.org.uk.

Age Concern Scotland, Tel: 0845 833 0200; e-mail: enquiries@acscot.org. uk; website: www.ageconcernscotland.org.uk.

Age Concern Northern Ireland, Tel: 028 9024 5729; e-mail: info@agecon cernni.org; website: www.ageconcernni.org.

Carers UK is a mine of information for family, partners or friends who need help because they look after an ill, frail or disabled person at home. With around 80 local branches, it provides information and advice through a CarersLine, and campaigns for a better deal for carers. Administrative help is needed at its London office and at its branches, whose members meet to discuss mutual problems. Contact Carers UK on 020 7378 4999; e-mail: info@carersuk.org; website: www. carersuk.org.

Contact the Elderly offers a way of making new friends while at the same time providing much needed companionship for lonely elderly people living nearby. Contact volunteers keep a personal link with isolated elderly people by taking them on one Sunday afternoon each month to have tea in the home of a volunteer host. Help is needed with driving (one Sunday a month) and/or hosting a tea party for about 10 elderly visitors once or twice a year. There are Contact groups nationwide; call 020 7240 0630; e-mail: info@contact-the-elderly.org.uk; website: www.contact-the-elderly.org.

Help the Aged aims to improve the quality of life for older people here and overseas. In the UK, it provides funds for day centres, community transport, home safety devices, emergency alarm systems and sheltered housing. It also produces a range of advice leaflets and operates a Freephone advice line. Overseas, it advises on social policy for older people and supports projects in combating destitution and ill health. Help the Aged is a major fundraising charity and has five regional offices. Volunteer help is needed to staff charity shops and to assist local fundraising committees. Contact Help the Aged on 020 7278 1114; e-mail: info@helptheaged.org.uk; website: www.helptheaged.org.uk.

IndependentAge helps older people on low incomes to remain independent by giving practical and financial support. Local volunteers keep in touch with beneficiaries through regular visits and telephone calls and by offering friendship to alleviate loneliness. Volunteers are also very much welcomed to participate in local fundraising events. Contact IndependentAge on 020 7605 4200; e-mail the development director: madeleine.jones@independentage.org.uk; website: www.independentage.org.uk.

The Princess Royal Trust for Carers is the largest provider of carers' support services in the UK. It gives information, advice and support to carers of all ages through its network of 130 independently managed carers' centres and two interactive websites. Volunteers are wanted to run aromatherapy and relaxation sessions. Help is also needed to provide telephone and administrative help in the centres. There are also openings for people with accountancy, fundraising and other business skills to serve on their local management committee. Contact the Trust on 0844 8004 361; e-mail: info@carers.org; website: www.carers.org.

The family

Marriage Care runs pre-marriage courses and also provides a professional counselling service for anyone with relationship problems. Help is required in running and administering its 56 centres. New potential counsellors are also sought. Contact Marriage Care on 020 7371 1341; e-mail: info@marriagecare.org.uk; website: www.marriagecare.org.uk.

Relate works to support marriage and family life. There are about 88 local Relate centres, which offer counselling to anyone with relationship problems; some also undertake education work in schools. Volunteers who would like to become counsellors receive training. There are also openings to serve on committees and help in the office. The work is most likely to appeal to people who have been previously involved with social or community activity of some kind. Contact Relate on 0300 100 1234; e-mail: enquiries@relate.org.uk; website: www.relate.org.uk.

SSAFA Forces Help provides a welfare and advisory service for the families of service- and ex-servicemen and women. There are 7,000 volunteers in branches throughout the UK and overseas, as well as professionals wherever service families are stationed. Case workers deal with every kind of problem – domestic, financial, legal and compassionate. Training is given, and although there is no minimum time commitment it is obviously critical to see a case through to the end. Help is particularly needed in inner cities. There is also a requirement for assistance in the counties as chair, treasurer, administrative helper, IT professional and publicity and fundraising officer. A service background is not necessary. Contact SSAFA Forces Help on 0845 1300 975; e-mail: info@ssafa.org.uk; website: www.ssafa.org.uk.

Health

Attend (formerly the National Association of Hospital and Community Friends) is the representative body for Friends groups throughout the UK. Each group is autonomous, and all work to improve the comfort and dignity of patients in both hospitals and the community. Volunteers, of whatever age, are always welcomed. Opportunities for voluntary work vary, but all groups are concerned with both service to patients and fundraising. Attend can put new volunteers in touch with their local Friends group. Contact Attend on 0845 450 0285; e-mail: info@attend. org.uk; website: www.attend.org.uk.

BackCare funds research into the causes and treatment of back pain. It teaches children and adults how to use their bodies sensibly and runs a network of local self-help branches. BackCare needs volunteers to start local branches and to provide practical help for back pain sufferers. Particular activities include organizing exercise and hydrotherapy classes, arranging talks and demonstrations, and running social and fundraising events. Contact BackCare on 0845 130 2704; website: www.backcare.org.uk

British Heart Foundation (BHF) funds research into the causes, prevention, diagnosis and treatment of heart disease. Its educational role includes promoting training in simple life-saving skills, informing the medical and scientific community about the results of its research and making the information known to the general public. BHF also provides life-saving cardiac care equipment to hospitals and other health providers, and helps support rehabilitation courses and heart support groups. With a national network of over 400 branches, BHF helps fund this vital work through a wide variety of fundraising schemes. Contact BHF on 020 7554 0000; e-mail: internet@bhf.org.uk; website: www.bhf.org.uk.

Calibre is a national lending library of recorded books on ordinary standard cassette tapes for use by 'anyone unable to read'. Volunteers are needed to help run the library, which is maintained entirely from donations. Publicity and fundraising help are also required. Contact Calibre on 01296 432 339; to e-mail fill in the enquiry form on its website: www.calibre.org.uk.

Cancer Research UK's aim is to bring hope to all those touched by cancer through pioneering research into the prevention, treatment and cure of the disease. It is almost entirely dependent on the generosity of the general public, and your support, whether helping to raise funds or sparing a few hours of your time, will contribute towards the work of its scientists in their efforts to conquer cancer. Thousands of volunteers organize local fundraising events, help in Cancer Research UK's shops (sorting, serving, pricing and ironing) or assist with general work in its office. For more information, contact Cancer Research UK on 020 7121 6699; to e-mail fill in the enquiry form on their website: www.cancerresear chuk.org.

Disability Snowsport UK, the skiers and boarders charity, provides opportunities for people with a disability to participate in skiing and snowboarding. Its goal is to help individuals improve their quality of life and transfer the benefits that they can derive from taking part to their everyday life. For more information contact Disability Snowsport UK on 01479 861 272; e-mail: admin@disabilitys nowsport.org.uk; website: www.disabilitysnowsport.org.uk.

Leonard Cheshire Disability is the UK's largest voluntary sector provider of support services to disabled people, helping them to live their lives as they choose. Its many services throughout the UK are supported by local people via regional offices, who make an enormous contribution. There are endless ways in which you can lend a hand, including driving, gardening, befriending individuals and fundraising, or you might like to help on the campaigning side. For further information contact Leonard Cheshire Disability on 020 3242 0200; e-mail: info@LCDisability.org; website: www.lcdisability.org.

Mind, The National Association for Mental Health, works for a better life for people with experience of mental distress. It has offices in England and Wales and more than 200 local associations. While these vary in size and the scope of their work, all raise their own funds and provide information and practical support. Their activities include running social clubs and day centres, befriending schemes, an advocacy service and self-help groups. If you would like to help, contact the Information Helpline on 0845 766 0163; e-mail: contact@mind.org. uk; website: www.mind.org.uk.

RDA (Riding for the Disabled Association) aims to help provide opportuni- ties for riding for disabled children and adults. You do not have to be horsey to help in one of the 520 local groups. Legal and financial knowledge is particularly valuable in connection with the opening of new groups and with keeping the accounts. For those with experience of horses (which may be supplemented by training courses), the main jobs are leading or walking beside the ponies while they are being ridden and accompanying parties on riding holidays. Contact the Association on 0845 658 1083; or by e-mail via the enquiry form on their website: www.riding-for-disabled.org.uk.

Royal National Institute of Blind People (RNIB) aims to help blind and partially sighted people lead full and independent lives. Among many other initi- atives, it runs schools for blind children, provides careers advice, offers training and assists with finding suitable employment. It also manages some rehabilita- tion centres and special homes, has a welfare advisory service, sells specially designed or adapted goods to make life easier and safer for blind or partially sighted people, publishes books and magazines in Braille and runs the Talking Book service. Contact the RNIB on 020 7388 1266; e-mail: helpline@rnib.org.uk; website: www.rnib.org.uk.

Scope works to promote equality and create education and employment oppor- tunities for people with cerebral palsy and related disabilities. There are also over 250 local groups offering information, confidential support and advice. Volunteers are particularly needed for helping in Scope shops, supporting local groups and participating in fundraising events. Contact Scope on 0808 800 3333; e-mail: response@scope.org.uk; website: www.scope.org.uk.

St John Ambulance is best known for its first aid role at public events. St John Ambulance volunteers also carry out care within the community. Volunteers receive a special induction training, tailored to their needs according to their chosen activity, which could variously be: care, transport, communications, support work at public events, the library service or first aid. Scope for volunteers is hugely varied and includes such activities as youth work, fundraising, public relations and community care, as well, of course, as first aid. Contact the national headquarters on 08700 10 49 50; or by e-mail via its website: www.sja.org.uk.

Heritage and the arts

There is scope for becoming involved in the arts in a volunteer capacity through community arts projects, arts centres, local arts councils and other arts activities associated with special groups such as the youth services or people with disabilities. All kinds of abilities are needed, from painting and other creative skills to accounting and clerical know-how. For addresses and other information about local arts organizations, contact your local authority or library, or search the internet.

Council for British Archaeology. Various archaeological excavations take place throughout the UK, mainly from March to September. The work will probably involve lifting, stooping and wheeling barrows, so this is not suitable for people with bad backs. No training is necessary. A two-week stay is the average. Accommodation will vary according to the site but may be pretty basic. Information on the various digs is given in *British Archaeology* magazine. Contact the Council on 01904 671 384; e-mail: info@britarch.ac.uk; website: www.britarch.ac.uk.

National Trust Central Volunteering involves volunteers in many aspects of the work of conservation in the great houses open to the public and on 248,000 hectares of coast and countryside properties. Inevitably, the needs will vary according to the location and time of the year. However, over 40,000 volunteers a year work alongside Trust staff in the regions. If you are interested, contact the Volunteering Enquiry Line on 01793 817 632; e-mail: volunteers@nationaltrust.org.uk; website: www.nationaltrust.org.uk.

SPAB (Society for the Protection of Ancient Buildings) promotes the sensitive repair of old buildings. Volunteers are needed in London and around the country to help with organizing events, administration, and cataloguing the archive. SPAB would also very much like to hear from qualified architects, building surveyors and structural engineers to assist with specific projects. For further information, contact SPAB on 020 7377 1644; e-mail: info@spab.org.uk; website: www.spab.org.uk.

The needy

Alexandra Rose Charities, founded in 1912 by Queen Alexandra, helps small charities that lack the internal resources themselves to raise funds. Such charities then benefit from the national profile, expertise and organizational support given to them. For further details, contact Alexandra Rose Charities on 01252 726 171; e-mail: enquiries@alexandrarose.org.uk; website: www.alexandrarose.org.uk.

Elizabeth Finn Care gives grants to needy British and Irish people from a wide range of backgrounds. Volunteers meet regularly with beneficiaries and applicants in their own home, both to ensure that they are receiving the right help and to maintain links between the charity and those in its care. Contact Elizabeth Finn Care on 020 7396 6700; e-mail: info@elizabethfinn.org.uk; website: www. elizabethfinntrust.org.uk.

OXFAM works with others to overcome poverty and suffering. Over 22,000 volunteers are involved in all parts of Great Britain. One of the main areas of need is help with the running of Oxfam shops: activities range from the day-to-day management to sorting and pricing, serving customers and arranging shop windows. Help is also needed to organize fundraising events, give administrative assistance and support the educational and campaigning aspects of Oxfam's work. Reasonable travel and meal expenses can be reimbursed. For further information, contact Oxfam on 0300 200 1300; e-mail via the enquiry form on the website: www.oxfam.org.uk.

Royal British Legion was founded to help needy ex-service men and women and also their dependants. Today, with over 2,000 branches in the UK, it runs care homes, maintains sheltered workshops for the disabled, gives pension counselling, provides training for jobseekers, offers advice and friendship and, through its welfare service, gives financial help. It also organizes pilgrimages to war graves overseas and has a small business advice service. The Royal British Legion's most important fundraising activity for all this work is the Poppy Appeal, which takes place during the fortnight leading up to Remembrance Day on the second Sunday in November. Contact the Head of the Poppy Appeal, Tel: 01622 717172; website: www.britishlegion.org.uk. If you would like to help in other ways, phone 0845 7725 725.

Samaritans aim to offer 24-hour emotional support to the suicidal and the despairing. Much of the work is done on the telephone and, while no special qualifications are required, an unshockable disposition and complete reliability are essential qualities in a volunteer. Training is given – often at weekends – and those who are selected will be expected to attend further courses from time to time. The minimum time commitment is about four hours a week plus one night duty a month. Apart from this work, there is need for fundraising help from anyone with a little time and a lot of enthusiasm. Contact the Samaritans, Tel: 08457 90 90 90; e-mail: jo@samaritans.org; website: www.samaritans.org.

Offenders and the victims of crime

Nacro strives to make society safer by finding practical solutions to reducing crime. It provides housing, training and resettlement services for prisoners and ex-offenders, supports disadvantaged families and communities, and steers young people away from crime. Opportunities for voluntary work, which are organized on a local basis, tend to be limited to juvenile justice, football and other activities for young people. For further information, contact Nacro on e-mail: supportnacro@nacro.org.uk; website: www.nacro.org.uk.

New Bridge Foundation offers friendship and support to people in prison and on their release, with the aim of giving them the encouragement and practical skills to lead responsible and law-abiding lives in the future. It achieves this by running vocational and parenting courses, as well as managing a befrienders' scheme. This involves hundreds of volunteers who visit offenders in prison and keep in touch through letter writing. Volunteers devote as much or as little time as they can spare. However, all are required to do an initial weekend training and to attend a local monthly group meeting. If you would be interested in participating in this valuable work, contact the Foundation, Tel: 020 7976 0779; e-mail: info@newbridgefoundation.org.uk; website: www.newbridgefoundation.org.uk.

Supporting Others through Volunteer Action (SOVA) works in England and Wales with the Prison Service and many other organizations to strengthen communities by involving local volunteers in strengthening communities and reducing crime. Organized on a regional basis, you can contact SOVA on 020 7793 0404; e-mail: london@sova.org.uk; or via the website: www.sova.org.uk.

Victim Support offers information, support and practical help to over a million people affected by crime every year. Volunteers play a crucial role in this delicate work. Some devote a couple of hours a week to visiting victims in their own home to allow them to talk through their feelings about the crime and work out ways of dealing with the effects. Others do a regular four-hour weekly shift in staffing the London-based Victim Supportline. A number, based in magistrates' and crown court buildings, act as Witness Service volunteers, offering emotional support and advice about court procedures to people appearing in court. Victim Support also very much welcomes volunteers with IT expertise to work in their offices, as well as enthusiasts able to assist with publicity, fundraising and interpreting. No qualifications are necessary to become a volunteer but, because of the nature of the work, you will need to provide references, and Victim Support will also carry out a Criminal Records Bureau check. For further information, contact the National Centre on 020 7268 0200; e-mail: supportline@victimsupport.org.uk; website: www.victimsupport.org.uk.

Politics

You may not immediately think of political parties in the context of voluntary work, but all of them use vast numbers of volunteer helpers. Between elections the help is mostly required with fundraising, committee work and staffing the constituency offices. At election time, activity is obviously intense: delivering literature, addressing and stuffing envelopes, recording canvass returns, driving elderly and disabled people to the polls and, for the politically informed, canvassing. Contact your constituency office, which can be found on the internet, or, if you have difficulty, get in touch with the national party headquarters. Contact details for the major parties are:

Conservative Party, Tel: 020 7222 9000; website: www.conservatives.com.
Green Party, Tel: 020 7272 4474; website: www.greenparty.org.uk.
Labour Party, Tel: 0870 5900 200; website: www.labour.org.uk.
Liberal Democrats, Tel: 020 7222 7999; website: www.libdems.org.uk.
Plaid Cymru, Tel: 029 2047 2272; website: www.plaidcymru.org.
Scottish National Party, Tel: 0131 525 8900; website: www.snp.org.
Social Democratic and Labour Party (SDLP),Tel: 028 9024 7700; website: www.sdlp.ie.
UKIP, Tel: 01626 831 290; website: www.ukip.org.uk.
Ulster Unionist Party, Tel: 028 9076 5500; website: www.uup.org.

Work after work

British Chambers of Commerce, the organizations representing the local business community, are highly active in a wide range of projects to promote local economic development and renewal in the wider community. Many Chambers, for example, take the lead in initiatives for inner-city regeneration, crime prevention, industry-education links, training schemes and similar activities, and very much welcome input from retired businesspeople to contribute to their special working parties. There are also opportunities for involvement in the representational role of Chambers on behalf of business, as a committee or panel member looking into such areas as transport, the environment and industrial affairs. For further information, contact your local Chamber direct, or contact the national body on 020 7654 5800; e-mail: info@britishchambers.org.uk; website: www.britishchambers.org.uk.

The National Federation of Enterprise Agencies. For those in England who would like to continue to work in business after retirement, an enterprise agency may be the answer. Set up as a partnership between government, employers, trade unions and the voluntary sector, it aims to encourage the greater local involvement of businesses in the communities in which they operate. In practice the work will involve advising and helping new small firms at the start-up stage and as they further develop. The time involved is likely to be of the order of one day a week. Expenses are paid. Contact can be made through your nearest local enterprise agency or the national network on 01234 831 623; e-mail: enquiries@nfea.com; website: www.nfea.com. For those in Scotland who are interested in Enterprise Trusts, which are similar partnerships, contact Scottish Business in the Community on 0131 451 1100; e-mail: info@sbcscot.com; website: www.sbcscot.com.

Long-term volunteering

If you are thinking of a long-term, probably residential, commitment there are a number of organizations both in the UK and abroad in need of voluntary help for a wide variety of projects. Some require specialist skills, such as engineering or medicine; others essentially need people with practical qualities, common sense and enthusiasm. As an indication of the kinds of opportunities that exist, there are broadly speaking four major groups, all of which require a two-year minimum period of service. General conditions are similar for all of them; travel is paid, plus a living allowance or salary that is based on local levels rather than on expatriate rates; couples without dependent children are welcome, as long as both have the necessary skills. National Insurance Contributions are provided, and a resettlement grant is paid on completion of the tour.

Overseas

There are four main organizations for overseas volunteering: Voluntary Service Overseas (VSO), Skillshare International, Progressio and International Service, details of which have already been provided on page 255. See Chapter 11 (Looking for Paid Work – Working in developing countries).

Volunteering abroad is also known as 'grey gapping'. It is a growth area, and this new trend is popular amongst baby boomers (those people who are 50–60 years old and born at the end of or just after WWII). A number of people are now taking a year out, sometimes immediately after retirement, to travel abroad and have a life-changing experience. If the idea of doing some voluntary work abroad before or just after you retire appeals to you, contact **Gapadvice.org**, which gives independent advice on gap years for people of all ages, on 01494 673448; e-mail: info@gapadvice.org; website: www.gapadvice.org. (This is further described in Chapter 14, Holidays.)

In the UK

Although the groups that we have listed in this section are primarily concerned with schemes requiring volunteer help for between two weeks and six months, they would also welcome shorter-term help with administration and fundraising:

Sue Ryder Care centres provide hospice and neurological care. They are run as far as possible as family homes in the true sense of the word. Volunteers are needed for work in a variety of jobs, including the general running of the 17 care centres and help in the 430 Sue Ryder Care charity shops. Contact Sue Ryder Care on 0845 050 1953; e-mail: info@suerydercare.org.uk; website: www.suerydercare.org.

Vitalise. Volunteers of all ages are needed all months of the year at the five accessible residential centres. Volunteers support and provide companionship to the guests. No formal qualifications are required. Stay is for one or two weeks. Board and lodging are free and fares are refunded for UK travel. Volunteers are also needed in the charity's two day centres, and to act as sighted guides for visually impaired people on holidays. Contact Vitalise on 0845 345 1972; e-mail: info@vitalise.org.uk; website: www.vitalise.org.uk.

Careways Trust Limited, website: www.carewaystrust.org.uk , 1st Floor, Burfree House, Teville Road, Worthing, West Sussex, BN11 1AZ, 01903 276030. e-mail: enquiries@carewaystrust.org.uk

Careways Trust, formerly known as Crossways Trust, was formed in 1949 by a consortium of Benevolent Funds to provide care and nursing homes for their elderly members and beneficiaries.

13

Health

Keeping fit

Have you ever enviously commented when meeting a recently retired friend: 'Goodness, he looks a different man? Fit, relaxed, contented – retirement must suit him'? It probably does, and why not? Perhaps more than any other period since your 20s, retirement is a time for positive good health. You have more chance to be out in the fresh air and take up sport again. You won't have to rush your meals so much and, without the need for business lunches or sandwiches day after day, will probably knock off a few pounds without any effort at dieting. At the same time, there will be less temptation to drop into the pub on the way home, so you will feel brighter and more alert at the start of the evening.

A major gain is that there will be no more fighting your way to work in the rush hour. Those interminable journeys on buses and trains, jam-packed with people in various states and conditions. Think of the winter months with people next to you coughing and sneezing, or of sitting in stuffy carriages with no fresh air. What about the delays, on public transport and in traffic, which had the effect of raising your blood pressure? Once free of the strains and pressures that are part of any job, you will feel less harassed and look better. If you are cutting down on fattening snacks too, you will find you have the energy to devote to new interests and activities.

People can get aches and pains, of course, as they become older. Doctors will tell you, again and again, that this is far less likely if you remain physically and mentally active. In other words, the days for putting on slippers and regarding retirement as the onset of old age are definitely gone. Today's recently retireds are often younger in age, looks and behaviour than any previous generation. They can therefore look forward to many healthy years ahead.

As with anything else, however, bodies do require a modicum of care and attention if they are to function at their best. Just as your car needs regular servicing, routine checks such as eye testing and dental appointments are obviously sensible. Also moderation, middle-aged as it may sound, is generally a wiser policy than excess. This has nothing to do with treating yourself as a premature geriatric – quite the reverse. It means enjoying small vices without paying the penalty for over-indulgence. By keeping trim instead of getting out of shape, and making the effort to look good and keep alert, you are likely to have a far longer and more enjoyable retirement.

Exercise plays an important part in keeping you healthy whatever age you are. It tones up muscles and improves the circulation. It reduces flab, helps ward off illnesses such as heart disease and, above all, can be a great deal of fun. The experts' motto is: little and often. For those not accustomed to regular exercise, it is essential to build up gradually. If you are planning to run a marathon or win the local tennis competition, start gently. If you rush off to play squash with your son or grandson, or to recapture the sporting feats of your youth, you may get carted off to hospital or the doctor's surgery still wearing your track suit.

Training in a whole range of sports is available around the country, with beginners in their 50s and older especially welcomed. Details of some of the many facilities, together with other keep fit options, are listed in Chapter 9, Leisure Activities. In addition to some of the more exotic choices, swimming has long been recognized as one of the best forms of exercise. Some people say there is nothing to beat a good brisk walk. Gardening is also recommended. With the explosion of sports clubs, leisure centres and adult keep fit classes run by local authorities and other organizations, opportunities have never been better for athletes of all ability levels – and none.

At the top end of the market, there are deluxe health clubs located in hotels, sports clubs and other commercial operators. These offer, amongst other things, facilities such as a fitness centre, swimming pool, massage and beauty salon. They have qualified staff who can advise on – and supervise – personal fitness programmes. However, at a fraction of the price, many local authority leisure centres offer a marvellous range of sports. They also usually run regular classes in everything from self-defence to badminton.

Emphasis on, and availability of, every type of keep fit activity is on the increase. It is a welcome innovation, as there are a growing number of opportunities for older people and those with disabilities. If you cannot find out the information locally, search the internet. Otherwise the following organizations may be able to help you:

Extend, which celebrated its 30th year in 2009, aims to enhance the quality of life for over-60s and disabled people of all ages by providing structured recreational movement sessions to music. For information about classes in your area contact Extend, Tel: 01582 832760; e-mail: admin@extend.org.uk; website: www.extend.org.uk.

Fitness League is a national organization whose aim is to promote fitness in an atmosphere of 'happy informality'. Emphasis is on exercise and movement to music, with special regard to individual ability. There are classes suitable for all ages, with some participants in their 70s. For further details contact the League, Tel: 01344 874 787; e-mail: tfl@thefitnessleague.com; website: www.thefitness league.com.

Medau Movement was developed in Germany at the beginning of the 20th century. Recreational movement classes aim to provide enjoyable lessons that improve posture and muscle tone, while developing suppleness, strength and stamina. There are also special breathing exercises, influenced by yoga, which are designed to aid respiration and stimulate the circulation. Classes are held all over the country. For further information contact Medau Movement, Tel: 01403 266 000; e-mail: medau@emdp.org; website: www.medau.org.uk.

Yoga

The number of yoga enthusiasts is increasing year by year, and it is estimated that over half a million people in Britain regularly practise yoga as a means of improving fitness and helping relaxation. Classes are provided by a great many local authorities. There are also a number of specialist organizations. Two that arrange courses in many parts of the country are the following:

British Wheel of Yoga is the governing body for yoga in Great Britain. It has over 2,000 teachers around the country and runs classes suitable for all levels of ability. Fees vary according to class size and area of the country. Some classes have special rates for retired people. For further information contact the British Wheel of Yoga, Tel: 01529 306 851; e-mail: office@bwy.org.uk; website: www.bwy.org.uk.

Iyengar Yoga Institute runs classes at all levels, including remedial for those with medical conditions. Of special interest is the 59-plus class for people who would like to start gently. For further details contact the Institute, Tel: 020 7624 3080; e-mail: office@iyi.org.uk; website: www.iyi.org.uk.

Sensible eating

A trim, well-kept body is one of the secrets of a youthful appearance. Excess weight and being out of condition tend to add years to anyone's age. Regular exercise is one-half of the equation, sensible eating the other. It is reported that over one in four adults in Britain is obese – that is, seriously overweight. No one is going to worry about the odd two or three pounds, but half a stone or more not only begins to look unsightly but starts to become a health risk. Middle-aged men in particular run the increased risk of a heart attack. But carrying excess weight can lead to other illnesses and makes operations more difficult. The older one gets, the greater the likelihood of restricted mobility.

Before embarking on a serious diet, it is important first to consult your doctor. But medical advice does not need to be sought if you are thinking of cutting out or cutting down on sweets, cakes, sticky buns, deep-fried foods, alcohol and rich sauces. Healthy foods that most people (except of course those on a special doctor's diet) can eat in almost unlimited quantities are fruit, salad, vegetables, fish and white meat such as chicken.

You should also keep an eye on your cholesterol level. Excess cholesterol (fatty deposits that collect in the arteries) is a great concern because, although it is regarded as a problem affecting the overweight, slimmer people can also suffer from it. The basic health message is to eat low-fat, healthy food and include plenty of roughage such as wholemeal bread in the diet. It is important to cut down on dishes with a high sugar, salt and animal fat content – this particularly includes cream, butter and red meat.

As every health magazine advises, crash diets are no solution for long-term fitness. This is because, unless individuals re-educate their eating habits, the weight comes back within a few days or weeks. Many people need a boost to get started, and one increasingly popular method is sponsored dieting for charity. Another possibility, which some people swear by and others reject, is going to a health spa. As opposed to starvation, the emphasis today is on a few days' general fitness eating (but usually enough to avoid being hungry). If nothing else, the experience is very relaxing, though not cheap. There are many advertisements for such places in the national press and at the back of glossy magazines. Your friends would probably be happy to recommend their favourite places, or you can search the internet.

Cheaper and arguably more successful for long-term slimmers are Weight Watchers meetings, held across the UK. The aim of Weight Watchers is to help members establish a healthy, balanced approach to weight loss, with emphasis on making small, lifetime changes that can be maintained for the long term. There are two different food plans: a 'points' plan, where all food is given a points value, allowing members flexibility in their food choices; and a 'no count' plan, where members can eat three meals a day from a prescribed list of foods from each food group. For details contact **Weight Watchers** Customer Service, Tel: 0845 345 1500; e-mail: uk.help@weightwatchers.co.uk; website: www.weight watchers.co.uk.

Of particular interest to women is the Natural Health Advisory Service, formerly known as the Women's Nutritional Advisory Service. This organization maintains that many of the problems associated with the menopause can be alle-viated without recourse to hormone replacement therapy (HRT) by healthy eating and exercise. For further information contact the **Natural Health Advisory Service**, Tel: 01273 609 699; e-mail: enquiries@naturalhealthas.com; website: www.naturalhealthas.com.

If you are single, you may find that living on your own presents a number of issues regarding food. Some people tend to get weight problems, perhaps because they cannot be bothered to cook for themselves, so snack off the wrong kinds of food such as jam sandwiches and chocolate biscuits. Alternatively, they neglect themselves and do not take enough nourishment. Elderly women, in particular, sometimes quite literally hardly eat enough to keep alive. In consequence, not only do they undermine their health but because of their general frailty they are more susceptible to falls and broken bones. Two excellent gifts for anyone living alone or for couples whose family has flown the nest are *Easy Cooking for One or Two* by Louise Davies (Penguin, £6.99) and *Leith's Cooking for One or Two* by Polly Tyrer (Bloomsbury, £12.99). Self-help to avoid trouble is one thing, but those who suspect that they could have something wrong with them should not hesitate to consult their doctor.

Food safety

No discussion about food and eating would be complete without a word or two on the subject of food safety. As most readers will know, it is inadvisable for anyone to eat raw eggs, whether consumed steak tartar fashion or used in uncooked dishes such as mayonnaise and mousses. To be on the safe side, elderly people as well as the very young should probably also avoid lightly cooked eggs. Likewise if, as was the case several summers ago, there is an official warning about certain seafood, then it is only common sense to refrain from eating the items in question.

However, when it comes to food poisoning, eggs and seafood are far from being the only culprits. It's been widely reported in the press that people tend to shop only once a week for perishable food, so the risks are high of eating items that are no longer as fresh as they should be. 'Cook-chill' foods in particular, including ready-cooked chickens and pork pies, are a breeding ground for bacteria, especially in the summer when many foods – even vegetables – are liable to deteriorate more quickly. Storage and cooking also play a major part in warding off the dangers of food poisoning. The government leaflet *Preventing Food Poisoning* gives the following basic advice:

- Keep all parts of your kitchen clean.
- Aim to keep your refrigerator temperature at a maximum of 5°C.
- Keep raw and cooked foods separate and use within the recommended dates.
- Cook foods thoroughly.
- Do not reheat food more than once and don't keep cooked food longer than two days.

Drink

Most doctors cheerfully maintain that 'a little bit of what you fancy does you good'. The majority of healthy adults can enjoy a drink at a party or a glass of wine with dinner without any ill effects, and retirement is no reason for giving up these pleasures. In small quantities alcohol can be a very effective nightcap and can also help to stimulate a sluggish appetite. However, where problems begin is when people fancy more than is good for them. Alcoholism is the third great killer after heart disease and cancer.

The condition is far more likely among those who are bored or depressed and who, perhaps almost without realizing it, drift into the habit of having a drink to cheer themselves up or to pass the time when they have nothing else to do. The trouble is that the habit can become insidious. At the beginning it does not feel that way, so individuals can quite quickly start becoming dependent on drink. Because the early symptoms appear fairly innocuous, the danger signs are apt to be ignored. These can include: needing a drink as a confidence boost; having 'just one more' out of misplaced conviviality at the end of a party; drinking in the morning to cure a hangover; drinking on your own; keeping a spare bottle 'just in case'; and having sneak drinks when you think no one is noticing.

Whereas most people are sensible enough to be able to control the habit themselves, others may need help. The family doctor will be the first person to check with for medical advice. But additionally, for those who need moral support, the following self-help groups may be the answer:

Alcoholics Anonymous has over 3,000 autonomous groups all over the country, designed to help those with a serious alcohol problem learn how to stay sober. Through friendship and mutual support, sufferers assist each other in coping, which is made easier by meeting others with the same problem. Meetings take two forms: some are for members only; others are open to relatives and friends. Membership is free, although a voluntary collection is taken towards the cost of renting meeting rooms. For more information contact Alcoholics Anonymous, Tel: 0845 769 7555; e-mail: help@alcoholics-anonymous.org.uk; website: www.alcoholics-anonymous.org.uk.

Al-Anon Family Groups UK & Eire offers support and understanding where a relative or friend's drinking is causing concern. Of possible interest to worried grandparents, Alateen, a part of Al-Anon, is specifically for young people aged 12–20 whose lives are or have been affected as a result of someone else's drinking. There are over 850 groups throughout the UK and Eire. Contact Al-Anon, Tel: 020 7403 0888; e-mail: enquiries@al-anonuk.org.uk; website: www.al-anonuk.org.uk.

Alcohol Concern is a charity, a national umbrella body for 500 local agencies tackling alcohol-related problems. It aims to promote better understanding and improve services for those in need of help. It publishes a quarterly magazine, has a library and a small bookshop, and can supply addresses of local advice and information centres. Contact Alcohol Concern, Tel: 020 7264 0510; e-mail: contact@alcoholconcern.org.uk; website: www.alcoholconcern.org.uk.

Smoking

Any age is a good one to cut back on smoking or preferably to give up altogether. The gruesome facts are that smokers are 20 times more likely to contract lung cancer; they are at more serious risk of suffering from heart disease, particularly coronary thrombosis; and additionally they are more liable to chronic bronchitis, as well as various other ailments.

Most people agree that it is easier to give up completely than attempt to cut back. Every habitual smoker knows that after the first cigarette of the day you can always think of a thousand excuses for lighting another. Aids to willpower include the recent ban on smoking in restaurants, bars and pubs and other designated areas, and leaving your cigarettes behind when you go out. Also helpful is not buying cigarettes for guests to smoke in your home, which they leave but you take. Finally, the best tip is refusing as a personal point of honour to cadge off friends. Many hardened smokers also swear by nicotine patches, available from most chemists. Working out how much money you could save in a year and promising yourself a holiday or other reward on the proceeds could help. Thinking about your health in years to come should be an even more convincing argument.

Dozens of organizations concerned with health publish leaflets giving the facts, including the harm you can do to non-smokers. To list just a couple that provide information:

Quitline offers information, advice and counselling for smokers and ex-smokers alike. Contact Quitline, Tel: 0800 00 22 00; e-mail: stopsmoking@quit.org.uk; website: www.quit.org.uk.
Smokeline (Scotland only) offers free advice, counselling and encouragement to those wishing to give up smoking. It is available noon to midnight, seven days a week. Contact Smokeline, Tel: 0800 848 484.
NHS Smoking Helpline offers help and advice to smokers who want to quit. It can give information about local cessation services, which include nicotine replacement therapy, one-to-one counselling and group support. The service also welcomes calls from ex-smokers who have given up but need a little support to help them not return to smoking. Contact 0800 022 4 332; website: www.nhs.uk/gosmokefree.

Accident prevention

One of the most common causes of mishap is an accident in the home. In particular this is due to falling and incidents involving faulty electrical wiring. The vast majority of these could be avoided by taking normal common sense precautions. This could be something as simple as repairing or replacing worn carpets and installing better lighting near staircases. For a list of practical suggestions, see 'Safety in the home', in Chapter 8, Your Home.

If you are unlucky enough to be injured in an accident, whether in the street or elsewhere, the Law Society offers a free service called the Accident Line to help you decide whether you can make a claim. You will be entitled to a free consultation with a local solicitor specializing in personal injury claims. He or she will inform you whether you have a good case, how to go about claiming and how much you might claim. Should you decide to pursue the matter, you are under no obligation to ask the same solicitor to act for you. A similar service is offered by the National Accident Helpline. For further details contact: **Accident Line**, Tel: 0800 19 29 39; website: www.accidentlinedirect.co.uk; **National Accident Helpline**, Tel: 0800 376 0185; website: www.national-accident-helpline.co.uk.

Aches, pains and other abnormalities

There is nothing about becoming 50, 60 or even 70 that makes aches and pains an inevitability. Age in itself has nothing to do with the vast majority of ailments. However, a big problem is that many people ignore the warning signs when something is wrong, on the basis that this symptom or that is only to be expected as one becomes older. More often than not, treatment when a condition is still in its infancy can either cure it altogether or at least help to delay its advance. The following should always be investigated by a doctor, to allay fear or to get treatment at an early stage:

- any pain that lasts more than a few days;
- lumps, however small;
- dizziness or fainting;
- chest pains, shortness of breath or palpitations;
- persistent cough or hoarseness;
- unusual bleeding from anywhere;
- unnatural tiredness or headaches;
- frequent indigestion;
- unexplained weight loss.

Health insurance

An increasing number of people are covered by private health insurance or provident schemes during their working lives. If you wish to continue this benefit, and you are unable to remain in your company scheme after retirement, you will normally be welcomed as an individual client by most of the main groups provided you are under the age of 70 (or in some cases even older). You can then renew your membership when you do reach 70. Even if you have not previously been insured, it is not too late to consider doing so. Although obviously this will be an extra expense, should you be unfortunate enough to fall ill or need an operation and want to be treated as a private patient, insurance will save you a great deal of worry and expense.

The terms and conditions of the different schemes offered by health insurance groups vary to some extent. All the major ones offer to pay, if not all, at least the greatest part of the costs. These include inpatient accommodation, treatment and medical fees, as well as outpatient charges for specialists, X-rays and similar services. They do not normally cover GPs' costs. Subscription levels largely depend on the area in which you live and on the type of hospital to which you choose to be admitted. The top figure is usually based on charges in private hospitals in London; the next is based on private hospitals outside London; and the lowest rate is based on charges in NHS pay beds and some private hospitals.

Other factors that can substantially affect the price are your age, the extent of the cover offered and the various restrictions or exclusions that may apply. Many insurers have recently introduced a range of budget policies, which while they have the advantage of being less costly are naturally also less comprehensive. For example, some policies confine cover to surgery or cover only certain specified procedures. Particular illnesses or conditions may be excluded, as may outpatient treatment. There may be an annual cash limit or the policy may include an excess – that is, the subscriber pays a fixed amount of every claim, typically between £100 and £500. Another popular saving is found in policies that restrict private care to cases where the wait for NHS treatment would exceed six (sometimes 12) weeks. As with all types of insurance, the small print matters, so look carefully at all the plans available before selecting the scheme that best suits your needs.

The NHS has, generally, an excellent record in dealing with urgent conditions and accidents. However, it sometimes has a lengthy waiting list for the less urgent and more routine operations such as hip replacements and hernias. By using health insurance to pay for private medical care you will probably get faster treatment, as well as greater comfort and privacy in hospital. The major organizations that provide cover are as follows:

AXA PPP offers a range of medical insurance policies to cover the cost of private health care. All include access to the Health at Hand counselling and health information line – a confidential 24-hour service staffed by nurses, pharmacists and counsellors, with whom customers can discuss any health issues that concern them. Benefits and monthly subscriptions vary according to an individual's health, lifestyle and geographical area. Customers who pay by single annual premium receive a 5 per cent discount. For further information contact AXA PPP, Tel: 0800 121 345; website: www.axappphealthcare.co.uk.

BUPA is the largest of the provident associations and offers a variety of choices for individuals under its Heartbeat plan. Customers are given a personalized price, according to which benefits they specifically choose to have included in their policy. It is possible to limit cover, for example just to cancer and heart conditions. Alternatively, you can opt for a more comprehensive policy covering a wider range of eventualities, including cover for most existing health problems. Guidance and support are available 24 hours a day from a team of nurses. Subscriptions can be reduced by electing to take an annual excess option, paid once, not for every claim you make in the year. For further information contact BUPA, Tel: 0800 600 500; website: www.bupa.co.uk.

The Exeter Friendly Society is a non-profit-making friendly society with subscribers throughout the UK and overseas. Its private health insurance has three distinguishing features that may make it particularly attractive to people of retirement age: it accepts new subscribers of any age up to 80; premiums are not increased on account of age, so rates for older people may be lower than in many other schemes; and making a claim will not result in an increase in your next premium. For further information contact the Society, Tel: 0300 123 3209; website: www.exeterfriendly.co.uk.

Two other groups that offer health insurance plans relevant to people over retirement age are **BCWA Healthcare**, Tel: 0800 197 6997; website: www.bcwa.co.uk, and **Saga Services Ltd**, Tel: 0800 857 857; website: www.saga.co.uk.

Help with choosing a scheme

With so many plans on the market, selecting the one that best suits your needs can be quite a problem. If you would welcome advice, you can either ask an independent financial adviser for help or approach a specialist insurance broker, such as the two listed below:

Medibroker offers advice on the best available health care plans. Contact Medibroker, Tel: 0800 980 1082; e-mail: ukclientservices@medibroker.com; website: www.medibroker.co.uk.

The Private Health Partnership will provide genuine, independent and unbiased advice or search out a cost-effective health scheme to match your specific needs. Contact the Partnership, Tel: 01274 588 862; e-mail: info@php.co.uk; website: www.php.co.uk.

Private patients – without insurance cover

If you do not have private medical insurance but want to go into hospital in the UK as a private patient, there is nothing to stop you, provided your doctor is willing and you are able to pay the bills. More and more people are forgoing insurance in favour of paying for themselves, if and when the need arises. The choice if you opt for self-pay lies between the private wings of NHS hospitals, hospitals run by charitable or non-profit-making organizations (such as the Nuffield Hospitals) and those run for profit by private companies. To help meet the cost, a number of health insurance providers have launched a variety of purpose-designed plans that normally consist of a regular savings account, plus optional insurance to provide cover towards part of the bill. Also helpful, if you cannot pay the full cost immediately, is to arrange an interest-free loan (for repayment within 10 months) for treatment at certain hospitals. One provider of such a service is **Nuffield Hospitals**, Tel: 0845 602 9262; e-mail via the contact form on the website: www.nuffieldhospitals.org.uk.

An interesting alternative

Have you ever thought of combining a holiday and having an operation at the same time? Sounds curious, but you could investigate one of the latest growth areas in health care – health tourism. Health and medical tourism is where you travel to take advantage of less expensive health treatments. These include cosmetic, dental and spa treatments and medical procedures (including joint replacement, heart surgery and other elective procedures). You can save usually over 50 per cent on the fees that you would pay for private treatment in the UK – and have a holiday as well. The destinations are extensive and sometimes exotic. Leading health tourism destinations include Eastern Europe, the Baltic region, Malta, Cyprus, Turkey, the Middle East, India, Malaysia, Singapore, South Korea, Costa Rica and Argentina. One way to find out about this new and growing market and to meet some of the providers of such services is to visit the annual Health Tourism Show held at Olympia. For further information on this subject, contact **The Health Tourism Show**, Tel: 01372 743 837; website: www.health tourismshow.com, or **Treatment Abroad**, Tel: 01442 817 817; website: www. treatmentabroad.com.

Long-term care insurance (LTCI)

An emergency operation is one thing; long-term care because an individual can no longer cope unaided is quite another. Over the past few years, a number of insurance companies have launched policies designed to help meet the costs in the event of people needing to stay long-term in a nursing home or requiring a carer to look after them in their own home. The days when the Welfare State automatically picked up the bill no longer exist. Increasingly people are having to contribute towards the costs of their own care and many have to support themselves from their savings. (*NB:* a married couple will not be forced into selling their home if the other partner is still living there.)

Nursing home fees are rising and good homes increasingly expensive. Care in your own home, if you were ever to become seriously incapacitated, is likely to be at least as expensive. It is advisable, if you can, to make some provision against long-term care. The big advantages of insurance cover of this type are that it buys peace of mind and helps safeguard your savings should care ever become a necessity in the future. An additional plus-point is that benefits paid out to a policy-holder are tax-free.

However, although a godsend in case of need, none of the policies is exactly cheap, and in most cases the criteria for paying out are pretty stringent. Cover normally applies only if an illness is diagnosed after joining and, while some plans cover a wide range of eventualities, others specifically exclude some of the critical illnesses, such as cancer. The premiums, which can be paid on a regular annual basis or as a lump sum, vary considerably, as of course does the amount of financial assistance given. In all cases, the charges are largely determined by the subscriber's age at the time of first joining and, as you would expect, are very much cheaper at 55 than 75.

To avoid wrangles over eligibility for benefit, most of the schemes have adopted a system known as activities of daily living (ADLs). ADLs typically include: bathing and washing, dressing, feeding, going to the lavatory, and getting in and out of a bed or chair. The higher the number of these an individual is unable to manage on his or her own, the greater the benefit entitlement. In some policies, Alzheimer's disease is specifically covered.

Although pre-funded insurance is the cheapest way of buying care cover, a disadvantage is that if you never claim you lose all the money you have paid over the years. Some policies link the insurance with an investment, providing a payout on death if no claim has been made. Though initially more expensive, you can take your money out of the plan at any time. However, if the investment growth is poor you could lose some of your capital.

A possible alternative to a conventional long-term care policy is *critical illness insurance*, which pays a lump sum if you are unfortunate enough to be struck by one of a specified number of dread diseases, such as cancer or a stroke. Rather than pay into a policy ahead of time, an alternative solution that has been growing in popularity is to buy a *care fee annuity* (sometimes known as an 'immediate-needs annuity') as and when the need arises. Such annuities can be bought with a lump sum and, as with other annuities, pay an income for life. The income is normally considerably higher than normal annuity rates, but with no return of capital to benefit your successors (capital protection is available with higher contributions). An advantage, however, is that you buy a care plan only at the time it would actually be useful. A further plus-point is that all money paid by the policyholder direct to the care provider, including a home nursing agency, is free of tax.

Despite these attractions, care fee annuities are not all win-win. First, you are investing a sizeable chunk of capital, which, depending on your life expectancy, may or may not prove good value in the long term. Also, as recent research by the Care Funding Bureau shows, prices quoted by different companies to provide exactly the same annual income often differ by many thousands of pounds and, while there may sometimes be a good reason for this, if you are interested in the idea you would be well recommended to obtain several quotes.

Deciding on your best option is not easy, since quite apart from the cost, all such policies are restrictive in one way or another. You are strongly advised to shop around and to read the small print extremely carefully before signing. If, as may be suggested, you are thinking of investing some of your lump sum to pay for the policy, it would be sensible to ask a lawyer or financial adviser to check the documentation for any hidden drawbacks. Alternatively, and this might be the best idea, you could ask an independent financial adviser (IFA) to recommend what would be your best choice.

However good the advice, only you can decide whether some form of long-term care cover would be a sensible precaution. As with most major items of expenditure, there will inevitably be arguments for and against. However, whereas in the past the market was something of a jungle, you may be reassured to know that, since October 2004, all LTCI products and services come under the compulsory jurisdiction of the Financial Ombudsman Service and the Financial Services Compensation Scheme. In accordance with the new rules, not only must the sales literature provide clear information about the key features of the policy, including whether premiums are subject to review, but all advisers will be required to pass an appropriate exam to ensure that they have the relevant competence to help customers make an informed choice about the type of product and amount of cover they need. The **Financial Services Authority (FSA)** also has a helpful fact sheet, *Choosing a Financial Adviser – How Key Facts Can Help You*, available from the FSA Money Made Clear helpline, 0845 606 1234; website: www.fsa.gov.uk.

Permanent health insurance (PHI)

PHI should not be confused with other types of health insurance. It is a replacement-of-earnings policy for people who are still in work and who, because of illness, are unable to continue with their normal occupation for a prolonged period and in consequence suffer loss of earnings. While highly recommended for the self-employed, many employees have some protection under an employer's policy. Either way, if you are close to retirement, PHI is unlikely to feature on your priority list.

Health screening

Prevention is better than cure, and most of the provident associations offer a diagnostic screening service to check general health and to provide advice on diet, drinking and smoking if these are problem areas. These tests show that roughly a quarter of patients aged over 55 have an unsuspected problem that can often be treated quickly and easily. Screening services normally recommend a check-up every two years, and centres are usually available to members of insurance schemes and others alike. Screening is provided by the following:

BMI Healthcare offers a range of screens at its hospitals. Screens, known as personal health profiles, cost slightly more for women than men. For further information contact BMI Healthcare, Tel: 0808 101 0337; e-mail: info@ bmihealthcare.co.uk; website: www.bmihealthcare.co.uk.

BUPA. There is a network of BUPA Wellness Centres up and down the country, offering a range of health assessments. In most cases, same-day results can be provided so you can discuss the findings with your health adviser and doctor there and then. Prices vary but tend to be less expensive for men than women. For further details, contact BUPA, Tel: 0800 600 500; website: www.bupa.co.uk/ wellness.

National Health Service. The NHS offers several different screening services of particular relevance to those aged 50-plus. Two are especially for women and the others are more general. First, all adults who have not been seen by a GP over the last three years can request an appointment for an assessment of their general health. This will include a few simple tests, such as checking your blood pressure, and the opportunity to discuss any health problems that could be worrying you, as well as discussion of factors to do with your lifestyle that could be affecting your health. All patients over 75 should be offered an annual health check by their GP, which can be arranged in their own home if they prefer. As well as their general state of health, the check will cover such matters as eyesight, hearing, possible mobility problems, worries that might be causing depression, use of medicines and similar. The special tests for women are to screen for breast cancer and abnormalities of the cervix. These tests are available in all parts of the country. All women aged between 25 and 64 who are registered with a GP are offered a smear test every three to five years, depending on their age. Women aged between 25 and 49 receive invitations every three years. Those aged between 50 and 64 receive invitations every five years. Tests are also available to women aged 65-plus who have not been screened since age 50 or who have had recent abnormal tests. All women aged between 50 and 70 years are invited for screening by breast X-ray every three years. Although women aged over 70 no longer receive routine invitations, if they have any reason for concern they should speak to their GP to arrange an appointment. If for some reason you have not been receiving invitations for screening, you should ask your GP for details or enquire at your local primary care trust. For further information, see leaflets *NHS Cervical Screening – The Facts* and *NHS Breast Screening – The Facts*, both obtainable from GPs and primary care trusts. For further details on NHS services see the website: www.nhs.uk.

Hospital care cash plans

These schemes provide a cash sum for every night the insured person spends in hospital. Premiums can start from just £1 a week, giving a payment of about £18 a night. All benefits are tax-free and are available to anyone joining before age 65.

A number of schemes cater for individuals aged over 65. About 20 organizations offer such schemes as well as a wide range of other health insurance, including cover for optical and dental treatment. A list can be obtained from the **British Health Care Association (BHCA Services Ltd)**, Tel: 0153 651 9960; website: www.bhca.org.uk.

National Health Service

Most readers will need no introduction to the National Health Service. However, there are one or two scraps of information that you may not know – or possibly have forgotten – that may come in useful around retirement. One area is the range of professionals, including district nurses and occupational therapists, who can provide invaluable support if you are caring for an elderly relative or if a member of the household needs to go into hospital. Most of what you need to know is described in Chapter 15, Caring for Elderly Parents.

Choosing a GP

If you move to a new area, you will need to find a new doctor. The best way to choose one is normally by recommendation. If you do not know whom to ask you can write to, or call in to, your local primary care trust or strategic health authority. Alternatively you can search the NHS website (www.nhs.uk).

You could ask to consult the local medical directory, where you will find details of GPs' qualifications and special areas of knowledge. This could be useful if someone in the household has a particular health problem and you would feel happier with a doctor who has more specialized experience.

Additional points you may want to consider are: how close the doctor is to your home; whether there is an appointments system; and whether it is a group practice and, if so, how this is organized. All GPs must have practice leaflets, available at their premises, with details about the service. The information should include: names, addresses, sex, year of qualification and type of qualifications, along with essential practice information such as surgery hours, services provided and arrangements for emergencies and night calls.

Having selected a doctor, you should take your medical card to the receptionist to have your name registered. This is not automatic as, first, there is a limit to the number of patients any one doctor can accept. Also, some doctors prefer to meet potential patients before accepting them on their list. If you do not have a medical card, you will need to fill in a simple form.

Changing your GP

If you want to change your GP, you go about it in exactly the same way. If you know of a doctor whose list you would like to be on, you can simply turn up at his or her surgery and ask to be registered; or you can ask your local primary care trust, or health board in Scotland, to give you a copy of its directory before making a choice. You do not need to give a reason for wanting to change, and you do not need to ask anyone's permission.

Two useful publications to read are *You and Your GP During the Day* and *You and Your GP at Night and Weekends*, available free from libraries, strategic health authorities and doctors' surgeries.

NHS Direct

If you need medical advice when you are on holiday or at some other time when it may not be possible to contact your doctor, you could ring NHS Direct, which offers a 24-hour free health advice service, staffed by trained nurses. The number to call is 0845 46 47; website: www.nhsdirect.nhs.uk.

Help with NHS costs

If you or your partner are in receipt of Income Support, income-based Jobseeker's Allowance or the Pension Credit Guarantee Credit, you are both entitled to free NHS prescriptions, NHS dental treatment, NHS wigs and fabric supports and an NHS sight test. You are both equally entitled to the maximum value of an optical voucher to help towards the cost of glasses or contact lenses and payment of travel costs to and from hospital for NHS treatment. You are also entitled to help if you and/or your partner are entitled to, or named on, a current tax credit NHS exemption certificate.

Even if you are not automatically entitled to help with the above costs, you and your partner may be entitled to some help on the grounds of low income. To find out, fill in claim form HC1 – obtainable from social security or Jobcentre Plus offices as well as many NHS hospitals, dentists, opticians and GPs – and send it to the Health Benefits Division in the prepaid envelope provided with the form. If you are eligible for help, you will be sent a certificate that is valid for up to 12 months according to your circumstances. Depending on your income, you may receive an HC2 certificate, which entitles you to full help with NHS costs, or alternatively an HC3 certificate, which will entitle you to partial help.

For more details see leaflet HC11, *Help with Health Costs*, available from Post Offices, some pharmacies and GP surgeries, or contact the **Department of Health Publications Orderline**, Tel: 0870 155 5455; website: www.dh.gov.uk.

Benefits

If you are on Income Support and have a disability, you may be entitled to certain premiums on top of your ordinary allowance. Various social security benefits are also available to those with special problems because of illness. These include:

- Attendance Allowance (see leaflet DS 702);
- Disability Living Allowance (see leaflet DS 704);
- Incapacity Benefit (see leaflet IB 1).

Employment and Support Allowance

Incapacity Benefit was replaced by Employment and Support Allowance (ESA) from October 2008. ESA is a new integrated contributory and income-related allowance. The government has brought forward 'Permitted Work' rules in Incapacity Benefit into both elements of the new Employment and Support Allowance benefit. All ESA claimants can work for fewer than 16 hours and earn up to £86 per week for up to 52 weeks without losing their entitlement. For further information, including the special concessions for voluntary and permitted work, see the website: www.dwp.gov.uk/esa.

Prescriptions

Both men and women aged 60 and over are entitled to free NHS prescriptions. Additionally, certain other groups are entitled to free prescriptions. These include those on low income (see 'Help with NHS costs', page 296) and people who suffer from a specified medical condition. If you are not sure if you qualify, you should pay and ask the pharmacist for an NHS receipt form FP57, which tells you how to claim a refund. For further information, see leaflet HC11, *Help with Health Costs*, obtainable from Post Offices, some pharmacies and GP surgeries.

People who do not qualify but who require a lot of prescriptions could save money by purchasing a prescription prepayment certificate. This costs £27.85 for three months, or £102.50 for a year. A prepayment certificate will work out cheaper if you are likely to need more than four prescription items in three months, or more than 14 items in 12 months, as there is no further charge regardless of how many prescription items you require. If you prefer, rather than pay for the 12-month certificate in one go, you can make 10 monthly direct debit payments. Application forms (FP95) are obtainable from pharmacies and GP surgeries, or contact **NHS Help With Healthcare Costs**, Tel: 0845 850 0030; website: www.nhsbsa.nhs.uk.

Going into hospital

Stories abound of people who wait months and months for an operation because of a shortage of beds. But while waiting lists for a hernia or hip replacement may be depressingly long in one area, hospitals in another part of the country may have spare capacity. Many patients are unaware that they can ask their GP to refer them to a consultant at a different NHS trust or even, in certain cases, help make arrangements for them to be treated overseas. Before you can become a patient at another hospital, your GP will need to agree to your being referred. A major consideration will be whether the treatment would be as clinically effective as the treatment you would receive locally.

Waiting lists have reduced considerably over the past few years, thanks to the government's initiatives in this area. This is of little comfort, however, if you are currently on a waiting list for treatment but feel that your condition has deteriorated and become more urgent. In this case you should speak to your GP, who may be able to arrange with the hospital for your appointment to be brought forward. (See also 'Complaints', below).

Those likely to need help on leaving hospital should speak to the hospital social worker, who will help make any necessary arrangements. Help is sometimes available to assist patients with their travel costs to and from hospital. If you receive Income Support, income-based Jobseeker's Allowance or Pension Credit Guarantee Credit, you can ask for repayment of 'necessary travel costs'. If you are not sure what would qualify, you can check with the hospital before you travel. If you have a war or MOD disablement pension, you may get help with travel costs for treatment of your pensionable disability. There are special schemes for people who live in the Isles of Scilly or the former Scottish Highlands and Islands Development Board area. Claims for help can also be made on the grounds of low income. For detailed information, see leaflet HC11, *Help with Health Costs*. Contact **NHS Help With Healthcare Costs**, Tel: 0845 850 0030; website: www.nhsbsa.nhs.uk.

If you go into hospital, you will continue to receive your pension as normal. This was not always the case. Your pension – as well as Incapacity Benefit, Severe Disablement Allowance, Income Support and Pension Credit Guarantee Credit – will continue to be paid in full, without any reductions, for the duration of your stay. For further information, see leaflet GL12, *Going into Hospital?* obtainable from social security or Jobcentre Plus offices and NHS hospitals. See website: www.jobcentreplus.gov.uk or www.dwp.gov.uk.

If you have any complaints while in hospital, you should speak to someone close to the cause of the complaint or to the complaints manager within the hospital; if the matter is more serious, you should write to the chief executive of the hospital. See also the information below.

Complaints

The NHS has a complaints procedure if you are unhappy about the treatment you have received. In the first instance, you should speak to someone close to the cause of the problem, such as the doctor, nurse, receptionist or practice manager. If, for whatever reason, you would prefer to speak to someone who was not involved in your care, you can speak to the complaints manager at your local NHS trust or strategic health authority instead; addresses will be in the telephone directory. In jargon terms, this first stage is known as *local resolution*.

If you are not satisfied with the reply you receive, you can ask the NHS trust or strategic health authority for an *independent review*. The complaints manager will be able to tell you whom to contact about arranging this. If you are still dissatisfied after the independent review, then the Health Service Ombudsman (known formerly as the Health Service Commissioner) might be able to help. The Ombudsman is independent of both government and the NHS. The Ombudsman investigates complaints of failure or maladministration across the whole range of services provided by, or for, the NHS, including pharmacists, opticians and dentists, as well as private hospitals and nursing homes if these are paid for by the NHS. The Ombudsman cannot, however, take up legal causes on a patient's behalf. Contacts are:

Health Service Ombudsman for England, Tel: 0345 015 4033; e-mail: phso. enquiries@ombudsman.org.uk; website: www.ombudsman.org.uk.
Health Service Ombudsman for Wales, Tel: 01656 641 150; e-mail: ask@ ombudsman-wales.org.uk; website: www.ombudsman-wales.org.uk.
Scottish Public Services Ombudsman, Tel: 0800 377 7330; e-mail: ask@spso. org.uk; website: www.spso.org.uk.

If you have a complaint, you should get on to the matter fairly speedily or your complaint may be dismissed on grounds of being 'out of time'. Time limits require you to register complaints within 12 months of the incident or within 12 months of your realizing that you have reason for complaint. These time limits may be waived if you have a very good reason why you could not complain sooner.

If you need further advice on the complaints procedure, contact **POhWER ICAS**, an independent complaints advisory service, Tel: 0845 337 3061; website: www.pohwer.net.

Rather than proceed through the formal channels described above, an alternative approach – which of course does not prevent you from also applying to the Ombudsman or to anyone else – is to contact the **Patients Association**. This is an independent advice centre that offers guidance to patients in the event of a problem with the health service. The Association also publishes a selection of useful leaflets and a quarterly magazine, *Patient Voice*. Contact the Association, Tel: 0845 608 4455; e-mail: helpline@patients-association.com; website: www. patients-association.com.

Useful reading

Your Guide to the NHS, obtainable from the Department of Health Publications Orderline, Tel: 0870 155 5455; website: www.dh.gov.uk.

Alternative medicine

Alternative medicine remains a very controversial subject. Some doctors dismiss it out of hand. Many patients claim that it is of great benefit. We list here some of the better-known organizations:

British Acupuncture Council (BAcC). Treatment, using fine needles, is claimed to be effective for a wide range of illnesses, including arthritis, rheumatism, high blood pressure and depression. The BAcC can provide you with a list of professionally qualified acupuncture practitioners in your local area. Contact: the BAcC, Tel: 020 8735 0400; e-mail: info@acupuncture.org.uk; website: www.acupuncture.org.uk.

British Chiropractic Association. Practitioners specialize in mechanical disorders of the spine and joints and the effects on the nervous system. Treatment is mainly by specific manipulation without drugs or surgery. For a list of members in your area, contact the Association, Tel: 0118 9505 950; e-mail: enquiries@chiropractic-uk.co.uk; website: www.chiropractic-uk.co.uk.

British Homeopathic Association. Homeopathy is essentially natural healing that follows the principle of looking at the whole person rather than just the illness. Homeopathy is available on the NHS, but as yet not many doctors are trained in this branch of medicine. The Association can supply a list of practising GPs as well as the names and addresses of pharmacies that stock homeopathic medicines. Patients wanting NHS treatment can apply only to GPs in their catchment area, or get a letter of referral to one of the homeopathic hospitals or to a GP able to take NHS referrals. Otherwise patients can be treated anywhere by doctors on a private basis. Contact the Association, Tel: 0870 444 3950; website: www.trusthomeopathy.org.

British Hypnotherapy Association. Hypnotherapy may help people with phobias, emotional problems, anxiety, migraine, psoriasis or relationship difficulties. For details of the nearest registered trained hypnotherapist, including his or her qualifications and fees, plus a pamphlet answering common questions about hypnotherapy, contact the Association, Tel: 020 8579 5533; website: www.hypnotherapy-association.org. When contacting the Association it would be helpful to indicate the nature of your problem.

Incorporated Society of Registered Naturopaths. Naturopaths are concerned about the underlying conditions that may cause illness, including, for example, diet, general fitness, posture, stress and the patient's mental outlook on life. The Society can put you in touch with your nearest practitioner. Contact the Society, Tel: 0131 664 3435; e-mail: info@naturecuresociety.org; website: www.naturecuresociety.org.

National Institute of Medical Herbalists. The practice of herbal medicine aims to offer the sufferer not just relief from symptoms but an improved standard of general health and vitality. For further information and a register of practitioners, contact the Institute, Tel: 01392 426 022; e-mail: info@nimh.org.uk; website: www.nimh.org.uk.

Osteopathic Information Service. Osteopathic treatment is often appropriate for those with back problems or with muscle or joint disorders. It can also provide pain relief from arthritis. Advice and leaflets are available on request, or you can telephone for a list of osteopaths in your area. Contact the Service, Tel: 020 7357 6655; e-mail: contactus@osteopathy.org.uk; website: www.osteopathy.org.uk.

Wessex Healthy Living Centre. The Centre is a non-profit-making registered charity which, as well as having an educative purpose, runs a clinic where all natural therapies are available under one roof. Members enjoy the benefit of reduced clinic fees and also receive a biannual newsletter and information leaflets. Contact the Centre, Tel: 01202 422087; e-mail: info@wessexhealthyliving centre.org; website: www.wessexhealthylivingcentre.org.

Eyes

It is advisable to have your sight checked at least every two years. Sight tests are now free on the NHS for all men, as well as women, aged 60 and over. If you are not yet 60, you can get a free NHS sight test only if: you are registered blind or partially sighted; you are prescribed complex lenses; you are diagnosed as having diabetes or glaucoma; you are over 40 and are a close relative of someone with glaucoma (ie parent, brother, sister, son or daughter); or you are a patient of the hospital eye service or have been referred by them to an optometrist. You are also entitled to a free sight test if you or your partner are getting Income Support, income-based Jobseeker's Allowance or Pension Credit Guarantee Credit. You may also be entitled to some help if you are entitled to, or named on, a valid NHS Tax Credit Exemption Certificate. For details, see leaflet HC11 (website: www.direct.gov.uk).

Even if you do not belong to any of these groups but are on a low income, you may be entitled to a free, or reduced-cost, sight test. To find out if you qualify for help, you should fill out claim form HC1, which you can get from social security or Jobcentre Plus offices (websites: www.dwp.gov.uk, www. jobcentreplus.gov.uk).

People with mobility problems who are unable to get to an optician can ask for a domiciliary visit to have their eyes examined at home. This is free for those with an HC2 certificate or who are in receipt of one of the benefits listed above. People with a (partial help) HC3 certificate can use this towards the cost of a private home visit by their optician. The going rate for private sight tests if you do have to pay is about £25. Many opticians, however, charge less for people who are retired, or run special promotions at various times of the year. Even if this is not advertised in the window, you have nothing to lose by asking before booking an appointment.

You do not need a doctor's referral to have your eyes tested. Simply book an appointment with a registered optometrist or ophthalmic medical practitioner. If you qualify for help with the cost, remember to take your HC2 or HC3 certificate, or other written evidence, to show to the optician. The sight test should establish whether or not spectacles are required and should also include an eye examination to check for signs of injury, disease or abnormality. Whether you have to pay or not, the optician must either give you a prescription identifying what type of glasses you require or give you a statement confirming that you have no need of spectacles. The prescription is valid for two years. If you do not use it straight away, you should keep it safe so that it is handy when you need to use it. When you do decide to buy spectacles or contact lenses, you are under no obligation to obtain them from the optician who tested your eyes but can buy them where you like.

There is a voucher system for helping with the purchase of glasses or contact lenses. If you or your partner are in receipt of Income Support, income-based Jobseeker's Allowance or Pension Credit Guarantee Credit, you will receive an optical voucher, with a cash value. The amount you get will depend on your optical prescription. If you do not get any of the above benefits but are on a low income, you may still be entitled to help. To find out, fill in claim form HC1, as explained above: see websites: www.adviceguide.org.uk and www.dwp.gov.uk.

The voucher might be sufficient to pay for your contact lenses or spectacles outright, or it may make only a small contribution towards the cost. Part of the equation will depend on the frames you choose. You will not be tied to any particular glasses: you can choose spectacles that cost more than the value of the voucher and pay the difference yourself. For further details, see leaflets HC11, *Help with Health Costs* (available in large print size), and HC12, *NHS Charges and Optical Voucher Values*. People who are registered blind are entitled to a special tax allowance of £1,890 a year.

A great deal of practical help can be obtained by contacting the **Royal National Institute of Blind People (RNIB)**. In addition to giving general advice and information, it can supply a range of special equipment, details of which are listed in a free catalogue. There are also a number of leaflets relating to blindness. For information, contact the RNIB, Tel: 0845 766 9999; e-mail: help@rnib.org.uk; website: www.rnib.org.uk.

Many elderly people with failing sight suffer from macular degeneration, which affects their ability to distinguish detail. Although there is no known cure, individuals can be helped to make the most effective use of their sight by special magnifiers and other aids, such as clip-on lenses that fit over normal spectacles. For further information contact the **Partially Sighted Society**, Tel: 0844 477 4966; e-mail: info@partsight.org.uk; website: www.partsight.org.uk.

Another helpful organization is the **National Library for the Blind and Talking Book Service**, which lends books and music scores in Braille and Moon free of charge, and post-free, to any blind reader who registers with the service. It also offers a wide range of electronic library and reference services through its website. For information, contact the National Library for the Blind and Talking Book Service, Tel: 0845 762 6843; e-mail: cservices@rnib.org.uk; website: www. rnib.org.uk.

Blind, visually impaired and print-disabled people can enjoy national newspapers and magazines on audiotape and audio CD, and in digital and electronic formats. Contact these two organizations: **Talking Newspaper Association of the United Kingdom (TNAUK)**, Tel: 01435 866 102; e-mail: info@tnauk.org. uk; website: www.tnauk.org.uk; and **Talking News Federation (TNF)**, Tel: 0871 226 5506; e-mail: enquiries@tnf.org.uk; website: www.tnf.org.uk.

For gardening enthusiasts, there is *Come Gardening*, a quarterly magazine available on audiotape and in Braille, and the *Cassette Library for Blind Gardeners*, which is offered as an auxiliary service to subscribers. There are also residential courses for blind gardeners. For further information, contact **Thrive**, Tel: 0118 988 5688; website: www.thrive.org.uk.

It is worth knowing that all the main banks will provide statements in Braille; and Barclaycard now also issues credit card statements in Braille, on request. Additionally, several institutions offer large-print chequebooks or templates for chequebooks, as well as other facilities, such as a taped version of their annual report. There is no extra charge for these services.

Finally, **BT** has a free directory enquiry service for customers who cannot read or handle a phone book. To use the service you first need to register with BT, which will issue you with a personal identification number. Full details and application forms can be obtained from the registration department by calling Freefone 195 or checking the website: www.bt.com.

Feet

Many people forget about their feet until they begin to give trouble. Corns and bunions, if neglected, can become extremely painful, and ideally everyone, especially women who wear high heels, should have podiatry treatment from early middle age or even younger. One of the problems of which podiatrists complain is that because many women wear uncomfortable shoes they become used to having painful feet and do not notice when something is more seriously wrong. The result can sometimes be ingrowing toenails or infections.

Podiatry is available on the National Health Service without referral from a doctor being necessary, but facilities tend to be very oversubscribed, so in many areas it is only the very elderly or those with a real problem who can get appointments. Private registered chiropodists are listed in the *Yellow Pages* or check the website: www.yell.com.

Alternatively, you can write to the **Society of Chiropodists and Podiatrists**, which is the professional association for registered chiropodists and podiatrists, asking for some local names from their list. In addition to keeping a list of members, the Society can supply a number of free leaflets on foot health. Contact the Society, Tel: 020 7234 8620; website: www.feetforlife.org.

Help the Aged has produced a helpful leaflet called *Fitter Feet*, which advises on how to avoid problems, gives tips on buying shoes and provides information on where to go for further help and treatment. It is available from Help the Aged, Tel: 020 7278 1114; e-mail: info@helptheaged.org.uk; website: www. helptheaged.org.uk.

Hearing

As they grow older, a great many people suffer some deterioration in their sense of hearing. Should you begin to have difficulty in hearing people speak, or find that you are having to turn up the television, it is probably worth having a word with your doctor. Your GP may well refer you to a consultant, who will advise whether a hearing aid would be helpful or alternatively may refer you direct to a hearing aid centre for examination and fitting. You can either obtain a hearing aid and batteries free on the NHS or buy them privately.

There are many other aids on the market that can make life easier. **BT**, for example, has a variety of special equipment for when a standard phone becomes too difficult to use. For further information, dial BT free on 0800 800 150 and ask for a free copy of *Communications Solutions* or see its website: www.bt.com.

There are also a number of specialist organizations that can give you a lot of help, both as regards hearing aids and on other matters:

British Deaf Association (BDA) works to protect the interests of deaf people and also provides an advice service through its regional offices. Contact the BDA, Tel: 02476 550 936; e-mail: headoffice@bda.org.uk; website: www.bda.org.uk.

British Tinnitus Association (BTA). Tinnitus is a condition that produces a sensation of noise, for example hissing or ringing, in the ears or head. The BTA helps to form self-help groups and provides information through its quarterly journal, *Quiet*. Contact the BTA, Tel: 0800 018 0527; e-mail: info@tinnitus.org. uk; website: www.tinnitus.org.uk.

Hearing Concern LINK – the newly united charity –provides support and information to people with hearing loss, as well as their families. For further information, Tel: 01323 638 230; e-mail: info@hearingconcernlink.org; website: www. hearingconcernlink.org.

RNID publishes a comprehensive range of free leaflets and fact sheets for deaf and hard-of-hearing people. Titles include: *The Facts – Hearing Aids*; *The Facts – Losing Your Hearing* and *The Facts: Equipment*. Contact the Institute, Tel: 0808 808 0123; e mail: informationlinc@rnid.org.uk; wcbsitc: www.rnid.org.uk.

Friends and family can do a great deal to help those who are deaf or hard of hearing. One of the essentials is not to shout but to speak slowly and distinctly.

You should always face the person, so he or she can see your lips, and avoid speaking with your hand over your mouth or when smoking. It could also be helpful if you, as well of course as deaf people themselves, were to learn British Sign Language. In case of real difficulty, you can always write down your message.

Teeth

Everyone knows the importance of having regular dental check-ups. Many adults, however, slip out of the habit, which could result in their having more trouble with their teeth as they become older. Dentistry is one of the treatments for which you have to pay under the NHS, unless you have a low income. If you or your partner are in receipt of Income Support, income-based Jobseeker's Allowance or Pension Credit, you are entitled to free NHS dental treatment. You may also receive some help if you are in receipt of the Working Tax Credit; for details, see leaflet HC11.

Even if you do not belong to any of these groups, you may still get some help if you have a low income. To find out if you qualify, fill in claim form HC1 (obtainable from social security or Jobcentre Plus offices, NHS hospitals and NHS dentists). To avoid any nasty surprises when the bill comes along, it is important to confirm with your dentist before he or she treats you whether you are being treated under the NHS. This also applies to the hygienist, should you need to see one. The best advice is to ask in advance what the cost of your treatment is likely to be.

Help with the cost is all very well, but for many an even bigger problem than money is the difficulty of finding an NHS dentist in their area. The best advice is to call the British Dental Health Foundation's Helpline (see below) or, if you are thinking of going private, ask friends and acquaintances for recommendations. You could also look in the *Yellow Pages* or on its website: www.yell.com, where you should find some names.

For those who like to be able to budget ahead for any dental bills, **Denplan** could be of interest. It offers two plans: Denplan Care, which for a fixed monthly fee entitles you to all routine and restorative treatment including crowns and bridges; and Denplan Essentials, for a lower monthly fee covers just normal routine care including examinations, X-rays and hygienists' visits. In both cases, patients' actual monthly fees are calculated by their own dentist after an initial assessment of their oral health. Registration must be with a Denplan member dentist, but as around a third of UK dentists participate this should not be a problem. For further information contact Denplan Ltd, Tel: 01962 828 000; e-mail: cae@denplan.co.uk; website: www.denplan.co.uk.

Prevention is always better than cure. If you want free, independent and impartial advice on all aspects of oral health and free literature on a wide range of topics, including patients' rights, finding a dentist and dental care for older people, contact the **British Dental Health Foundation**, Tel: 0845 063 1188; website: www.dentalhealth.org.uk.

A useful free fact sheet is *Dental Care*, from Age Concern, Tel: 0800 009 966; website: www.ageconcern.org.uk.

Personal relationships

Retirement, for couples, is a bit like getting married again. It involves a new lifestyle and fresh opportunities, and inevitably, as with marriage, a few compromises are needed. He may have to accustom himself to no longer going to a regular job. She may have to start thinking about another meal to prepare and may possibly feel compelled to reorganize her domestic or working routine. Of course, it could be the other way round. If the wife has given up her job, the husband who has long acted as manager of the household may be worrying at the prospect of someone carrying out spot checks on his activities at regular intervals.

After years of perhaps seeing each other no more than a couple of hours at the beginning and end of each weekday, suddenly almost the whole of every day can be spent together. He may feel hurt that she does not appear more delighted. She may feel guilty about wanting to pursue her normal activities. More and more women are nowadays working after the husband has retired. Sometimes too, with the children no longer at home, couples may feel they have nothing left in common. There is a sad statistic that indicates this may be true: there has been a recent increase in the over-60s divorce rate. It is possible, therefore, that one or other of the couple may be tempted to seek excitement elsewhere rather than trying to work out a solution together.

It is possible that, even in the most loving relationship, the first weeks of retirement – for either partner – can produce tensions. This may consequently affect their sex life in a way that neither had anticipated. Normally, with goodwill and understanding on both sides, difficulties are quickly resolved to allow an even deeper, more satisfying relationship to develop. However, for some couples it does not work out so easily, and it may be helpful to seek skilled guidance:

Albany Trust offers counselling for people facing change and with difficulties in relationships, depression or psychosexual problems. Costs vary, but fees are negotiable for those on low incomes. Contact Albany Trust, Tel: 020 8767 1827; e-mail: info@albanytrust.org; website: www.albanytrust.org.

Marriage Care offers a similar service, plus also a confidential telephone helpline, for those who are having problems with their marriage or other close personal relationship. Contact **Marriage Care England and Wales**, Tel: 0845 6606 000; website: www.marriagecare.org.uk or **Scottish Marriage Care**, Tel: 0141 222 2166; website: www.scottishmarriagecare.org.

Relate offers a counselling service to people who are experiencing difficulties in their marriage or other personal relationships. Its clients are of all ages. Some have been married twice or more. Many are in the throes of actually seeking a divorce but are trying to prevent the bitterness that can develop. Some come for advice because of upsets with their stepchildren. Others may have sexual problems. Sometimes couples come together; sometimes, either the husband or the wife comes alone. Often, the emphasis is not on a particular crisis but instead on ways couples are seeking to make their marriage more positively enjoyable, as at retirement. Relate offers counselling through 88 centres around the country. Each counselling centre operates an independent pricing policy, and counsellors will discuss with clients what they can reasonably contribute. However, no one is turned away if they cannot afford to make a contribution. Local branches can be found by contacting **Relate England**, Tel: 0300 1001 234; website: www.relate.org.uk or **Relate Scotland**, Tel: 0845 119 6088; website: www.relatescotland.org.uk.

Help for grandparents

A sad result of today's divorce statistics is the risk to grandparents of losing contact with their grandchildren. While some divorcing parents lean over backwards to avoid this happening, others – maybe through force of circumstance or hurt feelings – deny grandparents access or even sever the relationship completely. Until 1989 grandparents had very few rights. However, following the introduction of the Children Act, grandparents may, with the leave of the court, seek an order for contact with the child or for residence so that the child may live with them. Generally, a fee is payable to the court for the making of such applications unless the grandparent is in receipt of Community Legal Service funding (formerly Legal Aid). In reaching a decision the paramount consideration for the court must be what action, if any, is in the best interest of the child. If the court feels that the child is of sufficient age and understanding, it will take into account his or her views in reaching a decision.

Recourse to the law is never a step to be taken lightly and should obviously be avoided if there is the possibility that a more conciliatory approach could be successful. An organization that has considerable experience of advising grandparents and that can also offer a mediation service in London, as well as practical help and support with legal formalities, is the **Grandparents' Association.** The helpline telephone number is 0845 434 9585; e-mail: info@grandparents-association.org.uk; website: www.grandparents-association.org.uk.

Depression

Depression is a condition that is often akin to problems in a marriage and other personal crises. It is fairly common after giving birth, as well as after bereavement. It can be caused by worries or may occur after an operation. Sometimes too, as a number of retired people find, it develops as a result of loneliness, boredom or general lack of purpose. Usually people manage to deal with it alone. They come out of it in their own way and in their own time, depending on how quickly time heals sorrow or the scars of a relationship that has gone wrong. In the case of those who are temporarily bored and fed up, they will recover as soon as they find new interests and outlets for their talents.

If the condition persists for more than a few days, a doctor should always be consulted, as depression can create sleeping difficulties. It also affects the appetite and leads to an overall feeling of physical malaise. The sufferer can be caught in a vicious circle of being too listless to enjoy anything, yet not having done enough during the day to be able to sleep at the proper time.

Another reason for consulting a doctor is that depression may be due to being physically run down. If you've recently suffered from flu, maybe all that is required is a good tonic – or perhaps a holiday. Sometimes, however, depression persists. In these cases it may be that, rather than medicines or the stimulus of a new activity, individuals need to talk to someone. Often it is better to find someone outside the family circle who has a deeper understanding of what the person is experiencing. There are several organizations that may be able to help:

Depression Alliance is a charity that offers assistance to anyone affected by depression. As well as a nationwide network of groups where individuals can meet to provide mutual support, the Depression Alliance has a penfriend scheme and also produces a quarterly newsletter and a wide range of free literature. For further information contact the Alliance, Tel: 0845 1232 320; e-mail: information@depressionalliance.org; website: www.depressionalliance.org.

Mind (National Association for Mental Health), works for a better life for people with experience of mental distress. It has offices in England and Wales and more than 200 local associations that offer a wide range of special facilities and services, including housing with care, day centres, social clubs, advocacy and self-help groups. Mind also runs a national information line and produces a variety of publications, including a bimonthly magazine. For further information contact Mind, Tel: 0845 766 0163; e-mail: contact@mind.org.uk; website: www.mind.org.uk.

Samaritans are available at any time of the day or night, every single day of the year. They are there to talk or listen for as long as an individual needs or wants to be able to speak to another person. Although most people think of the Samaritans as being a telephone service for those who feel they may be in danger of taking their own lives, anyone who would like to can visit their local branch. You do not need to feel actively suicidal before contacting the Samaritans; if you are simply depressed, they will equally welcome your call. The service is free and completely confidential. Just contact the Samaritans, Tel: 08457 90 90 90; e-mail: jo@samaritans.org; website: www.samaritans.org.

Sane is a mental health charity which, in addition to initiating and funding research, operates a helpline to give individuals in need of emotional support or practical information on the help they require. It can provide information about local and national mental health services, mental health law and the rights of both service users and carers. SANELINE is open every day, from 1 pm to 11 pm. Contact Sane, Tel: 0845 767 8000; e-mail: info@sane.org.uk; website: www.sane. org.uk.

Some common afflictions

You may be one of the lucky ones and the rest of this chapter will be of no further interest to you. It deals with some of the more common afflictions, such as back pain and heart disease, as well as with disability. However, if you are unfortunate enough to be affected, or have a member of your family who is, then knowing which organizations can provide support could make all the difference in helping you to cope.

Aphasia

Aphasia is a condition that makes it hard to speak, read or understand language. It typically affects individuals after a stroke or a head injury. **Speakability (Action for Dysphasic Adults)** is the national charity offering information and support to people with aphasia, their families and their carers. As well as a helpline, it has fact sheets, publications and videos. There is also a national network of self-help groups. For further information, contact Speakability, Tel: 080 8808 9572; e-mail: speakability@speakability.org.uk; website: www.speaka bility.org.uk.

Arthritis and rheumatism

Although arthritis is often thought of as an older person's complaint, it accounts for the loss of an estimated 70 million working days a year in Britain. **Arthritis Care** is a registered charity working with, and for, people with arthritis. It encourages self-help and has over 400 local branches offering practical support and social activities. There is a confidential helpline, staffed by professional counsellors, open 10 am to 4 pm weekdays. Arthritis Care also runs four specially adapted hotels and publishes various leaflets and booklets. For the addresses of local branches, contact Arthritis Care, Tel: 0808 600 6868; e-mail: info@arthritiscare.org.uk; website: www.arthritiscare.org.uk.

In addition to funding a major research programme, **Arthritis Research Campaign (arc)** publishes a large number of free booklets on understanding and coping with arthritis and also produces a quarterly magazine, *Arthritis Today*. Contact arc, Tel: 0870 850 5000; e-mail: info@arc.org.uk; website: www.arc.org.uk.

Back pain

Four out of five people suffer from back pain at some stage of their lives. While there are many different causes, doctors agree that much of the trouble could be avoided through correct posture, care in lifting heavy articles, a firm mattress, and chairs that provide support in the right places. Whether you have problems or are hoping to prevent them, the following two organizations could be helpful:

The Back Shop is a shop and mail-order business that sells ergonomically approved products that help prevent back trouble or may provide relief for those who suffer. The shop is staffed by assistants with specialized knowledge of back pain and related problems. Contact The Back Shop, Tel: 020 7935 9120; e-mail: info@thebackshop.co.uk; website: www.thebackshop.co.uk.

BackCare is a registered charity that funds research into the causes and treatment of back pain and also publishes a range of leaflets and fact sheets to help back pain sufferers. It has local branches around the country that organize talks, lectures and exercise classes, as well as social activities and fundraising events. Membership includes copies of the quarterly magazine, *Talkback*. Contact BackCare, Tel: 0845 130 2704; e-mail contact via form on the website: www. backcare.org.uk.

Cancer

One of the really excellent trends in recent years is a far greater willingness to talk about cancer. Quite apart from the fact that discussing the subject openly has removed some of the dread, increasingly one hears stories of many more people who have made a complete recovery. Early diagnosis can make a vital difference. Doctors recommend that all women should undergo regular screening for cervical cancer, and women over 50 are advised to have a routine mammography to screen for breast cancer at least once every three years.

Computerized cervical screening systems for women aged 25 to 64 and breast cancer screening units for women aged 50 to 70 are available nationwide. In both cases, older women can have access to the services on request. It also goes without saying that anyone with a lump or swelling, however small, should waste no time in having it investigated by a doctor. There are a number of excellent support groups for cancer sufferers:

Breast Cancer Care offers practical advice, information and emotional support to women who have, or fear they have, breast cancer or benign breast disease. Its services include a helpline, free leaflets, a prosthesis-fitting service, and one-to-one support from volunteers who have themselves experienced breast cancer or whose partner has been affected. Interactive support from both professionals and people affected by breast cancer is available via the website. Contact Breast

Cancer Care, Tel: 0808 800 6000; e-mail: info@breastcancercare.org.uk; website: www.breastcancercare.org.uk.

Cancerbackup offers a free and confidential telephone information service to help people affected by cancer. Calls are answered by a qualified nurse who has the time, knowledge and understanding to answer your questions and listen to how you may be feeling. Cancerbackup also produces many booklets and fact sheets on different types of cancer and their treatment. A publications list is available via its website. Contact Cancerbackup, Tel: 0808 800 1234; website: www.cancerbackup.org.uk.

Chest and heart diseases

The earlier sections on smoking, diet, drink and exercise list some of the most pertinent 'dos and don'ts' that can help prevent heart disease. The advice is not to be taken lightly. Latest statistics reveal that UK death rates from coronary heart disease are among the highest in the world, killing almost 120,000 people a year and responsible for one in five of all deaths. Although people tend to think of heart attacks as particularly affecting men, over four times as many women die from heart disease as from breast cancer. In an effort to reduce the casualty rate, the **British Heart Foundation** publishes a range of 'help yourself' booklets, designed to create greater awareness of how heart disease can best be prevented through healthy living. For further information, contact the British Heart Foundation, Tel: 0300 333 1333; website: www.bhf.org.uk.

Diabetes

Diabetes occurs when the amount of glucose in the blood is too high for the body to use properly. It can sometimes be treated by diet alone; sometimes pills or insulin may also be needed. Diabetes can be diagnosed at any age, although it is common in the elderly and especially among individuals who are overweight. **Diabetes UK** aims to improve the lives of people with diabetes. It offers information and support to affected individuals and their families and friends. There are around 430 nationwide branches that hold regular meetings and social activities. Contact Diabetes UK, Tel: 0845 120 2960; e-mail: info@diabetes.org.uk; website: www.diabetes.org.uk.

Migraine

Migraine affects over 10 million people in the UK. It can involve severe head pains, nausea, vomiting, visual disturbances and in some cases temporary paralysis. The **Migraine Trust** funds and promotes research, holds international symposia and runs an extensive support service. Contact the Migraine Trust, Tel: 020 7462 6601; e-mail: info@migrainetrust.org; website: www.migrainetrust.org.

Osteoporosis and menopause problems

Osteoporosis is a disease affecting bones, which become so fragile that they can break very easily, with injuries most common in the spine, hip and wrist. It affects one in two women (and one in five men) and often develops following the menopause, when body levels of oestrogen naturally decrease. The following may be useful:

Menopause Exchange produces a quarterly newsletter and number of fact sheets with the aim of providing reliable and easily understood information about the menopause and other health issues of concern to women in midlife. There is also an information service, and members have access to an 'Ask the Experts' panel. Contact the Menopause Exchange, Tel: 020 8420 7245; e-mail: info@meno pause-exchange.co.uk; website: www.menopause-exchange.co.uk.

National Osteoporosis Society offers help, support and advice on all aspects of osteoporosis. There is a medical helpline staffed by specialist nurses, a range of leaflets and booklets, and also a network of over 120 local support groups throughout the UK. Contact the Exchange on 0845 450 0230; e-mail: info@nos. org.uk; website: www.nos.org.uk.

Women's Health Concern (WHC) is a national charity, founded in 1972, to offer professional advice and counselling to women, in particular those with gynaecological and hormonal disturbance problems, as well as problems with the menopause. It runs a telephone and e-mail nurse counselling service. Fact sheets and general information about gynaecological conditions can be sourced from the website. As a charity, WHC charges no fee, but donations are very much appreciated. For further information, contact 0845 123 2319; e-mail: info@womens-health-concern.org; website: www.womens-health-concern.org.

Stroke

Over 130,000 people suffer a stroke every year in England and Wales. A stroke is a brain injury caused by the sudden interruption of blood flow. It is unpredictable in its effects, which may include muscular paralysis or weakness on one side, loss of speech or loss of understanding or language, visual problems or incontinence. Prevention is similar to the prevention of heart disease.

The **Stroke Association** works to prevent strokes and helps stroke patients and their families. It produces a range of publications and provides advice and welfare grants to individuals through its London office and regional centres. Its Community Services, Dysphasia Support and Family Support help stroke sufferers through home visits, and over 400 stroke clubs provide social and therapeutic support. Contact the Association on 0845 303 3100; e-mail: info@stroke.org.uk; website: www.stroke.org.uk.

Disability

Disability is mainly covered in Chapter 15, Caring for Elderly Parents, so if you or someone in your family has a problem you may find the answer you need there. In this section, there are simply one or two points that may be useful for younger people.

Local authority services

Social services departments (social work departments in Scotland) provide many of the services that people with disabilities may need, including:

- practical help in the home, perhaps with the support of a home help;
- adaptations to your home, such as a ramp for a wheelchair or other special equipment for your safety;
- meals on wheels;
- provision of day centres, clubs and similar;
- the issue of badges for cars driven or used by people with a disability (in some authorities this is handled by the works department or by the residents' parking department);
- advice about other transport services or concessions that may be available locally.

In most instances, you should speak to a social worker, who will either be able to make the arrangements or signpost you in the right direction. He or she will also be able to tell you of any special facilities or other help provided by the authority.

Occupational therapists, who can advise about special equipment and help teach someone with a disability through training and exercise how best to manage, also come within the orbit of the social services department.

Health care

Services are normally arranged through either a GP or the local authority health centre. Key professional staff include:

- health visitors (who are qualified nurses), who rather like social workers will be able to put you in touch with whatever specialized services are required;
- district nurses, who will visit patients in their home;
- physiotherapists, who use exercise and massage to help improve mobility, for example after an operation;
- medical social workers, employed in hospitals, who will help with any arrangements before a patient is discharged.

Employment

The disablement resettlement officer helps and advises people looking for work and can also give information about any available grants, for example towards the cost of fares to work and for special equipment that may make work life easier. Ask at your nearest Jobcentre or **Jobcentre Plus** office or check the website: www.jobcentreplus.gov.uk.

Council Tax

If someone in your family has a disability, you may be able to claim a reduction on your Council Tax. If you have an orange badge on your car, you may get a rebate for a garage. You would normally apply to the housing benefits officer, but different councils employ different officers to deal with this; see website: www. dwp.gov.uk.

Alcoholics Anonymous, National Helpline: 0845 769 7555. Po Box 1, 10 Toft Green, York, YO1 7NJ Tel: 01904 644 026.

Alcoholics Anonymous has over 4,000 groups throughout the UK, designed to help those with a serious alcohol problem. Through mutual support, sufferers assist each other in coping with their problem. There are no fees for membership of Alcoholics Anonymous and anonymity is carefully preserved.

14

Holidays

Holidays are so much better when you've retired. No longer do you need to plan months ahead in order to fit in with colleagues. You can avoid peak periods, which are almost invariably more expensive and crowded. You can enjoy real flexibility in a way that is usually not possible when you are working. Why not take several mini-breaks when you feel like it, or perhaps go away for a month or two at a time? One of the greatest things about retirement is the availability of concessionary prices. You can research cheaper fares and reduced charges for hotel accommodation.

Apart from these benefits, the fact that you've retired makes very little difference. You can do whatever you like: ride an elephant in India or take a caravan around Europe. If you've always wanted to sail on the Norfolk Broads or go bird-watching in Scotland, now is the time to do it. You could combine a holiday with a special interest, such as painting or music. There is ample opportunity for you to enrol for summer school, exchange homes with someone in another country or sign on for a working holiday. These are many and varied, such as voluntary conservation activity or home- and pet-sitting, for which you get paid. The choice is enormous.

The list of suggestions that follows here is by no means exhaustive. You can go to any travel agent or search the internet and collect further ideas by the hundred. However, there are two main criteria that have been used here to help decide which, amongst the thousands of options, to include. The first is the variety factor: holidays that one way or another offer some special attraction. The second is age: holidays that specifically cater for those aged 50 and above.

Some of the choices offered verge on the exotic, with prices to match. Others in contrast are extremely reasonable in cost. There are suggestions that are only suitable for the really fit and active. At the other extreme, there are a number of inclusions that would be of interest only to individuals in need of special care.

Some of the choices may strike you as mad, risky, humdrum, too demanding – or simply not your style. But retirement is a time for experimentation, and trying something entirely different is half the fun.

For ease of reference, entries are listed under such headings as 'Arts and crafts', 'Sport', 'Self-catering and other low-budget holidays', etc. Inevitably, some organizations are relevant in several sections but, to avoid repetition, the majority are featured only once in what it is hoped is the most logical place.

At the end of the chapter, there is a general information section with brief details about insurance, concessionary fares and other travel tips. Prices and some of the other detailed information, if provided, are as accurate as possible. Programme details do change (sometimes at very short notice), and it is impossible to guarantee that all are current. Website addresses and e-mail contact details are included wherever possible so that up-to-date information can be accessed easily.

Art appreciation

Many tour operators, clubs and other organizations that arrange group holidays include visits to museums, churches and other venues of artistic interest along with their other activities such as walking, bridge and general sightseeing. There is one that specializes in cultural tours that has been going for a long time: **Specialtours**. Alternatively, if you enjoy the performing arts, you could spend several glorious days attending some of the music and drama festivals held in many parts of the country, as well as some of the famous festivals overseas. Specialtours arranges accompanied cultural tours in association with numerous organizations, including the Art Fund. For further information contact Specialtours on 020 7386 4690; e-mail: info@specialtours.co.uk; website: www. specialtours.co.uk.

Festivals

There is a feast of music, drama and the arts. The most famous festivals are those held at Edinburgh and Aldeburgh. Over the years the number of festivals has been growing, and these are now a regular feature in many parts of the country. To find out what is going on where, contact the Arts Council or your regional Arts Council office. Look in the national press or search the internet for lists of major festivals at home and overseas:

Aldeburgh Music Festival in Suffolk is held annually during June. A varied programme of classical and contemporary music and opera at Snape Maltings Concert Hall, Jubilee Hall and other local venues is complemented by exhibitions, talks, walks and films. There are also three other festivals, at Easter, during August and in October. In addition, there is a year-round programme of concerts and master classes that are open to the public. For further details contact Aldeburgh Music on 01728 687100; e-mail: enquiries@aldeburgh.co.uk; website: www.aldeburgh.co.uk.

Edinburgh International Festival is held every August. Details of music, theatre, dance, opera and other events are available from early April. For further information on the Festival, e-mail: info@festivalsedinburgh.com; website: www. edinburghfestivals.co.uk.

Three Choirs Festival is an international classical music festival presented in August each year (since the early 18th century) by rotation in the Cathedral cities of Gloucester, Hereford and Worcester. Choral music is at its exhilarating and uplifting best, in a quintessentially English setting. Varied and inspiring programmes performed by world-class artists and ensembles – there is something for everyone at Three Choirs. For more information contact the Festival on 0845 652 1823; e-mail: info@3choirs.org; website: www.3choirs.org.

Arts and crafts

The focus here is on taking courses or just participating for the pleasure, rather than viewing the works of others. The choice includes wood carving and other crafts, painting and music. Further suggestions are also given in Chapter 9, Leisure Activities.

Benslow Music Trust provides exciting opportunities for music making and appreciation, with a year-round programme of weekend and midweek courses for adult amateur musicians of all standards. The programme includes chamber music, choral and solo singing, music appreciation, beginner courses, jazz, solo and ensemble wind, orchestras, big band and early music. For further details contact the Trust, Tel: 01462 459 446; e-mail: info@benslow.org; website: www. benslow.org.

The Crafts Council aims to position the UK as the global centre for the making, seeing and collecting of contemporary craft. This is a growing industry and contributes to the UK's reputation as a world leader in creativity. The Council works with a strategic choice of partners to make contemporary craft exciting and relevant to the widest possible audience and promotes the teaching and studying of contemporary craft. Contact the Council, Tel: 020 7806 2500; e-mail: education@craftscouncil.org.uk; website: www.craftscouncil.org.uk.

West Dean College, housed in a beautiful mansion surrounded by landscaped gardens and parkland, organizes short residential courses in contemporary and traditional crafts, the visual arts, photography, music and gardening – variously lasting from one to seven days. A typical programme includes calligraphy, textiles, woodcarving, picture framing, blacksmithing, sculpture, drawing and painting, stained glass, willow work and many more. There are also 10 full-time diploma programmes including, among others, the conservation and restoration of antique furniture, tapestry weaving and musical instrument making, all of which are validated by the University of Sussex. Contact the College, Tel: 01243 811 301; e-mail: enquiries@westdean.org.uk; website: www.westdean.org.uk.

Coach holidays

Some of the coach companies organize holidays, as distinct from simply offering a mode of transport. Advice note from other holidaymakers: before embarking on a lengthy coach tour, try a few shorter excursions to see how you cope with the journey.

National Express provides a scheduled coach network to over 1,000 destinations throughout the UK and also a wide choice of short-break holidays to most European countries. Passengers aged 60-plus travel for half-price, but this does not include the hotel costs. For further details contact National Express, Tel: 0871 7818 181; website: www.nationalexpress.com.

Historical holidays

Holidays with a particular focus on history are becoming increasingly popular. The choice includes battlefield tours, exploring famous archaeological sites of Britain and the highly imaginative 'production' at Kentwell Hall.

Holts Tours – Battlefields & History offers a choice of over 40 battlefield, historical and archaeological tours throughout the world. All are accompanied by a specialist guide-lecturer, and local experts are also used. The 2008 programme included: Cyprus – Aphrodite's Island; the Anglo-Zulu War; Normandy 1944; 1918 commemorative tour; and the Indian Mutiny. Most tours are half-board in good-standard hotels with private facilities. Every effort is made to cater for single travellers, many of whom are women. Special group tours can be arranged. Contact Holts Tours, Tel: 0845 375 0430; e-mail: info@holts.co.uk; website: www.holts.co.uk.

Kentwell Hall. Every summer Kentwell Hall in Suffolk recreates a living panorama of what life was like during the Tudor period. Participants are required to provide their own costumes and to enter into the role of a character living at the time: for example, this could be a 16th-century cook or haymaker. You are expected to prepare yourself by reading, and there are open days at Kentwell with briefing sessions. The event lasts for three weeks, and participants can stay for one, two or three complete weeks. The only cost involved is the provision of a suitable costume. All meals are free, and there is camping space available. Those requiring more comfort can book into one of the many local bed-and-breakfast hotels. Applications should ideally be made by the end of February at the latest.

Contact Kentwell Hall, Tel: 01787 310 207; e-mail can be sent via the enquiry form on their website: www.kentwell.co.uk.

Mike Hodgson Battlefield Tours. Military historian Mike Hodgson has over 25 years' experience in organizing guided coach tours for small groups (about 25 people) to visit European battlefields. Recent tours (variously between three and five nights) included Agincourt, Waterloo, Ypres, the Somme, Verdun and Normandy. Costs include all travel, hotel accommodation, meals and guiding services. Contact Mike Hodgson Battlefield Tours, Tel: 01526 342 249; e-mail: info@mhbattlefieldtours.co.uk; website: www.mhbattlefieldtours.co.uk. Should you wish to visit a particular grave, the **Commonwealth War Graves Commission** will help you identify the exact location. Contact the Commission, Tel: 01628 634 221; e-mail can be sent via the enquiry form on their website: www.cwgc.org.

Poppy Travel is the specialist travel arm of the Royal British Legion. This organization has been arranging visits to battlefields, war cemeteries and memorials since the 1920s. Its background in remembrance gives it a unique insight into the historical significance of destinations, which are then blended with its proven travel and holiday expertise. It now offers trips to almost every location where the British armed services have fought. Poppy Travel has established an unrivalled reputation for a sympathetic approach and professionalism. Contact Poppy Travel, Tel: 01622 716729; e-mail: info@poppytravel.org.uk; website: www. poppytravel.org.uk.

Language courses

If you are hoping to travel more when you retire, being able to speak the language when abroad will greatly add to your enjoyment. The quickest and easiest way to learn is in the country itself. There are attractive opportunities for improving your French, German, Italian, Spanish and even Japanese.

British Institute of Florence is situated in the historic centre of Florence, offering courses in Italian language and art history as well as in life drawing, watercolour painting, Tuscan cooking and Italian opera. Classes are timetabled to allow students to take as many different courses as they wish. The British Institute also runs a summer school in Massa Marittima, near the Tuscan coast, during the first two weeks of August. A regular programme of events including lectures, concerts and films is held in the Institute's magnificent library overlooking the River Arno. Contact the Institute, Tel: (from the UK) 00 39 055 267 781; e-mail: info@ britishinstitute.it; website: www.britishinstitute.it.

Goethe-Institut London offers a variety of German-language courses, from beginners to examination level, at 16 centres in Germany. The instruction is designed so that you can follow from one level to another in all centres. Course fees include such items as excursions and cultural events as well as the help of course assistants. For full details contact Goethe-Institut London, Tel: 020 7596 4000; e-mail: info@london.goethe.org; website: www.goethe.de.

Instituto Cervantes provides courses for studying Spanish in London and also discovering the cultures of Spain and Latin America. Contact Instituto Cervantes, Tel: 020 7235 0353; e-mail: cenlon@cervantes.es; website: www.londres.cervantes.es.

Other people's homes

Living in someone else's home free is one of the cheapest ways of enjoying a holiday. There are two ways of arranging this. You can exchange your home with another person, in this country or abroad. The onus is on you to select a suitable property and to decide whether the person with whom you are swapping is likely to care for your home properly. The alternative is to become a homesitter and, for a modest payment, mind someone else's property while they are away.

Home exchange

Unless you are lucky enough to hear about someone through a personal recommendation, probably the easiest method of finding a swap (and of advertising your own home) is through a specialized directory or website listing. In most cases, this is not an introduction service as such. The exchanges are normally arranged direct between the two parties concerned, who agree the terms between themselves. Some people even exchange their cars and pets. Here are some organizations that may be useful:

Home Base Holidays operates an international home exchange agency. Accommodation varies from small city apartments to large country homes complete with swimming pool. Your own exchange offer is included on the website, and you can search the other homes registered on the site. Home Base Holidays does not get involved in the actual arrangements but is happy to give advice. For further information contact Home Base Holidays, Tel: 020 8886 8752; website: www.homebase-hols.com.

HomeLink International offers around 14,000 home exchange possibilities in nearly 70 countries. Register, and your home is included on the website with a photo and is entered in the twice-yearly directory. For further information contact HomeLink International, Tel: 01962 886 882; e-mail: mail@homelink.org.uk; website: www.homelink.org.uk.

Homesitting

Retired people are generally considered ideal homesitters. Homesitting means that you provide a caretaking service and get paid for doing so. Duties variously involve light housework, plant watering, care of pets and sometimes tending the garden. First-class references are naturally required. Here are some contacts:

Absentia sitters variously offer a holiday care service, provide long-term specialized care (as, for example, when a property is vacant during probate) or care for a home and any pets if owners have to go into hospital. In that case sitters will also visit the patients, take in mail and generally keep them in touch with domestic events during their absence. Pay varies, depending on duties. For further information contact Absentia, Tel: 01279 777 412; e-mail: theteam@home-and-pets. co.uk; website: www.home-and-pets.co.uk.

Homesitters are looking for mature, responsible people who are non-smokers with no children or pets. Assignments may be for short or long periods. It is useful to have your own car. Payment rates vary depending on responsibilities, and there is a (non-taxable) food allowance plus travel expenses. With agreement, a homesitter can take his or her partner. The houses can be anything from a city centre apartment to an isolated country mansion. Contact Homesitters, Tel: 01296 630 730; e-mail: admin@homesitters.co.uk; website: www.homesit ters.co.uk.

Universal Aunts organize a home- and pet-sitting service for absent owners and recruit single or pairs of mature, responsible people for this work. All applicants for the homesitters' panel are interviewed before acceptance on the list. For further information contact Universal Aunts, Tel: 020 7738 8937; e-mail: aunts@ universalaunts.co.uk; website: www.universalaunts.co.uk.

Overseas travel

Many of the big tour operators make a feature of offering special holidays designed for the over-55s. We have also included companies that specialize in arranging cruises and packaged motoring holidays, and also information about timesharing. For up-to-date details, you should check the websites:

Explore Worldwide arranges more than 400 tours to over 130 countries. Accommodation varies from camping to modest hotels and rustic lodges. To view the wide range of holidays on offer, contact Explore Worldwide, Tel: 0845 013 1537; e-mail: res@explore.co.uk; website: www.explore.co.uk.

Relais du Silence is a French group of independently owned hotels with a network of about 230 hotels throughout Europe, including Britain. It offers tranquil, rural settings in two-, three- and four-star comfort at reasonable prices, with good food and a family-like atmosphere. For more information, contact Relais du Silence, Tel: 0033 1 44 49 90 00; e-mail: info@relaisdusilence.com; website: www.relaisdusilence.com.

Saga Holidays are exclusively for people aged 50 and over. There is a large range of options worldwide including, among others, ocean and river cruising (including Saga's own cruise ships, *Saga Rose* and *Saga Ruby*), safaris, short- and long-stay resort holidays and multi-centre tours. There is also a selection of special interest holidays including, for example, gardens, music, walking and art appreciation. Saga Holidays are sold direct and not through a travel agent. For further information contact Saga Holidays, Tel: 01303 771 111; website: www.saga.co.uk/travel.

Cruises

Cruises are an exotic option and appeal to many people. There are a great variety of programmes and the following are recommended:

Carnival Group cruise brands include P&O Cruises, Cunard Line, Princess Cruises, Ocean Village and the Yachts of Seabourn. For further information contact Carnival Group, Tel: 023 8065 5000; website: www.carnivalukgroup.com.

Fred. Olsen Cruise Lines operates four ships, with departures mostly from Dover, Southampton, Leith, Greenock, Liverpool, Newcastle and Dublin. Choices include a winter season of Caribbean fly-cruises from London and Manchester, as well as from regional airports on selected dates. Itineraries range from a two-night mini-cruise to a world cruise. Prices range from the modest to the luxurious. For further information contact Fred. Olsen Cruise Lines, Tel: 01473 746 175; e-mail: internet@fredolsen.co.uk; website: www.fredolsencruises.com.

NCL (Norwegian Cruise Line) offers fly-cruise and stay holidays in the Caribbean, Alaska, New England and Canada, Bermuda, South America, the Panama Canal, Hawaii, Mexico and Europe. For further information contact Norwegian Cruise Line, Tel: 0845 201 8907; e-mail: longuestservices@ncl.com; website: www.ncl.co.uk.

P&O Cruises offer a wide range of destinations, including two round-world cruises, the Mediterranean, the Atlantic isles, the Baltic and the Caribbean. For further information contact P&O Cruises, Tel: 0845 678 0014; e-mail: reservations@pocruises.com; website: www.pocruises.com.

Page & Moy Ltd. Choosing the cruise most likely to offer what you want no longer entails elaborate detective work if you consult tour operator Page & Moy. Discounts are offered on every booking, and there are also many exclusive special offers. Cruise specialists are available seven days a week to give assistance. For further information contact Page & Moy, Tel: 0800 567 7400; e-mail via the contact form on their website: www.pageandmoy.com.

Princess Cruises. Choose from 17 ships cruising to Alaska, the Far East and Australia, the Caribbean, the Panama Canal, Mexico, South America, Hawaii and the South Pacific, New England, the Mediterranean and Scandinavia. For further information contact Princess Cruises, Tel: 0845 3555 800; e mail: enquiry@princesscruises.co.uk; website: www.princess.com.

Cargo ship cruises

If price is one of the main considerations and you don't mind sacrificing the dressing up and organized activity, a happy solution could be to travel via cargo ship. Accommodation and facilities (there is often a swimming pool) vary according to the size and type of vessel, which could be a roll-on roll-off container or a banana boat going to South America and back. A few of the best are:

Andrew Weir Cruises, Tel: 020 7575 6480; website: www.aws.co.uk.
Cargo Ship Voyages, Tel: 01473 736265; e-mail: cargovoyager1@btconnect. com; website: www.cargoshipvoyages.co.uk.
Strand Voyages, Tel: 020 7921 4340; e-mail: voyages@strandtravel.co.uk; website: www.strandtravel.co.uk.

Motoring holidays abroad

A number of organizations – including in particular some ferry operators – offer packages for the motorist that include ferry crossings, accommodation and insurance. While these often provide very good value, some people prefer to make all their own arrangements in order to get exactly what they want. Whatever your preference, if a main concern is carefree motoring, maybe one of the options suggested below could provide a happy solution:

Automobile Association (AA). The AA offers several helpful products and services for motoring at home and abroad, including route planning, maps, AA Five Star Europe Breakdown Assistance and travel guides. For further details contact the AA, Tel: 0870 600 0371; website: www.theaa.com.
Brittany Ferries offers short-break holidays in France and Spain including accommodation, breakfast and return car ferry crossings. There is also a selection of gite holidays in France. For further details contact Brittany Ferries, Tel: 0871 244 0744; website: www.brittany-ferries.co.uk.
RAC Motoring Services. As well as motoring breakdown cover for Europe, the RAC offers a range of overseas single trip or annual travel insurance, plus international driving permits, camping cards and other essential documents. For further details contact the RAC, Tel: 08705 722 722; website: www.rac.co.uk.

Tips when motoring abroad

These are all basic common sense but, given the tales of woe one hears, many holidaymakers forget the obvious precautions:

- Have your car thoroughly serviced before you go.
- Take the following with you: a tool kit, the manual for your car, a rented spares kit, a fuel can, a mechanic's light that plugs into the cigarette lighter socket and at least one extra set of keys.

- Always lock your car and park it in a secure place overnight (nearly 75 per cent of luggage thefts abroad are from cars).

Unless you are taking one of the packages that include insurance, you should contact your insurance company or broker well ahead of time to arrange special insurance cover. The ABI information sheet, *Holiday Insurance and Motoring Abroad* summarizes the essentials you need to know when taking your car overseas. Contact either the AA or the RAC overseas travel department. Both have facilities for helping you if you become stranded, and welcome non-members. See:

Association of British Insurers, Tel: 020 7600 3333; e-mail: info@abi.org.uk; website: www.abi.org.uk.
Europ Assistance, Tel: 0844 338 5533; e-mail: customerservices@europ-assistance.co.uk; website: www.europ-assistance.co.uk.
Green Flag, Tel: 0845 246 1557; e-mail: member-queries@greenflag.com; website: www.greenflag.com.

Advice from seasoned travellers is to have information about garages, spare parts and the legal rules of the country, or countries, through which you are driving. The requirements – and documents you need to carry – are not the same for all European countries, and failure to have the right bond, special permit or spares could mean a fine, or even imprisonment.

If your main purpose in taking your car is to enjoy the freedom it offers when you reach your destination, rather than the journey itself, it is worth looking at the Motorail facilities to Southern France and Italy and the long-range ferries to Spain and Portugal, which save on wear and tear and may be no more expensive than the extra cost of petrol plus overnight stays.

If, instead of taking your own car, you plan to hire a car or motor scooter overseas, you will probably have to buy special insurance at the time of hiring the vehicle. Make sure that this is properly comprehensive (check for any excesses or exclusions) and that at the very least it gives you adequate third-party cover. If in any doubt, you would be recommended to seek advice from the local motoring organization as to the essential requirements – including any foreign words or terms you particularly need to understand before signing.

Short breaks

A very large number of organizations offer short-break holidays all year round, with special bargain prices in spring and autumn. Many British hotels have winter breaks from November to April, when full board can be considerably cheaper than the normal rates. Likewise, many overseas travel operators slash prices during the off-peak seasons. While the websites contain plenty of suggestions, including some glorious city breaks, for very best value (and often all the more fun for being unplanned) look in the newspapers and on the internet for last-minute bargains.

Timesharing

Timesharing is an investment in long-term holidays and, as with other investments, should not be undertaken lightly. The idea is that you buy the use of a property for a specific number of days each year, either for an agreed term or in perpetuity. Your timeshare can be lent to other people, sublet or left eventually in your will. Most timeshare schemes allow you to swap your week(s) for one in other developments throughout the world for your annual holiday, via one of the exchange companies.

A week's timeshare will cost from about £7,000 to over £40,000 depending on the location, the size of the property, the time of year and the facilities of the resort. The average is around £7,500 for one bedroom (peak season). Maintenance charges could cost another £250-plus a week, and you should always check that these are linked to some form of cost-of-living index such as the RPI and ascertain – item by item – precisely what the charges cover. Another useful point to check is that there is an owners' association linked to the property.

While the great majority of people enjoy very happy experiences, stories about unscrupulous operators still occur. You should be on your guard against dubious selling practices which, despite efforts by industry watchdogs, have not been entirely stamped out. In particular, you should beware timeshare scratch cards and fraudulent holiday clubs that are not protected by the Timeshare Directive. Also be wary of such enticing promotional gifts as a 'free' holiday flight to visit the property. Above all, do not be stampeded into signing any commitment until you have had the validity of all aspects of a proposed contract thoroughly vetted by a solicitor. You might also like to check whether the operator is a member of the Resort Development Organisation.

For some years, buyers signing contracts in the UK have had a 14-day cooling-off period. Now, thanks to the 1994 Timeshare Directive, all EU member countries must provide a 10-day minimum cooling-off period and a full prospectus to residents of EU member countries in their own language. In the UK, there is now also a ban on timeshare providers taking a deposit during the cooling-off period. However, this may not apply to deposits signed outside the UK, and buyers who are asked to give a deposit to a third party, such as a trustee, should check carefully before parting with their money.

Among the terms you need to be especially careful about are the future management and maintenance charges (these have been known to sky-rocket within a year or so of purchase) and the potential resale value of a property – or its timeshare weeks or timeshare points – which sometimes has been found to be very substantially below the initial purchase price.

The **Resort Development Organisation** (formerly the Organisation for Timeshare in Europe AISBL) is the regulatory body dedicated to promoting the interests of all with a legitimate involvement in the industry. It offers potential buyers free advice and information and also has an arbitration scheme, run in conjunction with the Chartered Institute of Arbitrators, to handle complaints that are not resolved through its standard complaints-handling procedure. Contact the Resort Development Organisation on www.rdo.org. Most reputable companies also belong to one of two worldwide exchange organizations: **RCI Europe** (Tel: 0845 60 86 363; website: www.rci.com) or **Interval International Ltd** (Tel: 0844 7014 444; website: www.intervalworld.com).

Existing owners wishing to sell their property should be on their guard against unknown resale agents contacting them 'on spec' and offering, in exchange for a registration fee, to act on their behalf. While some may be legitimate, the RDO has received complaints about so-called 'agents' taking money and doing nothing further. A telephone call to the RDO will establish whether the company is a member body. If not, leave well alone.

Retreats

Some people want to have no more than peace and quiet for a few days. If you would welcome the idea of a retreat you might like to contact the **Retreat Association**, which gives details of 240 retreat centres in Britain and Ireland, together with its programmes. Tel: 01494 433 094; e-mail: info@retreats.org.uk; website: www.retreats.org.uk.

Self-catering and other low-budget holidays

If you cannot quite manage to survive on a tenner a day, some of the suggestions in this section need hardly cost you very much more. This applies especially if you are camping, caravanning or renting very simple accommodation with friends. The list includes farm cottages, hostels, university accommodation and other rentals of varying degrees of sparseness or comfort:

Camping and Caravanning Club offers a national network of nearly 100 high-standard club sites, most of which are open to non-members. There are, however, many advantages in joining the Club. Members receive several free publications, including the monthly magazine *Camping and Caravanning* and the *Big Sites Book*, which lists details of over 4,000 places where you can camp in the UK. The Club also offers members a wide range of services including an exclusive RAC break-down and recovery scheme, insurance and an overseas travel service providing competitive ferry bookings and overseas site reservations. Members aged over 55 pay reduced fees on Club sites. Contact the Club, Tel: 0845 130 7632; or e-mail via the online enquiry form on the website: www.campingandcaravanningclub. co.uk.

English Country Cottages, Tel: 0845 268 0785; website: www.english-country-cottages.co.uk.

Holiday Cottages in Scotland, Tel: 01738 451610; e-mail: holidays@ckdgal braith.co.uk: website: www.scottish-holiday-cottages.co.uk.

Venuemasters is a consortium of university and college venues that let residential accommodation during the vacation periods and some other times of the year. Ensuite accommodation is available at competitive B&B rates. For further information contact Venuemasters, Tel: 0114 249 3090; e-mail: info@venuemasters.co.uk; website: www.venuemasters.co.uk.

The 'cottages' offered by English Country Cottages and Holiday Cottages in Scotland, above, range enormously in size, style and location and are variously capable of sleeping between 2 and 22. Many are available for long or short breaks all year round, with low out-of-season prices from November to March. There are many more sites to choose from if you search on the internet:

Farm Stay UK Ltd. Many farms take paying guests, let holiday cottages or run sites for tents or caravans. Farm Stay members offer a range of high-quality accommodation, all Tourist Board inspected, plus a glimpse of life on a farm. The *Farm Stay* guide contains information on over 1,100 good-value farm holidays all over Great Britain and Northern Ireland. Self-catering cottages or bed-and-breakfast facilities with many farms providing an evening meal, if required, are listed. Contact Farm Stay UK Ltd, Tel: 024 7669 6909; e-mail: admin@farmstayuk. co.uk; website: www.farmstayuk.co.uk.

Individual Travellers Company Ltd offers a large range of self-catering holidays in France, Italy, Sicily, Spain, Majorca, Portugal and New England. Properties vary widely in price, size and amenities, from chateaux complete with swimming pools to modest but comfortable apartments. Some in Spain and Southern France are suitable for short or long winter booking. Travel, car hire and insurance can be arranged. Contact Individual Travellers Company Ltd, Tel: 0845 604 3877; website: www.individualtravellers.com.

Landmark Trust is a building preservation charity that restores historic buildings and lets them for holidays. Prices vary considerably over the 183 available buildings. These include castles, timber and thatched cottages, moated properties, towers and follies. For further details contact Landmark Trust, Tel: 01628 825 925; e-mail: bookings@landmarktrust.org.uk; website: www.landmarktrust.org.uk.

Lee Abbey is a holiday, retreat and conference centre, run by a Christian community. It is set in a 280-acre coastal estate, and accommodation is either in the house or in self-catering units. Depending on the time of the year, visitors can stay for either a short-break weekend or up to a fortnight. There is a Christian content to the holidays, and guests can be involved as much or as little as they please. Costs vary according to season and choice of room. There are reductions for clergy and their families. Contact Lee Abbey, Tel: 01598 752 621; website: www.leeabbey.org.uk.

National Trust Holiday Cottages has a wide variety of holiday cottages and flats in many areas of England, Wales and Northern Ireland with varying accommodation for two to 14 people. Although they are very popular in the high holiday seasons, there are usually plenty of vacancies at other times of year. For more information contact National Trust Holiday Cottages, Tel: 0844 800 2070; e-mail: cottages@nationaltrust.org.uk; website: www.nationaltrustcottages.co.uk.

National Trust for Scotland has a large number of holiday cottages available in all areas, as well as cruises. For further information contact the National Trust for Scotland, Tel: 0844 493 2108; e-mail: holidays@nts.org.uk; website: www. ntsholidays.com.

YHA (England and Wales) Ltd welcomes people of all ages. There are over 200 youth hostels in England and Wales and over 4,000 worldwide. Most hostels provide a meals service, cycle storage, lounge areas and self-catering facilities. The accommodation ranges from shared rooms to private rooms with en-suite bathroom. Overnight prices vary according to the location and facilities. For further information, contact the YHA, Tel: 01629 592 700; e-mail: reservations@ yha.org.uk; website: www.yha.org.uk.

Special interest holidays

This section includes weekend courses and more formal summer schools, between them offering a huge variety of subjects, including crafts, computer studies, drama, archaeology, creative writing, photography and many others. It also includes holidays in the more conventional sense, both in Britain and abroad, but with the accent on a hobby such as bridge, dancing, yoga, photography, antiques and other pastimes. They are impossible to categorize other than alphabetically, because many of the organizations offer such a wide range of choices:

Centre for Alternative Technology features interactive displays and working examples of sustainable living, renewable energy, environmentally responsible building and organic gardening. It is open daily to the public throughout the year, except Christmas and mid-January. Short residential courses are held frequently, ranging from two to five days, and subjects covered include renewable energy systems, organic gardening, environmental building and green sanitation. Accommodation is in simple two- to six-person bedrooms; there are also a few single rooms. Pensioners and those on low incomes are charged less. Opportunities also exist for voluntary work during the spring and summer. For a week or fortnight, volunteers live and work as members of staff, gardening and maintaining the site. Volunteers pay about £10 a day towards bed and board. For further details contact the Centre, Tel: 01654 705 981; e-mail: courses@cat.org. uk; website: www.cat.org.uk.

City & Guilds offers special interest day, weekend and summer school courses at many colleges and universities throughout the country. The choice of subjects is enormous, ranging from yoga to astronomy, creative writing to digital photography. Prices vary widely. For further information contact City & Guilds, Tel: 020 7294 2800; e-mail: learnersupport@cityandguilds.com; website: www.cityandguilds.com.

Denman College is the WI's residential adult education college. It runs over 500 short courses (two, three and four nights) each year. The courses are open to both WI and non-members and include full board and tuition. Most of the accommodation is in single rooms, many with en-suite bathrooms. Courses cover such subjects as art, antiques, IT, dance, drama, literature, crafts, aromatherapy and many others. For further information contact the College, Tel: 01865 391 991; e-mail: info@denman.org.uk; website: www.thewi.org.uk.

Earnley Concourse is a residential centre near Chichester that holds weekend and week-long courses throughout the year on such subjects as arts and crafts, music, wildlife, computer studies, keep fit, yoga and others. For more details contact Earnley Concourse, Tel: 01243 670 392; e-mail: info@earnley.co.uk; website: www.earnley.co.uk.

Field Studies Council (FSC) offers over 600 leisure and special interest courses at its 14 centres throughout the UK. The courses cover a wide variety of subjects, including walking, outdoor pursuits, ecology and conservation, botany, birds and animals, history and archaeology, painting and drawing, photography, crafts and traditional skills, and many other general interest activities. The centres are based in the Lake District, Yorkshire Dales, Snowdonia, Shropshire, Pembrokeshire, Exmoor, South Devon, Suffolk, the North Downs, Epping Forest, County Fermanagh and the Scottish Highlands. The courses vary in length from a weekend to a week. For more information contact the FSC, Tel: 0845 345 4071; e-mail: enquiries@field-studies-council.org; website: www.field-studies-council.org.

HF Holidays Ltd offers walking and special interest holidays in a wide range of locations throughout Britain and abroad. The choice of activities includes, among others, golf, bridge, bowls, ballroom dancing, yoga, painting, photography, music making and birdwatching. There are also discovery coach tours and holidays, with gentle rambles and excursions, for those who want a more leisurely break. The walking holidays range from easy walking to rock scrambling. Overseas destinations include France, Majorca, Malta, Switzerland, Italy, Canada, the United States, New Zealand and Peru. For more details contact HF Holidays Ltd, Tel: 0845 470 7558; e-mail: info@hfholidays.co.uk; website: www.hfholidays.co.uk.

Mercian Travel Centre Ltd specializes in arranging bridge and bowling holidays to over 15 countries throughout the world, lasting from four nights to a fortnight. Mercian also arranges a wide choice of cruises. For further information contact Mercian, Tel: 01562 883795; e-mail: JDowning@merciantravel.co.uk; website: www.merciantravel.co.uk.

The Peak District National Park Centre for Environmental Learning offers weekend and week-long special interest breaks, including painting and illustration, natural history, birdwatching, navigation, photography and rambling. Losehill Hall is set in beautiful countryside with comfortable single and twin-bedded en-suite accommodation. Prices are fully inclusive of meals, accommodation, transport and tuition. For further information contact the Centre, Tel: 01433 620 373; e-mail: enquiries.losehill@peakdistrict.gov.uk; website: www.peakdistrict.org.

Vegi-Ventures is a holiday tour company that specializes in catering for vegetarians, offering an attractive range of destinations in Britain, Europe and wider afield. Accommodation is chosen very much with the food in mind and is in hotels, special guest houses and retreat centres with their own cook. Destinations range from relaxing Turkey to challenging Peru. Flights are willingly arranged but are not part of the package. For further details contact Vegi-Ventures, Tel: 01760 755 888; e-mail: holidays@vegiventures.com; website: www.vegiventures.com.

Sport

Holidays with on-site or nearby sporting facilities exist all over the country. However, if sport is the main objective of the holiday, it is often more difficult to know where to apply. The list that follows is limited to organizations that can advise you about organized residential courses or can offer facilities, rather than simply put you in touch with, say, your nearest tennis club. For wider information, see Chapter 9, Leisure Activities, which lists some of the many national sports associations.

Sportscotland runs three national sports centres that offer courses for all levels in sports such as golf, hill-walking, skiing and sailing. For more information contact Sportscotland, Tel: 0141 534 6500; e-mail: sportscotland.enquiries@sportscotland.org.uk; website: www.sportscotland.org.uk.

Boating

One or two ideas for holidays afloat are included, as well as organizations that offer serious sailing instruction:

Blakes Holiday Boating offers holiday boating throughout all the main waterways of Britain and also in France and Ireland. Basic boating tuition is provided for novices. Costs vary according to season and the size and type of accommodation. Pets are normally allowed on British holidays. For holidays abroad, Blakes will quote an inclusive price with travel arrangements. For further information contact Blakes, Tel: 0845 604 3985; e-mail: bbh.enquiry@holidaycottagesgroup.com; website: www.blakes.co.uk.

Hoseasons Boating Holidays. Choose from the Norfolk Broads, the Cambridgeshire waterways, the Thames, and the canals of England, Scotland and Wales, as well as boating holidays in France, Belgium, Holland, Italy and Ireland. Prices vary; travel and insurance can also be arranged. For further details contact Hoseasons, Tel: 0844 847 1356; website: www.hoseasons.co.uk.

Royal Yachting Association (RYA) can supply a list of recognized schools that offer approved courses in sailing, windsurfing, motor cruising and power boating. For further information contact the Association, Tel: 0845 345 0400; website: www.rya.org.uk.

Cycling

CTC organizes cycling tours in Britain and overseas and can also provide a great deal of extremely helpful information for cyclists wishing to arrange their own holiday, including advice on accommodation and scenic routes. There are organized UK cycle tours, with hostel accommodation or bed-and-breakfast accommodation with evening meal. Overseas tours vary from a fortnight's camping in Southern France to three weeks' holiday in South Africa. CTC also offers members free third-party insurance, free legal aid and introductions to local cycling groups. For further information contact CTC, Tel: 0845 045 1121; e-mail: info@cyclingholidays.org; website: www.cyclingholidays.org.

Cycling for Softies. Susi Madron's Cycling Holidays offer over 50 holiday options in 10 regions of France from three to 14 nights, cycling between a network of small country hotels, with terrain varying from very easy to quite a few hills. Travel, which is extra, can be arranged. For further information contact Cycling for Softies, Tel: 0161 248 8282; e-mail: info@cycling-for-softies.co.uk; website: www.cycling-for-softies.co.uk.

Railways. Cycles are allowed on some trains. However, it is normally necessary to make an advance reservation, and there is usually a small charge to pay. The best advice if you are hoping to take your cycle by rail is to ring National Rail Enquiries, Tel: 0845 7484 950; website: www.nationalrail.co.uk.

Golf

Many clubs will allow non-members to play on weekdays when the course is less busy, on payment of a green fee. (A telephone call to the secretary before arrival is normally advisable.) Better still, if you can spare the time, many hotels around the country offer special golfing weekends and short-break holidays.

Lotus Supertravel Golf offers a wide choice of golfing holidays overseas. Favourite destinations include Florida, Spain and the Algarve in Portugal. For further information contact Lotus Supertravel Golf, Tel: 020 7459 2984; website: www.golf.supertravel.co.uk.

Rambling

Rambling features on many special interest and other programmes as one of the options on offer. Three organizations that specialize in rambling holidays are described below:

ATG Oxford. Forget staying in cheap hostels and lugging around a rucksack with all your possessions for a week. Walking ATG Oxford style means staying in the most comfortable hotels in the area, having your luggage transported and enjoying the option of a ride on days when you feel like taking it easy. The emphasis is on visiting places of historical, cultural or artistic interest, exploring the scenic highlights and dining out on the best local cuisine. Groups are limited to a maximum of 16, and most holidays last between five days and two weeks, with Italy a favourite destination. Other choices include France, Turkey, Spain, the Czech Republic, India, South Africa and many others. There are also walking and cycling holidays for those who prefer to travel more independently, yet who would welcome the services of a local representative, including having their luggage transported. For further details contact ATG Oxford, Tel: 01865 315 678; e-mail: trip-enquiry@atg-oxford.com; website: www.atg-oxford.co.uk.

Exodus offers a wide choice of graded walking holidays in Europe (from about four hours a day) throughout the year. Accommodation is in hotels and guest houses and includes half-board. Costs vary depending on the country and time of year. Cross-country skiing holidays are also offered during the winter. For more information contact Exodus, Tel: 0845 863 9600; e-mail: sales@exodus.co.uk; website: www.exodus.co.uk.

Ramblers Holidays Ltd organizes guided walking tours at home and abroad, ranging in choice from just four or five hours a day relatively gentle exercise to maybe nine hours a day hard mountain trekking. Some trips focus on a special interest such as birdwatching or flowers, or make a particular feature of visiting places of cultural interest. There is also a huge choice of destinations including New Zealand, North America, China, South Africa, the Far East and most of Europe. For further details contact Ramblers Holidays Ltd, Tel: 01707 33 11 33; e-mail: info@ramblersholidays.co.uk; website: www.ramblersholidays.co.uk.

Skiing

Disability Snowsport UK. A disability, including blindness or even an amputated leg, need no longer be a bar to skiing, thanks both to the availability of special equipment and to the efforts of Disability Snowsport UK. This provides opportunities for people with a disability to participate in skiing and snowboarding. It is the goal of Disability Snowsport to help individuals improve their quality of life and transfer the benefits that they can derive from taking part to their everyday life. For more information, contact Disability Snowsport UK, Tel: 01479 861 272; e-mail: admin@disabilitysnowsport.org; website: www.disabilitysnowsport.org.uk.

Ski Club of Great Britain runs skiing holidays in Austria, France, Italy, Switzerland, Canada and the United States for over-50s who have some skiing experience. Qualified leaders accompany each group and will ski with you and offer advice, if wanted. One and two weeks' holidays are available. For further information contact the Ski Club of Great Britain, Tel: 0845 45 807 80; e-mail: skiers@skiclub.co.uk; website: www.skiclub.co.uk.

Tennis

The **Lawn Tennis Association (LTA)** can provide details of residential courses at home and abroad. For more information contact the LTA, Tel: 020 8487 7000; e-mail: contactus@lta.org.uk; website: www.lta.org.uk.

For other sporting holidays, see 'Tourist boards' (page 338). Their websites give lots of information on golfing, sailing and fishing holidays, pony trekking in Wales, skiing in Scotland and many others.

Wine tasting

Wine-tasting holidays are becoming more popular every year. The best guided tours ensure plenty of variety, with a mix of visits, talks, convivial meals, free time for exploring and memorable tastings:

Arblaster & Clarke Wine Tours operates tours to France, Spain, Portugal, Italy, California, Australia, Hungary, Chile, South Africa and New Zealand. Most of the chosen regions are places of interest in their own right, famous for their historic buildings or picturesque scenery. Guides accompany every tour and, though groups can be as large as 36, every effort is made to give personal attention and to create a friendly, informal atmosphere. For more information contact Arblaster & Clarke Wine Tours, Tel: 01730 263 111; e-mail: contact@winetours.co.uk; website: www.winetours.co.uk.

Winetrails offers wine-tasting holidays, combined with walking or cycling, in France, Italy, Spain, Hungary and many other countries. Most last between 6 and 12 days, and groups are limited to a maximum of 14 people. Trips for independent travellers and private groups can also be arranged. Contact Winetrails, Tel: 01306 712 111; e-mail: sales@winetrails.co.uk; website: www.winetrails.co.uk.

Working holidays

There is scope for volunteers who would like to engage in a worthwhile project during their holidays. Activities vary from, for example, helping run play schemes to conservation work. In order to avoid repetition, only a few suggestions are listed here (for more information and ideas, see Chapter 12, Voluntary Work):

The British Trust for Conservation Volunteers (BTCV) welcomes anyone who would like a working holiday in conservation. BTCV organizes over 500 conservation holidays each year throughout the UK. Projects usually last either a week or a weekend, and the work can vary from hedge-laying to repairing dry-stone walls. No experience is necessary, only plenty of enthusiasm plus reasonable fitness. There are also over 70 international BTCV holidays, with projects ranging from restoring historic gardens in Italy to building footpaths in Iceland. For further information contact BTCV, Tel: 01302 388 888; e-mail: informa tion@btcv.org.uk; website: www.btcv.org.uk.

BTCV Scotland offers training in conservation skills and opportunities to work as a conservation volunteer for as much or as little time as you can spare. There are 7- to 10-day conservation projects called 'action breaks', as well as weekend and single-day events across Scotland. The type of work varies from conservation proper – dry-stone dyking, fencing, footpath conservation, historic building resto-ration and habitat management – to office jobs in BTCV Scotland's local centres. For further information contact BTCV Scotland, Tel: 01786 479697; e-mail: scot land@btcv.org.uk; website: www2.btcv.org/scotland.

National Trust Working Holidays organizes around 450 week and weekend working holidays each year on Trust properties in England, Wales and Northern Ireland. Full guidance and instruction is given by Trust wardens, and many of the projects are suitable for the reasonably fit and active of all ages. For further details contact the Trust, Tel: 0844 800 3099; e-mail: enquiries@thenational trust.org.uk; website: www.nationaltrust.org.uk.

Toc H organizes short residential events throughout the year, normally lasting between a weekend and three weeks. Scope for volunteers includes running play schemes, activities with disabled people, conservation and manual work. For further information, contact Toc H, Tel: 01296 331099; e-mail: info@toch.org. uk; website: www.tochparticipation.co.uk.

Grey gapping

There is a new trend amongst baby boomers (the 55–65 year-olds born at the end of and just after WWII): it's called grey gapping. Increasingly popular for this age group is taking a year out, sometimes immediately after retirement, to travel and possibly change your life.

If you have experienced first-hand the gap-year student – maybe one of your children or a friend of the family – the memories of it may be redolent of hairy, unwashed, backpack-laden youths of either sex, hiking around the world. Barely a word of communication is uttered to their anxious families in the intervening months. The only time they do seem to make contact is when their credit card doesn't work or their mobile phone has been lost or stolen. The idea of getting your own back on your relatives by taking off around the world in bohemian fashion may well appeal to some readers. In fact it's big business, and a lot of people are getting in on the act.

It's not as crazy as it sounds. After years of working in a high-pressure environment, the idea of taking a year out (rather like a sabbatical) to experience a complete contrast of culture and work ethic can be revitalizing. Imagine going from a job in the city to volunteer work with an Aids charity in Africa – there's no greater contrast than that.

An online survey published by the *Independent* showed that, of 1,500 people aged over 65, a staggering 57 per cent wished they had travelled more and 45 per cent regretted that they had never given up their jobs or changed profession. But things are changing. Whether or not they are getting a good press (they are known in the travel industry as 'denture venturers' or 'Saga louts'), there are a lot of grey gappers out there. There are an estimated 200,000 pre-retirement gappers in the UK alone. Some of these people are both wealthy and adventurous. They were hippies in the 1960s and now have good earnings behind them. They have financial security, children who are now adults themselves and mortgage-free properties. No wonder the younger generation refer to them as SKINs – spending kids' inheritance now.

Of course there have been huge changes in the decades since they were children, with few 'jobs for life' these days. Employees do not feel compelled to offer total loyalty to their employers and are taking the opportunity to explore the world while they can. There is something intensely emotional for someone who has been working for decades in air-conditioned offices about going off to a developing country and working with a team helping deliver water to a remote village by digging a well. It focuses on a real-life situation that may come as a complete shock to most of us, unless they have worked in the charity sector.

If you are interested in getting more information about joining the ranks of grey gappers, try **Gapadvice.org**, which offers independent advice on gap years, for people of all ages; Tel: 01494 673 448; e-mail: info@gapadvice.org; website: www.gapadvice.org.

Holidays for singles

There are a number of people, who, if being completely honest, admit they would rather not go on holiday if it means travelling alone. It wasn't all that long ago that single people, especially women over 50, were virtually ignored by the holiday industry. For a start, tour operators arranging group parties would often impose an age limit with the aim of keeping the sexes roughly in balance. There was (and still is) almost invariably a supplement for single rooms. And worst of all was the prospect of dining alone or of receiving unwanted attentions that could become embarrassing.

Over the past few years, however, the outlook has been improving considerably. Many of the special interest holidays listed on pages 328 to 330 are ideal for those without a partner, as are some of the working holidays (see 'Working holidays' above and also Chapter 12, Voluntary Work). Additionally, one or two organizations are now springing up that cater specifically for solo holidaymakers. Ones that have been in existence for a number of years and are not essentially biased towards the under-35s (as many are) include:

Just You organizes worldwide escorted holidays, including cruises, for single travellers. Groups usually include around 20 to 30 people, with ages ranging from approximately mid-30s to 70-plus. All room prices are based on sole occupancy without a single room supplement. There are optional pre-tour get-togethers, the evening before, on holidays flying from Heathrow and Gatwick. For more information contact Just You, Tel: 0870 252 8008; e-mail: telesales@justyou.co.uk; website: www.justyou.co.uk.

Solo's Holidays specializes in arranging group holidays for single people, including a good selection for those aged 45-plus. A vast choice of special interests is catered for, including opera, golf, cruises, walking holidays and many others. All tours are escorted 24 hours a day, and most hotels are three- or four-star, without a single room supplement. For further details contact Solo's Holidays, Tel: 0844 815 0005; e-mail: travelsolos@solosholidays.co.uk; website: www.solosholidays.co.uk.

Travel Companions is an organization for individuals aged 20 to 80 seeking a congenial companion with whom to go on holiday. All applicants complete a form online listing their special interests and the type of destination they have in mind, as well as other requirements, and Travel Companions will then put them in contact with like-minded people. All personal information is handled in strict confidence. Travel Companions emphasizes that it is not a dating service and makes the point that people often prefer to travel with someone of their own sex. For further information contact Travel Companions, Tel: 020 8762 9933; e-mail: e-mail@single-living.com; website: www.singleagain.co.uk.

Holidays for those needing special care

Over the past few years, facilities for infirm and disabled people have been improving. More hotels are providing wheelchairs and other essential equipment. Transport has become easier. Specially designed self-catering units are more plentiful and of a higher standard. Also, an increasing number of trains and coaches are installing accessible loos. As a result of these improvements, many people with disabilities can now travel perfectly normally, stay where they please and participate in the entertainment and sightseeing without disadvantage. This section lists general sources of advice plus one or two organizations that arrange special care holidays.

Travel and other information

If you need help getting on and off a train or plane, inform your travel agent in advance. Arrangements can be made to have staff and, if necessary, a wheelchair available to help you at both departure and arrival points. If you are travelling independently, you should ring the airline and/or local station: explain what assistance you require, together with details of your journey in order that facilities can be arranged at any interim points, for example if you need to change trains.

A useful free leaflet is *Rail Travel for Disabled Passengers*, available from mainline stations. A couple of other helpful publications are *The Disabled Travellers' Guide*, free, obtainable by calling the AA Disability Helpline (Tel: 0800 262 050; website: www.theaa.com) and *Holidays in Britain and Ireland*, £14.50, available from the RADAR (the disability network) (Tel: 020 7250 3222; e-mail: radar@radar.org.uk; website: www.radar.org.uk).

Age Concern. Many local Age Concern groups are a mine of information. They can often put individuals in touch with organizations that can assist with, say, transport or that organize special care holidays, as do a number of Age Concern groups themselves. Age Concern England also publishes a free information sheet, *Planning a Holiday*, available from Age Concern, Tel: 0800 009 966; website: www.ageconcern.org.uk.

ATS Travel. If, rather than simply wanting someone to point you in the right direction, you are looking for an agency that can make all the practical arrangements, get on to ATS Travel. This organization specializes in planning tailor-made holidays for people with disabilities. Among other services, it will arrange the journey from door to door. This includes booking suitable accommodation according to your requirements. It will also organize the provision of special equipment and generally take care of any other details to make your holiday as enjoyable and trouble-free as possible. For further information, contact ATS Travel, Tel: 01708 863 198; e-mail: aatstravel@aol.com; website: www.assisted holidays.com.

Tourism for All/Vitalise is the UK voice for accessible tourism. It can provide details about a wide range of suitable accommodation, facilities and services both in the UK and overseas. It also has information about hiring equipment for holiday use, accessible attractions and respite care centres, plus a list of hotels that offer substantial discounts. For further information contact Tourism for All/Vitalise, Tel: 0845 1249 971; e-mail: info@tourismforall.org.uk; website: www.tourismforall.org.uk.

Virgin Holidays. Another company that has been much recommended, especially for the United States, is Virgin Holidays. Winner two years running of the EASE awards, as the best tour operator for travellers with disabilities, it offers a wide range of hotels with wheelchair-accessible rooms, will arrange transport including adapted cars for hire and (subject to availability) will also book whatever medical equipment may be needed in-flight and during the holiday stay. For further information, contact Virgin Holidays, Tel: 0844 557 5825; e-mail: customer.care@virginholidays.co.uk; website: www.virginholidays.co.uk.

Another source to contact is your local social services department. Some local authorities arrange holidays or give financial help to those in real need.

Examples of special holidays

Arthritis Care runs four holiday hotels specially adapted for people with arthritis. Specialist holidays include painting weeks, whist, Scrabble and birdwatching. Family weeks are also a feature. For further information contact Arthritis Care, Tel: 020 7380 6500; e-mail: info@arthritiscare.org.uk; website: www.arthritis-care.org.uk.

Diabetes UK provides information for holidaymakers who want to manage their diabetes confidently. For further information contact Diabetes UK, Tel: 020 7424 1000; e-mail: info@diabetes.org.uk; website: www.diabetes.org.uk.

Parkinson's Disease Society. Rather than arrange its own holidays, the Society produces a brochure listing holiday accommodation that can cater for individuals with Parkinson's disease. For further information contact the Helpline: 0808 800 0303; website: www.parkinsons.org.uk.

Vitalise provides essential breaks for disabled people and carers in five accessible residential centres, providing 24-hour care on-call and personal support. There is a choice of over 500 activities and excursions throughout the year, with evening entertainment laid on. Over 35 different theme weeks focus on particular activities. For further information contact Vitalise, Tel: 0845 345 1972; e-mail: info@vitalise.org.uk; website: www.vitalise.org.uk.

Tourist boards

England's regional tourist boards and the Scottish and Wales tourist boards are the main sources of information for all aspects of holidays in their areas. They can advise about accommodation, transport, highlights to see, special events and festivals, sporting facilities, special interest holidays – in short, almost everything you could possibly want to know. All produce excellent leaflets and guide books:

Regional tourist boards. England's regional tourist boards cover the following areas:

East of England Tourism. Area covered: Bedfordshire, Cambridgeshire, Essex, Hertfordshire, Norfolk and Suffolk. For further information, Tel: 01284 727 470; website: www.visiteastofengland.com.

Visit London. Area covered: the Greater London area. For further information, Tel: 020 7234 5800; website: www.visitlondon.com.

North East Tourist Board. Area covered: Durham, Northumberland, the Tees Valley, and Tyne and Wear. For further information, Tel: 0870 1601781; website: www.visitnortheastengland.com.

Tourism South East. Area covered: Berkshire, Buckinghamshire, East Sussex, Hampshire, the Isle of Wight, Kent, Oxfordshire, Surrey and West Sussex. For further information, Tel: 023 8062 5400; website: www.visitsoutheastengland. com.

South West Tourism. Area covered: Bath, Bristol, Cornwall, Devon, Dorset, Gloucestershire, the Isles of Scilly, Somerset and Wiltshire. For further information, Tel: 01392 360 050; website: www.swtourism.co.uk.

Heart of England Tourism. Area covered: Birmingham, Herefordshire, Shropshire, Staffordshire, Warwickshire, the West Midlands and Worcestershire. For further information, see the website: www.visithear tofengland.com.

Yorkshire Tourist Board. Area covered: Northern Lincolnshire and Yorkshire. For further information, see the website: www.yorkshire.com.

North West Regional Development Agency. Area covered: Cheshire, Cumbria, Greater Manchester, Lancashire and Merseyside. For further information, Tel: 01925 400100; website: www.nwda.co.uk.

East Midlands Tourism. Area covered: Derbyshire, Leicestershire, Lincolnshire, Northamptonshire, Nottinghamshire and Rutland. For further information, Tel: 0115 988 8546; website: www.eastmidlandstourism.co. uk.

Visit Scotland. There are a number of guides to hotels and guest houses, bed-and-breakfast, self-catering accommodation and camping and caravanning sites. For further information, Tel: 0845 22 55 121; website: www.visitscot land.com.

Wales Tourist Board. For further information, Tel: 0870 830 0306; website: www.visitwales.co.uk.

Long-haul travel

The two specialist organizations below can offer a great deal of practical information and help, as well as assist in obtaining low-cost fares, if you are planning to travel independently. Round-the-world air tickets are an excellent buy. Travel agents may also achieve savings by putting together routes using various carriers. Most airlines offer seasonal discounts that sometimes include a couple of nights' concessionary hotel stay, if you want to break your journey or visit another country at minimum extra travel cost:

Trailfinders Travel Centre will plan a tailor-made itinerary for you to any destination worldwide; book hotels, car hire and low-cost flights; and arrange comprehensive travel insurance. There is also a one-stop shop with information centre, visa and passport service, inoculation facilities plus guidebooks and handy travel accessories. For further information contact Trailfinders Travel Centre, Tel: 0845 058 58 58; website: www.trailfinders.com.

WEXAS. As well as providing a comprehensive travel service for independent holidaymakers, WEXAS offers a variety of trips to long-haul destinations, including such places as the Antarctic, China and the Nile Valley. Members enjoy flight, hotel and car hire discounts and receive *Traveller* magazine. Those booking a long-haul flight economy class, plus at least two nights' accommodation through WEXAS, are entitled to VIP lounge access with their family at 23 UK airports. For further information contact WEXAS, Tel: 0845 645 6568; e-mail: mship@wexas.com; website: www.wexas.com.

Visa and passport requirements

All too many people get caught out at the airport by not keeping up to date with the visa and other requirements of the country to which they are travelling. These sometimes change without much warning and, at worst if you get it wrong, can result in your being turned away on arrival.

Health and safety advice

This sometimes changes, and travel agents are not always as good as they should be about keeping customers informed. The best advice, especially if you are travelling out of Europe, including to the United States, is to check the Foreign Office website (www.fco.gov.uk) several weeks before departure, to allow time for inoculations, and again just before you leave.

Insurance

Even the best-laid holiday plans can go wrong. It is therefore only sensible to take out proper insurance cover before you depart. Regrettably, once you are over the age of 65, holiday insurance not only is more difficult to obtain but also tends to be considerably more expensive. However, were you unfortunate enough to fall ill or experience some other mishap, it would almost certainly cost you very much more than paying a bit extra for decent insurance. Eagle Star and Netcoverdirect are recommended as offering among the most competitive rates for older travellers.

Nevertheless, you are strongly recommended to shop around and get several quotes before paying for an unnecessarily expensive policy. For example, Help the Aged is enhancing its insurance policies for the over-60s and apparently will provide travel insurance up to any age. It currently has one customer aged 106 and will provide liability insurance for skiers in their 80s. Other firms who cater for people in their 60s and 70s are American Express and Saga.

Many tour operators try to insist that, as a condition of booking, you either buy their inclusive insurance package or make private arrangements that are at least as good. While this suggests that they are demanding very high standards, terms and conditions vary greatly. Before signing on the dotted line, you should read the small print carefully. Be careful to check that the package you are being offered meets all the eventualities and provides you with adequate cover should you make a claim. If for any reason you are unable to see an actual copy of the policy, ask any questions you think might be relevant. This should include in particular any special conditions you would have to satisfy in making a claim (eg whether there are medical conditions or possibly sporting or other activities that the policy would not cover).

If you are travelling independently, if anything it is even more important to be properly insured. Under these circumstances you will not be protected by the normal compensation that the reputable tour operators provide for claims for which they could be held liable in the event of a mishap.

Holiday insurance should cover you for:

- medical expenses, including hospital treatment and the cost of an ambulance, an air ambulance and emergency dental treatment, plus expenses for a companion who may have to remain overseas with you should you become ill (see 'Medical insurance', page 344);
- personal liability cover, should you cause injury to another person or property;
- personal accident leading to injury or death (check the small print, as some policies have reduced cover for older travellers);
- additional hotel and repatriation costs resulting from injury or illness;
- loss of deposit or cancellation (check what emergencies or contingencies this covers);
- the cost of having to curtail your holiday, including extra travel expenses, because of serious illness in the family;
- compensation for inconvenience caused by flight cancellations or other travel delays;
- cover for baggage and personal effects and for emergency purchases should your baggage be delayed;
- cover for loss of personal money and documents.

If you are planning to take your car abroad (see 'Motoring holidays abroad', page 323), you will need to check your existing car insurance to ensure that you are properly covered. Alternatively, if you are planning to hire a car or motor scooter overseas, you will need to take out fully comprehensive insurance cover (which you may need to purchase while on holiday).

Before purchasing new insurance, check whether any of the above items are already covered under an existing policy. This might well apply to your personal possessions and to medical insurance. Even if the policy is not sufficiently comprehensive for travel purposes, it will be better and cheaper in the long run to pay a small supplement to give you the extra cover you need than to buy a holiday insurance package from a tour operator. This could be especially true if you are over 65, as many travel agents load premiums against older holidaymakers on the basis of more costly medical insurance.

A cost-effective plan may be to extend any existing medical insurance to cover you while abroad. Then take out a separate policy (without medical insurance) to cover you for the rest of your travel needs.

Although many travel agents would like you to believe otherwise, *you are under no obligation to buy insurance from a travel company.* For a number of years, travel companies have not been able to oblige customers to buy their insurance as a condition of obtaining a special deal or discount. Also, whereas most companies selling insurance now need to be authorized by the Financial Services Authority, this does not apply to travel insurance when bought as part of a holiday package from a tour operator or travel agent.

When assessing holiday insurance, and especially inclusive packages, it pays to do a bit of mental arithmetic. Although at first glance the sums look enormous, the likelihood is that should you have to claim you will end up being out of pocket. A sum of £750 or even £1,000 in respect of lost baggage might well be insufficient if, as well as your clothes, you had to replace your watch, camera and other valuables.

The Association of British Insurers suggests the following guidelines in respect of the amount of cover holidaymakers should be looking for in their policy:

- *Cancellation or curtailment of holiday:* the full cost of your holiday, as well as the deposit and any other charges paid in advance, plus cover for any extra costs should you be forced to return early. Depending on the policy, cover is normally limited to a maximum of £5,000 per person.
- *Money and travel documents:* £500. Some companies offer additional cover for lost or stolen documents. Normally there is a limit of £200 to £300 for cash.
- *Luggage/belongings:* £1,500 (NB: check the limit on single articles).
- *Delayed baggage:* £100 for emergency purchases in the event that luggage is lost en route and arrives late.
- *Delayed departure.* Policies vary greatly. A number pay around £20 to £30 if departure is delayed by more than a certain number of hours. Some will allow you to cancel your holiday once departure has been delayed by over 12 hours, with cover normally limited to the same as for cancellation. If risk of delay is a serious concern, you should check the detail of your policy carefully.
- *Personal liability:* up to £2 million.

It is essential that you take copies of the insurance documents with you, as losses or other claims must normally be reported immediately. You will also be required to quote the reference number and/or other details given on the docket. Additionally, there may be particular guidelines laid down by the policy. For instance, you may have to ring a helpline before incurring medical expenses. Failure to report a claim within the specified time limit could nullify your right to compensation. The best advice is to check that you have the 24-hour helpline number and to keep it with you at all times.

Be sure to get a receipt for any special expenses you incur – extra hotel bills, medical treatment, long-distance phone calls and so on. You may not get all the costs reimbursed, but if your insurance covers some or all of these contingencies you will need to produce evidence of your expenditure. Some other pointers are:

The Association of British Insurers publishes a free information sheet on holiday insurance and motoring abroad, explaining the key points you should know in simple language. For further information contact the Association, Tel: 020 7600 3333; website: www.abi.org.uk.

The Association of British Travel Agents (ABTA) operates a Code of Conduct for all travel agents and tour operators that are members of ABTA and also runs a consumer advisory service for holidaymakers on how to seek redress if they are dissatisfied with their travel company. For further information contact ABTA, Tel: 020 3117 0500; website: www.abta.com.

Compensation for lost baggage. If the airline on which you are travelling loses or damages your baggage, you should be able to claim compensation up to a maximum value of about £850. (The figure may vary slightly up or down, depending on currency fluctuations.)

Also useful to know about is the *Denied Boarding Regulation,* which entitles passengers who cannot travel because their flight is overbooked to some immediate cash payment. This applies even if the airline puts them up in a hotel or books them on to an alternative flight a few hours later. To qualify, passengers must have a confirmed reservation and have checked in on time. Also, the airport where they were 'bumped off' must be in an EU country. (It may sometimes also be possible to get compensation in the United States.)

If, as opposed to being overbooked, your flight is cancelled, you are entitled to get a refund if you decide not to travel. Alternatively, you can request to be re-routed. You may, additionally, get compensation of between £125 and £600, depending on the length of your journey and how long you are delayed. If the delay is more than two hours, you will also be entitled to meals or refreshments plus two free telephone calls, e-mails or faxes. If it is overnight and you have more than five hours' wait, you will be put up in a hotel and given free transfers. Compensation is not, however, obligatory if the cancellation is due to 'extraordinary circumstances which could not have been avoided'. For further information, or if you have trouble in obtaining your compensation, contact the **Air Transport Users Council**, Tel: 020 7240 6061; website: www.caa.co.uk.

If you miss your flight or have to cancel your trip, you may be able to get a refund on at least a small part of the ticket cost. Most airlines will reimburse non-fliers for the air passenger duty and overseas government taxes. This applies even to normal non-refundable tickets. However, you have to make a claim, and in most cases there is an administration charge. This may vary somewhere between £15 and £20. If you booked through a travel agent, there could be a second administration charge. Even so, especially for long-haul travel and family holidays, the savings could be quite considerable.

Medical insurance

This is one area where you should never skimp on insurance. Although many countries now have reciprocal arrangements with the UK for emergency medical treatment, these vary greatly in both quality and generosity. Some treatments are free, as they are on the National Health Service; others, even in some EU countries, may be charged for as if you were a private patient.

The Department of Health leaflet *Health Advice for Travellers* (T7) explains what is entailed and what forms you should obtain. In particular you should get a European health insurance card (EHIC), which has replaced the old E111 forms. In practice, you are unlikely to notice very much difference. Similarly to the E111, the card entitles you to free or reduced-cost emergency medical treatment throughout EU countries, as well as in Switzerland, Norway, Iceland and Liechtenstein.

If you had a 2005 E111 form and ticked the relevant box, you should automatically have been issued with the new European card. If you have not received one, call 0845 605 0707. If you are applying for a form for the first time, you should be able to obtain one from any main Post Office or download a copy from the Department of Health website on www.dh.gov.uk. Alternatively, phone 0845 606 2030. Each member of the family requires his or her own individual card.

However, even the very best reciprocal arrangements may not be adequate in the event of a real emergency. Moreover, they certainly will not cover you for any additional expenses you may incur. These could include the cost of having to prolong your stay, extra hotel bills if a companion has to remain with you, special transport home should you require it and so on. Additionally, since in an emergency you may need or want private treatment, you would be advised to insure for this – even if you are going to a country where good reciprocal arrangements exist.

In the United States the cost of medical treatment is astronomical. For peace of mind, most experts recommend cover of £1 million for most of the world and up to £2 million for the United States. Some policies offer higher, or even unlimited, cover.

Most insurance companies impose various terms and let-out clauses as a condition of payment. You should read these very carefully because, whereas some are obviously sensible, others may be very restrictive or, for whatever reason, you may not be able to satisfy the requirements, for example if you have a chronic heart condition. Even though this may result in your having to pay a higher premium, you should declare any pre-existing illnesses or conditions. Failure to do so could nullify your claim if you had to make one.

Although theoretically there is no upper age limit if you want to take out medical insurance, some insurance companies are very difficult about insuring older travellers. Many request a note from a qualified medical practitioner stating that you are fit to travel if you are over 75, or require you to confirm that you are not travelling against medical advice.

Another common requirement is that the insured person should undertake not to indulge in any dangerous pursuits, which is fine in theory but in practice (depending on the company's interpretation of 'dangerous') could debar you from any activity that qualifies as 'strenuous'.

Book through a reputable operator

Many of the sad tales of woe one hears could have been avoided, or at least softened by compensation. It is essential that holidaymakers check to ensure that their travel agent or tour operator is affiliated to either ABTA or the Association of Tour Operators (ATO). Both organizations have strict regulations that all member companies must follow, and both run an arbitration scheme in the event of complaints. No one can guarantee you against every mishap, but a recognized travel company plus adequate insurance should go a long way towards giving you at least some measure of protection.

Travel and other concessions

Buses, coaches, some airline companies and especially the railways offer valuable concessions to people of retirement age. Some of the best-value savings that are available to anyone aged 60 and over are provided by train companies. These include:

Disabled Persons Railcard. This costs £18 for one year or £48 for three years and entitles the holder and one accompanying adult to reduced train fares. Details and eligibility criteria are shown in the *Rail Travel for Disabled Passengers* booklet available from your local staffed station. Tel: 08457 48 49 50; website: www.rail card.co.uk.

Family Friends Railcard. This costs £24 for a whole year and entitles up to four adults to a third off most fares (including cheap day singles and returns, Savers and SuperSavers) when travelling with between one and four children, aged 5 to 15. The children get 60 per cent off the normal child fare (subject to a minimum fare of £1); under-5s go free. Tel: 08457 48 49 50; website: www.railcard.co.uk.

Network Railcard. This costs £20 and is available only in South-East England. It gives a one-third reduction on most standard-class fares after 10 am, Monday to Friday, subject to a £10 minimum fare. The same reduction applies at weekends and Bank Holidays, when happily there is no minimum fare and when passengers can travel at any time, as opposed only to after 10 am. Up to four adults (including the card holder) can travel at a discount, and up to four children aged 5 to 15 will get 60 per cent off the normal child fare (subject to a minimum fare of £1); under-5s travel free. Tel: 08457 48 49 50; website: www.railcard.co.uk.

Railplus Cards. These are available to people from age 60 who are also British Senior Railcard holders. They cost £12 and entitle you to savings of up to 25 per cent on first- and standard- or second-class full fares on cross-border journeys within Europe. Reductions on cross-Channel Seacats and ships are allowed only if these services are part of rail-sea combined tickets to or from the Continent. The cards also allow you to purchase discounted international tickets for cross-border travel on the Continent. Railplus Cards can be obtained via Rail Europe appointed travel agencies, and International Rail, Tel: 0870 084 1410; e-mail: sales@internationalrail.com; website: www.internationalrail.com.

Senior Railcard. This costs £24 for one year and entitles you to a third off most fares, including: cheap day singles and returns; Savers and SuperSavers returns and most Rail Rover tickets; first-class single and return tickets; and all-zone off-peak Travelcards on the London underground, subject to a minimum fare. Discounts are also available on some ferry services for through rail-sea journeys. Tel: 08457 48 49 50; website: www.railcard.co.uk.

Buses and coaches

There are often reduced rates for senior citizens on long-distance buses and coaches. For example, discounts of 33 per cent apply on National Coaches on both ordinary and Rapide services. If you are planning to travel by coach, *Good Non Retirement Guide* readers have advised that it is worth shopping around to find out what bargains are available.

Airlines

Several of the airlines offer attractive discounts to older travellers. The terms and conditions vary, with some carriers offering across-the-board savings and others limiting them to selected destinations. Likewise, in some cases the qualifying age is 60; in others, it is a couple of years older. A particular bonus is that concessions are often extended to include a companion travelling at the same time.

These discounts are not particularly widely advertised and may well not be suggested by airline staff, often because they do not know a passenger's age. The best advice is to ask your travel agent or the airline at the time of booking what special discounts, if any, are offered.

Overseas

Many countries offer travel and other reductions to retired holidaymakers including, for example, discounts for entry to museums and galleries, day excursions, sporting events and other entertainment. As in Britain, provisions are liable to change, and for up-to-date information probably the best source to contact is the national tourist office of the country to which you are travelling. All EU countries – as well as most lines in Switzerland – give 25 per cent reductions on international rail fares. These are available to holders of a Railplus Card purchasing international rail travel tickets and are applicable to both first- and second-class travel.

Airport meet-and-greet services

These are an extravagance admittedly, but if you hate the hassle of parking your car in the long-term car park and collecting it again on your return after a long journey then a firm that will do the job for you could be worth paying for. **BCP**, which operates a meet-and-greet service at six airports (Heathrow, Gatwick, Stansted, Birmingham, Manchester and Edinburgh), will arrange for a rep to meet you at the terminal at both ends of your journey, park the car, deliver it back and, if you would like, give it a wash while you are on holiday. Price varies according to how long you will be away and the particular airport charges. For further details contact BCP, Tel: 0871 360 1013; e-mail: communications@park ing-bcp.co.uk; website: www.parkbcp.co.uk.

A number of other firms offer a similar service but, whereas some are reputable, others are cowboy operators who park owners' vehicles on unauthorized sites, risking damage to the car or even its theft. As a basic precaution at the time of booking, enquire where your car will be parked, and when dropping it off it would be sensible to ask for a 'conditions form' to complete, to avoid disputes if you find any damage on your return.

Health tips for travellers

Most are plain common sense – but worth repeating for all that:

- Remember to pack any regular medicines you require: even familiar branded products can be difficult to obtain in some countries.
- Take a mini first aid kit, including plasters, disinfectant, tummy pills and so on.
- If you are going to any developing country, consult your doctor as to what pills (and any special precautions) you should take.
- One of the most common ailments among British travellers abroad is an overdose of sun. In some countries it really burns, so take it easy, wear a hat and apply plenty of protective lotion.
- The other big travellers' woe is 'Delhi belly', which unhappily can occur in most hot countries, including Italy and Spain. Beware the water, ice, salads, seafood, ice cream and any fruit that you do not peel yourself. Department of Health advice is only to eat freshly cooked food that is thoroughly cooked and still piping hot.

- Always wash your hands before eating or handling food, particularly if you are camping or caravanning.
- Travelling is tiring and a sudden change of climate more debilitating than most of us admit. Allow plenty of time during the first couple of days to acclimatize before embarking on an activity programme that would exhaust a 17-year-old.
- Have any inoculations or vaccinations well in advance of your departure date.
- When flying, wear loose clothes and above all comfortable shoes, as feet and ankles tend to swell in the air.
- To avoid risk of deep vein thrombosis, which can be fatal, medical advice is to do foot exercises and walk around the plane from time to time. For long-haul travel especially, wear compression stockings, which can be bought at most chemists. Unless advised otherwise by your doctor, taking an aspirin before flying is also recommended.
- On long journeys, it helps to drink plenty of water and remember the warning that 'an alcoholic drink in the air is worth two on the ground'. If you have a special diet, inform whoever makes your booking. Most airlines, especially on long-distance journeys, serve vegetarian food.
- Department of Health leaflet T7, *Health Advice for Travellers*, contains essential information and advice on what precautions to take when you travel abroad and how to cope in an emergency. Contact the Department of Health, Tel: 020 7210 4850; website: www.dh.gov.uk.
- Finally, the old favourite, don't drink and drive.

Keep fit and have a wonderful holiday!

15

Caring for elderly parents

Many of us sooner or later have some responsibility for the care of elderly parents. An increasing number of people now live well into their 80s and beyond. The vast majority can manage, with a little help, to remain in their own homes rather than go into residential care. While there is no hiding the fact that with a very elderly person this can impose strains, many families cope exceedingly well. Evidence shows that this is the undoubted preference of most older people themselves. The main bias of this chapter is towards helping aged parents remain as independent as possible for as long as possible.

Knowing what facilities are available and what precautions you can take against a mishap occurring is an important factor. Being aware of whom you can turn to in an emergency can make all the difference, both to you and to parents who may fear becoming a burden. Over the last few years provisions for the elderly have enormously improved. Everything from simple gadgets, such as alarm systems that can buy peace of mind, to full-scale nursing care is available, if you know where to find it. Becoming familiar with how to access such things is half the battle.

A basic choice for many families is whether parents should move in with them or continue to live on their own. While the decision will depend on individual circumstances, in the early days at least the majority choice on all sides is usually to 'stay put'. Later in the chapter we cover sheltered housing, which some people see as the best of all worlds. Meanwhile, an alternative solution to any move may be simply to adapt the home to make it safer and more convenient.

Ways of adapting a home

Many even quite elderly people will not require anything more complicated than a few general improvements. These could include better lighting, especially near staircases, a non-slip mat and grab-rail in the bathroom, and safer heating arrangements. For some it might be necessary perhaps to lower some kitchen and other units to place them within easy reach.

Another sensible plan worth considering is to convert a downstairs room into a bedroom and bathroom, should managing the stairs later become difficult. These and other common sense measures are covered in more detail in Chapter 8, Your Home.

For some people, however, such arrangements are not really sufficient. In the case of a physically handicapped or disabled person, more radical improvements will usually be required. Far from presenting a major problem as used to be the case, today these are normally fairly easy to organize.

Local authority help

Local authorities have a legal duty to help people with disabilities and, depending on what is required and the individual's ability to pay, may assist with the cost. Your parents can either approach their GP or contact the social services department direct. A sympathetic doctor will be able to advise what is needed and supply any prescriptions such as for a medical hoist. Your GP will also be able to suggest which unit or department to approach as well as make a recommendation to the housing department, should rehousing be desirable.

The social services department may be able to supply kitchen, bathroom and other aids for the home. They can also arrange an appointment with an occupational therapist and support an application for a grant, should major adaptations be required.

If only relatively small changes are necessary, such as a handrail on the stairs or a ramp for a wheelchair, the occupational therapist may be able to arrange for these to be done by the local authority. This can take months, however, so if your parents cannot wait and want the work done privately the occupational therapist will give you names of local firms.

Help with home repair and adaptations

The Regulatory Reform Order (RRO) gives local authorities greater discretionary powers to provide assistance – such as low-cost loans and grants – to help with renovations, repairs and adaptations to the home. If it is more appropriate, they are also empowered to help someone move to more suitable accommodation. In particular, the RRO replaces the previous legislation governing renovation grant, common parts grant, HMO grant and home repair assistance. It allows local authorities greater flexibility to determine their particular eligibility criteria, whether means-testing should be involved and also the type of assistance available. Any assistance given, however, must be in accordance with the authority's published policy.

Disabled facilities grant

This is designed to adapt or provide facilities for a home (including the common parts where applicable) to make it more suitable for occupation by a disabled person. It can cover a wide range of improvements to enable the disabled to manage more independently. This includes work to facilitate access either to the property itself or to the main rooms, the provision of suitable bathroom or kitchen facilities, the adaptation of heating or lighting controls, improvement of the heating system, and various other works where these would make a home safe for a disabled person. Provided the applicant is eligible, a mandatory grant of up to £30,000 in England, £25,000 in Northern Ireland and £36,000 in Wales may be available. For further information and an application form, contact the environmental health or housing department of your local authority. See the website: www.direct.gov.uk/en/disabledpeople or www.communities.gov.uk.

Home improvement agencies (HIAs)

HIAs are small not-for-profit organizations that assist older, disabled and vulnerable homeowners or private sector tenants to repair, maintain or adapt their homes. Many also give advice about benefits and operate schemes for energy efficiency, crime prevention and other ways of making a home safer and more comfortable. By improving people's living conditions, HIAs enhance their quality of life and enable them to remain in their home in greater comfort and security. For details of your nearest HIA it would be sensible to contact the national coordinating body for HIAs, whose website provides a directory of home improvement agencies and the services each provides. If there is no HIA in your area, you might usefully try contacting your local authority, Citizens Advice Bureau or Age Concern group.

Other sources of help

Assist UK heads up a UK-wide network of locally situated disabled living centres. Each centre includes a permanent exhibition of products and equipment that provide people with opportunities to see and try products and equipment and get information and advice from professional staff. There are over 325 advisers working at over 60 member centres. Assist UK is the only organization in the UK to connect clients, manufacturers, regulators and professionals. For details of your nearest centre, contact the headquarters, Tel: 0870 770 2866; e-mail: general.info@assist-uk.org; website: www.assist-uk.org.

Both the **British Red Cross** (Tel: 0844 871 11 11; e-mail: information@redcross.org.uk; www.redcross.org.uk) and **Age Concern** (Tel: 0800 00 99 66; e-mail: customer.relations@acent.co.uk; www.ageconcern.org.uk) can loan equipment in the short term and may also be able to advise on local stockists. Larger branches of Boots, for example, sell a wide range of special items for people with disabilities, including bath aids, wheelchairs and crutches.

CAE (Centre for Accessible Environments) runs the House Adaptations Advisory Service and can recommend local architects with experience of designing for disabled people. When contacting the Centre, you should give broad details of the type of work required. For further details contact the Centre, Tel: 020 7840 0125; e-mail: info@cae.org.uk; website: www.cae.org.uk.

DEMAND (Design & Manufacture for Disability) is an independent charity that supplies as many disabled people as possible with one-off pieces of equipment where no off-the-shelf solution exists. It does not charge clients for its services. For further information contact DEMAND, Tel: 01923 681 800; website: www.demand.org.uk.

Disabled Living Foundation (DLF) is a charity concerned with the practical daily living problems of disability. As well as running a telephone enquiry service, DLF has an equipment centre where gadgets of all kinds can be demonstrated and tried out by visitors. The range includes special equipment for the bathroom, kitchen, bedroom and living room, and hoists, wheelchairs and gadgets to assist reading and writing. None of the items is for sale, but the centre can provide information on suppliers and prices. The centre is staffed by information advisers who show visitors round and discuss individual needs. To arrange an appointment, contact the DLF, Tel: 0845 130 9177; e-mail: advice@dlf.org.uk; website: www.dlf.org.uk.

Disability Wales/Anabledd Cymru is another helpful source of advice. Tel: 029 2088 7325; e-mail: info@disabilitywales.org; website: www.disabilitywales.org.

Hearing and Mobility operates a chain of 28 specialist shops across the country, which stock a wide range of gadgets and equipment to make life easier for elderly and less able people. Professional advice is available in all the shops, and home visits can be arranged without obligation. For further information contact Hearing and Mobility, Tel: 0844 888 1338; e-mail: customerservices@hearingand mobility.co.uk; website: www.hearingandmobility.co.uk.

REMAP can often help design or adapt goods to suit individuals where there is no commercially available product to meet their particular needs. For further information contact REMAP, Tel: 0845 130 0456; website: www.remap.org.uk.

Alarm systems

Alarm systems have become much more widespread in recent years. The knowledge that help can be summoned quickly in the event of an emergency is reassuring in its own right to many elderly or disabled people. In practical terms it can enable many people to remain independent far longer than would otherwise be sensible. Some local authorities have alarm systems that now allow people living in their own homes to be linked to a central control. Types of alarm vary greatly. Some have a telephone link, enabling personal contact to be made. Others simply signal that something is wrong. In other systems, a relative or friend who has been nominated will be alerted, or sometimes the alarm will go through to the police. To find out whether your parents' local authority operates such a system, contact the social services department. See the website: www.dh.gov.uk.

Commercial firms

A number of firms install and operate alarm systems. Price, installation cost and reliability can vary quite considerably. For advice on choosing an alarm, plus a list of suppliers, contact the **DLF (Disabled Living Foundation)**, Tel: 0845 130 9177; e-mail: advice@dlf.org.uk; website: www.dlf.org.uk.

Community alarms

Telephone alarm systems operated on the public telephone network can be used by anyone with a direct telephone line. The systems link into a 24-hour monitoring centre and the individual has a pendant that enables help to be called even when the owner is some distance from the telephone. Grants may be available in some cases to meet the costs. One of the most widely used systems is SeniorLink, run by Help the Aged and Age Concern. For further information, contact **Help the Aged and Age Concern**, Tel: 020 7278 1114; e-mail: seniorline@helptheaged.org.uk; website: www.helptheaged.org.uk.

Age Concern Aid-Call

This is another highly recommended alarm system. The subscriber has a small radio transmitter, worn as a pendant or like a watch, which contacts a 24-hour monitoring centre. The centre then alerts a list of nominated relatives or friends, or the emergency services, that something is wrong. Help can be on its way in a matter of minutes. For more details contact **Age Concern Aid-Call**, Tel: 0800 77 22 66; e-mail: info@aidcall-alarms.co.uk; website: www.aidcall.co.uk.

Main local authority services

Quite apart from any assistance with housing, local authorities supply a number of services that can prove invaluable to an elderly person. The two most important are meals on wheels and home helps. Additionally, there are social workers and various specialists concerned with aspects of health.

Since the introduction of Community Care, local authority social services departments have taken over all responsibility for helping to assess and coordinate the best arrangements for individuals according to their particular requirements.

Meals on wheels

The meals on wheels service is sometimes run by local authorities direct and sometimes by voluntary organizations, such as WRVS, acting as their agents. The purpose is to deliver a hot lunch (or batch of frozen lunches) to individuals in their own homes. Different arrangements apply in different areas, and schemes variously operate from two to seven days a week, or possibly less frequently when frozen meals are supplied. Cost also varies. For further information, contact the social services department.

WRVS also runs a private frozen meals scheme that delivers complete frozen meals direct to customers' doors. For further information, contact **WRVS**, Tel: 029 2073 9000; website: www.wrvs.org.uk.

Home helps

Local authorities have a legal obligation to run a home help service to help frail and housebound elderly people with such basic household chores as shopping, tidying up, a little light cooking and so on. In many areas the service is badly overstretched, so the amount of help actually available varies considerably, as does the method of charging. Different local authorities have different policies and, while some may charge nothing or just a small weekly amount, as a rule people are means-tested according to their ability to pay. If your parents can afford to do so, this could mean paying the full cost. Apply through the social services department. Some of the larger authorities have a special telephone number that may be listed as either 'Home help services' or 'Domiciliary services'; see website: www.dh.gov.uk.

Specialist helpers

Local authorities employ a number of specialist helpers, variously based in the social services department or health centre, who are there to assist:

- *Social workers* are normally the first people to contact if you have a problem. They can put you in touch with the right person, if you require a home help or meals on wheels, or have a housing difficulty or other query and are not sure whom to approach. Often, even if ultimately it is the responsibility of another department, a social worker may come and discuss the matter with you – or with your parents direct. You should ring the social services department or, in Scotland, the social work department.
- *Occupational therapists* have a wide knowledge of disability and can assist individuals via training, exercise, or access to aids, equipment or adaptations to the home. Ring the social services department.
- *Health visitors* are qualified nurses with a broad knowledge both of health matters and of the various services available through the local authority.

Rather like social workers, health visitors can put you in touch with whatever specialized facilities are required. Contact is through the local health centre.

- *District nurses* are fully qualified nurses who will visit a patient in the home, change dressings, attend to other routine nursing matters, monitor progress and help with the arrangements if more specialized care is required. Contact is through the health centre.
- *Physiotherapists* use exercise and massage to help improve mobility and strengthen muscles, for example after an operation or to alleviate a crippling condition. They are normally available at both hospitals and health centres.
- *Medical social workers (MSWs)* (previously known as almoners) are available to consult, if patients have any problems – whether practical or emotional – on leaving hospital. MSWs can advise on coping with a disablement, as well as such practical matters as transport, after-care and other immediate arrangements. They work in hospitals, and an appointment should be made before the patient is discharged.

Good neighbour schemes

A number of local authorities have an organized system of good neighbour schemes. In essence, these consist of individuals contracting with the authority to act as good neighbours to one or several elderly people living close by. Depending on what is required, they may simply pop in on a daily basis to check that everything is all right, or they may give more sustained assistance such as providing help with dressing, bathing, shopping or preparing a light meal. In some authorities, the service may largely be run by volunteer organizations. In others, 'good neighbours' are paid by the authority according to the number of hours they commit. To find out whether such a scheme exists locally, enquire at the social services department.

Key voluntary organizations

Voluntary organizations complement the services provided by statutory health and social services in making life easier for elderly people living at home. The range of provision varies from area to area but can include:

- lunch clubs;
- holidays and short-term placements;
- day centres and clubs;
- friendly visiting;
- aids such as wheelchairs;
- transport;
- odd jobs and decorating;
- gardening;

- good neighbour schemes; ·
- prescription collection;
- advice and information;
- family support schemes.

The particular organization providing these services depends on where you live, but the Citizens Advice Bureau (website: www.citizensadvice.org.uk) will be able to advise you whom to contact. The following are the key agencies:

In April 2009 the four national **Age Concerns** in the UK joined forces with **Help the Aged** to form a new charity called **Age UK**, dedicated to improving the lives of older people. They provide any or all of the voluntary services listed above in your local area. Many local groups recruit volunteers to do practical jobs and provide friendship. They also give advice and information and when necessary refer enquirers to a more appropriate agency. At the time of writing the contacts details are as follows:

Age UK, Tel: 0800 009 966; website: www.ageconcern.org.uk.

Age Scotland, Tel: 0845 1259 732; website: www.ageconcernscotland.org.uk.

Age Wales, Tel: 029 2043 1555; website: www.accymru.org.uk.

Age Northern Ireland, Tel: 028 9024 5729; website: www.ageconcernni.org.

British Red Cross supplies some important services to elderly people. The principal ones available from many branches include:

- helping sick, disabled or frail people make essential journeys;
- loaning medical equipment for short-term use at home and on holiday;
- providing home-from-hospital support: easing the transition of patients to their own home after discharge and giving support to both them and their carers;
- 'signposting' vulnerable people towards the statutory or voluntary services by which their needs may best be met.

Contact the **British Red Cross**, Tel: 0844 8711 111; e-mail: information@redcross.org.uk; website: www.redcross.org.uk.

St John Ambulance has over 45,000 volunteers who provide first aid and care services. They help in hospitals and in some areas will also come to people's homes to assist with various practical tasks such as shopping, collecting pensions, staying with an elderly person for a few hours or providing transport to and from hospital. It is emphasized, however, that the kind of help that the volunteers can provide (if any) varies enormously from county to county and depends on the local resources available. In some areas, loan of equipment such as wheelchairs can be arranged. St John Ambulance gives advice on caring and runs courses locally for carers looking after elderly people. Anyone wishing to enlist the help of St John Ambulance should contact the national headquarters, Tel: 08700 10 49 50; website: www.sja.org.uk.

WRVS runs many local projects:

- books on wheels;

- social transport;
- meals on wheels;
- good neighbour schemes;
- lunch clubs;
- Darby and Joan clubs;
- a meal delivery service for those not qualifying for meals on wheels.

For further information contact **WRVS**, Tel: 029 2073 9000; website: www.wrvs. org.uk.

Other sources of help and advice

Age UK runs SeniorLine, a free advice and information service, available throughout the UK for older people and their carers. Trained advice workers can help with enquiries about welfare or disability benefits, community or residential care, and housing options. For further information, contact Age UK, Tel: 0207 278 1114; e-mail: seniorline@helptheaged.org.uk; website: www.helptheaged.org.uk.

The Civil Service Retirement Fellowship runs a home visiting service for those who are housebound or living alone. It has an extensive network of branches and local groups throughout the country. These offer a wide range of social activities for retired civil servants and their partners and dependants. For further information contact the Fellowship, Tel: 020 8691 7411; e-mail: info@csrf.org.uk; website: www.csrf.org.uk.

Counsel and Care provides a free confidential advisory service for older people and their relatives. Advice workers liaise with all the statutory services and private and voluntary organizations. They also work with charities and benevolent funds to inform families of the various options. There is a range of fact sheets. Limited funds are also available to help with an exceptional needs payment. For further information contact Counsel and Care, Tel: 0845 300 7585; e-mail: advice@counselandcare.org.uk; website: www.counselandcare.org.uk.

The Disability Alliance publishes a number of free fact sheets and also an annual *Disability Rights Handbook*, which is packed with information on benefits and services for all people with disabilities and their families. For further information contact the Alliance, Tel: 020 7247 8776; e-mail: office.da@dial.pipex. com; website: www.disabilityalliance.org.

Jewish Care provides services for elderly Jewish people, including those who are mentally ill, in London and the South-East of England. Principal facilities include: special day care centres for people with dementia; residential and nursing homes in North London, Redbridge, Brighton and Southend; community centres; a home care service for the housebound; and short-term respite care to give carers a break or to give frail, elderly people the opportunity of a short holiday, particularly during the Jewish festivals. There is also a kosher meals on wheels service. Enquire through the local authority social services department, or contact Jewish Care head office for further information, Tel: 020 8922 2222; e-mail: jcdirect@ jcare.org; website: www.jewishcare.org.

Transport

Difficulty in getting around is often a major problem for elderly and disabled people. In addition to the facilities run by voluntary organizations already mentioned, there are several other very useful services:

The Forum of Mobility Centres provides information on a network of independent organizations throughout England, Scotland, Wales and Northern Ireland to help individuals who have a medical condition or are recovering from an accident or injury that may affect their ability to drive. For details of your nearest centre, contact the Forum, Tel: 0800 559 3636; e-mail: mobility@rcht. cornwall.nhs.uk; website: www.mobility-centres.org.uk.

London Taxi Card Service. This is a scheme whereby disabled people can use a taxi on weekdays and weekends at a much reduced rate, subsidized by their local authority. Prices may vary depending on the borough in which the person is resident. The fleet includes taxis capable of accommodating wheelchairs. Leaflets and application forms are obtainable from local authority social services departments, or the Association of London Government Taxi Card, Tel: 020 7934 9791; e-mail: taxicard@londoncouncils.gov.uk; website: www.taxicard.org.uk.

Motability is a registered charity set up to assist recipients of the war pensioners' mobility supplement and/or the higher-rate mobility component of Disability Living Allowance to use their allowance to lease or buy a car or a powered wheelchair or scooter. Motability's charitable fund can help those unable to afford the advance payment on some lease vehicles – or necessary adaptations to the vehicle. Grants are available for the least expensive option to meet individuals' basic mobility needs. Contact Motability, Tel: 0845 456 4566; website: www.motability.co.uk.

Driving licence renewal at age 70

All drivers aged 70 are sent a licence renewal form to have their driving licence renewed. The licence has to be renewed at least every three years. Depending on the individual's health, including in particular eyesight, the driver might be sent a new form to complete after only one or two years. If you have any queries or if, three weeks after returning the form, the new licence has not arrived, contact **DVLA Customer Enquiries**, Tel: 0870 240 0009; website: www.dvla.gov.uk.

Holidays

Many people in their late 70s and older travel across the world, go on activity holidays and see the great sights in the UK and abroad without any more difficulty than anyone else. They will find ideas galore in Chapter 14, including information about how to obtain assistance at airports and railway stations.

However, some elderly people, especially those who are in any way disabled, need special facilities if a stay away from home is to be possible. A number of organizations can help:

ATS Travel specializes in arranging holidays for people with disabilities, whether travelling alone, with a companion or in a group. It will fix all the necessary arrangements to make travel, whether in the UK or overseas, as easy as possible. This includes organizing the journey, booking suitable accommodation, ensuring the availability of special diets, and arranging for the provision of aids or equipment that may be needed, together with any other requirements. For further information, contact ATS Travel, Tel: 01708 863 198; e-mail: aatstravel@aol.com; website: www.assistedholidays.com.

Tourism for All/Vitalise is the UK voice for accessible tourism. It can provide details about a wide range of suitable accommodation, facilities and services both in the UK and overseas. It also has information about hiring equipment for holiday use, accessible attractions and respite care centres, plus a list of hotels that offer substantial discounts for people with special needs, including the frail elderly and those with disabilities. For further information contact Tourism for All/Vitalise, Tel: 0845 124 9971; e-mail: info@tourismforall.org.uk; website: www.tourismforall.org.uk.

A number of the specialist voluntary organizations run holiday centres or provide specially adapted self-catering accommodation. In some cases, outings and entertainment are offered. In others, individuals plan their own activities and amusement. Guests requiring assistance usually need to be accompanied by a companion, although in a few instances care arrangements are inclusive. Most of the organizations can advise about the possibility of obtaining a grant or other financial assistance. For further details, contact the following:

Arthritis Care runs four holiday hotels specially adapted for people with arthritis. Prices start from about £200 a week, depending on the time of year. Specialist holidays include painting weeks, whist, Scrabble and birdwatching. Family weeks are also a feature. For further information contact Arthritis Care, Tel: 020 7380 6500; e-mail: info@arthritiscare.org.uk; website: www.arthritiscare.org.uk.

Diabetes UK provides information for holidaymakers who want to manage their diabetes confidently. For further information contact Diabetes, UK Tel: 020 7424 1000; e-mail: info@diabetes.org.uk; website: www.diabetes.org.uk.

Parkinson's Disease Society. Rather than arrange its own holidays, the Society produces a brochure listing holiday accommodation that can cater for individuals with Parkinson's disease. For further information contact the Helpline: 0808 800 0303; website: www.parkinsons.org.uk.

Vitalise provides essential breaks for disabled people and carers in five accessible residential centres, providing 24-hour care on-call and personal support. There is a choice of over 500 activities and excursions throughout the year, with evening entertainment laid on. Over 35 different theme weeks focus on particular activities. For further information contact Vitalise, Tel: 0845 345 1972; e-mail: info@vitalise.org.uk; website: www.vitalise.org.uk.

There are also a couple of useful publications, listing a wide choice of holiday venues where disabled travellers can go in the normal way but with the advantage of having special facilities provided. *Disabled Travellers' Guide*, by the AA, gives information on holiday accommodation suitable for disabled individuals and their families, together with advice on travelling in Europe. Contact the AA Disability Helpline: 0800 262 050; website: www.theaa.com. *Holidays in Britain and Ireland*, £14.50, is available from RADAR (Royal Association for Disability and Rehabilitation), Tel: 020 7250 3222; website: www.radar.org.uk.

Finally, a number of organizations provide rent-assisted (or sometimes free) holidays for the financially needy. Local Citizens Advice Bureau, Age Concern/Help the Aged groups and county branches of the British Red Cross will often know what, if anything, is available to residents in the area.

Power of attorney

After retirement many perfectly fit men and women wonder whether it might be sensible to give power of attorney to someone they trust. This involves authorizing another person to take business and other financial decisions on their behalf, on the basis that any such decisions would reflect the action that they themselves would have taken. Until a few years ago, the power could be used only where the individual was unwilling rather than incapable of acting for him- or herself. So, in effect, just at the time when the power was most needed, it ceased to exist.

Thanks to the Enduring Powers of Attorney Act 1985 and the more recent Lasting Powers of Attorney (see below), an enduring power is not automatically revoked by any subsequent mental incapacity, but can now continue, regardless of any decline, throughout the individual's life. (*NB*: an ordinary power of attorney would be revoked by subsequent mental incapacity.) To protect the donor and the nominated attorney, the Act clearly lays down certain principles that must be observed, with both sides signing a declaration that they understand the various rights and duties involved. The Act furthermore calls for the power to be formally registered with the Public Trust Office in the event of the donor being, or becoming, mentally incapable.

As stated above, the Enduring Powers of Attorney have been replaced by Lasting Powers of Attorney (LPA), to coincide with the implementation of the Mental Capacity Act 2005. In effect, LPAs enable individuals to give their attorney power to make decisions about their personal welfare, including health care, when they lack the capacity to make such decisions themselves. Enduring Powers of Attorney set up before October 2007 are still effective. However, if you have not set one up but are planning to do so, you will now need to apply for the new LPA instead.

As any lawyer would explain, the right time to give power of attorney is when the individual is in full command of his or her faculties, so that potential situations that would require decisions can be properly discussed and the donor's wishes made clear. For the Lasting Power of Attorney to be valid, the donor must in any event be capable of understanding what he or she is agreeing to at the time of making the power.

There are two ways of drawing up a Lasting Power of Attorney: either through a solicitor or by buying a standard form published by Oyez, available from **Oyez Forms Link**, Tel: 0870 7377 370. It is, however, highly recommended that people consult a solicitor.

Temporary living-in help

Elderly people living alone can be more vulnerable to flu and other winter ailments; they may have a fall; or, for no apparent reason, they may go through a period of being forgetful and neglecting themselves. Equally, as they become older, they may not be able to cope as well with managing their homes or caring for themselves. In the event of an emergency or if you have reason for concern – perhaps because you are going on holiday and will not be around to keep a watchful eye on them – engaging living-in help can be a godsend. Most agencies tend inevitably to be on the expensive side, although in the event of a real problem they often represent excellent value for money. A more unusual and interesting longer-term possibility is to recruit the help of a Community Service Volunteer.

Community Service Volunteers (CSV)

CSV has volunteers who are aged over 16 and are involved in a variety of projects nationwide. CSV's independent living projects match full-time helpers with individuals and families who need a high degree of support. The volunteers are untrained and work for periods of four to 12 months away from home. They take their instructions from the people for whom they are working, but are not substitutes for professional carers. In general they provide practical assistance in the home, including, for example, shopping, light cooking, tidying up, attending to the garden and sometimes decorating jobs. They also offer companionship.

Usually a care scheme is set up through a social worker, who supervises how the arrangement is working out. Volunteers are placed on a one month's trial basis. Contact your parents' local social services department, or approach CSV direct for further information, Tel: 020 7278 6601; e-mail: information@csv.org. uk; website: www.csv.org.uk.

Agencies

The agencies listed specialize in providing temporary help, rather than permanent staff. Charges vary, but in addition to the weekly payment to helpers there is normally an agency booking fee. As a rule payment is gross, so your parents will not be involved in having to work out tax or National Insurance:

Consultus Care & Nursing Agency Ltd, Tel: 01732 355 231; e-mail: office@ consultuscare.com; website: www.consultuscare.com.
Country Cousins, Tel: 0845 601 4003; e-mail: info@country-cousins.co.uk; website: www.country-cousins.co.uk.
Universal Aunts Ltd, Tel: 020 7738 8937; e-mail: aunts@universalaunts.co.uk; website: www.universalaunts.co.uk.

For a further list of agencies, see *The Lady* magazine, or search the internet under the heading 'Employment agencies' or 'Care agencies', or look at the website www.yell.com for addresses in your local area.

Nursing care

If one of your parents needs regular nursing care, the GP may be able to arrange for a community or district nurse to visit him or her at home. This will not be a sleeping-in arrangement but simply involves a qualified nurse calling round when necessary. If you want more concentrated home nursing you will have to go through a private agency. Some of those listed above can sometimes supply trained nurses. Additionally, there are many specialist agencies that can arrange hourly, daily or live-in nurses on a temporary or longer-term basis.

Terms of employment vary considerably. Some nurses undertake nursing duties only – and nothing else – and may even expect to have their meals provided. Others will do light housework and act as nurse-companions. Fees vary throughout the country, with London inevitably being most expensive. Private health insurance can sometimes be claimed against part of the cost, but this is generally only in respect of qualified nurses.

Your local health centre or social services department should be able to give you names and addresses of local agencies, or search the internet under the heading 'Nursing agencies', or look at the website www.yell.com for addresses in your local area.

Permanent living-in help

There may come a time when you feel that it is no longer safe to allow one of your parents to live entirely on his or her own. One possibility is to engage a companion or housekeeper on a permanent basis, but such arrangements are normally very expensive. However, if you want to investigate the idea further, many domestic agencies (see the *Yellow Pages* or the website www.yell.com) supply housekeeper-companions. Alternatively, you might consider advertising in *The Lady*, which is probably the most widely read publication for these kinds of posts. For further details contact *The Lady* magazine, Tel: 020 7379 4717; e-mail: editors@lady.co.uk; website: www.lady.co.uk.

Permanent help can also sometimes be provided by agencies (such as those listed under 'Temporary living-in help'), which will supply continuous four-weekly placements. This is an expensive option, and the lack of continuity can at times be distressing for elderly people, particularly at the changeover point. But it can also lead to a happier atmosphere, as the housekeeper comes fresh to the job and neither party has time to start getting on the other's nerves. See:

Consultus Care & Nursing Agency Ltd, Tel: 01732 355 231; e-mail: office@ consultuscare.com; website: www.consultuscare.com.
Country Cousins, Tel: 0845 601 4003; e-mail: info@country-cousins.co.uk; website: www.country-cousins.co.uk.
Universal Aunts Ltd, Tel: 020 7738 8937; e-mail: aunts@universalaunts.co.uk; website: www.universalaunts.co.uk.

Au pairs are cheaper: roughly £55 to £70 a week with full board and lodging. A drawback, however, is that most au pairs speak inadequate English (at least when they first arrive). As they are technically students living 'en famille', they must by law be given plenty of free time to attend school and study. An alternative solution for some families is to engage a reliable daily help who, in the event of illness or other problem, would be prepared to stay overnight.

Flexible care arrangements

One of the problems for many elderly people is that the amount of care they need is liable to vary according to the state of their health. There are other relevant factors including, for example, the availability of neighbours and family. Whereas after an operation the requirement may be for someone with basic nursing skills, a few weeks later the only need may be for someone to act as a companion. Under normal circumstances it may be as little as simply popping in for the odd hour during the day to cook a hot meal and check all is well. Few agencies cater for all the complex permutations that may be necessary in caring for an elderly person in his or her own home, but here are three that offer a genuinely flexible service:

Anchor Care workers can be engaged by the hour, or nightly, for temporary or longer periods, or on a more permanent residential basis. All staff are personally interviewed, their references are taken up, and training is given. Prices vary according to the area and duties required. For further information contact Anchor Care, Tel: 0845 140 2020; e-mail: contactus@anchor.org.uk; website: www. anchor.org.uk.
Cura Domi – Care at Home carers undertake all or any of the tasks traditionally managed by a reliable housekeeper-companion. These include shopping, cooking,

attending to the chores around the home, helping an elderly person bath or dress, reading aloud and generally providing whatever assistance may be needed. Where appropriate, carers can also provide all personal care and help needed with such problems as incontinence and dementia. Depending on what is required, they will come in for the hour or live in full time for a few days, a few weeks or longer. Great care is taken to try to match clients with a carer who possesses the right skills and temperament. All carers are backed by a team of RGN care managers on 24-hour call, seven days a week. There is a once-only non-returnable registration and assessment fee, with a list of varying prices according to whether the job is weekday, weekend, daytime, night-time or live-in. For further information contact Cura Domi, Tel: 01483 420 055; website: www.curadomi.co.uk.

UKHCA (United Kingdom Home Care Association) works for quality in home care and represents over 1,500 member branches throughout the country that specialize in providing care for elderly and/or disabled people in their own home. All requirements are catered for, including temporary and permanent posts, residential, daily, overnight and hourly work. UKHCA runs a Helpline – and also includes a 'Choosing care' section on its website – which can refer enquirers to local members committed to upholding the Association's Code of Practice. For further information contact the Association, Tel: 020 8288 5291; e-mail: helpline@ukhca.co.uk; website: www.ukhca.co.uk.

Although any of these suggestions can work extremely well for a while, with many families it may sooner or later come down to a choice between residential care and inviting a parent to live with you. Many families choose to care for an elderly parent in their own home. Sometimes, particularly in the case of an unmarried son or daughter or other relative, it is more practical to move into the parent's (or relative's) home if the accommodation is more suitable.

Emergency care for pets

For many elderly people a pet is a very important part of their lives. It provides companionship and fun as well as stimulating them into taking regular outdoor exercise. But in the event of the owner having to go into hospital or through some other emergency being temporarily unable to care for the pet, there can be real problems. These include not only the welfare of the animal but also the distress of the owner. To overcome these problems, two highly imaginative schemes have been set up. One operates throughout the UK and the other just in Scotland. Depending on what is required, volunteers will either simply feed or exercise the animal or will care for it in their own home until the owner can manage again:

The Cinnamon Trust. As well as the above services, the Cinnamon Trust also offers permanent care for pets whose owners have died, who had registered their pets with the Trust. Some animals stay at the Trust's havens in Cornwall and

Devon. Others are found alternative loving homes with a new owner. Either way, every effort is made to help pets adjust. Familiar possessions, such as the animal's basket or favourite toy, are very much encouraged, and as far as possible 'families' of pets are kept together to avoid the further distress of separating them from their companions. Emergency services can be called 24 hours a day. The Trust makes no charge, but donations, or a bequest, are very much appreciated. For further information contact the Trust, Tel: 01736 757 900; e-mail: admin@ cinnamon.org.uk; website: www.cinnamon.org.uk.

Pet Fostering Service Scotland. Here the focus is on temporary care. The only charges are the cost of the pet's food, litter (in the case of cats) and any veterinary fees that may be incurred during fostering. In the main the service caters for dogs, cats and birds, but some volunteers are willing to care for other species, such as rodents. If help is needed, contact the Service, Tel: 01877 331 496; e-mail: info@pfss.org.uk; website: www.pfss.org.uk.

Practical help for carers

If your parent is still fairly active – visits friends, does his or her own shopping, or enjoys some hobby that gets him or her out and about – the strains and difficulties may be fairly minimal. This applies particularly if your home lends itself to creating a granny flat, so everyone can retain some privacy and your parent can continue to enjoy maximum independence. However, this is not always possible, and in the case of an ill or very frail person far more intensive care may be required. If you have to go out to work, need time to attend to other responsibilities or quite understandably feel that if you are to remain human you must have time for your own interests, it is important to know what help is available and how to obtain it.

The many services provided by local authorities and voluntary agencies, described earlier in the chapter, apply as much to an elderly person living with a family as to one living alone. If there is nothing in the list that solves a particular problem you may have, there are other courses of action. It would be sensible to talk to the Citizens Advice Bureau and social services department, as there may be some special local facility that could provide the solution. It could also be useful to contact:

Age Concern/Help the Aged group and **WRVS**. Age Concern will be able to tell you about the possibility of voluntary sitters: people who come in and stay with elderly people for a few hours (or sometimes overnight), to prevent them from being on their own. Contact Age Concern/Help the Aged (website: www.agecon cern.org.uk) or WRVS (website: www.wrvs.org.uk).

Other sources to try include the local branch of the **British Red Cross** (website: www.redcross.org) or the **St John Ambulance** (website: www.sja.org.uk).

The Princess Royal Trust for Carers provides support services for carers throughout the UK and is a fund of practical information and advice. In particular, you might ask about day centres and clubs. Activities and surroundings vary, so you might wish to investigate. However, a responsible person will always be in charge, and transport to and from the venue is often provided. For further information contact the Trust, Tel: 0844 800 4361; e-mail: info@carers.org; website: www.carers.org.

Most areas now have, or are planning, respite care facilities to enable carers to take a break from their dependants from time to time. Depending on the circumstances, this could be for just the odd day or possibly for a week or two to enable carers who need it to have a real rest. A particularly welcome aspect of respite care is that many schemes specially cater for, among others, elderly people with dementia. For further information, contact your local health centre or social services department.

Another service well worth knowing about is **Crossroads – Caring for Carers**, which arranges for helpers to care for very frail or disabled people in their own home while the regular carer is away. The helpers will come in during the day, or stay overnight, and provide whatever practical help is required. Arrangements are planned very much on an individual basis and are tailored to meet particular family circumstances. Demand for the service is very high, so priority is given according to the strain imposed on the carer. Both the Citizens Advice Bureau and the social services department should be able to give you the address of the local branch. Alternatively, you could contact Crossroads directly, Tel: 0845 450 0350; website: www.crossroads.org.uk.

Holiday breaks for carers

There are various schemes to enable families with an elderly relative to go on holiday alone or simply to enjoy a respite from their caring responsibilities.

A number of local authorities run *fostering schemes*, on similar lines to child fostering. Elderly people are invited to stay in a neighbour's home and live in the household as an ordinary family member. Lasting relationships often develop. There may be a charge, or the service may be run on a voluntary basis (or be paid for by the local authority). Schemes are patchy around the country. The Citizens Advice Bureau and social services department will advise you if anything exists locally.

Some voluntary organizations, including **Age Concern** groups and sometimes the **Mothers' Union**, organize *holidays for older people* to give relatives a break. Different charities take responsibility according to the area where you live: the CAB, volunteer centre or social services department should know whom you should approach. As with most types of provision, priority is given to families in greatest need.

You might also usefully contact **Tourism for All/Vitalise**, which, as well as advising on holidays for elderly and disabled people, can also advise carers who need a holiday about suitable provision for their dependent relative while they are away. For further information contact Tourism for All/Vitalise, Tel: 0845 124 9971; e-mail: info@tourismforall.org.uk; website: www.tourismforall.org.uk.

Another solution is a *short-stay home,* which is residential accommodation variously run by local authorities, voluntary organizations or private individuals, catering specifically for elderly people. Style and facilities vary from the very luxurious to the rather decrepit. The different types of home are described in more detail under the heading 'Residential care homes' further on in this chapter. For information about local authority provision, ask the social services department.

If, as opposed to general care, proper medical attention is necessary, you should consult your parent's GP. Many *hospitals and nursing homes* offer short-stay care arrangements as a means of relieving relatives, and a doctor should be able to help organize this for you.

The best place to seek a solution on anything to do with caring is **Carers UK**. Set up to support and campaign for those caring for an ill, frail or disabled relative at home, Carers UK has around 80 self-help branches that are run for and by carers. Their useful and informative website gives information about all aspects of caring. For further information contact Carers UK, Tel: 0808 808 7777; e-mail: info@carersuk.org; website: www.carersuk.org.

Jewish Care runs a number of carers' groups, mostly in London. Contact Jewish Care head office for further information, Tel: 020 8922 2222; e-mail: jcdirect@jcare.org; website: www.jewishcare.org.

Useful reading

Caring for Someone? (SD4), available free from social security or Jobcentre Plus (website: www.jobcentreplus.gov.uk).

Benefits and allowances

There are a number of benefits or allowances available to those with responsibility for the care of an elderly person and/or to elderly people themselves.

Entitlements for carers

Home Responsibilities Protection

This is a means of protecting your state pension if you are unable to work because of the necessity to care for an elderly person. For further details, see under 'State pensions' at the start of Chapter 3, or ask for leaflet CF411 at any pension centre.

Carer's Allowance

This used to be known as Invalid Care Allowance, but the name has been changed to highlight the fact that the allowance is paid as a benefit to carers. Men and women who spend at least 35 hours a week looking after a severely disabled person (ie someone who gets Attendance Allowance, Constant Attendance Allowance or the two higher care components of Disability Living Allowance) may qualify for Carer's Allowance. You do not need to be related to the person, nor do you need to live at the same address. Claimants may earn up to £95 a week after deduction of allowable expenses without loss of benefit.

NB: the previous age limit for entitlement to the allowance has been removed and, since October 2002, carers aged 65 and older who are not in receipt of a full State pension or bereavement benefits are now equally eligible to claim. For further details, enquire at your local **Jobcentre Plus** office or ring the Benefit Enquiry Line on 0800 882 2000; website: www.jobcentreplus.gov.uk.

Entitlements for elderly or disabled people

Higher personal tax allowance

People over 65 receive a higher personal allowance – £9,490 for those aged 65–74 and £9,640 for those aged 75 and over. The full amount is given only to people whose income does not exceed £22,900. People with higher incomes will have the age-related element of their personal allowance reduced by £1 for every £2 of income above the income limit. For further information, see IR leaflet 121, *Income Tax and Pensioners*. See website: www.hmrc.gov.uk.

Higher married couple's tax allowance

A higher married couple's allowance is similarly available to those couples where the elder partner is over 75. The current amount is £6,965, compared with the normal minimum of £2,670. The full amount is given only to those whose income does not exceed £22,900. All married couple's allowances are restricted to 10 per cent tax relief.

Attendance Allowance

This is paid to people aged 65 or over who are severely disabled, either mentally or physically, and have needed almost constant care for at least six months. (They may be able to get the allowance even if no one has actually given them that help.) An exception to the six months' qualifying period is made in the case of those who are terminally ill, who can receive the allowance without having to wait.

There are two rates of allowance: £70.35 a week for those needing 24-hour care, and £47.10 for those needing intensive day or night-time care. The allowance is tax-free and is generally paid regardless of income (although payment might be affected by entering residential care). For further details, together with a claim form, obtain leaflet DS702 from social security offices and advice centres, or ring the **Benefit Enquiry Line** on 0800 882 2000; website: www.directgov.uk.

Disability Living Allowance (DLA)

This benefit is paid to people up to the age of 65 inclusive who become disabled. It has two components: a mobility component and a care component. A person can be entitled either to one or to both components. The level of benefit depends on the person's care and/or mobility needs. There are two rates for the mobility component and three rates for the care component. The higher-rate mobility component, for people who are unable or virtually unable to walk, is £49.10 a week; the lower rate, for those who owing to physical or mental disability need guidance or supervision in getting around, is £18.65. The three rates for the care component are: higher rate, £70.35; middle rate, £47.10; and lower rate, £18.65. DLA is tax-free and is generally paid regardless of income (although payment may be affected by entering residential care). Except in the case of people who are terminally ill, who can receive the higher-rate care component of DLA immediately, there is a normal qualifying period of three months.

For further information see leaflet DS704, obtainable from Post Offices, Citizens Advice Bureau and social security offices. The leaflet contains a reply slip, which you should complete and return as soon as possible in order to obtain the necessary claim pack. The pack includes a questionnaire with space for you to explain how the disability is making your life more difficult.

Cold weather payments

These are designed to give particularly vulnerable people extra help with heating costs during very cold weather. Anyone aged 60 and over who is in receipt of the guaranteed element of Pension Credit, Income Support or income-based Jobseeker's Allowance qualifies automatically. The payment is made by post as soon as the temperature in an area is forecast to drop – or actually drops – to zero degrees Celsius (or below) for seven consecutive days, so people can turn up their heating secure in the knowledge that they will be receiving extra cash help. The amount paid is £25.00. Those eligible should receive it without having to claim. In the event of a problem, contact your local **Jobcentre Plus** or social security office. See website: www.jobcentreplus.gov.uk.

Winter fuel payments

This is a special annual tax-free payment of between £125 to £400, given to all households with a resident aged between 60 and 80 and over. For further information see www.thepensionservice.gov.uk.

Free off-peak bus travel

People over the age of 60 and also disabled people can travel free on any bus service in the country.

Free TV licence

People aged 75 and older no longer have to pay for their TV licence.

Financial assistance

A number of charities give financial assistance to elderly people in need. These include the following:

Counsel and Care gives advice on ways to fund care, whether this is for nursing or other residential care, or for care in the home. Single needs payments are sometimes available to help towards holidays, special equipment, telephone installations and other priority items. For further information contact Counsel and Care, Tel: 0845 300 7585; e-mail: advice@counselandcare.org.uk; website: www.counselandcare.org.uk.

Elizabeth Finn Care gives grants to enable British and Irish people to remain in their own home and can also provide weekly grants to top-up private care homes fees. For further information contact Elizabeth Finn Care, Tel: 020 7396 6700; e-mail: info@elizabethfinn.org.uk; website: www.elizabethfinntrust.org.uk.

Guild of Aid for Gentlepeople can assist those 'of gentle birth or good education' who want to stay in their own home and who cannot call on any professional or trade body. The Guild will also consider long-term help with fees in care homes. For further information contact the Guild, Tel: 020 7935 0641; e-mail: thead@pcac.org.uk; website: www.aco.uk.net.

Independent Living Fund (ILF) is a trust fund set up with government backing to assist people – aged 16 to 65 – with severe disabilities pay for domestic or personal care to enable them to remain in their own homes. To become eligible, applicants must first approach their local authority for assistance under the Community Care scheme and be successful in obtaining care services to the value of about £200 a week. The Trust may top this up, provided: 1) they are living on their own or with someone who is unable to provide all the care they need; 2) they are receiving Income Support (or have a similar level of income once care has been paid); 3) they have minimal savings; and 4) they receive the highest-rate care component of Disability Living Allowance. For further information contact the Independent Living Fund, Tel: 0845 601 8815; e-mail: funds@ilf.org.uk; website: www.ilf.org.uk.

IndependentAge helps older people to remain independent by providing small lifetime annuities, financial help in times of crisis, and equipment to aid mobility. It provides residential and nursing care and assistance with fees. For further information contact IndependentAge, Tel: 020 7605 4200; e-mail: charity@independentage.org.uk; website: www.independentage.org.uk.

Motability is a registered charity set up to assist recipients of the war pensioners' mobility supplement or the higher-rate mobility component of DLA to use their allowance to lease or buy a car, a powered wheelchair or a scooter. Motability's charitable fund can help those unable to afford the advance payment on some lease vehicles – or necessary adaptations to the vehicle. Grants are available for the least expensive option to meet individuals' basic mobility needs. For further information contact Motability, Tel: 0845 456 4566; website: www.motability.co.uk.

RABI (Royal Agricultural Benevolent Institution) supports retired disabled or disadvantaged members of the farming community and their families, in England, Wales and Northern Ireland. Assistance includes a range of grants, help towards fees in residential and nursing homes, and advice on other available support. RABI has two residential care homes and also sheltered flats available at Bury St Edmunds and Burnham-on-Sea, and nomination rights to other homes across England and Wales. For further information contact RABI, Tel: 01865 727 888; e-mail: info@rabi.org.uk; website: www.rabi.org.uk.

SSAFA Forces Help is restricted to those who have served in the armed forces (including reservists and those who have done National Service) and their families. Grants can be made to meet immediate needs, including rent, wheelchairs and similar essentials. Contact via the local branch is preferred. For further details contact SSAFA Forces Help, Tel: 0845 1300 975; e-mail: info@ssafa.org.uk; website: www.ssafa.org.uk.

Wireless for the Bedridden Society loans radios and televisions on a permanent basis to elderly housebound people who cannot afford sets. Application should be made through a health visitor, social worker or officer of a recognized organization. In the event of any queries about the procedure, contact the Society, Tel: 01708 621 101; e-mail: info@w4b.org.uk; website: www.w4b.org.uk.

Useful reading

For other sources of financial help, ask your library for *A Guide to Grants for Individuals in Need*, published by the Directory of Social Change, and *The Charities Digest*, published by Waterlow Professional Publishing.

Helpful guidance

For many people, one of the main barriers to getting help is knowing which of the many thousands of charities to approach. **Charity Search** exists to help elderly people in need overcome their problem by putting them in contact with those charities most likely to be able to assist. For further information contact the secretary, Tel: 0117 982 4060; e-mail: info@charitysearch.org.uk; website: www.charitysearch.org.uk.

Special accommodation

Retired people who need particular support, assistance or care may choose or need to move to accommodation where special services are provided. This can be either sheltered housing or a care home. Both kinds of accommodation cover an enormous spectrum, so anyone considering either of these options should make a point of investigating the market before reaching a decision.

An all-too-common mistake is for people to anticipate old age long before it arrives. Sometimes they move into accommodation that is either too small or quite unnecessarily 'sheltered' years before they have need of the facilities. By the same token, some individuals buy or rent sheltered housing with a minimum of support services. Often they find they have to move a few months later because they need rather more help than is available.

Choosing the right accommodation is critically important, as it can make all the difference to independence, lifestyle and general well-being. It can also of course lift a great burden off families' shoulders to know that their parents are happy and comfortable, in congenial surroundings and with on-the-spot help, should this be necessary.

Sheltered housing

Sheltered housing is usually a development of independent, purpose-designed bungalows or flats within easy access of shops and public transport. It generally has a house manager and an alarm system for emergencies, and often some common facilities. These could include a garden, possibly a launderette, a sitting room and a dining room, with meals provided for residents, on an optional basis, either once a day or several days a week.

Residents normally have access to all the usual range of services – home helps, meals on wheels and so on – in the same way as do any other elderly people. Sheltered housing is available for sale or rental, variously through private developers, housing associations or local authorities. It is occasionally also provided through gifted housing schemes, or on a shared ownership basis.

Sheltered housing for sale

Some developers specialize in this kind of housing, and there are of course new companies joining the market. With the current conditions in the housing market it is not possible to predict whether the sale of sheltered housing is on the increase. One thing is for certain: the good developments are always sought after and can require you to join a waiting list. Although this is emphatically not a reason for rushing into a decision you might regret, if you were hoping to move in the fairly near future it could be as well to start looking sooner rather than later.

There are many companies offering sheltered housing for sale, with standards and facilities varying enormously. Some also provide personal care services as an adjunct to their retirement home schemes. Flats and houses are usually sold on long leases (99 years or more) for a capital sum, with a weekly or monthly service charge to cover maintenance and resident support services.

Should a resident decide to move, the property can usually be sold on the open market, either through an estate agent or through the developer, provided the prospective buyer is over 55 years of age. Most developers impose a levy of 1 per cent of the sale price for checking the credentials of an incoming resident, irrespective of whether the property is sold through them. Look carefully at any schemes that enable you to buy the property at a discount. Some of these entitle the developer or estate agent to retain a proportion of the equity on resale.

Occupiers normally have to enter into a management agreement with the house builder, and it is important to establish exactly what the commitment is likely to be before buying into such schemes. Factors that should be considered include: who the managing agent is; the house manager's duties; what the service charge covers; the ground rent; the arrangements for any repairs that might prove necessary; whether there is a residents' association; whether pets are allowed; what the conditions are with regard to reselling the property – and the tenant's rights in the matter.

Although the rights of sheltered housing residents have been strengthened over the years, you would nevertheless be strongly recommended to get any contract or agreement vetted by a solicitor before proceeding.

Prices

The range of prices is very wide, depending on size, location and type of property. Weekly service charges vary widely too. Additionally, there is usually an annual ground rental – and Council Tax is normally excluded.

The service charge usually covers the cost of the house manager, alarm system, maintenance, repair and renewal of any communal facilities (external and internal) and sometimes the heating and lighting costs. It may also cover insurance on the building (but not the contents). A particular point to watch is that the service charge tends to rise annually, sometimes well above the inflation level. Be wary of service charges that seem uncommonly reasonable in the sales literature, as these are often increased sharply following purchase. Owners of sheltered accommodation have the same rights as other leaseholders, and charges can therefore be challenged by appeal to a leasehold valuation tribunal.

A further safeguard is the Sheltered Housing Code operated by the **NHBC**, which is mandatory for all registered house builders selling sheltered homes. The Code, which applies to all new sheltered dwellings in England and Wales registered on or after 1 April 1990, has two main requirements. One is that all prospective purchasers should be given a purchaser's information pack (PIP), clearly outlining all essential information that they will need to enable them to decide whether or not to buy. The second is that the builder and management organization enter into a formal legal agreement giving purchasers the benefit of the legal rights specified in the Code. For further information contact the NHBC, Tel: 0844 633 1000; e-mail: cssupport@nhbc.co.uk; website: www.nhbc.co.uk.

For those on lowish incomes, it may also be possible to get housing benefit to meet some or all of the service charge. The local authority housing department will advise on this.

The following organizations can provide information about sheltered housing for sale:

AIMS offers impartial information, legal advice and a mediation service to residents of both private retirement and rented sheltered housing across England and Wales. For further information contact AIMS, Tel: 020 8765 7465; e-mail: aims@ace.org.uk; website: www.ageconcern.org.uk.

Elderly Accommodation Counsel maintains a nationwide database of all types of specialist accommodation for elderly people and gives advice and detailed information to help enquirers choose the support and care most suited to their needs. For further information contact Elderly Accommodation Counsel, Tel: 020 7820 1343; e-mail: sheila.coles@eac.org.uk; website: www.eac.org.uk.

Retirement Homesearch is an estate agent that specializes in retirement homes for sale. It operates nationwide and deals in all types of property including flats, houses and bungalows, in all price ranges. For further information contact Retirement Homesearch, Tel: 0845 880 5560 for properties in England and Wales, or 0141 248 2846 for properties in Scotland; e-mail: enquiries@retirem enthomesearch.co.uk; website: www.retirementhomesearch.co.uk.

Useful reading

New Choices in Retirement Housing, published by Age Concern/Help the Aged. This is an excellent guide to the sort of questions you should ask before committing yourself. It is available from Age Concern Books, Tel: 0870 442 2120; website: www.ageconcern.org.uk.

Private companies with sheltered housing for sale

New developments are constantly under construction. Properties tend to be sold quickly soon after completion, so it pays to find out about future developments and to get on any waiting lists well in advance of a prospective purchase. Firms specializing in this type of property include the following:

Beechcroft Developments offers one-, two- and three-bedroom cottages and apartments located in towns and villages in Southern England: Berkshire, Dorset, Gloucestershire, Hampshire, Hertfordshire, Surrey and Wiltshire. Each development is maintained by a site secretary, employed to take care of the day-to-day management and provide high levels of security and service. For further information, including current prices, contact Beechcroft Developments, Tel: 01491 825 522; e-mail: info@beechcroft.co.uk; website: www.beechcroft.co.uk.

Bovis Homes Retirement Living offers one- and two-bedroom apartments in Cambridgeshire, Hertfordshire, Suffolk, Surrey and Wiltshire. Developments include 24-hour staffing. For further information, including current price list and availability, contact Bovis Homes Retirement Living, Tel: 01474 876 200; website: www.bovishomes.co.uk.

English Courtyard Association (ECA) offers architecturally award-winning 'courtyard-style' schemes throughout England, with two- and three-bedroom houses, cottages and flats for sale on 150-year leases. For further information and prices, contact English Courtyard Association, Tel: 01491 615 960; website: www.englishcourtyard.co.uk.

McCarthy & Stone Retirement Living builds over 2,000 new retirement apartments a year in all parts of England, Scotland and Wales. For further information contact McCarthy & Stone (Developments) Ltd, Tel: 0800 919 132; website: www.mccarthyandstone.co.uk.

Pegasus Retirement Homes plc offers one-, two- and three-bedroom apartments in the Midlands and South-East and South-West of England. For further information contact Pegasus Retirement Homes plc, Tel: 0800 583 8844; e-mail: sales@pegasus-homes.co.uk; website: www.pegasus-homes.co.uk.

Housing associations with sheltered housing for sale

Housing associations build sheltered housing for sale and also manage sheltered housing developments on behalf of private construction companies:

Guardian Retirement Housing (now part of the Anchor Trust) has nearly 200 estates of mainly one- and two-bedroomed flats, bungalows and cottages, comprising almost 7,000 properties countrywide. For further details contact the Customer Enquiries Team, Tel: 01274 386 035; website: www.anchor.org.uk.

RLHA Group (formerly Retirement Lease Housing Association) is a not-for-profit provider of housing and care services to elderly people and others. It offers a leasehold retirement scheme, shared ownership and domiciliary care services. For further information contact the Association, Tel: 01252 356 000; e-mail: info@rlha.org.uk; website: www.rlha.org.uk.

Rented sheltered housing

This is normally provided by local authorities, housing associations and certain benevolent societies. As with accommodation to buy, quality varies.

Local authorities

This is usually only available to people who have resided in the area for some time. There is often an upper and lower age limit for admission, and prospective tenants may have to undergo a medical examination, since as a rule only those who are physically fit are accepted. Should a resident become infirm or frail, alternative accommodation will be found. Apply to the local housing or social services department or via a housing advice centre.

Housing associations

Housing associations supply much of the newly built sheltered housing. Both rent and service charges vary around the country. In case of need, Income Support or Housing Benefit may be obtained to help with the cost. Citizens Advice Bureau and housing departments often keep a list of local housing associations. Or you could look on the websites: www.housingnet.co.uk, or www.clickhousingassociations.co.uk. There are hundreds to choose from; here are just a few:

Abbeyfield Society has supported sheltered houses nationwide, providing independent accommodation, a resident house manager and main meals of the day. It also has houses providing 24-hour registered personal care facilities. For further information contact the Society, Tel: 01727 846 168; e-mail: enquiries@abbeyfield.com; website: www.abbeyfield.com.

Anchor Retirement Housing provides flats and bungalows for older people located throughout England. Most of the developments have a communal area, laundry, alarm system and guest room. There are also a number of special developments for frail older people who require extra assistance with everyday living. For further information contact Anchor Retirement Housing, Tel: 01274 381 600; e-mail: contactus@anchor.org.uk; website: www.anchor.org.uk.

Habinteg Housing Association provides homes that are accessible, adaptable and affordable. With over 30 years' experience in housing and disability, Habinteg uses its expertise to create neighbourhoods that allow everyone to live as independently as possible. All are fully accessible for wheelchair users, and most of the schemes have an on-site community assistant to offer support if needed. For further information contact the Association, Tel: 020 7822 8700; e-mail: info@habinteg.org.uk; website: www.habinteg.org.uk.

Hanover Housing Association. Whether you wish to rent or buy, Hanover offers one of the widest choices of housing options available in the UK to the over-55s, in towns, cities and rural locations. There are also more than 40 extra-care housing estates where care is available 24 hours a day. Applications are encouraged from people over 60. Tel: 0800 280 2575; e-mail: service.centre@hanover.org.uk; website: www.hanover.org.uk.

Jewish Community Housing Association Ltd has some 600 sheltered flats primarily for Jewish people in housing need. Properties are located in London,

Hemel Hempstead and Margate. Tel: 020 8381 4901; e-mail: info@jcha.org.uk; website: www.jcha.org.uk.

Servite Houses has around 18,000 homes for over 30,000 people in some 70 sheltered housing schemes with resident scheme managers in and around London, West Sussex, the West Midlands and Merseyside. For further information contact Servite Houses, Tel: 020 8333 6000; e-mail via the contact form on their website: www.servitehouses.org.uk.

Southern Housing Group is one of Southern England's largest housing associations. Founded over 100 years ago, it owns and manages 24,000 homes with more than 66,000 residents. It provides a range of options for rent and home ownership, including sheltered accommodation, across the South of England and the Isle of Wight. For further information contact the Southern Housing Group, Tel: 0300 303 1771; e-mail: service.centre@shgroup.org.uk; website: www. shgroup.org.uk.

Benevolent societies

These all cater for specific professional and other groups:

Housing 21 is a major national provider of housing, care and support services for older people. Established over 40 years ago, this not-for-profit organization with charitable status provides over 13,000 properties in 350 sheltered and extra-care housing schemes throughout England. Tel: 0370 192 4000; e-mail: enquiries@ housing21.co.uk; website: www.housing21.co.uk.

Royal Alfred Seafarers' Society, established as a charity in 1865 to help 'worn out and infirm seamen', provides quality long-term care for seafarers and their widows and dependants. For further details, contact the Society, Tel: 01737 353 763; e-mail: royalalfred@btopenworld.com; website: www.royalalfredseafarers. com.

SSAFA Forces Help is restricted to those who have served in the armed forces (including reservists and those who have done National Service) and their families. The Association's Housing Advisory Service provides advice about sheltered accommodation to retired ex-service people. Tel: 0845 1300 975; e-mail: info@ ssafa.org.uk; website: www.ssafa.org.uk.

Alternative ways of buying sheltered accommodation

For those who cannot afford to buy into sheltered housing either outright or through a mortgage, there are a variety of alternative payment methods.

Shared ownership and 'Sundowner' schemes

Part-ownership schemes are now offered by a number of developers. Would-be residents, who must be over 55 years, part-buy or part-rent, with the amount of rent varying according to the size of the initial lump sum. Residents can sell at any time, but they only recoup that percentage of the sale price that is proportionate to their original capital investment, with no allowance for any rental payments made over the intervening period.

'Investment' and gifted housing schemes

Some charities and housing associations operate these schemes, for which a capital sum is required, to obtain sheltered accommodation. They work as follows. The buyer puts in the larger share of the capital, usually 50 to 80 per cent, and the housing association puts in the remainder. The buyer pays rent on the housing association's share of the accommodation and also service charges for the communal facilities.

Gifted housing schemes differ in that an individual donates his or her property to a registered charity, in return for being housed and cared for in his or her own home. The attraction is that the owner can remain in his or her own property with none of the burden of its upkeep. However, it is advisable to consult a solicitor before signing anything, because such schemes have the big negative of reducing the value of the owner's estate, with consequent loss for any beneficiaries.

Age Concern/Help the Aged run SeniorLine, a free advice and information service, available throughout the UK for older people and their carers. Trained advice workers can help with enquiries about community or residential care and housing options. Contact Help the Aged and Age Concern, Tel: 020 7278 1114; website: www.helptheaged.org.uk.

Almshouses

Most almshouses are endowed by a charity for the benefit of older people of reduced means who live locally or have a connection with a particular trade. There are now over 2,000 groups of almshouses, providing about 35,000 dwellings. Although many are of considerable age, most of them have been modernized, and new ones are being built. Rents are not charged, but there will be a maintenance contribution towards upkeep and heating.

A point you should be aware of is that, like Abbeyfield and some other charitable housing associations, almshouses do not provide the same security of tenure as some other tenancies. You would be well advised to have the proposed letter of appointment checked by a lawyer or other expert to ensure you understand exactly what the beneficiary's rights are.

There is no standard way to apply for an almshouse, since each charity has its own qualifications for residence. Some housing departments and advice centres keep lists of local almshouses. Another organization that could help is the **Almshouse Association**, which supplies information on almshouses and contact details in the county in which you are interested. To contact the Association, Tel: 01344 452 922; e-mail: naa@almshouses.org; website: www.almshouses.org.

Granny flats

A granny flat or annexe is a self-contained unit attached to a family house. A large house can be converted or extended for this purpose, but planning permission is needed. Enquire at your local authority planning department. Some councils, particularly new towns, have houses to rent with granny flats.

Housing for ethnic groups

LHA-ASRA is a not-for-profit organization with over 20 years' experience in providing affordable housing to meet the needs of single people and families of all ages, including Asian elders and single Asian women. There are also general family homes. For further information contact LHA-ASRA, Tel: 020 7940 6600; or 0116 257 6700; website: www.lha-asra.org.uk.

Salvation Army homes

The Salvation Army has 18 homes for elderly people in various parts of the UK, offering residential care for men and women unable to manage in their own homes. Christian caring is given within a family atmosphere, in pleasant surroundings, but the homes are not nursing homes. Fees are determined by negotiation with local authority social services. Tel: 0845 634 0101; e-mail: info@ salvationarmy.org.uk; website: www.salvationarmy.org.uk.

Extra-care schemes

A number of organizations that provide sheltered accommodation also have extra-care sheltered housing, designed for those who can no longer look after themselves without assistance. Cost ranges from about £100 to £450 a week. Although expensive, it is cheaper than most private care homes and often more appropriate than full-scale nursing care. A possible problem is that tenants of some of these schemes do not have security of tenure and, should they become frail, could be asked to leave if more intensive care were required. Among the housing associations that provide these facilities are Housing 21, Hanover Housing Association, Anchor, Abbeyfield, and Servite Houses (see the details listed earlier in this chapter).

Community Care

Since the start of Community Care in April 1993, anyone needing help in arranging suitable care for an elderly person should contact his or her social services department. Before making suggestions, the department will assess what type of provision would best meet the needs of the individual concerned. This could be services or special equipment to enable the person to stay in his or her own home, residential home accommodation or a nursing home. If residential or nursing home care is necessary, the department will arrange a place in either a local authority or other home, pay the charge and seek reimbursement from the individual according to his or her means. (See 'Financial assistance for residential and nursing home care', page 383.) The general range of choices is the same as for individuals making their own private arrangements, which of course anyone – provided he or she can afford it – is free to do.

Care homes

Until recently, care homes were variously known as 'residential care homes' and 'nursing homes'. Most people likely to be concerned knew in general terms what the difference was and the type of care that each provided. Today, both kinds of home are officially classified as care homes. For those needing to know whether nursing is provided or not, former nursing homes are now registered as 'care homes to provide nursing care', while former residential care homes are now registered as 'care homes to provide personal care'. To avoid confusion, we have mainly stuck to the old terminology on the basis of this being more familiar.

The government is proposing a range of measures to help cover the costs of care home fees in future. There are three options:

1. The government would pay a quarter to a third of all future personal care, leaving the recipient to pay the rest of the board and lodging costs.
2. A voluntary state-backed insurance scheme could cover all of the personal care element. Here a person would pay £20–25,000 up-front at 65, weekly through deferred pension payments, or on death via their estate.
3. Those with assets in excess of £23,000 would have to join a compulsory state-backed insurance scheme, which would enable everyone to get free personal care.

None of these options includes payment for accommodation costs. Whichever option is finally to be used, anyone with assets of less than £23,000 would not have to pay personal or accommodation costs. The Green Paper consultation ran until November 2009, with the chosen option expected to be published in a White Paper sometime in 2010.

Residential care homes (care homes registered to provide personal care)

There may come a time when it is no longer possible for an elderly person to manage without being in proper residential care. In a residential care home, sometimes known as a 'rest home', the accommodation usually consists of a bedroom plus communal dining rooms, lounges and gardens. All meals are provided, rooms are cleaned, and staff are at hand to give whatever help is needed. Most homes are fully furnished, though it is usually possible to take small items of furniture. Except in some of the more expensive private homes, bathrooms are normally shared. Intensive nursing care is not usually included.

Homes are run by private individuals (or companies), voluntary organizations and local authorities. All homes must be registered with the Commission for Social Care Inspection to ensure minimum standards. An important point to note is that any unregistered home should not be considered.

No home should ever be accepted 'on spec'. It is very important that the individual should have a proper chance to visit it and ask any questions. Before reaching a final decision, it is a good idea to arrange a short stay to see whether the facilities are suitable and pleasant. It could also be sensible to enquire what long-term plans there are for the home. Over the past couple of years, many private and voluntary care homes have been closing owing to the increasing expense of running them.

While in the event a move may turn out to be a blessing in disguise, equally it can be a highly distressing experience for an elderly person who has become attached to the staff and made friends among the other residents. Though a move can never be totally ruled out, awareness of whether the home is likely to remain a going concern could be a deciding factor when making a choice. Possible clues could include whether the place is short-staffed or in need of decoration. If it is run by a company or charity, you could request to see the latest accounts.

Private homes

Private care homes are often converted houses, taking up to about 30 people. As more companies move into the market, they can be purpose-built accommodation, which may include a heated swimming pool and luxury facilities. The degree of care varies. If a resident becomes increasingly infirm, a care home will normally continue to look after him or her if possible. It may, however, become necessary at some point to arrange transfer to a nursing home or hospital. Fees vary enormously.

Voluntary care homes

These are run by charities, religious bodies or other voluntary organizations. Eligibility may be determined by age, background or occupation, depending on the criteria of the managing organization. Income may be a factor, as may general fitness, and individuals may be invited to a personal interview before acceptance on to the waiting list. Priority tends to be given to those in greatest need. Homes are often in large converted houses, with accommodation for under 10 people or up to 100. Fees vary depending on locality.

Local authority homes

These are sometimes referred to as 'Part III accommodation', and admission will invariably be arranged by the social services department. If someone does not like the particular accommodation suggested, he or she can turn it down and ask the department what other offers might be available. Weekly charges vary around the country. In practice, however, individuals are charged only according to their means.

Nursing homes (care homes registered to provide nursing care)

Nursing homes provide medical supervision and fully qualified nurses, 24 hours a day. Most are privately run, with the remainder being supported by voluntary organizations. All nursing homes in England must be registered with the Commission for Social Care Inspection, which keeps a list of what homes are available in the area. In Wales, the inspectorate is called the Care Standards Inspectorate for Wales, and in Scotland it is called the Scottish Commission for the Regulation of Care.

Private

These homes normally accommodate between 15 and 100 patients. Depending on which part of the country, charges can vary. Some fees rise depending on how much nursing is required. For information about nursing homes in the UK, contact the following:

Elderly Accommodation Counsel has a nationwide database with details of all types of specialist accommodation suitable to meet the needs of retired or elderly people, including sheltered housing for sale or rent, residential care and nursing homes. For further information contact Elderly Accommodation Counsel, Tel: 020 7820 1343; e-mail: sheila.coles@eac.org.uk; website: www.eac.org.uk.
NHFA Ltd runs a free helpline that offers advice to individuals and their families on specialist accommodation and how to pay for care home fees, what State benefits are available to them and other related matters. Contact the Care Advice Line on 0800 99 88 33; e-mail: enquiries@nhfa.co.uk; website: www.nhfa.co.uk.
RNHA (Registered Nursing Home Association) is an organization that provides support for nursing home owners, requiring its members to meet high levels of standards and service. Patients in nursing homes that are members of the RNHA can expect to receive some of the best standards of service available from a nursing home in the UK. Tel: 0121 451 1088; e-mail: info@rnha.co.uk; website: www.rnha.co.uk.

Voluntary organizations

These normally have very long waiting lists, and beds are often reserved for those who have been in the charity's care home. Voluntary organizations that run care homes include:

Careways Trust, Tel: 01903 276 030; e-mail: enquiries@carewaystrust.org.uk; website: www.carewaystrust.org.uk.
Catholic Old People's Homes are listed in the *Catholic Directory*, available in libraries.
Friends of the Elderly, Tel: 020 7730 8263; e-mail: enquiries@fote.org.uk; website: www.fote.org.uk.
IndependentAge, Tel: 020 7605 4200; e-mail: charity@independentage.org.uk; website: www.independentage.org.uk.
Jewish Care , Tel: 020 8922 2222; website: www.jewishcare.org.

Free nursing care

Since October 2001, the nursing costs of being in a home have been made free to all patients. This does not include the personal care costs (eg help with bathing, dressing or eating), nor the accommodation costs, both of which individuals will continue to be assessed for under the rules described below. In Scotland, exceptionally, the personal care costs are also free.

The provision of free nursing care may make only a fairly limited contribution to the cost of being in a home. Patients are assessed according to their needs and the amount of actual nursing care they require.

Financial assistance for residential and nursing home care

Under the Community Care arrangements, people needing to go into a residential or nursing home may receive help from their local authority social services department. As explained earlier, the department will make the arrangements direct with the home following its assessment procedure and will seek reimbursement from the person towards the cost, according to set means-testing rules.

People who were already in a residential or nursing home before April 1993 used to receive special levels of Income Support. This arrangement, known as 'preserved rights', ended in April 2002, and instead the full cost of residential care is now met by the individual's local authority.

People who had been or are currently paying for themselves but can no longer afford to do so may have the right to claim help, now or in the future, if they qualify on grounds of financial need. Help is provided on a sliding scale for those with assets. Even those on a very low income are required to make some contribution towards the cost of being in a home.

For further information enquire at your local Citizens Advice Bureau or contact **Elderly Accommodation Counsel**, Tel: 020 7820 1343; e-mail: sheila.coles@ eac.org.uk; website: www.eac.org.uk. See also leaflet GL15, *Help if You Live in a Care Home*, from your local **Jobcentre Plus** or social security office. Website: www.jobcentreplus.gov.uk.

Age Concern/Help The Aged also publishes a useful fact sheet, *Local Authority Charging Procedures for Care Homes*, which applies to care homes in England. See website: www.ageconcern.org.uk. A separate Scottish version is also available.

Additional help

A major worry for many people going into residential care is the requirement to sell their home to cover the costs. While this may still eventually be necessary, the rules have been made slightly more flexible to allow a short breathing space for making decisions. Under the rules introduced in April 2001, the value of a person's home is disregarded from the means-testing procedure in assessing their ability to pay for the first 12 weeks of their going into care. Also, instead of selling, you may be able to borrow the money (secured against your home) from the local council, which will eventually reclaim the loan at a later stage or from your estate.

Further information

Key sources of information about voluntary and private homes are: the *Charities Digest* (available in libraries, housing aid centres and Citizens Advice Bureau) and the *Directory of Independent Hospitals and Health Services* (available in libraries). The *Charities Digest* also includes information about hospices. Here are some sources of advice:

Action on Elder Abuse was founded to help prevent physical, psychological or financial exploitation and other types of abuse of elderly people. As well as providing guidance and training for professionals engaged in the care of vulnerable older people, it also runs a free confidential helpline offering advice and support to individuals who feel that they are the victims of abuse as well as to other members of the public who have grounds for concern about someone's welfare. For further information contact Action on Elder Abuse, Tel: 0808 808 8141; e-mail: enquiries@elderabuse.org.uk; website: www.elderabuse.org.uk.

The Cinnamon Trust maintains a register of care homes that allow pets to be kept. For further information contact the Trust, Tel: 01736 757900; e-mail: admin@cinnamon.org.uk; website: www.cinnamon.org.uk.

Elderly Accommodation Counsel provides a nationwide database with details of all types of specialist accommodation suitable to meet the needs of retired or elderly people, including sheltered housing for sale or rent, residential care and nursing homes. Tel: 020 7820 1343; e-mail: sheila.coles@eac.org.uk; website: www.eac.org.uk.

Help the Aged/Age Concern runs a Care Fees Advice Service, offering free financial advice on how to meet the costs of ongoing care. Recommendations, tailored according to individual circumstances, cover the full range of possibilities, from help with claiming benefits to choosing a suitable savings plan for long-term care. Depending on the enquiry, advice can be given over the telephone or in face-to-face discussion with an adviser. For further details, contact Help the Aged/Age Concern, Tel: 020 7278 1114; website: www.helptheaged.org.uk.

NHFA Ltd runs an advice line for individuals and their families on how to pay for care home fees, what State benefits are available to them, and other related matters including, for example, Enduring Power of Attorney and Inheritance Tax planning. Contact the Care Advice Line on 0800 99 88 33; e-mail: enquiries@nhfa.co.uk; website: www.nhfa.co.uk

R&RA (Relatives & Residents Association) offers a support service to families and friends of older people in, or considering, long-term care. There are local groups around the country where relatives can meet and discuss any practical or emotional worries they may have about opting for residential care, and there is also a helpline that can give advice on most questions, from finding a home to concerns about the standard of care. For further information contact the Association, Tel: 020 7359 8136; e-mail: info@relres.org; website: www.relres.org.

Social services departments keep lists of both voluntary and private homes. See website: www.dh.gov.uk.

Useful reading

Finding Care Home Accommodation, a free fact sheet obtainable from Help The Aged/Age Concern, Tel: 0800 009 966; website: www.ageconcern.org.uk.

Some special problems

A minority of people, as they become older, suffer from special problems that can cause great distress. Because families do not like to talk about them, they may be unaware of what services are available and so may be missing out on practical help and sometimes also on financial assistance.

Hypothermia

Elderly people tend to be more vulnerable to the cold. If the body drops below a certain temperature, it can be dangerous, because one of the symptoms of hypothermia is that sufferers no longer actually feel cold. Instead, they may lose their appetite and vitality and may become mentally confused. Instead of doing all the sensible things like getting a hot drink and putting on an extra sweater, they are liable to neglect themselves further and can put themselves at real risk.

Although heating costs are often blamed, quite wealthy people can also be victims by allowing their home to become too cold or not wearing sufficient clothing. For this reason, during a cold snap it is very important to check up regularly on an elderly person living alone.

British Gas, electricity companies and the Solid Fuel Association are all willing to give advice on how heating systems can be used more efficiently and economically. Insulation can also play a very large part in keeping a home warmer and cheaper to heat. It may be possible to obtain a grant from the local authority, although normally this would only be likely on grounds of real need.

Additionally, elderly and disabled people in receipt of Income Support may receive a cold weather payment to help with heating costs during a particularly cold spell – that is, when the temperature is forecast to drop to zero degrees Celsius (or below) for seven consecutive days. Those eligible should receive the money automatically. In the event of any problem, ask at your social security office. In the event of an emergency, such as a power cut, contact the Citizens Advice Bureau or Help The Aged/Age Concern.

Finally, every household with someone aged 60 or older will get an annual tax-free winter fuel payment of £250, while those with a resident aged 80 or older will receive £400. For further information, call the **Winter Fuel Payment Helpline**, Tel: 0845 915 1515; website: www.direct.gov.uk.

Incontinence

Bladder or bowel problems can cause deep embarrassment to sufferers as well as inconvenience to relatives. The problem can occur in an elderly person for all sorts of reasons, and a doctor should always be consulted, as it can often be cured or at least alleviated by proper treatment. To assist with the practical problems, some local authorities operate a laundry service that collects soiled linen, sometimes several times a week. The person to talk to is the health visitor or district nurse (telephone your local health centre), who will be able to advise about this and other facilities.

B&BF (Bladder and Bowel Foundation) is the charity for people with bladder and bowel dysfunction. The charity operates a helpline that is staffed by nurses with specialist knowledge; Tel: 0845 345 0165; e-mail: info@bladderandbowel foundation.org; website: www.bladderandbowelfoundation.org.

Dementia

Sometimes an elderly person can become confused or forgetful, suffer severe loss of memory or have violent mood swings and at times be abnormally aggressive. It is important to consult a doctor as soon as possible, as the cause may be depression, stress or even vitamin deficiency. All of these can be treated and often completely cured. If dementia is diagnosed, there are ways of helping a sufferer to cope better with acute forgetfulness and other symptoms.

The most common type of dementia is Alzheimer's disease, which is usually found in people aged over 65. Approximately 24 million people worldwide have dementia, of which the majority (over 60 per cent) is due to Alzheimer's. Clinical signs are characterized by progressive cognitive deterioration, together with a decline in the ability to carry out common daily tasks, and behavioural changes. The first readily identifiable symptoms of Alzheimer's disease are usually short-term memory loss and visual-spatial confusion. These initial symptoms progress from seemingly simple and fluctuating to a more pervasive loss of memory, including difficulty navigating familiar areas such as the local neighbourhood. This advances to loss of other familiar and well-known skills, as well as recognition of objects and persons.

Since family members are often the first to notice changes that might indicate the onset of Alzheimer's (or other forms of dementia) they should learn the early warning signs. They should serve as informants during initial evaluation of patients clinically. It is important to consult your doctor as soon as you have concerns. It is also a good idea to talk to the health visitor, as he or she will know about any helpful facilities that may be available locally. The health visitor is also able to arrange appointments with other professionals, such as the community psychiatric nurse and the occupational therapist.

Other sources of help and support for people with dementia and their carers are:

The national charity **Mind**. You can contact Mind Information Line, 0845 766 0163, e-mail: contact@mind.org.uk; website: www.mind.org.uk.
Alzheimer's Society offers help and support for sufferers and their carers. Tel: 0845 300 0336; e-mail: enquiries@alzheimers.org.uk; website: www.alzheimers. org.uk.
Alzheimer Scotland – Action on Dementia has local services throughout Scotland. Contact the helpline, 0808 8083 000; e-mail: alzheimer@alzscot.org; website: www.alzscot.org.

Useful reading

Caring for the Person with Dementia, published by the Alzheimer's Society, website: www.alzheimers.org.uk, and *Understanding Dementia*, available from Mind, website: www.mind.org.uk.

16

No one is immortal

As they say, you only get one shot at life; there is no dress rehearsal. In Bali, death is celebrated with glorious processions, merry-making and days of feasting. In Western society, we go to the other extreme. Many couples never even discuss death or how it will affect them. Even more worrying, they ignore the financial practicalities, in the subconscious belief perhaps that to do otherwise would be tempting fate. For the same reason, many people put off making a will or rationalize that it does not really matter. They believe perhaps that, whatever happens, their possessions will eventually go to their family. However, as every widows' organization would testify, a great deal of heartbreak and real financial worry could be avoided if husbands and wives were more open with each other, in particular where their own mortality is concerned.

Wills

Anyone who is married, has children or is over the age of 35 should make a will. At the very least, should anything happen, this will ensure that the person's wishes are known and properly executed. But also very important, it will spare the family the legal complications that arise when someone dies intestate. A major problem, if someone dies without leaving a will, is that the surviving husband or wife will usually have to wait very much longer for badly needed cash. The legal formalities are infinitely more complex. There will be no executor. Also, the individual's assets will be distributed according to a rigid formula, which may be a far cry from what he or she had intended, and may perversely result in the partner's security being quite unnecessarily jeopardized.

Laws of intestacy

The rules if you die without leaving a will are as follows:

- If there is *a surviving spouse but no surviving children, parents, brothers, sisters or direct nephews or nieces* of the deceased, the widow or widower inherits the whole of the estate.
- If there are *children but no surviving spouse,* the estate is divided equally among the children. If one child has died, his or her share goes to his or her own children.
- If there are *a spouse and children,* the partner receives all personal possessions, a maximum of £125,000 (if the estate is a large one) and a life interest in half of the remainder. The other half goes to the children.
- If there are *no children* but other close members of the family still living (parents, brothers, sisters or direct nephews or nieces), the surviving spouse receives all personal possessions, up to £200,000 where there is a large estate, and half of the remainder of the estate. The other half is divided between the rest of the family.
- *Non-married partners* do not inherit automatically; they have to make a court application.
- *Same-sex partners* who have entered into a civil partnership (see page 72) have the same inheritance rights as married spouses.
- If *a couple are separated* but not divorced, they are still legally married and, therefore, the separated partner could be a major beneficiary.

Making a will

You have three choices: you can do it yourself, you can ask your bank to help you, or you can use a solicitor or a specialist will-writing practitioner.

Doing it yourself

Home-made wills are not generally recommended. People often use ambiguous wording which, while perfectly clear to the individual who has written it, may be less than obvious to others. This could result in the donor's wishes being misinterpreted and could also cause considerable delay in settling the estate.

You can buy forms from WH Smith and other stationers which, while helpful, are not perfect and still leave considerable margin for error. For individuals with sight problems, **RNIB** has produced a comprehensive guide to making or changing a will that is available in large print size, in Braille and on tape, as well as in standard print size. This is obtainable free by contacting the donor development department at RNIB, Tel: 0845 766 9999; website: www.rnib.org.uk.

Two witnesses are needed, and an essential point to remember is that beneficiaries cannot witness a will, nor can the spouses of any beneficiaries. In certain circumstances, a will can be rendered invalid. A sensible precaution for those doing it themselves is to have it checked by a solicitor or by a legal expert from the Citizens Advice Bureau.

Banks

Advice on wills and the administration of estates is carried out by the trustee companies of most of the major high street banks. In particular, the services they offer are to provide general guidance, to act as executor and to administer the estate. They will also introduce clients to a solicitor and keep a copy of the will – plus other important documents – in their safe, to avoid the risk of their being mislaid. Additionally, banks (as solicitors) can give tax planning and other financial guidance, including advice on Inheritance Tax. Some banks will draw up a will for you.

Solicitors

Solicitors may offer to draw up a will, act as executors and administer the estate. Like banks, they will also keep a copy of your will in safe keeping (most will not charge for storing a will). If you do not know a solicitor, you can look in the *Yellow Pages* or on the website: www.yell.com, or ask the Citizens Advice Bureau. Or you can contact the **Law Society,** Tel: 020 7242 1222; e-mail: contact@lawso ciety.org.uk; website: www.lawsociety.org.uk.

Alternatively, if you simply want help in writing a will, you could consult a specialist will-writing practitioner. The best approach is to contact one of the following organizations:

The Society of Will Writers will be pleased to send you an information pack, together with details of up to three of their members in your area. Contact the Society, Tel: 01522 687 888; website: www.willwriters.com.

Trust Inheritance Limited provides a home-visit will-writing service, and all work is professionally drafted by a solicitor-led team. Contact on 0800 097 8012; e-mail: info@trustinheritance.com; website: www.trustinheritance.com.

The Will Bureau writes wills, offers estate planning advice and, once it has written your will, regularly updates you with developments in the law that could affect your estate and Inheritance Tax. For further information contact the Bureau, Tel: 020 8920 3360; e-mail: info@twb.org.uk; website: www.twb.org.uk.

Charges

These can vary enormously, depending on the size and complexity of the will. A basic will could cost around £120 or, if your affairs are more complicated, the cost could run into many hundreds of pounds. Always ask for an estimate before proceeding. Remember too that professional fees normally carry VAT. Some solicitors charge according to the time they spend on a job, so, although the actual work may not take very long, if you spend hours discussing your will or changing it every few months the costs can escalate very considerably. However, nowadays, many solicitors will give you a fixed-fee estimate for a will, so you should have a good idea from the outset what it will cost. The fees for will-writing practitioners are broadly in line with those of solicitors.

Community Legal Service funding (Legal Aid)

Financial assistance for legal help and advice is available to certain groups of people for making a will. These include people aged over 70, disabled people, and a parent of a disabled person whom the parent wishes to provide for in his or her will. Additionally, to qualify, the people will need to satisfy the financial eligibility criteria. For further information enquire at your Citizens Advice Bureau or other advice centre.

Executors

You will need to appoint at least one executor to administer your will. An executor can be a beneficiary under the estate and can be a member of your family or a friend whom you trust to act impartially, always provided of course that he or she is willing to accept the responsibility. Alternatively, and this is generally advisable for larger estates, you could appoint your solicitor or bank.

The fees will be additional. They are not paid at the time of making the will but instead come out of the estate. Pretty significant sums could be involved, so the advice on obtaining an estimate is, if anything, even more relevant. In certain instances, banks can be more expensive; in others, solicitors can be. The only way to discover is to get an estimate from each.

Banks publish a tariff of their charges. Solicitors render bills according to the time involved so, although it is impossible for them to be precise, they should nevertheless be able to give a pretty accurate assessment – at least at the time of quoting. Both banks' and solicitors' fees may increase during the interval between their being appointed and their fulfilling their duties as executor.

Other points

Wills should always be kept in a safe place – and their whereabouts known. The most sensible arrangement is for the solicitor to keep the original and for both you and the bank to have a copy.

A helpful initiative devised by the Law Society is a mini-form, known as a *personal assets log*. This is for individuals drawing up a will to give to their executor or close relatives. It is, quite simply, a four-sided leaflet with space to record the essential information: name and address of solicitor; where the will and other important documents, for example share certificates and insurance policies, are kept; the date of any codicils and so on. Logs should be obtainable from most solicitors.

Wills may need updating in the event of an important change of circumstances, for example a divorce, a remarriage or the birth of a grandchild. An existing will normally becomes invalid in the event of marriage or remarriage and should be replaced. Any changes must be by codicil (for minor alterations) or by a new will, and must be properly witnessed.

Another reason why you may need, or wish, to change your will is in consequence of the new Inheritance Tax rules affecting accumulation and maintenance trusts, as well as interest-in-possession trusts. The Law Society had been advising all owners of homes and other assets worth more than the nil-rate band (£325,000 for the 2009/10 tax year) to review their will if any of their assets have been left in trust.

Partners who wish to leave all their possessions to each other should consider including a 'survivorship clause' in their wills, as an insurance against the intestacy rules being applied were they both to be involved in the same fatal accident. Legal advice is strongly recommended here.

If you have views about your funeral, it is sensible to write a letter to your executors explaining your wishes and to lodge it with your will. If you have any pets, you may equally wish to leave a letter filed with your will explaining what arrangements you have made for their immediate and long-term welfare.

Over the years there has been increased interest in living wills. For those who would like information, **Dignity in Dying** supplies a free information pack. The advanced decisions (formerly known as living wills) pack is available at a cost of £25. It contains all the necessary forms to complete a living will. Contact Dignity in Dying, Tel: 020 7479 7730; e-mail: info@dignityindying.org.uk; website: www.dignityindying.org.uk.

If you would be willing to donate an organ that might help save someone else's life, you could indicate this in your will or alternatively obtain an organ donor card. These are available from most hospitals, chemists and Jobcentre Plus offices, as well as some charities.

Finally, **Help the Aged/Age Concern** has a team of locally based wills and legacy advisers who provide confidential, impartial advice to older people in their own homes about all aspects of making or revising a will. The advice service is available free of charge to anyone of retirement age.

Useful reading

Will information pack, free from the Wills and Legacies Department, Help the Aged/Age Concern, Tel: 020 7278 1114; website: www.helptheaged.org.uk.

Provision for dependent adult children

A particular concern for parents with a physically or mentally dependent son or daughter is what plans they can make to ensure his or her care when they are no longer in a position to manage. There is no single right answer, as each case is individual, depending on the severity of the disability or illness, the range of helpful voluntary or statutory facilities locally, and the extent to which they, as parents, can provide for their child's financial security long-term.

While social services may be able to advise, parents thinking ahead might do better to consult a specialist organization experienced in helping carers in this situation to explore the possible options available to them. Useful addresses are:

Carers UK, Tel: 0808 8087 777; e-mail: info@carersuk.org; website: www. carersuk.org.
The Princess Royal Trust for Carers, Tel: 0844 8004 361; e-mail: info@carers. org; website: www.carers.org.

Parents concerned about financial matters such as setting up a trust or making alternative provision in their will would also be advised to consult a solicitor or accountant.

Money and other worries – and how to minimize them

Many people say that the first time they really think about death, in terms of what would happen to their nearest and dearest, is after the birth of their first baby. As children grow up, requirements change, but key points that anyone with a family should consider – and review from time to time – include life insurance and mortgage protection relief. Both husbands and wives should have *life insurance cover.* If either were to die, not only would the partner lose the benefit of the other's earnings, but the partner would also lose the value of the other's services: home decorating, gardening, cooking and so forth.

Most banks and building societies urge homeowners to take out *mortgage protection schemes.* If you die, the loan is paid off automatically and the family home will not be repossessed. Banks also offer *insurance to cover any personal or other loans.* This could be a vital safeguard to avoid leaving the family with debts.

Many people worry about *funeral costs.* Burial service costs can vary, according to different parts of the country, with the average price about £5,000 or even more depending on the choice of coffin and other arrangements. Although you may well hear of cheaper estimates, these are normally exclusive of disbursements, which include minister's fees, cremation fees, medical certificate fees and other items. While cremations are cheaper, prices have increased by at least 15 per cent over the past few years, with £2,500 being a rough average. But here again, costs can vary significantly according to both area and how grand, or simple, the arrangements are.

As a way of helping, a number of insurance companies offer policies to cover funeral costs. While these could be sensible, a drawback is that you are budgeting today against an unknown cost in the future. Over the past four or five years, funeral costs have soared by over 20 per cent. There is no guarantee even with the best policies that the eventual payout would be sufficient to cover the expenses.

A rather different type of scheme, which overcomes the uncertainties and is growing in popularity, is the prepaid funeral plan, which is designed so you pay all the costs in advance, at present-day prices. In other words, if you join today, the funeral is paid at today's price, whenever the service is actually required and whatever the prices are at the time. Funeral plans are offered by the following:

Co-operative Funeralcare, a nationwide network of more than 600 funeral homes and founder member of the Funeral Planning Council, offers the choice of prepaid tailor-made arrangements or a selection of funeral plan packages, with the option to pay in monthly instalments or in a single payment. For details contact Co-operative Funeralcare, Tel: 0800 328 7083; e-mail via the contact form on its website: www.co-operativefuneralcare.co.uk.

Dignity Caring Funeral Services offers a varied range of choices to suit different requirements, with in all cases the option of paying in a single payment or by monthly instalments. For further information contact Dignity Funeral Plans, Tel: 0800 38 77 17; e-mail: planinfo@dignity.co.uk; website: www.dignityfuneralp lans.co.uk.

Help The Aged/Age Concern Funeral Plan, Tel: 0800 00 99 66; website: www. ageconcern.org.uk.

Perfect Choice Funeral Plans, offered by the National Association of Funeral Directors (NAFD) has three standard plans and a 'bespoke' scheme, enabling you to choose all the details you want. Contact the NAFD, Tel: 0845 230 1343; e-mail: info@nafd.org.uk; website: www.nafd.org.uk.

As with insurance policies, a point to check is whether there are any exclusions. Because of the large increases in fees being charged by some cemeteries and crematoria, as well as the rising cost of other disbursements, a number of funeral plan providers are now restricting their guarantee on price to those services within the control of the funeral director. This does not necessarily mean that there would be an excess to pay. For example, **Golden Charter** – the UK's largest independent funeral plan provider – allows provision to be made for increased disbursement costs, and the family would only be charged any extra in the event of these exceeding the amount provided for in the plan at the time of need. The company, which is recommended by the National Society of Allied and Independent Funeral Directors, offers a selection of four plans that can all be tailored to individual requirements, plus a totally bespoke plan. The family has complete freedom of choice of funeral director. Golden Charter plants a tree with the Woodland Trust for each plan sold. For further information, contact Golden Charter, Tel: 0800 833 800; e-mail: mailbox@golden-charter.co.uk; website: www.golden-charter.co.uk.

If you are thinking of giving the idea serious consideration, as with any other important purchase it is sensible to compare the different plans on the market to ensure that you are choosing the one that best suits your requirements.

While most prepaid funeral schemes are problem-free, as an Office of Fair Trading report warned there can be pitfalls – including the risk of losing your money if the company that sold you the plan should go out of business. Happily this is far less likely today, as the government has introduced new regulations designed to ensure that customers' money is properly safeguarded and will be available to pay for the funeral when the time comes.

Another welcome development is the setting up of the **Funeral Planning Authority**. This is a self-regulatory organization that monitors members' compliance procedures. It has rules and a Code of Practice, laying down strict professional standards that all funeral plan providers registered with the Authority are expected to observe. For further details and a list of approved funeral plan providers, contact the Funeral Planning Authority, Tel: 0845 6019 619; e-mail: info@ funeralplanningauthority.co.uk; website: www.funeralplanningauthority.com.

Helpful as these new measures are, before making any advance payment you would still be wise to investigate the following points:

- whether your money will be put into an insurance policy or trust fund or, if not, whether the plan provider is authorized by the Financial Services Authority;
- what fees are deducted from the investment;
- what exact expenses the plan covers;
- what freedom you have if you subsequently want to change any of the details of the plan; and
- if you cancel the plan, whether you can get all your money back – or only a part.

Before paying, you should receive a letter confirming the terms and conditions together with full details of the arrangements you have specified. It is important to check this carefully and inform your next of kin where the letter is filed.

Those in receipt of Income Support, Housing Benefit or Council Tax Benefit may qualify for a payment from the Social Fund to help with funeral costs. For details of eligibility and how you claim, see leaflet D49, *What to Do after a Death*, obtainable from any social security or Jobcentre Plus office. If the matter is urgent, make a point of asking for form SF200.

A very real crisis for some families is the need for immediate money while waiting for the estate to be settled. At least part of the problem can be overcome by couples having a *joint bank account,* with both partners having drawing rights without the signature of the other being required. Sole-name bank accounts and joint accounts requiring both signatures are frozen.

For the same reason, it may also be a good idea for any savings or investments to be held in the joint name of the couple. However, couples who have recently made any changes – or were planning to do so – as a result of independent taxation could be advised to discuss this point with a solicitor or qualified financial adviser.

Additionally, an essential practical point for all couples is that any financial and other *important documents should be discussed together* and understood by both husband and wife. Even today, an all-too-common situation is for widows to come across insurance policies and other papers that they have never seen before and do not understand, often causing quite unnecessary anxiety. A further common sense 'must' is for both partners to *know where important papers are kept.* The best idea is either to lock them, filed together, in a home safe, or to give them to the bank to look after.

If someone dies, *the bank manager should be notified as soon as possible,* so he or she can assist with the problems of unpaid bills and help work out a solution until the estate is settled. The same goes for the *suppliers of essential services:* gas, electricity, telephone and so on. Unless they know the situation, there is a risk of services being cut off if there is a delay in paying the bill. Add, too, any credit card companies, where if bills lie neglected the additional interest could mount up alarmingly.

Another organization that may be able to help you after a loved one has died is the **Bereavement Register**. This organization has one aim: to reduce the amount of direct mail to those who are deceased. Originally launched in the UK in 2000, this service has since expanded into France and Canada. Coming to terms with the loss of a loved one takes time; receiving direct mail bearing the name of the deceased is often painful and unnecessary. The Bereavement Register puts an end to such occurrences. Contact the Bereavement Register, Tel: 0800 082 1230; website: www. the-bereavement-register.org.uk.

Useful reading

What to Do after a Death, a free booklet, from any social security office, and *Planning for a Funeral,* a free fact sheet for those in England from Help The Aged/ Age Concern, Tel: 0800 009 966; website: www.ageconcern.org.uk. A separate Scottish version is available.

State benefits, tax and other money points

Several extra financial benefits are given to widowed people. Most take the form of a cash payment. However, there are one or two tax and other points that it may be useful to know.

Benefits paid in cash form

There are three important cash benefits to which widowed people may be entitled: Bereavement Benefit, Bereavement Allowance and Widowed Parent's Allowance. These have replaced the former widows' benefits, as all benefits are now payable on equal terms to men and women alike.

To claim the benefits, fill in form BB1, obtainable from any social security or **Jobcentre Plus** office; see website: www.jobcentreplus.gov.uk. You will also be given a questionnaire (BD8) by the Registrar. It is important that you complete this, as it acts as a trigger to speed up payment of your benefits.

Bereavement Benefit

This has replaced what used to be known as Widow's Payment. It is a tax-free lump sum of £2,000, paid as soon as people are widowed, provided that: 1) the widowed person's spouse had paid sufficient NI Contributions; 2) the widowed person personally is under State retirement age; or 3) if over State retirement age, the widowed person's husband or wife had not been entitled to retirement pension.

Bereavement Allowance

This has replaced the Widow's Pension. Women already in receipt of Widow's Pension before 6 April 2001 are not affected and will continue to receive it as normal.

Bereavement Allowance is for those aged between 45 and State pension age who do not receive Widowed Parent's Allowance. It is payable for 52 weeks and, as with Widow's Pension before, there are various levels of payment: the full rate and age-related allowance. Receipt in all cases is dependent on sufficient NI Contributions having been paid.

Full-rate Bereavement Allowance is paid to widowed people between the ages of 55 and 59 inclusive. The weekly amount is £95.25, which is the same as the current pension for a single person.

Age-related Bereavement Allowance is for younger widows or widowers, who do not qualify for the full rate. It is payable to those who are aged between 45 and 54 inclusive when their partner dies. Rates depend on age and vary from £28.58 for 45-year-olds to £88.58 for those aged 54.

Bereavement Allowance is normally paid automatically once you have sent off your completed form BB1, so if for any reason you do not receive it you should enquire at your social security office. In the event of your being ineligible, owing to insufficient NIC having been paid, you may still be entitled to receive Income Support, Housing Benefit or a grant or loan from the Social Fund. Your social security or **Jobcentre Plus** office will advise you. See website: www.jobcentreplus.gov.uk.

Widowed Parent's Allowance

This is paid to widowed parents with at least one child for whom they receive Child Benefit. The current value (2009/10) is £95.25 per week. The allowance is usually paid automatically. If for some reason, although eligible, you do not receive the money, you should inform your social security office.

Retirement pension

Once a widowed person reaches State retirement age, he or she should receive a State pension in the normal way. An important point to remember is that a widow or widower may be able to use the late spouse's NIC to boost the amount he or she receives. See leaflet RM1, *Retirement – A Guide to Benefits for People Who Are Retiring or Have Retired*.

Problems

Both pension payments and bereavement benefits are dependent on sufficient NIC having been paid. Your social security office will inform you if you are not eligible. If this should turn out to be the case, you may still be entitled to receive Income Support, Housing Benefit, Council Tax Benefit or a grant or loan from the Social Fund – so ask. If you are unsure of your position or have difficulties, ask at your Citizens Advice Bureau, which will at least be able to help you work out the sums and inform you of your rights.

Particular points to note

- Most widowed peoples' benefits are taxable. However, the £2,000 Bereavement Benefit is tax-free, as are pensions paid to the widows or widowers of armed forces personnel.
- Widowed people will normally be able to inherit their spouse's additional pension rights, if they contributed to SERPS (see the note below) and/or the Second State Pension (S2P), or at least half their guaranteed minimum pension, if their spouse was in a contracted-out scheme. Additionally, where applicable, all widowed people are entitled on retirement to half the gradu-ated pension earned by their husband or wife. *NB:* SERPS benefits paid to surviving spouses are due to be halved over the coming years. The cuts will be completed by October 2010. Anyone over State pension age before 6 October 2002 is exempt from any cuts and will keep the right to pass on his or her SERPS pension in full to a bereaved spouse. Equally, any younger widow or widower who inherited his or her late spouse's SERPS entitlement before 6 October 2002 will not be affected and will continue to receive the full amount.

- Women in receipt of widow's pension who remarry, or live with a man as his wife, lose their entitlement to the payment, unless, that is, the cohabitation ends, in which case they can claim it again. If a woman is aged over 60, the fact that she is living with a man will not affect her entitlement to a retirement pension based on her late husband's contribution record.
- Widows and widowers of armed forces personnel whose deaths were a direct result of their service are now entitled to keep their armed forces attributable pension for life, regardless of whether they remarry or cohabit.

Tax allowances

Widows and widowers receive the normal single person's tax allowance of £6,475 and, if in receipt of married couple's allowance, are also entitled to any unused portion of the allowance in the year of their partner's death. Those aged 65 and older may be entitled to a higher personal allowance (see page 368).

Advice

Many people have difficulty in working out exactly what they are entitled to – and how to claim it. The Citizens Advice Bureau is always very helpful. Additionally, Cruse and the National Association of Widows (see below) can assist you.

Organizations that can help

Problems vary. For some, the hardest thing to bear is the loneliness of returning to an empty house. For others, money problems seem to dominate everything else. For many older women, in particular, who have not got a job, widowhood creates a great gulf where for a while there is no real sense of purpose. Many widowed men and women go through a spell of feeling enraged against their partner for dying. Most are baffled and hurt by the seeming indifference of friends, who appear more embarrassed than sympathetic.

In time, all these feelings soften, problems diminish and individuals are able to recapture their joy for living with all its many pleasures. Talking to other people who know the difficulties from their own experience can be a tremendous help. The following organizations not only offer opportunities for companionship but also provide an advisory and support service:

Cruse Bereavement Care offers free help to anyone who has been bereaved by providing both one-to-one and group support through its 150 local branches throughout the UK. A list of publications and a newsletter are available. Tel: 0844 477 9400; e-mail: helpline@cruse.org.uk; website: www.crusebereavement care.org.uk.

The National Association of Widows is a national voluntary organization. Its many branches provide a supportive social network for widows throughout the UK. Tel: 0845 838 2261; e-mail: info@nawidows.org.uk; website: www.nawidows.org.uk.

Many professional and other groups offer a range of services for widows and widowers associated with them. These include:

The Civil Service Retirement Fellowship, Tel: 020 8691 7411; e-mail: info@csrf.org.uk; website: www.csrf.org.uk.
The War Widows Association of Great Britain, Tel: 0845 2412 189; e-mail: info@warwidowsassociation.org.uk; website: www.warwidows.org.uk.

Many local Help The Aged/Age Concern groups offer a counselling service. Trade unions are often particularly supportive, as are Rotary Clubs, all the armed forces organizations and most benevolent societies.

Index

Index of advertisers